Table of Contents

Introduction

Learn the Message

Live the Message

Spread the Message

Spirituality

World Apostolate of Fatima, USA

Spiritual Guide for the Salvation of Souls and World Peace

Introduction

Pope Benedict the XV reigned during WWI and had a very strong devotion to the Blessed Mother. It is to her that the Holy Father appealed to end the War which claimed over 40 million lives and that he called the "suicide of Europe." Three shepherd children from Fatima, Portugal; Francisco, Jacinta and Lucia were prepared by the Angel of Peace to receive a message from Heaven that was delivered by the Virgin Mary on the 13th of the months between May and October in 1917.

God wants all people to know that hell exits and that war is a consequence of spiritual decay, He also wants us to save souls and bring peace to the earth. The Blessed Mother delivered a message of Hope, she taught us how to avoid the fire and pain of hell not only for ourselves, but also for our loved ones, our friends, and others and how to avoid war; war so devastating that nations will be annihilated if we don't follow Heaven's Peace Plan. On October 13, 1917, God performed the greatest miracle since Jesus Christ walked the face of the earth, the only miracle ever predicted as to time and place; this miracle was witnessed by a crowed estimated to number over 70,000. The miracle was so profound because the message is so profound.

During the cold war and for over 60 years The World Apostolate of Fatima, previously known as the Blue Army has helped millions and millions of people from around the world learn, live, and spread Heaven's powerful message, a message so powerful that if followed it can overcome war without firing a shot and pluck souls from Satan's grip.

At the request of Pope John Paul II, who said the Message of Fatima is More Important Now Than Ever, the World Apostolate of Fatima took the steps to become a Public Association of the Faithful under the Pontifical Council for the Laity. This means that under Church law we are one of only a few lay organizations that are officially part of the Church and we are the only Fatima organization. With this designation comes much responsibility to help people Learn, Live, and Spread Heaven's plan for the Salvation of Souls and World Peace.

This booklet is a compilation of some of the information we have made available over the past 60 years, we also publish SOUL magazine which provides timely information on the relevance of Our Lady's message in today's world, as well as insightful articles about the message. As a member nation of the International World Apostolate of Fatima we establish what we call Divisions; Divisions are organizations of people like you that work within a diocese with the approval of the Bishop and a spiritual director who is appointed by the Bishop.

We ask that you join us in this very important work by Learning, Living, and Spreading the message of Fatima and helping others Learn, Live, and Spread this message. As you do this, you will provide much spiritual nourishment for a world in great need. As explained by Our Blessed Mother in Fatima, the salvation of Souls and World Peace is what's at stake.

DIOCESAN IMPRIMATUR

In accord with Canon 827 of the New Code of Canon Law, this publication has been submitted to a censor of the Diocese and nothing being found contrary to faith and morals, we hereby grant permission in accord with Canon 824 that it be published.

Rev. Msgr. William Benwell, J.C.L.
Vicar General
Diocese of Metuchen
August 5, 2008

N.B. The imprimatur implies nothing more than the material contained in the publication has been examined by diocesan censors and nothing contrary to faith and morals has been found therein.

2008 Edition

© 2008 World Apostolate of Fatima, USA/
Blue Army, USA

Blue Army History

On a November day in 1946, Msgr. Harold V. Colgan, pastor of St Mary's Parish in Plainfield, NJ was rushed to the hospital with a heart attack. The middle-aged priest had recently celebrated his twenty-fifth anniversary of ordination.

The consensus of opinion among the doctors was that he would soon die. With absolute rest he might survive six months.

As he lay in his hospital room on December 8, 1946, Father Colgan asked for a statue of Our Lady and spent the day in prayer. He made a promise to the Mother of God that if she would intercede with her Son to postpone his death, he would spend the rest of his life promoting devotion to her.

His prayer was answered and one week later he walked out of the hospital to the amazement of the doctors. He was gradually able to resume his parish ministry.

Then, one day in 1947 Monsignor Colgan read an article about Fatima in a magazine. He decided to make Fatima the focus of the Marian devotion upon which he would expend his life's energies.

He preached the message of Fatima for ten consecutive weeks in his parish. One day he said, "We in this parish will be the Blue Army of Our Lady against the Red Army of Communism." The Cold War had begun and the Communist Red Army personified the evil power of militant atheism. His words that day launched the Blue Army, now also known as the World Apostolate of Fatima.

He stressed amendment of life, frequent Confession, devotion to the Immaculate Heart of Mary, the daily Rosary and the First Saturday devotion in reparation to the Immaculate Heart of Mary and for the conversion of sinners. He asked his Apostolate members to wear something blue as a point of conversation to interest others in Fatima.

After preaching the Fatima message to his parishioners, Monsignor Colgan invited Mr. John Haffert to his parish to speak. Mr. Haffert had developed a pledge listing conditions that would fulfill the basic requirements of the Fatima message. He did this in cooperation with Sister Lucia, the surviving Fatima witness. Monsignor

Colgan adopted this pledge and it has since become known as the World Apostolate of Fatima Pledge.

Mr. Haffert introduced the idea of the World Apostolate of Fatima to the Bishop of Fatima who embraced the organization and encouraged the construction of an International Center at Fatima. Mr. Haffert subsequently became the National Director of the Apostolate and did yeoman's work in establishing it throughout the United States and around the world.

The Priests of the Archdiocese of Newark played a key role in the establishment of the Apostolate's International Center, Domus Pacis (House of Peace), at Fatima. At one point in his life Monsignor Colgan had made the Marian consecration of St. Louis de Montfort. Through this consecration he committed everything to God through Mary. When funds were short for the construction of the center at Fatima, Monsignor Colgan approached his brother priests in Newark who had also made the Marian consecration. Reminding them of their consecration, he asked for a large donation to cover construction costs and they came through.

By May of 1950, interest in the Apostolate was such that Monsignor Colgan took the names of nearly a million persons who had signed the Blue Army Pledge to Fatima during his first visit there.

Progress on the International Center at Fatima continued and on October 13, 1956, Cardinal Eugene Tisserant, Papal Legate of Pope Pius XII, performed the blessing and dedication. The cardinal returned to Domus Pacis on August 28, 1963, (the date on which the Assumption is celebrated in Russia) to dedicate the new Byzantine chapel.

Monsignor Colgan once met Padre Pio and asked the renowned Capuchin priest to accept Apostolate members as his spiritual children. The stigmatic priest reportedly replied that he would if they were faithful and he predicted Russia would be converted when there was an Apostolate member for every Communist.

Monsignor Colgan celebrated his fiftieth anniversary of ordination on April 11, 1970. The Fatima Apostolate founder credits the Virgin Mary with being the real founder of the Apostolate. Monsignor Colgan died on April 16, 1972. He is buried at the National Blue Army Shrine of the Immaculate Heart of Mary in Washington, NJ. Please remember him in your prayers.

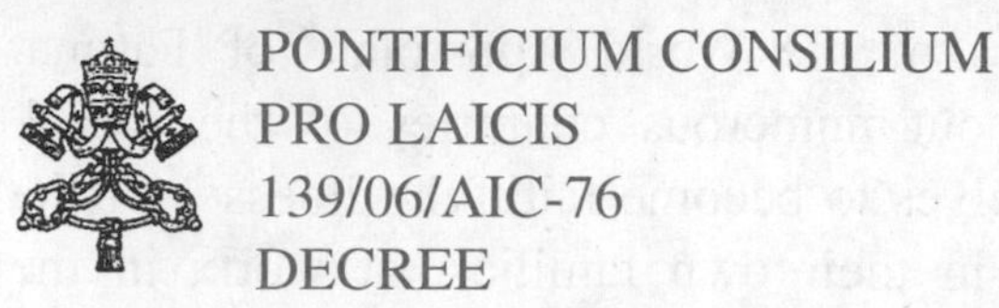

PONTIFICIUM CONSILIUM
PRO LAICIS
139/06/AIC-76
DECREE

The World Apostolate of Fatima is an association of the faithful that has as its general purpose the promotion of the authentic teaching of the Catholic Church and the strict adherence to the tenets of the Gospel; the personal sanctification of the adherents through faithful adherence to the message of Fatima and the promotion of the common good by the spreading of the message of Fatima. (Statutes, art. II, 1-3).

In the apparitions of 1917, the Blessed Virgin reaffirmed to the three little shepherds -Lucia dos Santos and the blessed Francisco and Jacinta Marto- the perennial Christian message of conversion, prayer and penance in reparation for sins and for the conversion of sinners, together with a more genuine devotion to the Eucharist, the devotion to the Rosary and the consecration to her Immaculate Heart.

At the same time, the World Apostolate has the specific purpose of promoting the Pledge given by each member of the World Apostolate of Fatima. (Statutes, art. II, 4).

The members of the World Apostolate of Fatima, spread throughout numerous countries of the world, commit themselves to become faithful witnesses of the Catholic faith in their own families, at work, in the parishes and communities, participating in this way in the "New Evangelization".

The Second Vatican Council, together with the post-conciliar teaching, has given special attention to the new forms of aggregation of the Christian faithful and their participation in the life of the Church. Deep esteem and consideration has been shown to them (cf. Decree on the Apostolate of the Laity Apostolicam actuositatem, 18, 19 and 21; John Paul II, Post-Synodal Apostolic Exhortation Christifideles Laici, 29).

In his Apostolic Letter, Novo millennio inuente, His Holiness Pope John Paul II wrote about the great importance of the promotion of forms of associations, whether of the more traditional kind or the newer ecclesial movements which continue to give the Church a vitality that is God's gift and a true "Springtime of the Spirit." (46).

PONTIFICIUM CONSILIUM
PRO LAICIS

Consequently:

Having examined attentively the request presented to this Dicastery, by Prof. Americo Pablo Lopez Ortiz, President of the World Apostolate of Fatima, that this association be erected as a public international association of the faithful and that its Statutes be approved;

Considering that the World Apostolate of Fatima is a suitable instrument for the formation of the lay people through the message of Fatima in view of the new evangelization proposed by the Holy Fathers John Paul II and Benedict XVI;

Valuing the commendatory letters received from many Dioceses around the world, which reflect the positive appreciation of the Bishops for the activities developed for the members of the World Apostolate of Fatima to benefit the Church;

In light of articles 131-134 of the Apostolic Constitution Pastor Bonus for the Roman Curia and according to canon 312, § 1, 1 ° of the Code of Canon Law, the Pontifical Council for the Laity decrees:

1 °. The erection of the World Apostolate of Fatima as a public international association of the faithful, according to canons 298-320 and 327-329 of the Code of Canon Law.

2°. The approval of the Statutes of this association, duly authenticated by this Dicastery and deposited in our Archives, for a period of five years ad experimentum.

Vatican City, 7 October 2005,
Memory of the Blessed Mary Virgin of the Rosary:

Stanislaw Rylko
President

Josef Clemens
Secretary

World Apostolate of Our Lady of Fatima

Before He chose the Twelve Apostles, Jesus prayed to the Father. He prayed during important moments throughout His ministry. By His example, He teaches us to pray so that we may grow in holiness and do God's Will in our lives. All are called to holiness: "Be perfect, as your heavenly Father is perfect" (Mt 5:48).

Personal Holiness

Holiness is at the heart of the World Apostolate of Fatima. It all began at Fatima, Portugal, in 1917, when the Mother of God appeared to three illiterate shepherd children. Revealing herself as the Lady of the Rosary, the Blessed Virgin requested daily prayer (the Rosary), personal conversion and reparation as a means for growth in personal holiness and world peace. The apparitions and Message of Fatima, approved by the Church, were confirmed by a solar miracle October 13, 1917, witnessed by more than 70,000 persons.

The effect of the Fatima apparitions and Message on the three children, Lucia dos Santos and her cousins, Jacinta and Francisco Marto, was profound. Following the apparitions they adopted an edifying lifestyle of persevering prayer, reparation for sin and great charity. Jacinta (d. February 20, 1920) and Francisco (d. April 4, 1919) were cited for heroic virtue and declared Blessed by the Church on May 13, 2000. Lucia entered the religious life and became a Carmelite nun.

Father Harold Colgan's Cure

Msgr. Harold V. Colgan

In 1946, Father Harold Colgan, a parish priest in Plainfield, New Jersey, was cured of a terminal heart condition through the intercession of the Blessed Virgin. In gratitude, he dedicated his life to promoting the Fatima Message. Father Colgan began a parish organization to live and promote the Fatima Message. The World Apostolate of Our Lady of Fatima was born. The group adopted a membership pledge developed earlier by Mr. John Haffert in cooperation with Sister Lucia, the surviving Fatima seer. The World Apostolate of Fatima expanded across the nation and around the world. After Monsignor Colgan's death in 1972, Mr. Haffert led the Apostolate until his retirement in 1987.

Today, the World Apostolate of Fatima, with its headquarters in Fatima, Portugal, is officially recognized as a Public Association of the Faithful by the Catholic Church. The WAF is active throughout the United States with divisions in 70 dioceses and in 120 countries around the world.

The World Apostolate of Fatima offers an excellent means for Catholics to respond to the Vatican II universal call to holiness and, in response to the Decree of the Apostolate of the Laity, to evangelize fellow Catholics through the Fatima Message. In their 1990 pastoral letter, "Heritage and Hope, Evangelization in the United States," the American Bishops observed, ". . . Our age expects of all believers simplicity of life, a spirit of prayer, charity toward all, obedience and humility, detachment and sacrifice. Without these marks of holiness, the evangelists will have difficulty touching the hearts of modern people."

The World Apostolate of Fatima spiritual program, embodied in the WAF Pledge, encourages each of these aspects of holiness in its members. Through the pledge, members offer the sacrifices of daily life in reparation for sin; pray the Rosary each day; and wear the Brown Scapular as a sign of consecration to the Immaculate Heart of Mary.

In May of 1983, the bishops of the United States issued "The Challenge of Peace: God's Promise and Our Response," a pastoral letter on war and peace. The bishops say, "As believers, we understand peace as a gift of

God. This belief prompts us to pray constantly, personally and communally, particularly through the reading of scripture and devotion to the Rosary especially in the family" (part iv, a). "Prayer by itself is incomplete without penance," the bishops continue, "Penance directs us toward our goal of putting on attitudes of Jesus Himself."

World Apostolate of Fatima Spirituality

Aren't prayer and penance central to the Fatima Message? The WAF promotes Eucharistic prayer and the Rosary. It promotes penance, especially the generous acceptance of the duties of our state in life.

The WAF offers a variety of spiritual programs for young people, individuals and parishes. These range from the Prayer Cells, where individuals meet for weekly prayer in the parish or home setting, to the Pilgrim Virgin Evangelization programs that introduce the Fatima Message and Rosary to schools, parishes, hospitals, nursing homes, colleges and prisons. They also include Parish First Saturday Devotions, All-Night Vigils, a Sacred Heart Home Enthronement Program and Family Consecrations to the Sacred Heart of Jesus and the Immaculate Heart of Mary. These and other WAF programs can revitalize and strengthen the faith of participants in local Church communities.

Our Savior tells us, "How narrow is the gate, and straight is the way that leads to life: and few there are that find it!" (Mt 7:14) The Mother of God came to Fatima in 1917 to lead us back to God with an evangelical Message of repentance conversion. On May 13, 1982, Pope John Paul II declared the Fatima Message to be more relevant and urgent than when it was first delivered.

The American Bishops echoed this sentiment in their 1990 evangelization pastoral: "Without the gospel, modern life with its immediacy, efficiency and speed, its constant changes and congestion at times has resulted in misery, increasing violence, controversy, and tension. Humanity is suffering from confusion, self-doubt, and uncertainty about fundamental values. Pragmatism, materialism, consumerism are the creeds of the age. There is a declining sense of moral values; there is fear, hopelessness, and a growing lack of respect for law and for life" (pp. 32-33).

A Spiritual Alternative

At Fatima, Our Lady predicted the moral and spiritual breakdown of our society if her requests were not heeded. She offered us a spiritual means for restoring the moral order and establishing peace in the world. Her Message is a message of hope and of sure guidance in this era of moral confusion. Our Lady promised that in the end her Immaculate Heart will triumph and an era of peace will be granted to mankind.

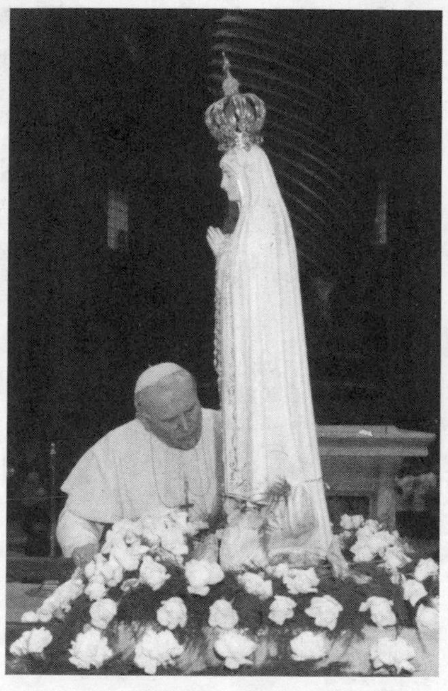

These dramatic prophecies were made to the children immediately after they were shown a vision of Hell on July 13, 1917. The vision of Hell is the first part of what has been called the Fatima Secret. The second part was the request for devotion to the Immaculate Heart of Mary. The keyword of the third part of the Secret is the threefold cry: Penance, Penance, Penance! It also reveals a terrifying image of war, as well as persecutions of the Church and the Holy Father.

The Miracle of the Sun and the prophecies serve to highlight the vital importance of the central Message of Fatima: return to God. The prayer, conversion and repa-

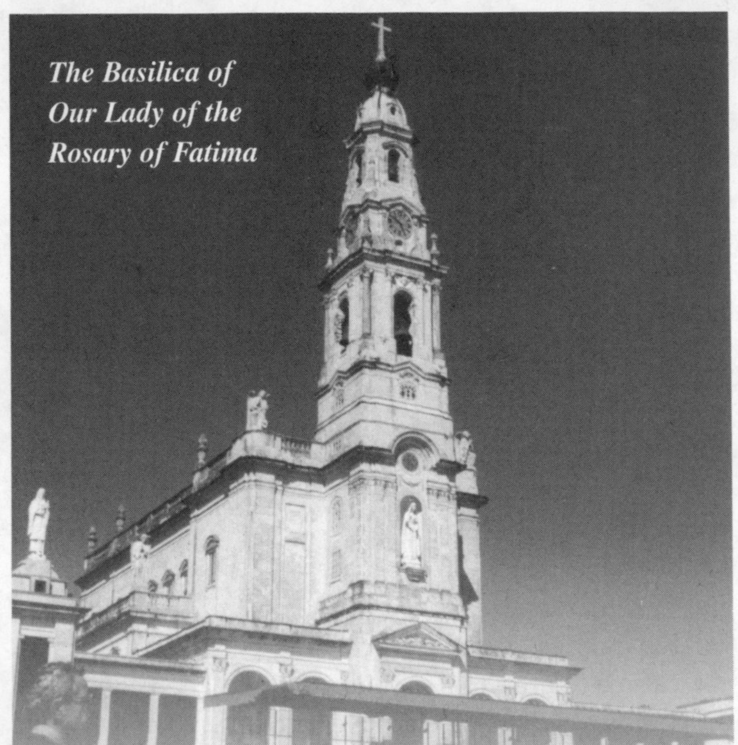
The Basilica of Our Lady of the Rosary of Fatima

ration implied in this are all elements of that Christian perfection to which each is called. But we must remember that "the way of perfection passes by way of the Cross. There is no holiness without renunciation and spiritual battle" (Catechism of the Catholic Church, no. 2015). The Fatima Message offers us a map from which to plan our life's journey to personal holiness. Join us in Our Lady's Apostolate in following her Son.

Contact your local World Apostolate of Fatima at:
www.wafusa.org

In accord with Canon 827 of the New Code of Canon Law, this publication has been submitted to a censor of the Diocese and nothing being found contrary to faith and morals, we hereby grant permission in accord with Canon 824 that it be published.

Rev. Msgr. John B. Szymanski, Vicar General
Diocese of Metuchen
March 20, 2003

N.B. The ecclesiastical permission implies nothing more than the material contained in the publication has been examined by diocesan censors and nothing contrary to faith and morals has been found therein.

Cover photo by foto iris. Jacinta, Francisco, and Lucia photo from *Fatima Archives. Photo of Father Colgan by Lou Caruso. Photo of Pope John Paul II from* Blue Army Archives.

Contact the National Center at:
World Apostolate of Fatima, USA
PO Box 976, Washington, NJ 07882

Telephone: 866-513-1917
Fax: 908-689-0721
E-mail: service@bluearmy.com
Website: www.wafusa.org

333295

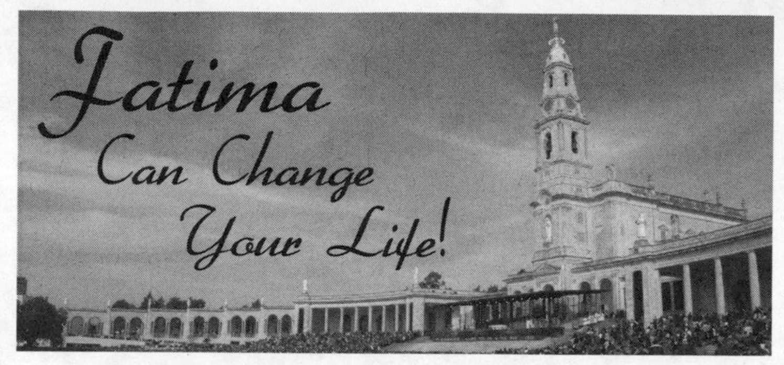
Fatima
Can Change
Your Life!

THE FATIMA MESSAGE CAN CHANGE YOUR LIFE!

It changed the lives of Jacinta and Francisco Marto who faithfully responded to the expectations of the Blessed Virgin. These two children, who the Church declared venerable on May 13, 1989, offer an excellent example for living the Fatima message to World Apostolate of Fatima members. The following highlights are excerpted from the Vatican decrees declaring the heroic virtue of the children.

JACINTA MARTO

...Jacinta Marto, who corresponded unreservedly to divine grace, rapidly attained to great perfection in the imitation of Christ and voluntarily consumed her short life in giving glory to God and cooperating in the salvation of souls through fervent prayer and assiduous penance.

...Afterwards...she changed completely and became a splendid model of humility, mortification and generosity.

What unexpectedly changed their life, came to pass in the year 1916. They said they had seen an angel three times, who urged them to pray and do penance for the remission of sins and to obtain the conversion of sinners. From that moment onward, the little Jacinta made use of every occasion to do what the angel had asked her.

...Full of joy and gratitude for the gift she had received, she wished to respond immediately with all her strength to the exhortation of the Virgin Mary, who asked their prayers and sacrifices in reparation for sins that offend God and the Immaculate Heart of Mary, and for the conversion of sinners. At the same time, docile to the action of grace, she separated herself from the things of earth in order to turn her attention to heavenly things, and voluntarily consecrated her life so as to enter paradise one day. She was constantly immersed in the contemplation of God, in intimate colloquy with Him. She sought silence and solitude, and at night she got out of bed to pray and freely express her love for Our Lord. In a little while, her interior life became distinguished by a great faith and by enormous charity.

Devotion to the Eucharist

...She nourished an ardent devotion to the Eucharist, which she visited frequently and for long periods in the parish church, concealing herself in the pulpit where no one could see or distract her. She longed to receive the Body of Christ, but that was not permitted because of her age. However, she found some consolation in spiritual communion. In the same way, she venerated the Virgin Mary with a tender, filial and joyful love, responding constantly to her words and desires, and honoring her many times with the recitation of the Rosary and with pious ejaculations.

...She conscientiously offered prayers and sacrifices for the Supreme Pontiff, for the salvation of souls and for the conversion of sinners. Even during the apparitions of Our Lady, she was already able to share in the Passion of the Lord....She was called a liar and a fraud; she was even beaten and put in prison for some days. She bore all of this in silence, happy to complete in the body what is lacking in Christ's sufferings for the sake of His Body, that is, the Church (cf. Col, 1:24).

Restraint of Will

...She bore many other crosses spontaneously, as if she had an insatiable hunger for immolation. She restrained her will and her temperament, and was obedient to her parents and to her older brothers and sister; she deprived herself of food to give it to the poor; she did not drink water, especially in the summer heat; as a form of penance she wore a rope around her waist; she endured everything that was disagreeable in a spirit of penance and oblation. She expressed her manner of acting in praying; "O my Jesus, it is for love of You, for the conversion of sinners, and in reparation for the sins committed against the Immaculate Heart of Mary."

Work of Redemption

...She multiplied her sacrifices, penances and privations as a way of cooperating to the fullest of her possibilities in the work of Redemption. But what cost her most was having to leave her family in order to undergo treatment in a hospital. Foreseeing that she would die alone, that is, far from her dear ones at home, she said: "O my Jesus, now You can convert many sinners, because this is really a big sacrifice!"

While the strength of her body was failing, her soul became more beautiful as the days passed by, through the resolute, constant, joyful and perfect exercise of the Christian virtues. Indeed her abandonment to the will of God was complete. Not only did her strength in surrendering to the Lord, in responding to his graces and in avoiding any kind of sin never fail her, rather it increased more and more. Even in adverse and difficult circumstances, she gave witness of possessing to a high degree the theological virtues and also the virtues of prudence, justice, fortitude, temperance, humility, sincerity and modesty. Therefore the words of Wisdom seem to be very appropriate: "Being made perfect in a short space, she fulfilled a long time." (Wis. 4:13).

On February 20, 1920,...she died in the Lisbon hospital where she had been a patient for some time. She had finally reached the goal of her desires: eternal life.

Francisco Marto

Francisco, in spite of his tender age, left us an eminent example of obedience to the will of God, of ardent love for the Immaculate Heart of Mary and of diligent attentiveness in consoling Our Lord, so offended by the sins of men, and of praying and suffering for the needs of the Church and for the conversion of sinners.

The Servant of God was born in a village called Aljustrel, belonging to the parish of Fatima, in Portugal, on June 11, 1908...

Meditation and Prayer

...He began to be more pious and reserved; he frequently recited the prayer taught by the angel; he was always ready to offer sacrifices for the salvation of those who do not believe, do not hope or do not love. After these apparitions he seemed to have received the vocation of an anchorite; he hid behind the rocks and trees in order to pray alone, while at other times he climbed to the highest and most solitary places and there gave himself so intensely to meditation and prayer that he did not hear the voices of those who called him. At the same time he felt a strong and continuous longing to approach the sacred Eucharistic table, which in fact was only permitted to him just before he died.

...From then on, ever more and more inflamed with love for God and for souls, he had only one aspiration: to pray and suffer according to Our Lady's request. If the measure of divine benevolence towards him was extraordinary, the manner in which he wished to correspond with divine grace, in joy, fervor, and constancy, was also extraordinary. He did not limit himself only to being a messenger, announcing penance and prayer, but more than that, with all his strength he conformed his life to the message which he announced, more by the goodness of works than by words. Thus he fulfilled the exhortation of Peter: "Each one of you has received a special grace, so, like good stewards responsible for all these different graces of God, put yourselves at the service of others." (1 Pet. 4:10).

...During the apparitions he bore with firm spirit and admirable fortitude the malicious interpretations, the injuries, the persecutions and even some days of imprisonment.

Resistance to Will

...He mortified his will and his character, overcoming fatigue, depriving himself of food in order to give it to the poor, not drinking water for entire days, especially in the hot weather, fasting during Lent, wearing a rope around his waist as a penance, giving up his favorite games in order to devote more time to prayer. He lost no occasion of uniting himself to the Passion of Christ and of cooperating in this manner in the salvation of souls and in the growth of the Church.

...He became conscious of being called to dedicate himself zealously and constantly to the duty of prayer according to the intentions of the Virgin Mary. He sought silence and solitude in order to immerse himself totally in contemplation and in dialogue with God.

Eucharistic Devotion

...He nurtured a special devotion to the Eucharist and spent much time in church, adoring the Sacrament of the Altar which he called the "Hidden Jesus." He recited the fifteen mysteries of the Rosary daily, and many more times besides, in order to fulfill Our Lady's desire. He prayed with the intention of consoling God, of honoring the mother of the Lord, whom he loved so much, of being useful to the hold souls who were expiating their penalties in the fire of purgatory, and of helping the Supreme Pontiff in the fulfillment of his important office as universal pastor; he prayed for the needs of the world ravaged by hatred and sin; he prayed for the Church and for eternal salvation of souls. He prayed alone, with his family, and with the pilgrims, manifesting a deep interior recollection and a sure confidence in the divine goodness.

Penance

With the firm resolve of desiring and doing only that

which was pleasing to God, he dedicated himself constantly in heart and soul to the immortal things of the spirit, avoiding every form of sin and, at the age of seven years, he began frequently and piously to approach the Sacrament of Penance. Docile to the precepts of the Lord and to the words of the most Holy Virgin Mary, he progressed continually on the path of sanctity and, in a short time, attained a great and solid Christian perfection. Indeed his was a living faith, his charity was tender and zealous and his hope was full of joy. He was upright in word and deed. He had total disregard for earthly goods and for his own life and health. Since it had been made known to him by the Virgin Mary that his life would be brief, he spent the days in ardent expectation of entering heaven...

The Joy of Suffering

...Once confined to bed he never managed to get up again; on the contrary, his state of health deteriorated in the year 1919. With great interior joy, he suffered his infirmity and severe pains as an oblation to God. When Lucia asked him if he was suffering he replied: "Quite a lot, but never mind. I am suffering to console Our lord, and afterwards, within a short time, I am going to heaven." In spite of being so sick, he nevertheless prayed many Rosaries, exhorting the others to pray with him...He piously entered into eternal life, which he so ardently desired, on April 4, 1919.

The Message of OUR LADY *of* FATIMA

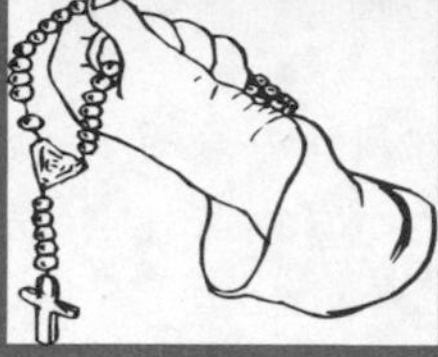

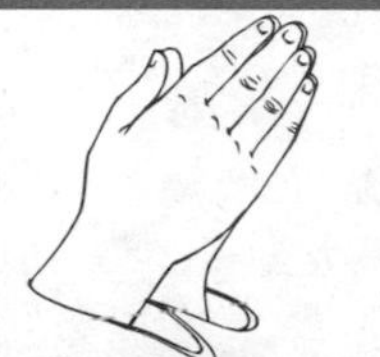

Pray the Rosary Every Day!

WORLD APOSTOLATE OF FATIMA, USA

In 1916, a new charism began to be realized in the hills of Fatima when Lucia dos Santos, age nine, and her cousins, Francisco Marto, age eight and Jacinta Marto, age six, met an angel for the first time.

"Do not be afraid. I am the Angel of Peace.
Pray with me."

Then he taught them this prayer:

"My God, I believe, I adore, I hope and I love You!
I ask pardon of You for those who do not believe,
do not adore, do not hope and do not love You!"

"Pray thus. The Hearts of Jesus and Mary
are attentive to the voice of your supplications."

As if concerned that this sublime invitation might not have entered into the souls of the little shepherds, the Angel came for the second time and insisted:

"Pray! Pray very much! The Hearts of Jesus and
Mary have designs of mercy on you. Offer prayers
and sacrifices constantly to the Most High."

"Make of everything you can a sacrifice, and offer it to God as an act of reparation for the sins by which He is offended, and in supplication for the conversion of sinners. You will thus draw down peace upon your country. I am its Angel Guardian, the Angel of Portugal. Above all, accept and bear with submission, the suffering which the Lord will send you."

He appeared to them yet a third time, carrying in his hand a chalice and a host. Prostrating on the ground with the little shepherds he repeated three times:

"Most Holy Trinity, Father, Son and Holy Spirit, I adore

You profoundly, and I offer You the most precious Body, Blood, Soul and Divinity of Jesus Christ, present in all the tabernacles of the world, in reparation for the outrages, sacrileges and indifference with which He Himself is offended. And, through the infinite merits of His most Sacred Heart, and the Immaculate Heart of Mary, I beg of You the conversion of poor sinners."

When giving them Holy Communion during the vision, the Angel uttered these moving words:

"Take and drink the Body and Blood of Jesus Christ, horribly outraged by ungrateful men. Repair their crimes and console your God."

On the thirteenth of six consecutive months, from May to October in 1917, the Queen of Angels herself came to crown this doctrine of reparation which is known simply as, the *Message of Fatima.* In October she identified herself as the Lady of the Rosary.

The Confirmation of the Doctrine of the Angel

In the first apparition on May 13, 1917, Our Lady said she had come to ask for reparation. She revealed these truths to the little shepherds through the light from her hands.

"O most Holy Trinity, I adore You! My God, my God, I love You in the most Blessed Sacrament!"

In the third apparition, on July 13, 1917, she opened her hands again as in the two previous months and the Little Shepherds saw in the reflection of the light, hell, the place of punishment for sins:

"You have seen hell where the souls of poor sinners go."

With total clarity the central truths about the Most Holy Trinity, the

Holy Eucharist and the function of Mary in the salvific plan of God were communicated to the seers.

The function of Mary in God's plan of salvation

First, Mary received from God a special mission for our time marked by grave errors and false doctrines, by wars and social changes: a century in which the Pope and the whole Church are subjected to serious trials and in which souls find themselves in grave danger of being eternally lost.

The Message of Fatima points to sin as the principal cause of these evils and reason for punishment. Hence the great request of Our Lady:

"They must amend their lives and ask forgiveness for their sins."

"Do not offend the Lord our God any more,
because He is already so much offended."

Secondly, Our Lady indicated one important means of avoiding these evils:

"God wishes to establish in the world devotion
to my Immaculate Heart."

Therefore, she asked for the consecration of Russia to her Immaculate Heart and reparatory devotion of the First Saturdays.

"Pray the Rosary every day!"

"When you pray the Rosary say after each mystery:
O my Jesus, forgive us, save us from the fire of hell. Lead all
souls to heaven, especially those who are most in need."

"Sacrifice yourselves for sinners, and say many times, especially whenever you make some sacrifice: O Jesus, it is for love of You, for the conversion of sinners, and in reparation for the sins committed against the Immaculate Heart of Mary."

The final result of the Message of Fatima:

"In the end, my Immaculate Heart will triumph."

The Godly Examples of the Fatima Seers

The seers Francisco and Jacinta Marto realized to a heroic degree in their short lives the requests of Our Lady for sacrifice and prayer. Their sufferings were rewarded when they were taken to heaven by Mary at an early age.

Their examples guide a great number of souls on the way of sanctity. The Church is making serious efforts to officially present the little shepherds as models of sanctity. Their beatification and canonization will help to increase knowledge and practice of the Message of Fatima in the world.

Our Lady came to Lucia again, as she promised, eight years later on December 10, 1925. She appeared with the Child Jesus in the Dorothean convent at Pontevedra, Spain. The Blessed Virgin revealed a heart encircled by thorns. The Child Jesus spoke these words:

"Have compassion on the heart of your most holy Mother, covered with thorns with which ungrateful men pierce it at every moment, and there is no one to make an act of reparation..."

Our Lady spoke next, saying:

"Look, my daughter, at my heart, surrounded with thorns with which ungrateful men pierce it at every moment by their blasphemies and ingratitude. You at least try to console me and say that I promise to assist at the hour of death, with all the graces necessary for salvation, all those who, on the first Saturday of five consecutive months, shall confess, receive Holy Communion, recite five decades of the Rosary, and keep me company for fifteen minutes while meditating on fifteen mysteries of the Rosary, with the intention of making reparation to me."

Catholics have always honored the Blessed Virgin on Saturday because of the pious tradition of her constant faith in Jesus on that first Holy Saturday before the Resurrection.

According to Sister Lucia, five first Saturdays of reparation were requested to atone for the five ways in which people offend the Immaculate Heart of Mary:

1. Attacks upon Mary's Immaculate Conception.
2. Attacks against her Perpetual Virginity.
3. Attacks upon her Divine Maternity and the refusal to accept her as the Mother of all mankind.
4. For those who try to publicly implant in children's hearts indifference, contempt and even hatred of this Immaculate Mother.
5. For those who insult her directly in her sacred images.

Consecration to the Immaculate Heart of Mary

Virgin Mary, Mother of God and our Mother, to your Immaculate Heart I consecrate myself entirely with all that I am and all that I possess.

Take me under your maternal protection, defend me from danger, help me to overcome temptations which lure me to evil and preserve the purity of my body and my soul.

May your Immaculate Heart be my refuge and the way that leads me to God. Obtain for me the grace of praying and sacrificing myself for the love of Jesus, for the conversion of sinners and in reparation for the offenses committed against your Immaculate Heart.

In union with You and through the Heart of your Divine Son, I wish to live for the Most Holy Trinity, in Whom I believe, Whom I adore, I hope and I love.

Based on a prayer by Sister Lucia dos Santos, witness to the Fatima Apparitions.

Printed with ecclesiastical permission by

World Apostolate of Fatima, USA
PO Box 976
Washington, New Jersey
866-513-1917
for more information visit
www.wafusa.org

99570 **6/2006**

Do You Know?

The requests of Our Lady of Fatima to bring peace to the world?

Do you know that when a suffcient number of people fulfill Our Lady's requests, "Russia will be converted and a period of peace will be granted to the world?"

Are you doing what Our Lady of Fatima asked you to do while there is still time?

1. Are you *offering up your daily tasks* as a sacrifice in reparation?
2. Are you praying the *Rosary* every day?
3. Are you wearing the *Brown Scapular* as a sign of personal consecration and making *acts of consecration* to the Immaculate Heart of Mary?
4. Are you making further reparation: *First Saturday requests* and *visits* to the Blessed Sacrament?

Morning Offering

O my God, in union with the Immaculate Heart of Mary *(here kiss your scapular as a sign of your consecration),* I offer Thee the Most Precious Blood of Jesus, present in all the tabernacles of the world, joining with It the offering of my every thought, word and action of this day.

O my Jesus, I desire today to gain every indulgence and merit I can and I offer them, together with myself, to Mary Immaculate, that she may best apply them to the interests of Thy most Sacred Heart. Precious Blood of Jesus, save us! Immaculate Heart of Mary, pray for us! Sacred Heart of Jesus, have mercy on us!

REMEMBER
OUR LADY OF FATIMA SAID:

(These quotations are in the exact order in which Our Lady of Fatima spoke them beginning with the first apparition on May 13. 1917.)

1. **OFFERING:** "Will you offer yourselves to God, and bear with submission all the sufferings He sends you, in reparation for the sins that offend Him, and for the conversion of sinners?"
2. **BLESSED SACRAMENT:** Our Lady opened her hands and flooded the children in light. They fell to their knees, repeating: "Most Holy Trinity, I adore Thee! My God, my God, I love Thee in the Most Blessed Sacrament."
3. **HEAVEN:** "I come down from heaven." Our Lady promised that the children to whom she appeared would go to heaven, but one of them would have to pray many Rosaries "first."
4. **PURGATORY:** "She is in purgatory.... " (In reference to a friend, Amelia, who had recently died.)
5. **ROSARY:** "Pray the Rosary every day to obtain peace for the world and the end of the war." *(In July.)* "O my Jesus, forgive us our sins, save us from the fires of hell; lead all souls to heaven, especially those most in need of Thy mercy."
6. **IMMACULATE HEART:** "My Immaculate Heart will be your refuge and the way that will lead you to God."
7. **SACRIFICES:** "Make sacrifices for sinners, and say often, especially while making a sacrifice: 'O Jesus, this is for love of Thee. for the conversion of sinners and in reparation for sins committed against the Immaculate Heart of Mary."
8. **HELL:** "You have seen hell, where the souls of poor sinners go. It is to save them that God wants to establish in the world devotion to my Immaculate Heart. If you do what I tell you, many souls will be saved, and there will be peace." Before Our Lady spoke these words, she opened her hands, as Lucia says in her Memoirs, and "we saw a sea of fire Plunged in this flame

were devils and souls that looked like transparent embers; others were black or bronze, and in human form; these were suspended in flames...."

9. **FIVE WARNINGS:** "If my requests are not heeded, Russia will spread her errors throughout the world, provoking wars and persecutions of the Church; the good will be martyred, the Holy Father will have much to suffer, and various entire nations will be annihilated."
10. **PEACE:** "If my requests are fulfilled, Russia will be converted and there will be peace.... Finally, my Immaculate Heart will triumph. . . an era of peace will be granted to mankind."
11. **PRAYER:** "Pray, pray a great deal and make sacrifices for sinners, for many souls go to hell because they have no one to pray and make sacrifices for them."
12. **AMENDMENT OF LIFE:** "I have come to ask the faithful to amend their lives and ask pardon for their sins. They must cease offending God, who is already too much offended!"
13. **ST. JOSEPH:** The only saint who appears at Fatima besides Our Lady. St. Joseph held the Child Jesus in his arms and blessed the people.
14. **SCAPULAR OF MOUNT CARMEL:** In the final vision, on October 13, 1917, Our Lady appeared in the Carmelite habit wearing the Brown Scapular, highlighting the importance of this sacramental.
15. **FIRST SATURDAY DEVOTION:** "I promise to assist at the hour of death, with all the graces necessary for salvation, to all who on the first Saturday of five consecutive months: (1) Confess, (2) Receive Holy Communion, (3) Pray five decades of the Rosary, and (4) Keep me company for fifteen minutes while meditating on the mysteries of the Rosary, all with the intention of making reparation to my Immaculate Heart."

Before her death, Jacinta revealed some little-known statements made by Our Lady:

16. **WAR:** "War is a punishment for sin."
17. **FASHIONS:** "Certain fashions will be introduced that will offend Our Lord very much."
18. **MATRIMONY:** "Many marriages are not good, they do not please Our Lord and are not of God."
19. **PRIESTS:** "Priests must be pure, very pure. They should not busy themselves with anything except what concerns the Church and souls. The disobedience of priests to their superiors and to the Holy Father is very displeasing to Our Lord."
20. **SIXTH COMMANDMENT:** "More souls go to hell because of sins of impurity than for any other reason."

I Pledge Myself to Our Lady

Dear Queen and Mother, who promised at Fatima to convert Russia and bring peace to all mankind, in reparation for my sins and the sins of the whole world, I solemnly promise to your Immaculate Heart: (1) To offer up every day the sacrifices demanded by my daily duty; (2) To pray part of the Rosary (five decades) daily while meditating on the mysteries; (3) To wear the Scapular of Mount Carmel as profession of this promise and as an act of consecration to you. * I shall renew this promise often, especially in moments of temptation.

Signature: ______________________________

(This pledge is not a vow and does not bind under pain of sin. Nevertheless it is a promise: your word to your heavenly Mother.)

*Note: Baptized Catholics must be formally invested in the Scapular of Mount Carmel to gain the promise. A non-Catholic may wear the scapular and will receive blessings for doing so.

Requests

1. Make the First Saturdays.
2. Mass—Communions—visits—holy hours—vigils.

A Guide to Action

1. Send the signed pledge to the World Apostolate of Fatima National Center.
2. Encourage others to join.
3. Wear something blue, preferably the Blue Army pin.

Benefits

1. You know you are fulfilling Our Lady's conditions to obtain the triumph of her Immaculate Heart and the peace of Christ for the world.
2. You obtain numerous indulgences through the Rosary and the Scapular.
3. You become eligible for the Sabbatine Privilege.
4. Your name is flown to Fatima and buried near the site of the apparitions.
5. You are remembered in special Masses at the site of the apparitions.
6. You share in the prayers of all WAF members throughout the world.

Printed with ecclesiastical permission
World Apostolate of Fatima, USA
PO Box 976
Washington. NJ 07882-0976
866-513-1917
www.wafusa.org

333338

Detach and send in only this slip – save the other section as your record and reminder and for your Morning Offering.

☐ I am signing my pledge and wish my name flown to Fatima and buried near the site of the apparitions.

☐ I request permission to pray the Rosary (instead of praying the Little Office) as a condition of obtaining the Sabbatine Privilege. (If you check this box, this permission is automatically extended to you through the World Apostolate of Fatima.)

☐ I wish to help spread the message of Fatima. Please send me more information.

☐ Enclosed is $7.95 for a one-year subscription to *SOUL* magazine. [Canadian subscribers: $10.95 per year and all other foreign subscribers: $11.95 per year - U.S. currency only.]

Name____

Address______________________________________

City ________________ State ______ Zip Code____________

Parish_______________________________________

American and Canadian residents, please detach this pledge and send to: ***World Apostolate of Fatima, Box 976, Washington, NJ 07882-0976.*** All others send to ***World Apostolate of Fatima, International Secretariat. P.O. Box 38. 2496 Fatima. Portugal***

Lucia Speaks

The Message of Fatima

THE MESSAGE OF FATIMA

Lucia Speaks

In accord with Canon 827 of the New Code of Canon Law, this publication has been submitted to a censor of the Diocese and nothing being found contrary to faith and morals, we hereby grant permission in accord with Canon 824 that it be published.

Rev. Msgr. John B. Szymanski,
Vicar General
Diocese of Metuchen,
November 3, 1997

N.B. The ecclesiastical permission implies nothing more than the material contained in the publication has been examined by diocesan censors and nothing contrary to faith and morals has been found therein.

THE MESSAGE OF FATIMA

Lucia Speaks

Sr. Maria Lucia
of the Immaculate Heart

Edited by John Hauf & Marie Ostermann

World Apostolate of Fatima
Blue Army Shrine, USA
Washington, New Jersey
www.wafusa.org (908) 689-1700

Cover: ©The World Apostolate of Fatima, USA / The Blue Army, USA.

Back cover: ©The World Apostolate of Fatima, The Blue Army, USA.

Texts excerpted from *Fatima in Lucia's Own Words,* edited by Fr. Louis Kondor, S.V.D. and translated from the Portuguese by the Dominican Nuns of the Perpetual Rosary, and from *Jacinta, the Flower of Fatima* by Fr. José Galamba de Oliveira. Translated from the Portuguese by Frs. Humberto S. Medeiros and William F. Hill. © 1982, 1972 by AMI Press.

©2007 Revised Edition

Texts compiled by Jeannette Koene & Marie Ostermann

Printed in the United States of America
All Rights Reserved

ISBN 1-56036-107-7

Editor's Note

This new and expanded edition of *The Message of Fatima* (popularly known as *Lucia Speaks*) was published on the occasion of the 80th anniversary of the Fatima apparitions and the 50th anniversary of the World Apostolate of Fatima. It differs slightly from previous editions in that the source of the quotations by Sister Lucia, the surviving Fatima witness, is the English edition of Sister Lucia's memoirs published by the Postulation Center for the Causes of Jacinta and Francisco Marto at Fatima. The memoirs were edited by Fr. Louis Kondor, S.V.D. vice postulator for the causes of the Blesseds Jacinta and Francisco Marto. They are widely recognized as a fundamental source of information on the Fatima message.

Quotations attributed to Jacinta after the 1917 apparitions are taken from Father Oliveira's biography, *Jacinta, the Flower of Fatima*.

Preface

The news of the great happenings at Fatima in 1917 have reached the most remote corners of the earth. Yet the heavenly message which Our Lady brought to earth is still unknown to many, the message that mankind must turn from its evil ways and return to God, our Creator and Lord.

The reason for this little booklet is to make Our Lady's message known to all the world, as far as possible. This is the true message of Fatima, which very accurately reflects the Gospels, and shows the way for everyone to return to our Father's house. May this small book, with the blessings of Our Heavenly Mother, achieve its mission.

Introduction

God prepares those souls whom He has chosen to perform some extraordinary mission in the world. The more carefully He prepares them, the greater is the importance of the mission for all mankind.

This is especially true in regard to the three little shepherds of Fatima to whom Our Lady appeared, and to whom she confided a message that crosses all frontiers, and is directed to all men of good will.

First of all, God willed that they should be born into deeply Christian families, where they were brought up and educated in the love of God and the fulfillment of his Commandments. Later, He sent them a celestial messenger who, during the three successive apparitions, formed and prepared them in order to receive, from the Blessed Virgin Mary herself, the great message of salvation so that men would come back once more to the ways of God.

Because it is of primary importance that all should know the facts, we now present them according to the account given by Sister Lucia in her memoirs. Sister was providentially left in the world to faithfully transmit to us the requests of Our Lady of the Rosary of Fatima.

The Apparitions of the Angel of Peace

In Lucia's Own Words

First Apparition of the Angel

The dates I cannot set down with certainty, because, at that time, I did not know how to reckon the years, the months, or even the days of the week. But I think it must have been in the spring of 1916 that the angel appeared to us for the first time in our Loca do Cabeço.

As I have already written in my account of Jacinta, we climbed the hillside in search of shelter. After having taken our lunch and said our prayers, we began to see, some distance off, above the trees that stretched away towards the east, a light, whiter than snow, in the form of a young man, transparent, and brighter than crystal pierced by the rays of the sun. As he drew nearer, we could distinguish his features more and more clearly. We were surprised, absorbed, and struck dumb with amazement.

On reaching us, he said:

"Do not be afraid. I am the Angel of Peace. Pray with me."

Kneeling on the ground, he bowed down until his forehead touched the earth. Led by a supernatural impulse, we did the same, and repeated the words which we heard him say:

"My God, I believe, I adore, I hope and I love Thee! I beg pardon of Thee for those who do not believe, do not adore, do not hope and do not love Thee!"

Having repeated these words three times, he rose and said:

"Pray thus. The Hearts of Jesus and Mary are attentive to the voice of your supplications." Then he disappeared.

The supernatural atmosphere which enveloped us was so intense, that we were for a long time scarcely aware of our own existence, remaining in the same posture in which he had left us, and continually repeating the same prayer. The presence of God made itself felt so intimately and so intensely that we did not even venture to speak to one another. Next day, we were still immersed in this spiritual atmosphere, which only gradually began to disappear.

It did not occur to us to speak about this apparition, nor did we think of recommending that it be kept secret. The very apparition itself imposed secrecy. It was so intimate, that it was not easy to speak of it at all. The impression it made upon us was all the greater perhaps, in that it was the first such manifestation that we had experienced.

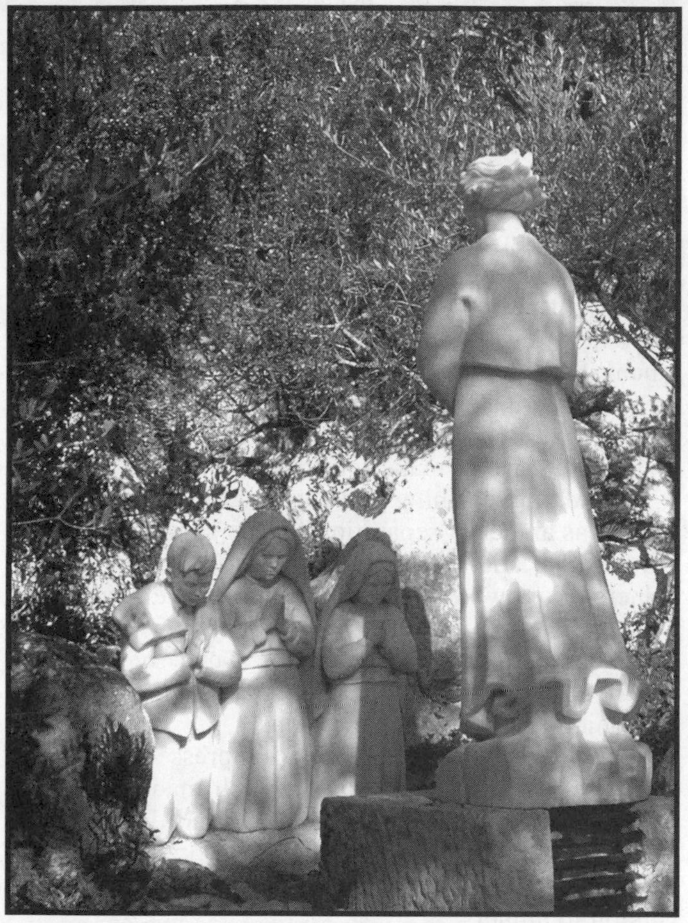

The Apparition of the Angel of Peace is depicted in this monument located in the Loca do Cabeço, the location in which the event occurred.

Second Apparition of the Angel

The second apparition must have been at the height of summer, when the heat of the day was so intense that we had to take the sheep home before noon and only let them out again in the early evening.

We went to spend the siesta hours in the shade of the trees which surrounded the well that I have already mentioned several times. Suddenly, we saw the same angel right beside us.

"What are you doing?" he asked. "Pray! Pray very much! The Hearts of Jesus and Mary have designs of mercy on you. Offer prayers and sacrifices constantly to the Most High."

"How are we to make sacrifices?" I asked.

"Make of everything you can a sacrifice, and offer it to God as an act of reparation for the sins by which He is offended, and in supplication for the conversion of sinners. You will thus draw down peace upon your country.

"I am its Angel Guardian, the Angel of Portugal. Above all, accept and bear with submission, the suffering which the Lord will send you."

These words were indelibly impressed upon our minds. They were like a light which made us understand who God is, how He loves us and desires to be loved, the value of sacrifice, how pleasing it is to Him and how, on account of it, He grants the grace of conversion to sinners.

It was for this reason that we began, from then on, to offer to the Lord all that mortified us, without, however, seeking out other forms of mortification and penance, except that we remained for hours on end with our foreheads touching the ground, repeating the prayer the angel had taught us.

Third Apparition of the Angel

It seems to me that the third apparition must have been in October, or towards the end of September, as we were no longer returning home for siesta.

As I have already written in my account of Jacinta, we went one day from Pregueira (a small olive grove belonging to my parents) to the Lapa, making our way along the slope of the hill on the side facing Aljustrel and Casa Velha. We said our Rosary there and the prayer the Angel had taught us at the first apparition.

While we were there, the angel appeared to us for the third time, holding a chalice in his hands, with a Host above it from which some drops of Blood were falling into the sacred vessel. Leaving the chalice and the Host suspended in the air, the angel prostrated himself on the ground and repeated this prayer threc times:

"Most Holy Trinity, Father, Son and Holy Spirit, I adore You profoundly. I offer Thee the most precious Body, Blood, Soul and Divinity of Jesus Christ, present in all the tabernacles of the world, in reparation for the outrages, sacrileges and indifference with which He is offended by the infinite merits of the Sacred Heart, and the Immaculate Heart of Mary, I beg of Thee the conversion of poor sinners."

Then, rising, he once more took the chalice and the

Host in his hands. He gave the Host to me, and to Jacinta and Francisco he gave the contents of the chalice to drink, saying as he did so: "Take and drink the Body and Blood of Jesus Christ, horribly outraged by ungrateful men. Repair their crimes and console your God." Once again, he prostrated himself on the ground and repeated with us three times more, the same prayer "Most Holy Trinity, . . ." and then disappeared.

Impelled by the power of the supernatural that enveloped us, we imitated all that the angel had done, prostrating ourselves on the ground as he did and repeating the prayers that he said. The force of the presence of God was so intense that it absorbed us and almost completely annihilated us. It seemed to deprive us even of the use of our bodily senses for a considerable length of time. During those days, we performed all our exterior actions as though guided by that same supernatural being who was impelling us thereto. The peace and happiness which we felt were great but wholly interior, for our souls were completely immersed in God. The physical exhaustion that came over us was also great.

I do not know why, but the apparitions of Our Lady produced in us very different effects. We felt the same intimate joy, the same peace and happiness, but instead of physical prostration, an expansive ease of movement; instead of this annihilation in the Divine Presence, a joyful exultation; instead of the difficulty speaking, we felt a certain communicative enthusiasm. Despite these feelings, however, we felt inspired to be silent, especially concerning certain things.

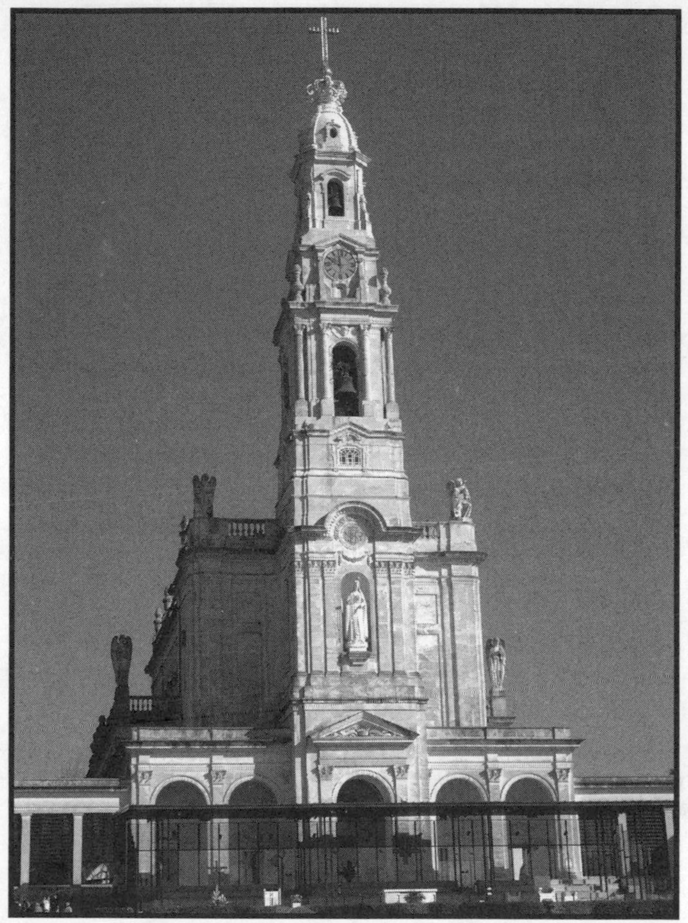

The Basilica of Our Lady of the Rosary of Fatima is a beacon of hope for millions of pilgrims from around the world each year.

Jacinta, Francisco and Lucia in a photograph from 1917. On May 13, 1989, Pope John Paul II venerated Jacinta and Francisco Marto, in a ceremony in Fatima.

The Apparitions of Our Lady

First Apparition of Our Lady

May 13, 1917

High up on the slope in the Cova da Iria, I was playing with Jacinta and Francisco at building a little stone wall around a clump of furze. Suddenly we saw what seemed to be a flash of lightning.

"We'd better go home," I said to my cousins, "that's lightning; we may have a thunderstorm."

"Yes, indeed!" they answered.

We began to go down the slope, hurrying the sheep along towards the road. We were more or less half-way down the slope, and almost level with a large holmoak tree that stood there, when we saw another flash of lightning. We had only gone a few steps further when, there before us on a small holmoak, we beheld a Lady all dressed in white. She was more brilliant than a crystal glass filled with sparkling water, when the rays of the burning sun shine through it.

We stopped, astounded, before the apparition. We were so close, just a few feet from her, that we were bathed in the light which surrounded her, or rather, which radiated from her. Then Our Lady spoke to us:

"Do not be afraid. I will do you no harm."

"Where are you from?"

"I am from heaven."

"What do you want of me?"

"I have come to ask you to come here for six months in succession, on the 13th day, at this same hour. Later on, I will tell you who I am and what I want. Afterwards, I will return here yet a seventh time."[1]

"Shall I go to heaven too?"

"Yes, you will."

"And Jacinta?"

"She will go also."

"And Francisco?"

"He will go there too, but he must say many Rosaries."

Then I remembered to ask about two girls who had died recently. They were friends of mine and used to come to my home to learn weaving with my eldest sister.

"Is Maria das Neves in heaven?"

"Yes, she is."(I think she was about 16 years old).

"And Amélia?"

"She will be in purgatory until the end of the world."

---

1. This "seventh time" refers to June 16, 1921, on the eve of Lucia's departure for Vilar de Oporto. The apparition in question was of a personal nature for Lucia. She did not consider it necessary to relate in her memoirs. (*Fatima in Lucia's Own Words*, ed. by Fr. Louis Kondor, S.V.D., p.187).

(It seems to me that she was between 18 and 20 years of age.)

"Are you willing to offer yourselves to God and bear all the sufferings He wills to send you, as an act of reparation for the sins by which He is offended, and of supplication for the conversion of sinners?"

"Yes, we are willing."

"Then you are going to have much to suffer, but the grace of God will be your comfort."

As she pronounced these last words ". . . the grace of God will be your comfort," Our Lady opened her hands for the first time, communicating to us a light so intense that, as it streamed from her hands, its rays penetrated our hearts and the innermost depths of our souls, making us see ourselves in God, Who was that light, more clearly than we see ourselves in the best of mirrors. Then, moved by an interior impulse that was also communicated to us, we fell on our knees, repeating in our hearts:

"O most Holy Trinity, I adore Thee! My God, my God, I love Thee in the most Blessed Sacrament!"

After a few moments, Our Lady spoke again:

"Pray the Rosary every day, in order to obtain peace for the world, and the end of the war."

Then she began to rise serenely, going up towards the east, until she disappeared in the immensity of space. The light that surrounded her seemed to open up a path before her in the firmament, and for this reason we sometimes said that we saw heaven opening.

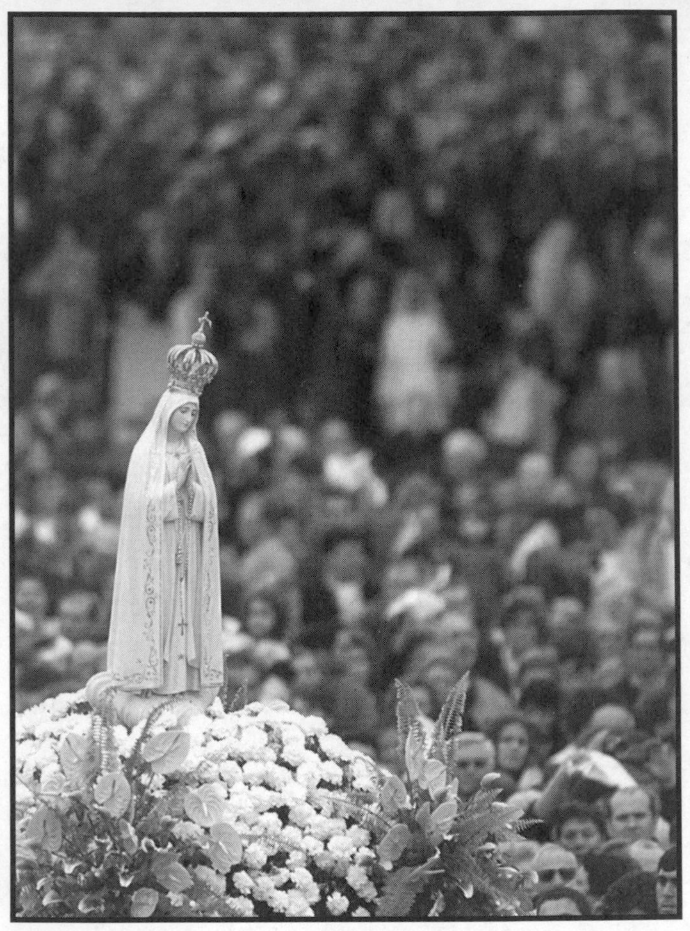

Thousands of pilgrims watch as the statue of Our Lady of Fatima is processed towards the Basilica of Our Lady of the Rosary in Fatima, Portugal.

Second Apparition of Our Lady

June 13, 1917

As soon as Jacinta, Francisco and I had finished praying the Rosary, with a number of other people who were present, we saw once more the flash reflecting the light which was approaching (which we called lightning). The next moment, Our Lady was there on the holmoak, exactly the same as in May.

"What do you want of me?" I asked.

"I wish you to come here on the 13th of next month, to pray the Rosary every day, and to learn to read. Later, I will tell you what I want."

I asked for the cure of a sick person.

"If he is converted, he will be cured during the year."

"I would like to ask you to take us to heaven."

"Yes. I will take Jacinta and Francisco soon. But you are to stay here some time longer.
Jesus wishes to make use of you to make me known and loved. He wants to establish in the world devotion to my Immaculate Heart."[1]

"Am I to stay here alone?" I asked, sadly.

"No, my daughter. Are you suffering a great deal?

Don't lose heart. I will never forsake you. My Immaculate Heart will be your refuge and the way that will lead you to God."[1]

As Our Lady spoke these last words, she opened her hands and for the second time, she communicated to us the rays of that same immense light. We saw ourselves in this light, as it were, immersed in God. Jacinta and Francisco seemed to be in that part of the light which rose towards heaven, and I in that which was poured out on the earth. In front of the palm of Our Lady's right hand was a heart encircled by thorns which pierced it. We understood that this was the Immaculate Heart of Mary, outraged by the sins of humanity, and seeking reparation.

You know now, Your Excellency, what we referred to when we said that Our Lady had revealed a secret to us in June. At the time, Our Lady did not tell us to keep it secret, but we felt moved to do so by God.

---

1. Because she was in a hurry, Lucia omitted the end of the paragraph which, in other documents, reads as follows: "I promise salvation to those who embrace it, and those souls will be loved by God like flowers placed by me to adorn His throne." (*Fatima in Lucia's Own Words*, ed. by Fr. Louis Kondor, S.V.D., p. 187).

Third Apparition of Our Lady

July 13, 1917

A few moments after arriving at the Cova da Iria, near the holmoak, where a large number of people were praying the Rosary, we saw the flash of light once more, and a moment later Our Lady appeared on the holmoak.

"What do you want of me?" I asked.

"I want you to come here on the 13th of next month, to continue to pray the Rosary every day in honor of Our Lady of the Rosary, in order to obtain peace for the world and the end of the war, because only she can help you."

"I would like to ask you to tell us who you are, and to work a miracle so that everybody will believe that you are appearing to us."

"Continue to come here every month. In October, I will tell you who I am and what I want, and I will perform a miracle for all to see and believe."

I then made some requests, but I cannot recall now just what they were. What I do remember is that Our Lady said it was necessary for such people to pray the Rosary in order to obtain these graces during the year. And she continued:

"Sacrifice yourselves for sinners, and say many times, especially whenever you make some sacrifice: O Jesus, it is for love of Thee, for the conversion of sinners, and in reparation for the sins committed against the Immaculate Heart of Mary."

As Our Lady spoke these last words, she opened her hands once more, as she had done during the two previous months. The rays of light seemed to penetrate the earth, and we saw as it were a sea of fire. Plunged in this fire were demons and souls in human form, like transparent burning embers, all blackened or burnished bronze, floating about in the conflagration, now raised into the air by the flames that issued from within themselves together with great clouds of smoke, now falling back on every side like sparks in huge fires, without weight or equilibrium, amid shrieks and groans of pain and despair, which horrified us and made us tremble with fear. (It must have been this sight which caused me to cry out, as people say they heard me.)

The demons could be distinguished by their terrifying and repellent likeness to frightful and unknown animals, black and transparent like burning coals. Terrified and as if to plead for succor, we looked up at Our Lady, who said to us, so kindly and so sadly:

"You have seen hell where the souls of poor sinners go. To save them, God wishes to establish in the world devotion to my Immaculate Heart. If what I say to you is done, many souls will be saved and there will be peace. The war is going to end; but if people do not cease offending God, a worse one will break out during the pontificate of Pius XI. When you see a night illumined by an unknown light,[1] know that this is the great sign given you by God that he is about to punish the world for its crimes, by means of war, famine, and persecutions of the Church and of the Holy Father.

"To prevent this, I shall come to ask for the consecration of Russia to my Immaculate Heart, and the Communion of Reparation on the First Saturdays. If my requests are heeded, Russia will be converted, and there will be peace; if not, she will spread her errors throughout the world, causing wars and persecutions of the Church. The good will be martyred, the Holy Father will have much to suffer, various nations will be annihilated. In the end, my Immaculate Heart will triumph. The Holy Father will consecrate Russia to me, and she will be converted, and a period of peace will be granted to the world. In Portugal, the dogma of the Faith will always be preserved; etc. . . .[2] Do not tell this to anybody. Francisco, yes, you may tell him.

"When you pray the Rosary, say after each mystery: O my Jesus, forgive us our sins, save us from the fires of hell. Lead all souls to Heaven, especially those most in need of Thy mercy."

After this, there was a moment of silence, and then I asked:

"Is there anything more that you want of me."

---

1. This was the aurora borealis on the night of January 25 - 26, 1938, which was unusual, and always regarded by Lucia as the God-given sign which had been promised. (*Fatima in Lucia's Own Words*, ed. by Fr. Louis Kondor, S.V.D., p. 187).

2. It was at this point that Our Lady revealed what has become known as the Third Secret of Fatima. The secret is discussed in the appendices.

“No, I do not want anything more of you today.”
Then, as before Our Lady began to ascend towards the east, until she finally disappeared in the immense distance of the firmament.

Fourth Apparition of Our Lady

August 19, 1917

As I have already said what happened on this day, I will not delay over here, but pass on to the apparition which, in my opinion, took place on the 15th[1] in the afternoon. As at that time I did not yet know how to reckon the days of the month, it could be that I am mistaken. But I still have an idea that it took place on the very day that we arrived back from Vila Nova de Ourém.

I was accompanied by Francisco and his brother John. We were with the sheep in a place called Valinhos, when we felt something supernatural approaching and enveloping us. Suspecting that Our Lady was about to appear to us, and feeling sorry lest Jacinta might miss seeing her, we asked her brother to go and call her. As he was unwilling to go, I offered him two small coins, and off he ran.

Meanwhile, Francisco and I saw the flash of light, which we called lightning. Jacinta arrived, and a moment

---

1. Lucia mentions here and also elsewhere, that the apparition occurred at Valinhos on August 15, that is, on the day of her return from Vila Nova de Ourém. This is a mistake; the day of her return from Ourém was certainly August 15, but the apparition occurred on the following Sunday, August 19, 1917 (*Fatima in Lucia's Own Words*, edited by Fr. Louis Kondor, S.V.D., p. 100).

later, we saw Our Lady on a holmoak tree.

"What do you want of me?"

"I want you to continue going to the Cova da Iria on the 13th, and to continue praying the Rosary every day. In the last month, I will perform a miracle so that all may believe."

"What do you want done with the money that the people leave in the Cova da Iria?"

"Have two litters made. One is to be carried by you and Jacinta and two other girls dressed in white; the other is to be carried by Francisco and three other boys. The money from the litters is for the "festa" [feast] of Our Lady of the Rosary, and what is left over will help towards the construction of a chapel that is to be built here."

"I would like to ask you to cure some sick persons."

"Yes, I will cure some of them during the year."

Then looking very sad, Our Lady said:

"Pray, pray very much, and make sacrifices for sinners; for many souls go to hell, because there are none to sacrifice themselves and to pray for them."

And she began to ascend as usual towards the east.

Fifth Apparition of Our Lady

September 13, 1917

As the hour approached, I set out with Jacinta and Francisco, but owing to the crowds around us we could only advance with difficulty. The roads were packed with people, and everyone wanted to see us and speak to us. There was no human respect whatsoever. Simple folk, and even ladies and gentlemen, struggled to break through the crowd that pressed around us. No sooner had they reached us than they threw themselves on their knees before us, begging us to place their petitions before Our Lady. Others who could not get close to us shouted from a distance:

"For the love of God, ask Our Lady to cure my son who is a cripple!" Yet another cried out: "And to cure mine who is blind! . . . To cure mine who is deaf! . . . To bring back my husband, my son, who has gone to war! . . . To convert a sinner! . . . To give me back my health as I have tuberculosis!"

All the afflictions of poor humanity were assembled there. Some climbed up to the tops of trees and walls to see us go by, and shouted down to us. Saying yes to some, giving a hand to others and helping them up from the dusty ground, we managed to move forward, thanks to some gentlemen who went ahead and opened a passage for us through the multitude.

Now, when I read the New Testament about those enchanting scenes of Our Lord's passing through Palestine, I think of those which Our Lord allowed me to witness, while yet a child, on the poor roads and lanes from Aljustrel to Fatima and on to the Cova da Iria! I give thanks to God, offering Him the faith of our good Portuguese people, I think: "If these people so humbled themselves before three poor children, just because they were mercifully granted the grace to speak to the Mother of God, what would they not do if they saw Our Lord Himself in person before them?"

Well, none of this was called for here! It was a distraction of my pen, leading me away where I did not mean to go. But, never mind! It's just another useless digression. I am not tearing it out, so as not to spoil the notebook.

At last, we arrived at the Cova da Iria, and on reaching the holmoak we began to say the Rosary with the people. Shortly afterwards, we saw the flash of light, and then Our Lady appeared on the holmoak.

"Continue to pray the Rosary in order to obtain the end of the war. In October Our Lord will come, as well as Our Lady of Dolors and Our Lady of Carmel. Saint Joseph will appear with the Child Jesus to bless the world. God is pleased with your sacrifices. He does not want you to sleep with the rope on, but only wear it during the daytime."

"I was told to ask you many things, the cure of some

sick people, of a deaf-mute . . ."

"Yes, I will cure some, but not others. In October I will perform a miracle so that all may believe."

Then Our Lady began to rise as usual, and disappeared.

Witnesses of the October 13, 1917, Miracle of the Sun in Fatima, Portugal.

Sixth Apparition of Our Lady

October 13, 1917

We left home quite early, expecting that we would be delayed along the way. Masses of people thronged the roads. The rain fell in torrents. My mother, her heart torn with uncertainty as to what was going to happen, and fearing it would be the last day of my life, wanted to accompany me.

On the way, the scenes of the previous month, still more numerous and moving, were repeated. Not even the muddy roads could prevent these people from kneeling in the most humble and suppliant of attitudes. We reached the holmoak in the Cova da Iria. Once there, moved by an interior impulse, I asked the people to shut their umbrellas and say the Rosary. A little later, we saw the flash of light, and then Our Lady appeared on the holmoak.

"What do you want of me?"

"I want to tell you that a chapel is to be built here in my honor. I am the Lady of the Rosary. Continue always to pray the Rosary every day. The war is going to end, and the soldiers will soon return to their homes."

"I have many things to ask you: the cure of some sick persons, the conversion of sinners, and other things . . ."

"Some yes, but not others. They must amend their lives and ask forgiveness for their sins."

Looking very sad, Our Lady said:

"Do not offend the Lord our God any more, because He is already so much offended."

Then, opening her hands, she made them reflect on the sun, and as she ascended, the reflection of her own light continued to be projected on the sun itself.

Here, Your Excellency, is the reason why I cried out to the people to look at the sun. My aim was not to call their attention to the sun, because I was not even aware of their presence. I was moved to do so under the guidance of an interior impulse.[1]

---

1. Lucia refers here to the miracle promised by Our Lady on July 13. The miracle of the sun occurred at this point in Lucia's narration. Estimates of the crowd present at Fatima ranged from 50,000 to 100,000 persons. It was seen by people within a 600 square mile area (roughly 32 by 20 miles) and described by journalist Avelino de Almeida. "Before the astonished eyes of the crowd, whose aspect was biblical as they stood bareheaded, pale with fright, eagerly searching the sky, the sun trembled, made sudden incredible movements outside all cosmic laws—the sun 'danced' according to the typical expression of the people. . . . The great majority admitted to having seen the trembling and the dancing of the sun. Others affirmed that they saw the face of the Blessed Virgin, while others swore that the sun whirled on itself like a giant catherine wheel and that it lowered itself to the earth as if to burn it with its rays. Some said they saw it change colors successively." *Fatima, the Great Sign*, Francis Johnston, Washington, N.J., AMI Press, 1980, pp. 58-66.

After Our Lady had disappeared into the immense distance of the firmament, we beheld St. Joseph with the Child Jesus and Our Lady robed in white with a blue mantle, beside the sun. St. Joseph and the Child Jesus appeared to bless the world, for they traced the Sign of the Cross with their hands. When, a little later, this apparition disappeared, I saw Our Lord and Our Lady; it seemed to me that it was Our Lady of Dolors. Our Lord appeared to bless the world in the same manner as St. Joseph had done. This apparition also vanished, and I saw Our Lady once more, this time resembling Our Lady of Carmel.

© Reproducta Co. Inc, New York

An artist's rendering of the vision of the Trinity and Our Lady as seen by Sister Lucia in the Dorothean convent at Tuy, Spain on June 13, 1929. The representation of the Trinity is similar to an illustration of the Trinity in a Psalter from Engelburg, Switzerland dating to 1335.

Apparitions after 1917

Francisco Marto died at his home in Aljustrel near Fatima on April 4, 1919. His sister Jacinta died in a Lisbon hospital on February 20, 1920. This chapter about Jacinta is excerpted from the book, *Jacinta, the Flower of Fatima* by Father Oliveira.

"Our Lady came to see us and said that she is coming very soon for Francisco to take him up to heaven. But she asked me if I still wanted to convert more sinners. I told her that I did. She told me that I was going to a hospital, and that I was going to suffer very much there, and that I should suffer for the conversion of sinners, in reparation for the sins committed against the Immaculate Heart of Mary and for the love of Jesus. . . . "

"Our Lady wants me to go to two hospitals, but it is not to be cured; it is only to suffer more for the love of Our Lord and for sinners."

The last days of Jacinta's life were spent in intimate union with the Mother of God. Because the Lady told her before she entered the hospital that she was going to die, Jacinta objected to surgical treatment. A successful operation was performed, however, and yet Jacinta grew worse. Violent pains racked her little body. Then as if by magic, four days before she died, the pains disappeared. Jacinta explained that Our Lady had again visited her, promising that in a short time she would come for her and relieve her of all pain. From that day until the moment of her death she showed no more signs of suffering.

The Lady told her that the sin which leads most people to perdition is the sin of impurity; that luxuries have to be put aside, and that people must not be obstinate in sin as they have been until now; that people must perform great penances. The Lady was very sad as she said these words.

For that reason Jacinta used to say again and again, "Oh, I feel so sorry for Our Lady! I feel so sorry for her!"

Our Lady's Words

These quotations are in the exact order in which Our Lady of Fatima spoke them beginning with the first apparition on May 13. 1917.

1. **OFFERING:** "Will you offer yourselves to God, and bear with submission all the sufferings He sends you, in reparation for the sins that offend Him, and for the conversion of sinners?"
2. **BLESSED SACRAMENT:** Our Lady opened her hands and flooded the children in light. They fell to their knees, repeating: "Most Holy Trinity, I adore Thee! My God, my God, I love Thee in the Most Blessed Sacrament."
3. **HEAVEN:** "I come down from heaven." Our Lady promised that the children to whom she appeared would go to heaven, but one of them would have to pray many Rosaries "first."
4. **PURGATORY:** "She is in purgatory.... " (In reference to a friend, Amelia, who had recently died.)
5. **ROSARY:** "Pray the Rosary every day to obtain

peace for the world and the end of the war." *(In July.)* "O my Jesus, forgive us our sins, save us from the fires of hell; lead all souls to heaven, especially those most in need of Thy mercy."

6. **IMMACULATE HEART:** "My Immaculate Heart will be your refuge and the way that will lead you to God."
7. **SACRIFICES:** "Make sacrifices for sinners, and say often, especially while making a sacrifice: 'O Jesus, this is for love of Thee. for the conversion of sinners and in reparation for sins committed against the Immaculate Heart of Mary."
8. **HELL:** "You have seen hell, where the souls of poor sinners go. It is to save them that God wants to establish in the world devotion to my Immaculate Heart. If you do what I tell you, many souls will be saved, and there will be peace." Before Our Lady spoke these words, she opened her hands, as Lucia says in her Memoirs, and "we saw a sea of fire Plunged in this flame were devils and souls that looked like transparent embers; others were black or bronze, and in human form; these were suspended in flames.... "
9. **FIVE WARNINGS:** "If my requests are not heeded, Russia will spread her errors throughout the world, provoking wars and persecutions of the Church; the good will be martyred, the Holy Father will have much to suffer, and various entire nations will be annihilated."
10. **PEACE:** "If my requests are fulfilled, Russia will be converted and there will be peace.... Finally, my

Immaculate Heart will triumph. . . an era of peace will be granted to mankind."

11. **PRAYER:** "Pray, pray a great deal and make sacrifices for sinners, for many souls go to hell because they have no one to pray and make sacrifices for them."
12. **AMENDMENT OF LIFE:** "I have come to ask the faithful to amend their lives and ask pardon for their sins. They must cease offending God, who is already too much offended!"
13. **ST. JOSEPH:** The only saint who appears at Fatima besides Our Lady. St. Joseph held the Child Jesus in his arms and blessed the people.
14. **SCAPULAR OF MOUNT CARMEL:** In the final vision, on October 13, 1917, Our Lady appeared in the Carmelite habit wearing the Brown Scapular, highlighting the importance of this sacramental.
15. **FIRST SATURDAY DEVOTION:** "I promise to assist at the hour of death, with all the graces necessary for salvation, to all who on the first Saturday of five consecutive months: (1) Confess, (2) Receive Holy Communion, (3) Pray five decades of the Rosary, and (4) Keep me company for fifteen minutes while meditating on the mysteries of the Rosary, all with the intention of making reparation to my Immaculate Heart."

Before her death, Jacinta revealed some little-known statements made by Our Lady:

16. **WAR:** “War is a punishment for sin.”
17. **FASHIONS:** “Certain fashions will be introduced that will offend Our Lord very much.”
18. **MATRIMONY:** “Many marriages are not good, they do not please Our Lord and are not of God.”
19. **PRIESTS:** “Priests must be pure, very pure. They should not busy themselves with anything except what concerns the Church and souls. The disobedience of priests to their superiors and to the Holy Father is very displeasing to Our Lord.”
20. **SIXTH COMMANDMENT:** “More souls go to hell because of sins of impurity than for any other reason.”

These following quotes are also attributed to Jacinta:

"Tell everybody...that the Heart of Jesus wishes the Heart of Mary to be venerated at His side. Let them ask for peace through the Immaculate Heart of Mary, for God has given it to Her."

"Our Lady also said that we should pray much and that we should make many sacrifices of the senses, which please Our Lord so much; that we should love God with our whole heart; that we should respect priests, who are the salt of the earth and serve to direct souls onto the path to Heaven..."

The Five First Saturday Devotion of Reparation

Dorothean convent, Pontevedra, Spain,

December 10, 1925

On December 10, 1925, the most holy Virgin appeared to her,[1] and by her side, elevated on a luminous cloud, was a Child. The most holy Virgin rested her hand on her shoulder, and as she did so, she showed her a heart encircled by thorns, which she was holding in her other hand. At the same time, the Child said:

"Have compassion on the Heart of your most holy Mother, covered with thorns, with which ungrateful men pierce it at every moment, and there is no one to make an act of reparation to remove them."

Then the most holy Virgin said:

"Look, my daughter, at my Heart, surrounded with thorns with which ungrateful men pierce me at every moment by their blasphemies and ingratitude. You at least try to console me and say that I promise to assist at the hour of death, with the graces necessary for salvation, all those who, on the first Saturday of five consecutive

---

1. Sister Lucia is writing of herself in her memoirs in the third person.

months, shall confess, receive Holy Communion, recite five decades of the Rosary, and keep me company for fifteen minutes while meditating on the fifteen mysteries of the Rosary, with the intention of making reparation to me."

February 15, 1926

On February 15, 1926, the Infant Jesus appeared to her again. He asked her if she had already spread the devotion to his most holy Mother. She told Him of the confessor's difficulties, and said that Mother Superior was prepared to propagate it, but that the confessor had said that she, alone, could do nothing.

Jesus replied: "It is true that your Superior alone can do nothing, but with my grace, she can do all." She placed before Jesus the difficulty that some people had about confessing on Saturday, and asked that it might be valid to go to Confession within eight days. Jesus answered: "Yes, and it could be longer still, provided that, when they receive Me, they are in the state of grace and have the intention of making reparation to the Immaculate Heart of Mary."

She then asked: "My Jesus, what about those who forget to make this intention?" Jesus replied: "They can do so at their next Confession, taking advantage of the first opportunity to go to Confession."

May 29-30, 1930

On June 12, 1930, Sr. Lucia wrote to her priest confessor answering questions he had put to her, "Why should it be 5 Saturdays and not 9 or 7 in honor of the Sorrows of Our Lady?"

Sr. Lucia answered, "While staying in the chapel with Our Lord part of the night, between the 29th and 30th of this month of May 1930, and speaking to our good Lord...I felt myself being more possessed by the Divine Presence, and if I am not mistaken, the following was revealed to me:

"My daughter, the motive is simple: there are 5 ways in which people offend, and blaspheme against the Immaculate Heart of Mary:

1. The blasphemies against the Immaculate Conception,
2. Against Her Virginity,
3. Against Her Divine Maternity, refusing at the same time to accept Her as the Mother of all mankind,
4. Those who try publicly to implant in the children's hearts indifference, contempt and even hate against this Immaculate Mother,
5. Those who insult Her directly in Her sacred statues.

"Here, My daughter, is the motive why the Immaculate Heart of Mary made Me ask for this little act of reparation and due to it move My mercy to forgive those souls who had the misfortune of offending her. As for you, try incessantly with all your prayers and sacrifices to move Me into mercifulness toward those poor souls."

Sister Lucia further answered this question, "And if one could not accomplish all those obligations on a Saturday, would Sunday not do?"

"The practice of this devotion will be equally accepted on the Sunday following the first Saturday, when, for just motives, many priests will allow it."

On May 18, 1936, Sr. Lucia wrote to Fr. Gonzalvez, having asked Our Lord why He wouldn't convert Russia without the Holy Father making the Collegial Consecration:

"Because I want my whole Church to acknowledge that consecration as a triumph of the Immaculate Heart of Mary, so that it may extend its cult later on, and put the devotion to this Immaculate Heart beside the devotion to My Sacred Heart."

The Last Vision

Dorothean convent, Tuy, Spain, June 13, 1929

This vision was granted to Sister Lucia on June 13, 1929, in the chapel of her convent at Tuy, Spain.

It was at this time that Our Lady informed me that the moment had come in which she wished me to make known to Holy Church her desire for the Consecration of Russia, and her promise to convert it.

I had sought and obtained permission from my superiors and confessor to make a Holy Hour from eleven o'clock until midnight, every Thursday to Friday night. Being alone one night, I knelt near the altar rail in the middle of the chapel and, prostrate, I prayed the prayers of the angel. Feeling tired, I then stood up and continued to say the prayers with my arms in the form of a cross. The only light was that of the sanctuary lamp. Suddenly the whole chapel was illumined by a supernatural light, and above the altar appeared a cross of light, reaching to the ceiling. In a brighter light on the upper part of the cross, could be seen the face of a man and his body as far as the waist; upon his breast was a dove of light; nailed to the cross was the body of another man. A little below the waist, I could see a chalice and a large host suspended in the air, on to which drops of blood were falling from the face of Jesus Crucified and from the wound in His side. These drops ran down on to the host and fell into the chalice. Beneath the right arm of the cross was Our Lady and in her hand was her Immaculate Heart. (It was Our Lady of Fatima, with her Immaculate Heart in her left hand, without sword or roses, but with a crown of thorn and flames.) Under the left arm of the cross, large letters, as if of crystal clear water which ran down upon the altar, formed these words: "Grace and Mercy."

I understood that it was the Mystery of the Most Holy Trinity which was shown to me, and I received lights about this mystery which I am not permitted to reveal.

Our Lady then said to me: "The moment has come in which God asks the Holy Father, in union with all the bishops of the world, to make the consecration of Russia to my Immaculate Heart, promising to save it by this means. . . ."

The Rich Content of the Message of Fatima

The message of Fatima which springs from the apparitions of Our Lady, is a solid blueprint for life. It cries out to be put into practice for the good of the world, and the salvation of souls.

Its teachings are in harmony with the Gospel, calling to mind the following elements with new emphasis:

- The mystery of the Blessed Trinity;
- The providence of God, which directs and governs the world and presides over the events of human history;
- The omnipotence and omniscience of God, Who knows and realizes all things according to His exalted designs. It foretold future events and revealed miraculous signs to prove the truth of God's predictions;
- God, Who rewards or punishes, according to the good or evil done, though He is ever merciful towards sinners;
- The reality of heaven, hell and purgatory;
- The existence of Guardian Angels, not only of indi-

viduals but also of nations;

- The real presence of Christ in the Most Blessed Sacrament, and the necessity and value of Holy Communion;
- Sanctity as a condition of true happiness even on earth, and docility and correspondence to grace, the mysterious mixture of divine action and human effort;
- The reality of sin as an offense against God with its tragic consequences for sinners and nations;
- The flight from sin and amendment of life as an indispensable condition of the state of grace;
- The Christian solidarity of the Mystical Body of Christ;
- The intercession of the Mother of God as a powerful mediatrix and dispenser of grace;
- The necessity of penance and prayer, with their value of atonement and intercession;
- The love of the Heart of Jesus and of the Immaculate Heart of Mary—the great revelation of Fatima;
- The importance of Marian devotions, particularly, the excellence and efficacy of the Rosary, the new devotion of the first Saturdays, and the value of Consecration of the Immaculate Heart of Mary;
- The powerful action of grace, which so transformed the three little children at Fatima and led them to such a close union with God.
- Russia, simultaneously a scourge that punishes the sins of the world, and the object of Divine Mercy, by the promise of its conversion through the intermediary of the Heart of Mary;

- The sanctification of the family, in imitation of the vivid scene of the last apparition;
- Devotion to the Holy Father and the necessity of purity and modesty;
- The final triumph of the Immaculate Heart of Mary.

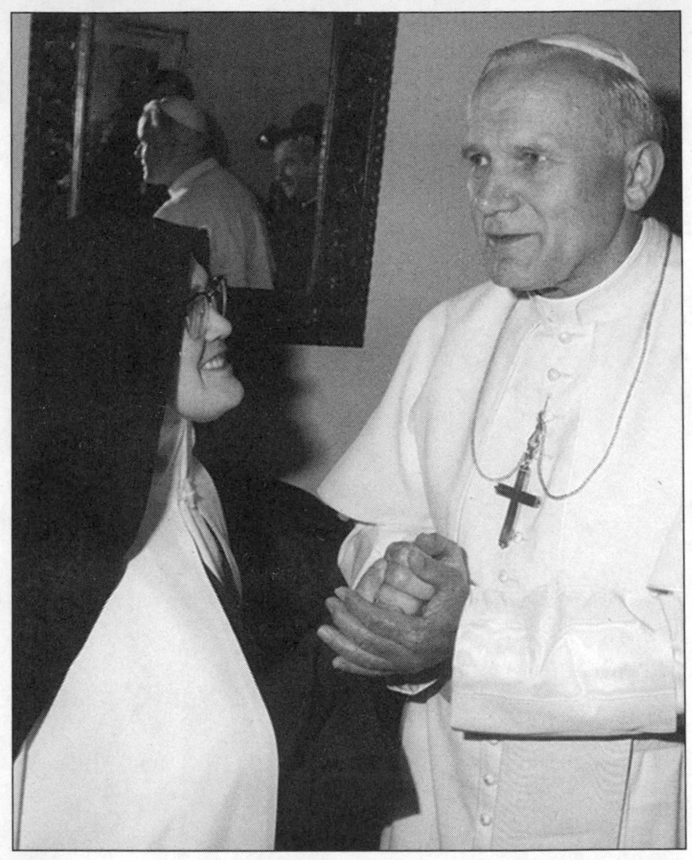

Pope John Paul's first encounter with Sr. Lucia took place exactly one year after the attempt on his life in St. Peter's Square in 1981. On that occasion he ordered the bullet that was found in the jeep in which he was riding, be set in the crown of the image of the Virgin of Fatima in gratitude to her for saving his life, as the Third Secret revealed.

Appendix I

The Third Secret of Fatima

Translation of the Original Text written by Sr. Lucia in 1944 to Bishop Leiria

J.M.J.

The third part of the secret revealed at the Cova da Iria-Fatima, on 13 July 1917.

I write in obedience to you, my God, who command me to do so through his Excellency the Bishop of Leiria and through your Most Holy Mother and mine.

After the two parts which I have already explained, at the left of Our Lady and a little above, we saw an Angel with a flaming sword in his left hand; flashing, it gave out flames that looked as though they would set the world on fire; but they died out in contact with the splendor that Our Lady radiated towards him from her right hand: pointing to the earth with his right hand, the Angel cried out in a loud voice: 'Penance, Penance, Penance!'. And we saw in an immense light that is God: 'something similar to how people appear in a mirror when they pass in front of it' a Bishop dressed in White 'we had the impression that it was the Holy Father'.

Other Bishops, Priests, men and women Religious going up a steep mountain, at the top of which there was a big Cross of rough-hewn trunks as of a cork-tree with the bark; before reaching there the Holy Father passed through a big city half in ruins and half trembling with halting step, afflicted with pain and sorrow, he prayed for the souls of the corpses he met on his way; having reached the top of the mountain, on his knees at the foot of the big Cross he was killed by a group of soldiers who fired bullets and arrows at him, and in the same way there died one after another the other Bishops, Priests, men and women Religious, and various lay people of different ranks and positions. Beneath the two arms of the Cross there were two Angels each with a crystal aspersorium in his hand, in which they gathered up the blood of the Martyrs and with it sprinkled the souls that were making their way to God.

Tuy-3-1-1944

Appendix II

The Third Secret of Fatima

Translation of the Pope John Paul II's Official Response to the Text of the Third Secret

To the Reverend Sister
Maria Lucia
of the Convent of Coimbra

In the great joy of Easter, I greet you with the words the Risen Jesus spoke to the disciples: "Peace be with you"!

I will be happy to be able to meet you on the long-awaited day of the Beatification of Francisco and Jacinta, which, please God, I will celebrate on 13 May of this year.

Since on that day there will be time only for a brief greeting and not a conversation, I am sending His Excellency Archbishop Tarcisio Bertone, Secretary of the Congregation for the Doctrine of the Faith, to speak with you. This is the Congregation which works most closely with the Pope in defending the true Catholic faith, and which since 1957, as you know, has kept your handwritten letter containing the third part of the "secret" revealed on 13 July 1917 at Cova da Iria, Fatima.

Archbishop Bertone, accompanied by the Bishop of Leiria, His Excellency Bishop Serafim de Sousa Ferreira e Silva, will come in my name to ask certain questions about the interpretation of "the third part of the secret".

Sister Maria Lucia, you may speak openly and candidly to Archbishop Bertone, who will report your answers directly to me.

I pray fervently to the Mother of the Risen Lord for you, Reverend Sister, for the Community of Coimbra and for the whole Church. May Mary, Mother of pilgrim humanity, keep us always united to Jesus, her beloved Son and our brother, the Lord of life and glory.

With my special Apostolic Blessing.

IOANNES PAULUS PP. II

From the Vatican, 19 April 2000.

PLEDGE OF
OUR LADY OF FATIMA

Dear Queen and Mother, who promised at Fatima to convert Russia and bring peace to all mankind, in reparation for my sins and the sins of the whole world, I solemnly promise to your Immaculate Heart:

1. To offer up every day the sacrifices demanded by my daily duty.

2. To pray part of the Rosary* daily while meditating on the Mysteries.

3. To wear the Scapular of Mount Carmel as profession of this promise and as an act of consecration to you.

4. To accomplish the devotion of the Five First Saturdays of the month, including fifteen minutes of meditation on the Mysteries of the Rosary.

I shall renew this promise often, especially in moments of temptation.

---

*Usually understood to mean at least five decades.

Note: This pledge is not a vow and does not bind under sin. Nevertheless, it is a promise of love; your word to your heavenly Mother.

Morning Offering

O my God, in union with the Immaculate Heart of Mary *(here kiss your Brown Scapular as a sign of your consecration—this carries a partial indulgence)*, I offer Thee the Precious Blood of Jesus from all the altars throughout the world, joining with It the offering of my every thought, word and action of this day.

O my Jesus, I desire today to gain every indulgence and merit I can, and I offer them, together with myself, to Mary Immaculate—that she may best apply them to the interests of thy most Sacred Heart. Precious Blood of Jesus, save us! Immaculate Heart of Mary, pray for us! Sacred Heart of Jesus, have mercy on us!

SOUL Magazine keeps you updated on the latest news from the World Apostolate of Fatima, the Blue Army and the Catholic Church. SOUL also carries lively features on faith, prayer, Church history, the lives of the saints, Scripture and Marian devotion. It makes a wonderful gift!

SUBSCRIPTION RATES

United States

1 Year (4 issues) - $13.00
3 Years (12 issues) - $34.95

Canada

1 Year (4 issues) - $15.95
3 Years (12 issues) - $43.95

Prices subject to change without notice.

To subscribe, fill out the form below and mail with your payment to:
***SOUL* Magazine, Box 976, Washington, NJ 07882.**
Subscribe by phone with your credit card: (866) 513-1917
or on our website: www.wafusa.org

- -

Name______________________________

Address______________________________

____

City ______________________________

State_______________ Zip _______________

Now that you know the Message of Fatima, why not make a difference in the world?

Join the World Apostolate of Fatima

Pope John Paul II has said that the Fatima message is more relevant today than ever (Fatima, May 13, 1982) and that it can be synthesized in Christ's own words: "The kingdom of God is at hand. Repent, and believe in the Gospel" (Vatican City, May 15, 1991).

WRITE: World Apostolate of Fatima, Box 976, Washington, NJ 07882
TOLL FREE: (866) 513-1917 **WEB:** www.wafusa.org

I wish to further the work of Our Lady of Fatima through the World Apostolate of Fatima.

Name ______________________________

Address ______________________________

City ______________________________

State ____________________ Zip ____________________

☐ Please send me the World Apostolate of Fatima Pledge and information about the Apostolate.

☐ Accept my donation of $ _______ to further the work of the World Apostolate of Fatima or donate online at wafusa.org.

☐ Please send me information on how to honor Our Lady in my Will.

ONE WORLD PRAYING
ORBIS UNUS ORANS
WORLD APOSTOLATE OF FATIMA

Would You Like to Grow in Holiness and Change the World?

Those Incredible Prayer Cells

Join a Blue Army of Our Lady of Fatima Prayer Cell!

What is a World Apostolate of Fatima Prayer Cell?

A World Apostolate of Fatima Prayer Cell (Cell Hour of Holiness) is a weekly spiritual gathering for small group prayer before the Blessed Sacrament or in a home. Members endeavor to grow in holiness by responding to Our Lady of Fatima's requests for prayer, penance and sacrifice in a spirit of reparation.

The Imperative to Pray

God has always required perseverance in prayer from the faithful in the Old and New Testaments (Sir. 17:24;18:22; Luke 21:36; Rom. 12:12; Eph. 6:18; Col. 4:2; 1 Thess. 17 and 1 Peter 4:7). At Fatima, the angel and the Blessed Virgin reinforced to the children and all Christians the scriptural imperative to remain constant in prayer. Participating in a Fatima Prayer Cell is an excellent means of putting these healthy spiritual admonitions into practice in our lives.

Origin

It may be said that the first prayer cell started with Our Lady and the three children at Fatima. During her six apparitions at Fatima in 1917, Our Lady and the children prayed together.

Why Are They Called "Cells"?

Just as the cells in a body divide and grow, a prayer

group should do the same after there are between eight and ten members. Part of the group splits and forms a new prayer cell.

What are the Added Advantages?

By participating in a World Apostolate of Fatima Prayer Cell, members experience the joy of weekly meetings for prayer, to discuss Our Lady's message and to experience her "presence." The prayer cell offers the joy of holy friendships, of praying together and helping each other to respond to Our Lady as did the children of Fatima.

How May I Join?

If there is an established World Apostolate of Fatima Prayer Cell in your parish or in a nearby home, you can join it. If not, please contact your diocesan division of the World Apostolate of Fatima and inquire about the location of prayer cells in your diocese. If a diocesan division does not exist, contact the national center. Interest others in participating in a prayer cell. By all means approach your pastor, show him the ten-point program and explain your reason for wanting to pray in a group. If you cannot obtain permission to meet in a church, begin a prayer cell in your home. Just one or two more with you is sufficient to form a prayer cell.

What Program Do We Follow?

We follow a ten-point program of prayer, based on the spiritual exercises of Saint Ignatius of Loyola, which includes the Rosary and prayers taught by Our Lady and the Angel of Peace at Fatima:

Opening Prayer

1. Eucharistic Prayer and Angel's Prayer
2. World Apostolate of Fatima Pledge
3. Meditative Rosary
4. Pardon Prayer
5. Motivation Report (prayer petitions)
6. Invocations to World Apostolate of Fatima Patrons
7. Spiritual Reading
   (a) *The Message of Fatima —Lucia Speaks*: one apparition at each meeting for beginners)
   (b) *Fatima in Lucia's Own Words* —(Sister Lucia's memoirs)
   (c) Articles from *SOUL* Magazine.
   (d) An approved catechism
8. Examination by cell members (report on previous week's resolution)
9. Resolutions for the week
10. Eucharistic Prayer and Angel's Prayer

Our Lady at Fatima

In World Apostolate of Fatima Prayer Cells, members will become more familiar with the message of Fatima. In 1917, Our Lady prophesied that Russia would spread her errors (militant atheism) throughout the world. She also prophesied the conversion of Russia, the triumph of her Immaculate Heart and promised an era of peace for mankind.

In all six of her apparitions, Our Lady of Fatima asked for prayer, penance and sacrifices and especially the daily recitation of the Rosary. She also requested the devotion of the First Saturdays. Our Lady said that God wishes to establish in the world devotion to her Immaculate Heart. She also said that certain fashions would be introduced that would offend Our Lord very much. And, with a sad expression, Our Lady of Fatima asked that we pray very much and make sacrifices for sinners, for many souls go to hell because there is no one to pray and make sacrifices for them.

You Can Make A Difference

Our Lady has brought about the overthrow of atheistic communism in Russia and opened the way for its conversion. The World Apostolate of Fatima has much to do to help Our Lady in converting Russia and the rest of the world from the corruption of materialism and immorality. Prayer and sacrifices are the tools needed to accomplish this. You can make a difference. Won't you join a prayer cell group today? These little islands of holiness are desired by Jesus and Mary and can help save the world.

Full Details

Full details are available in the World Apostolate of Fatima Adult Cell Kit (order #412063) which includes the Leader's Manual and a sample copy of all literature each prayer cell member should have for the meeting. You may obtain the kit from your diocesan division of the World Apotolate of Our Lady of Fatima or the World Apostolate of Our Lady of Fatima National Center, Washington, New Jersey 07882-0976 or call (908) 689-1700 or FAX (908) 689-0721 between 8:00 A.M. and 4:30 P.M. Eastern time. The office is closed weekends and on Holy Days of Obligation and major holidays.

printed with ecclesiastical permission

for more information, contact your local diocesan division or:

World Apostolate of Fatima, USA
P.O. Box 976, Washington, N.J. 07882
866-513-1917 www.wafusa.org

48323

Requirements for
FIRST FRIDAYS

In 1675, Our Lord appeared "out of a monstrance" before St. Margaret Mary Alacoque and showed the burning love of His Heart for men.

After revealing the now-famous promises to those who would venerate His Sacred Heart, Our Lord said:

"The all powerful love of my Heart will grant to those who shall receive Communion on the First Friday of nine consecutive months the grace of final repentance..."

Those who honor Our Lord in his Sacred Heart by attending Mass and receiving Communion for nine consecutive First Fridays would receive many graces from the Heart of Jesus and would not die without receiving the Sacraments.

A final promise was that the Sacred Heart would be an *"assured refuge at the last hour."* A similar promise was made by Our Lady for those who faithfully practice the First Saturday Devotion.

Promises of Our Lord to Those Who Honor His

SACRED HEART

1. I will give them all the graces necessary for their state in life.
2. I will establish peace in their families.
3. I will console them in all their difficulties.
4. I will be their assured refuge in life and most especially at death.
5. I will pour out abundant benedictions on all their undertakings.
6. Sinners will find in my Heart the source and infinite ocean of mercy.
7. Tepid souls shall become fervent.
8. Fervent souls shall advance rapidly to great perfection.
9. I will bless the houses in which the image of my Sacred Heart will be exposed and honored.
10. I will give to priests the power of moving the most hardened hearts.
11. Persons who propagate this devotion shall have their names inscribed in my Heart, and they shall never be effaced from it.
12. I promise thee, in the excess of the mercy of my Heart, to grant to all those who receive Communion on the First Friday of every month, for nine consecutive months, *the grace of final repentance and that they shall not die under my displeasure,* nor without receiving the sacraments, and my Heart will be their secure refuge at that last hour.

Requirements for

FIRST SATURDAYS

On December 10, 1925, Our Lady appeared with the Child Jesus to Lucia at the Dorothean convent in Pontevedra, Spain.

Our Lord asked Lucia to *"Have pity"* on the Heart of her *"Most Holy Mother"* and to offer acts of reparation.

Then Our Lady said: *"Look, my daughter, at my Heart encircled with thorns, with which ungrateful men pierce it at every moment by their blasphemies and ingratitude. You, at least, try to console me, and say that I promise to assist at the hour of death with all the graces necessary for salvation all those who, on the First Saturday of five consecutive months, confess, receive Holy Communion, recite five decades of the Rosary, and keep me company for fifteen minutes meditating on the mysteries of the Rosary, with the intention of making reparation to me."*

Promises of Our Lady to Those Who Honor Her

IMMACULATE HEART

Our Lady said: *"God wishes to establish in the world devotion to my Immaculate Heart. If what I say is done, many souls will be saved and there will be peace."*

In addition Our Lady made the following promises to those who, *on five consecutive First Saturdays,* will confess their sins, receive Holy Communion, say the Rosary and spend fifteen minutes with her in meditation in reparation for the offenses committed against her Immaculate Heart: *"I will assist at the hour of your death with all the grace necessary for salvation..."*

To Lucia, as promoter of devotion to her Heart, Our Lady promised: *"I will be with you always. My Immaculate Heart will be your refuge and the way that will lead you to God."*

Then Our Lord said to her: *"I desire that devotion to the Immaculate Heart of my Mother be placed alongside devotion to my own Sacred Heart."*

St. John Eudes said: *"Be united to the Heart of Mary that thus you may be more intimately united to the Heart of Jesus."* So united we will obtain all Their promises.

Printed with ecclesiastical permission.

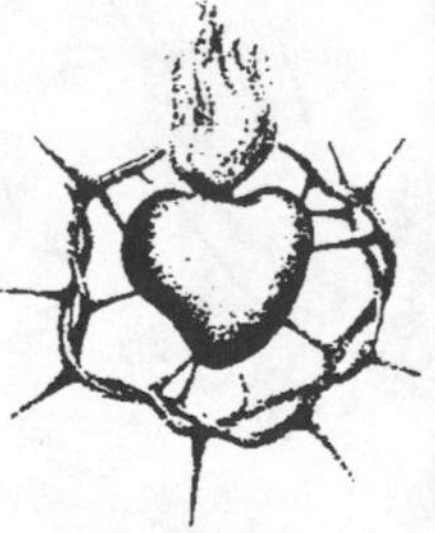

World Apostolate of Fatima,USA
P.O. Box 976
Washington, N.J. 07882
866-513-1917
www.wafusa.org

328621

WHY 5 FIRST SATURDAYS

The promise made by Our Lady to Lucia at Fatima on July 13, 1917, that there would be a future manifestation concerning the five First Saturdays, was fulfilled on December 10, 1925. Lucia was then a postulant in the Dorothean convent at Pontevedra, Spain. This time Our Lady appeared together with the Child Jesus. She addressed Lucia as follows:

Look, my daughter, at my heart encircled with thorns, with which ungrateful pierced it every moment by their blasphemies and ingratitude. Give me consolation, you, at least; and announce for me that I promise to assist at the hour of death, with the graces necessary for salvation, all those who on the first Saturday of five consecutive months shall confess, receive Holy Communion, recite five decades of the Rosary, and keep me company for fifteen minutes while meditating on the mysteries of the Rosary, with the purpose of making reparation to me.

Before Our Lady spoke these words, the Child Jesus had said to Lucia:

Have compassion on the Heart of your most holy Mother, covered with thorns with which ungrateful men pierce at every moment, and there is no one to make an act of reparation to remove them.

Saturday Is Traditionally Dedicated to Mary

Before studying the actual words of Mary's message, we should note that from ancient times the Holy Church has considered Saturday a day especially dedicated to intensifying Christians' devotion to the Blessed Virgin, Mother of God and our most loving Mother. Many people used to consecrate the first Saturdays of the months to Our Lady for this very intention and for making reparation for the blasphemies and outrages against her by sinners and false teachers. Pope St. Pius X, on June 12, 1905, issued a decree in which he praised this practice and offered indulgences for it.

That same year, in the month of November, the Holy Father again blessed and indulgenced the traditional practice of the Sons of the Heart of Mary and the Archconfraternity of the Immaculate Heart of Mary, to dedicate the first Saturdays of the months to the practice of this devotion with the purpose of making reparation to the Immaculate Heart of Mary.

Now, at Fatima, the Virgin herself wished to recommend this devotion, specifying five consecutive first Saturdays, and enriching the practice with her promise of salvation.

In the ultimate instance, it is God Who is offended by every sin. For this reason it is God, likewise, Who is the ultimate object of every act of Christian reparation. This shows clearly in all the manifestations of Fatima, and in a very concrete fashion in the apparition of July 13, 1917. But let us add, nevertheless, that one will not properly understand the "heavenly message of Fatima," in this essential point of the spirit of reparation, unless the meaning is extended to include also a direct reparation to the Immaculate Heart of Mary. It is Our Lord Himself Who tells us this: "Have compassion on the heart of your Most Holy Mother."

The predestination of Mary to the divine maternity, her active cooperation in all the work of Redemption, her mission to be spiritual Mother of the whole Church and of every person redeemed by the Precious Blood of Christ constitutes, as we have already said, one of the basic laws of divine providence for the effective application of the Redemption to souls. Therefore the Blessed Virgin tells us that it is God's design, to save the world and to save souls, that the devotion to her Immaculate Heart should be intensified and extended. Consequently, whoever does injury to Our Lady—whether by blasphemy, by denying her greatness or her saving mission, or by trying to depreciate the devotion to Our Lady in the Church or in souls—likewise does injury to God and His providence.

An aware Christian sees this disorder as an injury which is directed to the Mother of God and to God Himself and His providence, and he thus tries to make reparation for it by intensifying his personal devotion and his efforts to bring about the reign of the Heart of Mary. Both aspects of Christian reparation—that which looks directly to God, and that which, subordinately, looks directly to the Heart of Mary— are complementary manifestations of one and the same spirit of authentic Christian reparation. Both aspects of reparation are recommended and united in the manifestations of Fatima; and now, again, in the subsequent recommendation made to us concerning the practice of the five First Saturdays, in reparation.

Consider the Basic Elements of the Devotion

In this practice it is useful to consider four basic things: Confession, Communion, the Rosary and its meditation, and the promise of salvation.

In all true devotion to Our Lady (and devotion to her Immaculate Heart is the perfect expression of this true devotion), there is always an effective invitation for the return of hearts to Christ the Savior. Where it is concerned with sinners, it is a call to conversion to the ways of grace and eternal salvation. Where it is concerned with souls who already live in the grace of God, true devotion to Our Lady gives them a strong impulse to travel the pathway to sanctity, and creates in them the spirit of the Christian apostolate.

This is a constant law in the vitality of the Church. Marian institutions, Marian shrines, and Marian movements and pilgrimages which are carried in many cities—have always been, and are everywhere today, an irresistible call from the maternal Heart of Mary for a sincere return of souls to Jesus Christ. For example, Fatima is now, as Lourdes has been for more than a century, an important chapter of this history of the return of souls to God and to the paths of eternal salvation.

Five Excellent Reasons For This Devotion

The practice of the five First Saturdays in reparation belongs to this new chapter of the sanctification and the eternal salvation of the redeemed. Why precisely *five* First Saturdays?

In a letter given by Sister Lucia to Fr. Jose Bernardo Gonzalves on June 12, 1930, she said that while in the convent chapel on the night of May 29-30, Our Lord revealed the reason for five Saturdays.

"My daughter, the motive is simple: there are five ways in which people offend, and blaspheme against the Immaculate Heart of Mary.

1. The blasphemies against the Immaculate Conception.

2. Against her virginity.

3. Against the divine maternity, refusing at the same time to accept her as the Mother of all mankind.

4. Those who try publicly to implant in the children's hearts, indifference, contempt and even hate against this Immaculate Mother,

5. Those who insult her directly in her sacred images."

But be that as it may, it is clear that the practice of this devotion leads souls to habitual devotion, or the spirit of devotion to the Immaculate Heart of Mary, and to frequent or daily Holy Communion.

In order to succeed in introducing this spirit of devotion in souls, it is very useful to state some definite period of time—here the First Saturdays of five successive months—for the teaching and practice of that which should be acquired as a habit. The same thing occurs in the process of education in all aspects of faith and Christian life; and the same principle is followed in the liturgical cycle of the feasts of the Church, with their annual rotation. Thus, the first fruit of the practice of the First Saturdays is the cult of the divine Eucharist, in its threefold aspect of sacrifice, communion, and adoration.

The second requirement in the practice of the five First Saturdays is the Rosary, with meditation. In a strictly Christo-centric interpretation of the devotion of the Rosary we should have to define certain points, in the proper place. Here we will limit ourselves to underlining two aspects of the devotion of the Rosary: prayer and meditation. The Rosary whose recitation is here called for is not that of the complete fifteen decades, but of five mysteries only. In her testimony in the canonical investigation of the apparitions of Fatima, and later in her writings, the confidante of Our Lady always quotes her as saying "a third of the Rosary." And the Lady appeared with the five-decade rosary, not the fifteen decade one, in her hands.

Meditation's Role

The vocal prayer of the Rosary always has as its foundation the interior act of meditation upon the mysteries of the life, suffering, and glory of Our Lord and of the Blessed Virgin. But the fifteen-minute meditation specified in the practice of the First Saturdays is another thing. During these fifteen minutes the attention may be centered on one mystery only; or, if the time of this meditation is inserted between or distributed over the recitation of the decades, it can be directed to the mystery which is announced at the beginning of each of them. Any method is good.

Yet, let us consider it as more typical to make this meditation separately. Concerning Our Lady, the Gospel says, "His mother kept all these things in her heart." (Luke 2:51) This is the best model for a soul that proposes to know and imitate Jesus Christ. In the hands of a good director, this practice of the separate meditation will give the best opportunity for setting forth throughout the whole year the principal passages of the Gospel in their different aspects: historic, dogmatic, and ascetic.

A new detail of interest in the recitation of the Rosary is the ejaculation that Our Lady invites us to insert between the decades. The Portuguese text goes thus:

O meu Jesus! perdonai-nos, livrai do fogo da inferno e levai as alminhas todas para o ceu, e socorrei principalmente as que mais precisaren.

(O my Jesus; forgive us our sins: save us from the fires of hell. Lead all souls to heaven, especially those most in need of thy mercy.)

We have a correct version above. The expression *alminhas* (souls) has seemed to some to mean "the souls of Purgatory." One reads it thus in certain manuals. But Lucia herself, when expressly and repeatedly asked, has replied that the words never had that sense on the lips of Our Lady, but that it rather referred to the souls of sinners, for whose conversion and eternal salvation we are invited to pray.

To Think We Can Help Them!

But who are those "most in need?" Perhaps those who seem obstinately uprepentant, those who are exposed to an unforeseen death in the state of mortal sin, and finally, those who by circumstances of place, environment, or education, are farthest from any possible priestly influence and from the sacraments, even in the last moments of life. For all these poor souls, most in need of the mercy of God, should be poured out the efficacious prayers of Christian souls, interceding for them and making reparation, uniting themselves with the mediation of the Heart of Mary, Mother and Refuge of sinners.

To those who practice the devotion of the First Saturdays in reparation, Our Lady promises her assistance at the hour of death "with the graces necessary for salvation. . ." She does not promise them eternal salvation itself, but the divine graces necessary for salvation. It is not exactly the same thing. But is not this certainty of the special assistance of Our Lady a trustworthy guarantee that the soul, in that last hour upon which eternity depends, will respond to the call of divine grace with true contrition for its sins?

Frequent experience tells us that souls especially devoted to the Heart of Mary receive at that time an awareness from heaven that the hour of their parting is near. It is not precisely an announcement of death, but a new and gentle preoccupation with more frequent and more worthy reception of the sacraments, with a more pure intention in all one's actions, and with an intensification of one's charity and dedication to the apostolate. The Heart of Mary kindly goes about perfecting the souls of her children for their decisive encounter with the Divine Savior.

There are some who do not favor insisting upon the reminder of the great promise of the Sacred Heart of Jesus concerning the First Fridays, or the promise of the Heart of Mary concerning the practice of the First Saturdays. They fear that Christian piety and love for God will be depreciated and converted into a sentiment, or even a sentimentality, which is self-interested and egotistic. It is not impossible for such a deviation to arise in the practice of Christian piety and in the ways of inculcating it. But is this danger as great as that of the reaction against it, which would silence all reference to the divine promise?

Objection Answered

We have answered this objection before. It is not for man to give lessons to the Lord, or to correct the plan of the Savior's humane love, nor to straighten the paths traveled by his mercy, which is infinite, and infinitely delicate in the effective application of the fruit of his redemption to souls. The promises made by Divine Love in the Gospel, or in special manifestations to chosen souls at certain difficult moments in the history of salvation, are never the sole motive, nor the principal motive of the devotion of conscientious Christians. Yet their love of God, their faith, and their unshakable fidelity to God's commandments receive powerful aid from these promises, and from them they receive a firmer conviction in the supreme mystery of Divine Love and Divine Mercy. And more than a few times the memory of these divine promises was the effective point of departure for awakening in certain souls the first attention to the grave problem of their eternal salvation and their life in grace.

In conclusion, the promises made by the Hearts of Jesus and Mary are demonstrations of their love for us, and thus serve to enkindle love and gratitude in well-disposed souls. This is the experience of the Church concerning piety. Let us give one example. In keeping with the promise that the Heart of Mary made to them in her first apparition, the two younger shepherds of Fatima, Jacinta and Francisco, were well assured of their eternal salvation, and this prompted them to great undertakings of prayer and sacrifice, for the sake of reparation, so that they reached the summit of Christian holiness.

What Do I Have To Do?
A Helpful Guide

The devotion of First Saturdays, as requested by Our Lady of Fatima, carries with it the assurance of the graces necessary for salvation at the hour of death. However to derive profit from such a great promise of Our Lady, the devotion must be properly understood and duly performed. The requirements as stipulated by Our Lady are as follows:

(1) Confession, (2) Communion, (3) Five Decades of the Rosary (4) Meditation on one or more of the Rosary Mysteries for 15 minutes, (5) To do all these things in the spirit of Reparation to the Immaculate Heart of Mary, and (6) to observe these practices on the First Saturday of five consecutive months.

1. CONFESSION

A reparative confession means that the confession should not only be good (valid and licit), but also be offered in the spirit of reparation, in this case, to Mary's Immaculate Heart.

This confession may be made on the First Saturday itself or some days before or after the First Saturday, and may be associated with another devotion.

Thus the confession made in connection with First Friday devotion may be used for the First Saturdays.

2. COMMUNION

The Communion of reparation must be sacramental. No external action to express the intention is needed. The Communion must be made during the 24 hours of the First Saturday. For justifying reasons, approved by a priest, a person may receive the Communion the next day, the Sunday following the First Saturday. A spiritual communion does *not* satisfy this condition.

3. THE ROSARY

Five Decades Suffices

This too must be recited in the spirit of reparation. The important thing is to pray the Rosary well by doing one's best to be attentive. One should make the intention to offer the Rosary in reparation to the Immaculate Heart at least at the beginning of the Rosary.

4. MEDITATION FOR 15 MINUTES

Here the meditation on one mystery or more is to be made without simultaneous recitation of the Rosary decade. As indicated, the meditation may be either on one mystery alone for 15 minutes, or on all 15 mysteries spending about one minute on each mystery, or again, on two or more mysteries during the period. This can also be made before each decade spending three minutes or more in considering the mystery of the particular decade. This meditation has likewise to be made in the spirit of reparation to the Immaculate Heart.

Many find it difficult to meditate because they have not made any attempt before. But a start could be made by using pictures depicting different mysteries, or by reading slowly and devoutly appropriate meditations prepared for our use, or even by reading the Gospel narratives containing the mysteries with or without commentaries.

There have been many apparitions of Our Lady, but Fatima is the first where meditation on the Rosary mysteries is requested. It is obvious that this request is to help us to recite the Rosary properly and to derive many aids for the amendment of our lives and for our sanctification.

5. THE SPIRIT OF REPARATION

All these acts have to be done with the intention of offering reparation to the Immaculate Heart of Mary for the offenses committed against her. Everyone who offends her commits a twofold offense, for these sins also offend her Divine Son and endanger our salvation. Reparation emphasizes our responsibility towards sinners who, by themselves, will not pray and make reparation for their sins.

This devotion brings before us our social responsibilities and reminds us of the fact that to go to God we must love our neighbor and try to save his soul; it also shows us that one excellent way of doing this is through the spirit of reparation to the Immaculate Heart of Mary.

There are many who seem to be worried because, though they try to observe five First Saturdays in accordance with the requests of Our Lady of Fatima, they fail to remember to make the intention of reparation in due time for Confession, Communion, meditation, or the Rosary recitation. But this difficulty may be overcome by making a resolution at the very start when one decides to observe the First Saturdays for the next five consecutive months and resolve that all the acts or devotions connected with them will be offered in reparation to the Immaculate Heart.

6. FIVE CONSECUTIVE FIRST SATURDAYS

The idea of the five First Saturdays is to make us persevere in the devotional acts for these Saturdays. Our Lady knows that the person will become devoted to her Immaculate Heart and persist in practicing such devotion on all First Saturdays.

Unless Russia is converted, the movement against God will continue to spread, promoting wars and making the attainment of peace and justice impossible. One means of obtaining Russia's conversion is to practice the Fatima message. The stakes are so great that to encourage Catholics to practice the devotion of the First Saturday, Our Lady has assured us that she will obtain the graces necessary for salvation at the hour of death for all those who observe the First Saturdays for five consecutive months in accordance with her conditions.

At the supreme moment the departing person will be either in the state of grace or not. In either case Our Lady will be by his side. If in the state of grace, she will console and help him to resist whatever temptations the devil might put before him in his last attempt to take the person with him to hell. If not in the state of grace, Our Lady will help the person to repent in a manner agreeable to God and so benefit by the fruits of redemption and be saved.

NOTE: Our Lady asked that, whenever we pray the Rosary, the following prayer be inserted after each decade.

O my Jesus, forgive us our sins, save us from the fires of hell. Lead all souls to heaven, especially those most in need of thy mercy.

MARY'S REQUESTS

PRAYER

Do you pray Five Decades of her Rosary every day?

SACRIFICE

Do you extend your Morning Offering throughout the day in your daily duties?

REPARATION

Have you made an effort to make the Five First Saturdays?

CONSECRATION

Do you wear her Brown Scapular?

Imprimatur:
Most Rev. George W. Ahr,
Bishop of Trenton

World Apostolate of Fatima, USA
PO Box 976 - Washington, N.J. 07882-0976
866-513-1917 www.wafusa.org

96936 **5/2005**

A GUIDE TO
First Saturday REPARATION

During the second apparition of Our Lady to the children at Fatima on June 13, 1917, the Blessed Virgin Mary explained that Lucia would live longer than her cousins, Jacinta and Francisco Marto. *"Jesus wishes to make use of you to make me known and loved. He wants to establish in the world devotion to my Immaculate Heart. I promise salvation to those who embrace it, and those souls will be loved by God like flowers placed by me to adorn His throne."*

The next month the Blessed Virgin appeared again and showed the children a vision of hell. She then said, *"You have seen hell where the souls of poor sinners go. To save them, God wishes to establish in the world devotion to my Immaculate Heart. If what I say to you is done, many souls will be saved and there will be peace. The war [World War I] is going to end; but if people do not cease offending God, a worse one [World War II] will break out during the pontificate of Pius XI. . . To prevent this, I shall come to ask for the consecration of Russia to my Immaculate Heart and the Communion of Reparation on the First Saturdays. . ."*

Our Lady's Request

Eight years later, Our Lady returned to Lucia in the Dorothean convent at Pontevedra, Spain. She appeared with the Child Jesus who spoke: *"Have pity on the Heart of your Most Holy Mother. It is covered with the thorns with which ungrateful men pierce it at every moment, and there is no one to remove them with an act of reparation."*

The Blessed Mother then said: *"My daughter, look at my heart surrounded with the thorns with which ungrateful men pierce it at every moment by their blasphemies and ingratitude. You, at least, try to console me, and say that I promise to assist at the hour of death with all the graces necessary for salvation all those who, on the first Saturday of five consecutive months, go to confession and receive Holy Communion, recite five decades of the Rosary, and keep me company for fifteen minutes while meditating on the fifteen [now twenty] mysteries of the Rosary with the intention of making reparation to me."*

Why Five First Saturdays?

Christians have always honored the Blessed Virgin on Saturday because of her faith in Jesus on that first Holy Saturday before the Resurrection.

According to Sr. Lucia, Five First Saturdays of Reparation were requested to atone for the five ways in which people offend the Immaculate Heart of Mary:

attacks upon Mary's Immaculate Conception; attacks against her Perpetual Virginity; attacks upon her Divine Maternity and the refusal to accept her as the Mother of all mankind; for those who try to publicly implant in children's hearts indifference, contempt and even hatred of this Immaculate Mother; and for those who insult her directly in her sacred images.

First Saturday Devotion in Your Parish

First you must seek your pastor's permission to observe First Saturdays publicly. Inform him that an international effort is being made to respond to Jesus and Mary's request to Sister Lucia for reparation. Then assure him that there will be no work on his part and all that is needed is his permission for the Rosary to be recited in the church on the first Saturday of the month. Ask him if you can put a notice in the bulletin once a month and make a leaflet available to parishioners. It is the pastor's decision when the Rosary will be recited - it could be before or after any Saturday Mass.

In many parishes the Rosary is already recited daily. To formalize a First Saturday Devotion, all that is necessary is to announce the intention of making reparation to the Immaculate Heart of Mary at the start of the Rosary.

Parishioners who cannot attend a Saturday morning Mass may pray the Rosary for a half hour before or after the Saturday evening vigil Mass. Where there is no Saturday Mass, permission may be obtained from the priest to fulfill the conditions on the following Sunday. First Saturdays may also be observed as part of a valid Communion service instead of the Mass. This is especially helpful for those in mission churches or in institutions.

Devotion throughout the World

On March 24, 1984, Pope John Paul II consecrated the world to the Immaculate Heart of Mary as Our Lady requested. Since then, we have witnessed the collapse of Communism in Eastern Europe and the Soviet Union. This has opened the way for the conversion of Russia promised by Our Lady at Fatima.

Our goal is to continue our efforts to establish in the world devotion to the Immaculate Heart of Mary by responding to Jesus and Mary's request made to Sister Lucia for reparation. If we fulfill this request we may expect the fruition of Our Lady's promises: the salvation of sinners, her assistance with all the graces necessary for salvation at the hour of our death and an era of peace for mankind.

First Saturday Requirements

Sacrament of Penance

Confession may be made on the First Saturday itself or some days before or after the First Saturday. During an apparition of the Child Jesus, Sister Lucia presented the difficulty some persons had in going to Confession on Saturdays and asked that the Confession for the devotion be valid within eight days. Jesus answered, "*Yes. It can even be within many more days, provided that when they receive Me, they are in the state of grace and have the intention of offering reparation to the Immaculate Heart of Mary.*" She then asked, "My Jesus, what about those who forget about forming such an intention?" Jesus answered, "*They can form it in the following Confession at their first opportunity of receiving the Sacrament of Penance.*"

Communion of Reparation

Communion of Reparation must be sacramental (a spiritual Communion does not satisfy this condition) and must be made within the twenty-four hours of the First Saturday.

Sister Lucia asked Jesus, "And if one could not accomplish all those obligations on a Saturday, would Sunday not do?" She believed that Jesus revealed to her, *"The practice of this devotion will be equally accepted on the Sunday following the First Saturday when, for just motives, many priests will allow it."*

Intention of First Saturday Rosary

A full Rosary is made up of twenty decades —five Joyful Mysteries, five Luminous Mysteries, five Sorrowful Mysteries and five Glorious Mysteries. At Fatima and for the First Saturday Devotion, Our Lady asked that only five decades be recited in the vision to Sister Lucia. She also asked that we say the following prayer at the end of each Mystery:

> *"O My Jesus, forgive us, save us from the fire of Hell; lead all souls to Heaven, especially those who are most in need."*

Before beginning the public recitation of the First Saturday Rosary, the following should be said: "The intention of this First Saturday Rosary is to make reparation to the Immaculate Heart of Mary." The Joyful, Luminous, Sorrowful and Glorious Mysteries should be alternated each month so that all are covered. Exceptions would be using the Joyful at Christmas, the Sorrowful during Lent and the Glorious at Easter.

According to Sister Lucia, the fifteen-minute meditation and the Rosary recitation are two distinct requirements of the devotion. She has advocated that they be performed separately.[1] Our Lady asks us to keep her company for fifteen minutes while meditating on one or more Mysteries of the Rosary. Meditation entails thinking quietly and dwelling upon the Rosary Mysteries. It can be helpful to have a Rosary booklet with pictures, narratives or Gospel readings to bring the Mysteries to mind. The World Apostolate of Fatima has a booklet available for your use called, *First Saturday Aid.* It can be obtained by calling the numbers at the end of this brochure.

Let us recall the words Blessed Jacinta said when she had only a short time to live: "*Tell everybody that God grants us graces through the Immaculate Heart of Mary; that people are to ask her for them; and that the Heart of Jesus wants the Immaculate Heart of Mary to be venerated at His side. Tell them also to pray to the Immaculate Heart of Mary for peace, since God has entrusted it to her. . . .*"

[1]Joaquin Maria Alonso, *La Gran Promesa del Corazon Inmaculado de Maria en Pontevedra* (*The Great Promise of the Immaculate Heart of Mary at Pontevedra*), 3rd Edition, Madrid, EDITA, 1977, p 69.

First Saturday Devotion Requirements

1. Go to Confession
2. Receive Holy Communion
3. Pray five decades of the Rosary
4. Keep Mary company by meditating for fifteen minutes on the Rosary Mysteries

This should be done with the intention of making reparation to the Immaculate Heart of Mary.

Drawing by Ariel Agemian
© Confraternity of the Precious Blood
printed with ecclesiastical permission

World Apostolate of Fatima, USA
PO Box 976
Washington, NJ 07882
866-513-1917
www.wafusa.org

96916

Attach Great Importance to Your Scapular

It Is An Assurance of Salvation

> "Whosoever dies clothed in this scapular shall not suffer eternal fire."

- Mary's Promise to St. Simon Stock
July 16, 1251

The Brown Scapular of Our Lady of Mount Carmel should have deep meaning for you. It is a rich present brought down from heaven by Our Lady herself.

"Wear it devoutly and perseveringly," she says to each soul, "it is my garment. To be clothed in it means you are continually thinking of me, and I, in turn, am always thinking of you and helping you to secure eternal life."

St. Alphonsus Said:

"Just as men take pride in having others wear their livery, so the most holy Mary is pleased when her servants wear her scapular as a mark that they have dedicated themselves to her service, and are members of the family of the Mother of God."

By simply wearing the scapular, we tell Mary that we venerate her, love her and trust her every moment of the day.

The Scapular as a Prayer

Our Lord taught us to pray the **Our Father**. Mary taught us the value of the scapular. When we use it as a prayer, Our Lady draws us to the Sacred Heart of her Divine Son. It is well, therefore, **to hold the scapular in the hand** while addressing Our Lady.

A prayer thus uttered while holding the mystical scapular is as perfect as a prayer can be. It is especially in **time of temptation** that we need the powerful intercession of God's Mother. The evil spirit is utterly powerless when a scapular wearer, besides his silent devotion, faces temptation calling upon Mary.

"If you had recommended yourself to me, you would not have run into such danger," was Our Lady's gentle reproach to Blessed Alan de la Roche.

The Promise

In his book, *Brown Scapular of Mount Carmel,* Fr. Barry Bossa, S.A.C., observes that misunderstandings can arise about the nature of the scapular promise.

He says, "The very wording of the scapular promise

makes it absolutely clear that the Blessed Virgin never intended to substitute the wearing of brown cloth for living the Christian life." Instead, the scapular is a sign that its wearer is committed to living the Christian life after the perfect example of the Blessed Virgin Mary.

A former prior general of the Carmelite Order, the Most Rev. Kilian Lynch, warned against abusing the scapular devotion. "Let us not conclude," he said, "that the scapular is endowed with some kind of supernatural power which will save us no matter what we do or how much we sin... A perverse, sinful will can defeat the 'suppliant omnipotence' of the Mother of mercy." Fidelity to the commandments is required by those seeking "the special love and protection of Our Lady."

The Scapular Medal

The Scapular Medal bears an image of the Sacred Heart of Jesus on one side and an image of the Blessed Virgin Mary on the reverse. In 1910, Pope St. Pius X declared that a person already validly invested in a cloth scapular could wear or carry the Scapular Medal in its place. This concession was granted at the request of missionaries in the tropics where cloth scapulars deteriorated rapidly and wearing them was a real inconvenience.

Both Pius X and his successor Pope Benedict XV expressed their strong desire that people continue to wear the cloth scapular when practical and not substitute the medal without sufficient reason. Vanity and fear of making open profession of our affiliation with Our Lady would be wrong reasons for substituting the medal for the cloth.

Mary's Spiritual Motherhood

Mary's Motherhood is not limited to Catholics; it is extended to all people. Many miracles of conversion have been wrought in favor of good non-Catholics who practiced the scapular devotion.

"I wanted to know if Mary really and truly interested herself in me, and in the scapular she has given me the most tangible assurance. I have only to open my eyes. She has attached her protection to this scapular: 'Whosoever dies clothed in this shall not suffer eternal fire.'"

– *Saint Claude de la Colombiere*

World Apostolate of Fatima, USA
PO Box 976, Washington, NJ 07882
866-513-1917 www.wafusa.org

printed with ecclesiastical permission

99527

Questions & Answers

about the World Apostolate of Fatima and the Brown Scapular

Q. What is the World Apostolate of Fatima, USA?

The World Apostolate of Fatima, USA (WAF) is a worldwide movement of the faithful responding to the requests of the Mother of God made to three shepherd children at Fatima, Portugal, in 1917.

In 2006, the WAF was elevated to a Public Association of the Faithful by the Vatican and now serves as the only Fatima organization with that distinction. The Apostolate's goal is to teach people how to live, learn and spread the Message of Fatima in their personal lives, in thier local communities and throughout the world.

Q. What happened at Fatima?

Through a series of six apparitions from May 13 through October 13, the Blessed Virgin Mary invited all mankind to prayer, conversion, consecration and reparation as the sure means of obtaining world peace. Her message was validated by the Miracle of the Sun on October 13, 1917. More than 70,000 people within a thirty-mile radius of Fatima saw the sun make abrupt movements in the sky and plunge toward the earth.

Contained in Our Lady of Fatima's messages are

prophesies about the rise and fall of Communism, World War II and persecution for the Church, but she added that in the end, her Immaculate Heart would triumph and an era of peace would be granted.

Q. How is the Apostolate related to Fatima?

Members pray the Rosary daily as requested by the Virgin Mary at Fatima and frequently meet for a weekly Holy Hour called a Prayer Cell. They offer the penance of their daily trials in life for the conversion of sinners, and wear the Brown Scapular of Our Lady of Mount Carmel as a sign of consecration to the Immaculate Heart of Mary. They also make the Five First Saturdays Devotion of Reparation.

Q. How do I become a member of the World Apostolate of Fatima?

Simply sign a pledge in which you promise to fulfill the conditions for peace given by Our Lady at Fatima. The pledge is not a vow and does not bind under pain of sin.

Q. What are the conditions of the pledge?

(1) Pray the Rosary daily;
(2) wear the Brown Scapular as a sign of consecration to the Immaculate Heart of Mary; and

(3) offer reparation through the Morning Offering. To make the Five First Saturdays Devotion of Reparation.

Q. I am already fulfilling these basic conditions. What more can I do?

Attend Mass frequently; receive Holy Communion worthily; make visits to the Blessed Sacrament; participate in Prayer Cell Holy Hours and All-Night Vigils. Tell others about Our Lady of Fatima's requests and encourage them to join the World Apostolate of Fatima.

Q. What are the benefits of WAF membership?

You know you are fulfilling Our Lady's conditions for the conversion of sinners and world peace. You obtain numerous indulgences through the Rosary and the Scapular. Your name is flown to Fatima and buried near the site of the apparitions. You are remembered in Masses at the Shrine of the Immaculate Heart of Mary in Washington, New Jersey. You also share in the prayers of WAF members throughout the world.

Q. What are the conditions and benefits of the First Saturday Devotion?

Our Lady said: *"I promise to assist at the hour of death, with all the graces necessary for salvation, all those who, on the first Saturday of five consecutive months, shall confess, receive Holy Communion, recite five decades of the Rosary and keep me company for fifteen minutes while meditating on the fifteen Mysteries of the Rosary, with the intention of making reparation to me."*

Q. What is the Brown Scapular?

The Brown Scapular is a sacramental. It is part of the habit of Carmel. In miniature form, it consists of two small pieces of brown material connected by string or chain and worn over the shoulders. The Carmelite Order originated on Mount Carmel in the Holy Land near the cave of Elijah the Prophet, who was the inspiration of the early members of Carmel.

Q. What is the history of the Scapular?

"This shall be to you and all Carmelites a privilege, that anyone who dies clothed in this shall not suffer eternal fire; and if wearing it they die, they shall be saved."

The wearing of the Scapular must be understood to mean that one is striving earnestly to live up to all Christian ideals. It does not take the place of the Church's Sacraments, but is an outward sign of inward commitment to virtue and Christian piety, under the patronage of Mary.

Saints and pontiffs have often warned us of the folly of abusing Mary's promise. At the same time that Pope Pius XI joyfully professed: "I learned to love the Scapular Virgin in the arms of my mother," he also warned the faithful that " . . . although it is very true that the Blessed Virgin loves all who love her, nevertheless those who wish to have the Blessed Mother as a helper at the hour of death, must in life merit such a signal favor by abstaining from sin and laboring in her honor." To lead a willfully sinful life while trusting in the Scapular promise is to commit a sin of presumption.

Q. What privilege relates to wearing the Brown Scapular?

World Apostolate of Fatima members may take advantage of the spiritual priviledges associated to authentic devotees of Our Lady of Mount Carmel. Our Lady promised to release from purgatory soon after death all those who (1) wear the Brown Scapular, (2) observe chastity according to their state in life. You must be invested in the Brown Scapular and try to live a Christian Life.

Q. Do I simply begin wearing the Brown Scapular, or must I be invested in it first?

To obtain the full benefit of the Brown Scapular devotion, one must be validly invested in the Brown Scapular. The investiture "enrolls" the wearer in the Confraternity of Our Lady of Mount Carmel.

A Catholic can be invested in the Brown Scapular by a priest or deacon, using a Scapular blessed by a priest or deacon. After proper investiture in the Scapular, a person need not have subsequent Scapulars blessed. Once invested, you are invested until death.

Q. **May a non-Catholic wear the Brown Scapular?**

Yes, and in so doing, a non-Catholic will receive many graces and blessings with this special sign of devotion to the Mother of God. Although baptized Catholics are the only ones who can be officially invested in the Confraternity and share in the special Scapular privileges, non-Catholics are warmly encouraged to avail themselves of this special way of honoring Jesus' Mother.

Q. **I was once invested in the Brown Scapular but have failed to wear it for some time. Must I be reinvested in order to derive the Scapular benefits?**

Membership in the Confraternity is not forfeited by merely laying aside the Scapular. One need only begin wearing it again.

Q. Must I wear the Scapular around my neck?

Yes, the Scapular is a habit – Our Lady's habit. The Scapular must be worn over the shoulders in such a manner that one part hangs in front of the body and the other in back. Worn in any other way, it carries no indulgence or promise. It is usually worn under one's outer clothing but not necessarily next to the skin. Furthermore, the Scapular may be enclosed in some sort of case – metal, plastic, etc. – provided the case does not prevent the Scapular material from being attached to the braid or chain. A deteriorated Scapular should be burned or buried; any metal or plastic covering may be discarded.

Q. Must the Brown Scapular be made of wool?

At one time, this was a requirement. However, Carmelite regulations now permit the Scapular to be made from any suitable brown material.

Q. May I substitute the Scapular Medal for the cloth Scapular?

While the Scapular Medal, on one side the image of the Sacred Heart of Jesus, and on the other, the image of Mary, enjoys all the privileges granted to those wearing the cloth Scapular (except for the partial indulgence for kissing the Scapular granted by Pope Benedict XV), the substitution of the medal for the cloth should only be made for a good and serious reason. Saint Pius X insisted that he "...did not intend that the Scapular Medal should supplant the Brown Scapular in Europe and America." He said, "I wear the cloth; let us never take it off."

Q. There are many different Scapulars. Why does the World Apostolate of Fatima promote wearing the Brown Scapular?

The World Apostolate of Fatima promotes the Brown Scapular because Our Lady appeared at Fatima on October 13, 1917, as Our Lady of Mount Carmel.

The Ritual of Investiture admits the one being invested to a participation "in all the Masses, prayers and good works performed by the religious of Mount Carmel." This participation plus the great promise of salvation give an unspeakable spiritual value to the Brown Scapular devotion.

In 1950, Pope Pius XII wrote the now-famous words concerning the Scapular: "Let it be your sign of consecration to the Immaculate Heart of Mary, which We are particularly urging in these perilous times."

WORLD APOSTOLATE OF FATIMA, USA
WASHINGTON, NJ 07882
866-513-1917 WWW.WAFUSA.ORG

PLEDGE OF OUR LADY OF FATIMA

Dear Queen and Mother, who promised at Fatima to convert Russia and bring peace to all mankind, in reparation for my sins and the sins of the whole world, I solemnly promise to your Immaculate Heart:

1. To offer up every day the sacrifices demanded by my daily duty.

2. To pray part of the Rosary daily while meditating on the Mysteries.

3. To wear the Scapular of Mount Carmel as profession of this promise and as an act of consecration to you.

4. To accomplish the devotion of the Five First Saturdays of the month, including fifteen minutes of meditation on the Mysteries of the Rosary.

I shall renew this promise often, especially in moments of temptation.

____
NAME (PRINT CLEARLY)

____
ADDRESS

____
DIOCESE

____
SIGNATURE

* Usually understood to mean at least five decades.

PLEASE REGISTER YOUR PLEDGE BY EMAIL OR POSTAL MAIL AT THE ADDRESS ABOVE.

Note: This pledge is not a vow and does not bind under sin. Nevertheless, it is a promise of love; your word to your Heavenly Mother.

©2006 World Apostolate of Fatima, USA
Published with Ecclesiastical Permission.
99569
Revised 12/2006

The Children of Fatima

and Daily Duty

By Sr. Mary Joseph, A.M.I.

. . .the first and greatest responsbility of all Christians is to keep God's Commandments . . .

It is very well known that when Our Lady appeared at Fatima to Lucia, Francisco and Jacinta, she insistently asked them to pray the Rosary every day. Today, most people reflecting on Fatima immediately think of the Rosary, and if they have tried seriously to respond to Mary's requests, they have also begun to wear the Scapular of Mount Carmel. If asked about the message of Fatima, they would probably say that it primarily consists of praying the Rosary and offering sacrifices for the conversion of sinners and the salvation of souls, and, of course, this is very important.

However, it is interesting to note that when Sr. Lucia was asked about the message, she emphatically stated *that the most important element was the offering up of the sacrifices entailed in the accomplishment of daily duty!* She said that the Rosary and scapular were the prime means to help us to be faithful to the demands of daily duty.

Since the first and greatest responsibility of all Christians is to keep God's Commandments, we can see why daily duty is, indeed, the most fundamental element of Our Lady's requests.

Our Lord Himself told Sr. Lucia that the penance He now requires is the sacrifice necessary to keep His laws and to fulfill the duties required by our state in life. (Indeed, would Our Lady have had to come to Fatima in the first place if mankind had been faithful to the Commandments of God)?

The three little seers had received excellent religious training from their poor but pious parents. Young as they were, they well understood what was expected of them. We read in the many accounts of their lives of their ready compliance with their responsibilities, even before Our Lady appeared to them. They diligently took care of their families' sheep, were faithful to prayer (even when they were away from home), always told the truth, and obeyed their parents.

But after Our Lady visited them and they received even further enlightenment, the children of Fatima became even more zealous in fulfilling their daily duties. For example, the Rosary was offered in its entirety to replace the shortened version, which they had previously used, in order to provide more time for play. They were even ready to accept the fearful prospect of being boiled in oil rather than disobey Our Lady by telling the "secret" she had entrusted to them.

All three children suffered much after the apparitions. Countless visitors infringed upon their time and asked endless streams of questions.

The children patiently accepted these inconveniences as part of their daily duty and offered them as sacrifices to God for the conversion of sinners.

Lucia underwent a veritable martyrdom at home because of her mother's disbelief. Yet, she, offered this trial to God in a spirit of loving reparation. When little Jacinta and Francisco fell sick with the influenza which swept Europe, they accepted their sufferings with heroic patience and love, showing us how to accept *everything* that God permits to happen to us in the course of our daily lives. And how faithfully and obediently Lucia corresponded to the will of God . . . even to the point of leaving her home and loved ones to live with the Dorothean Sisters in Spain when it was recommended to her by her bishop.

Lucia was quick to realize that the difficulties God permitted to come into her life were simply a part of her daily duty, and she responded with great faith and virtue. Yes, she and her cousins understood in all simplicity what God expected of them, and they complied with love and generosity.

So Necessary Today

What is so desperately needed in our world today is that we realize the value of the sacrifices entailed in doing God's will and keeping His Commandments, even when doing so seems to turn our "own personal worlds" upside down!

Yes, it is necessary that the observance of the duties of our state in life in a spirit of sacrifice and reparation be restored.

Far too many people choose to run away from these responsibilities rather than humbly accept them.

Could this not be the reason for so many failures in marriage, so much delinquency and suicide among young people, and countless other serious moral problems that plague our nation and world? And have we as adults failed to teach our young people, by word and example, to be faithful to God and their duties?

Taking a strong stand in such matters does not always make us popular or loved, especially when we must censor or give unwelcome advice, but this is what God expects of us as parents, grandparents, aunts or uncles.

Even Jacinta, young as she was, found it necessary to remind Lucia not to concede to the wishes of friends who wanted her to arrange and take part in customary festivities and dancing which could have been occasions of sin.

Our Problems Solved

It has often been said that modern man has lost the sense of sin. But could this not have resulted from the fact that man for the most part has lost sight of God's Commandments and has become a law unto himself? Because the demands of daily duty entail sacrifice and suffering, man has chosen to ignore them and to free himself by specious reasoning. It is this neglect that has sown the seeds of the unprecedented permissiveness of modern society.

Our Lady's message at Fatima gives us the simple yet demanding solution to the world's problems: a return to the Commandments of God and to the faithful fulfillment of daily duty.

If enough people will comply and offer this sacrifice to God, moral order will be restored and there will be peace - peace in our hearts and peace in the world.

Morning Offering

0 my God, in union with the Immaculate Heart of Mary *(Here kiss your Brown Scapular as a sign of your consecration. This carries a partial indulgence.),* I offer Thee the Precious Blood of Jesus from all the altars throughout the world, joining with it the offering of my every thought, word and action of this day.

0 my Jesus, I desire today to gain every indulgence and merit I can, and I offer them, together with myself to Mary Immaculate - that she may best apply them to the interests

of Thy most Sacred Heart. Precious Blood of Jesus, save us! Immaculate Heart of Mary, pray for us! Sacred Heart of Jesus, have mercy on us!

Pledge

Dear Queen and Mother, who promised at Fatima to convert Russia and bring peace to all mankind, in reparation for my sins and the sins of the whole world, I solemnly promise to your Immaculate Heart:

1. To offer up every day the sacrifices demanded by my daily duty;
2. To pray part of the Rosary daily while meditating on the mysteries;*
3. To wear the Scapular of Mount Carmel as profession of this promise and as an act of consecration to you.
4. To accomplish the devotion of the Five First Saturdays of the month, including fifteen minutes of meditation on the mysteries of the rosary.

I shall renew this promise often, especially in moments of temptation.

*Usually understood to mean at least five decades daily.

Note: This pledge is not a vow and does not bind under pain of sin. Nevertheless it is a promise: your word to your heavenly mother.

Printed with ecclesiastical permission

The World Apostolate of Fatima, USA
PO Box 976
Washington, NJ 07882
(866) 513-1917 www.bluearmy.com

96073 8/2005
176

First Saturday Devotion

Photo courtesy Carmelo de Santa Teresa

Coimbra, Portugal

Origins

On June 13, 1917, when she appeared to three shepherd children at Fatima, Portugal, the Most Holy Mother of God told Lucia dos Santos, "Jesus wishes to make use of you to make me known and loved. He wants to establish in the world devotion to my Immaculate Heart. I promise salvation to those who embrace it, and these souls will be loved by God like flowers placed by me to adorn His throne."

The next month, on July 13, the Blessed Virgin Mary showed the children a terrifying vision of hell. Then she said, "You have seen hell where the souls of poor sinners go. To save them, God wishes to establish in the world devotion to my Immaculate Heart. If what I say to you is done, many souls will be saved and there will be peace.... I shall come to ask for... the Communion of reparation on the first Saturdays...."

Our Lady came to Lucia again, as she promised, on December 10, 1925, with the Child Jesus in the Dorothean convent at Pontevedra, Spain. She revealed a heart encircled by thorns. The Child Jesus said: "Have compassion on the heart of your most holy Mother, covered with thorns with which ungrateful men pierce it at every moment, and there is no one to make an act of reparation. . . ."

Conditions

Our Lady spoke next, saying: "Look, my daughter, at my heart, surrounded with thorns with which ungrateful men pierce it at every moment by their blasphemies and ingratitude. You at least try to console me and say that I promise to assist at the hour of death, with all the graces necessary for salvation, all those who, *on the first Saturday of five consecutive months, shall confess, receive Holy Communion, recite five decades of the Rosary, and keep me company for fifteen minutes while meditating on fifteen mysteries of the Rosary, with the intention of making reparation to me.*"

Why Five Saturdays?

Christians have always honored the Blessed Virgin on Saturday because of her constant faith in Jesus on that first Holy Saturday before the Resurrection.

According to Sister Lucia, five first Saturdays of reparation were requested to atone for the ways people offend the Immaculate Heart of Mary: (1) attacks upon Mary's Immaculate Conception; (2) attacks against her Perpetual Virginity; (3) attacks upon her Divine Maternity and the refusal to accept her as the Mother of all mankind; (4) for those who try to publicly implant in children's hearts indifference, contempt and even hatred of this Immaculate Mother, and (5) for those who insult her directly in her sacred images.

World Apostolate of Fatima, USA
Washington, NJ 07882-0976
www.wafusa.org

printed with ecclesiastical permission 6/05

419878

Stories *of the* Brown Scapular

REV. HOWARD RAFFERTY, O. CARM

Adapted from a filmstrip issued by Carmelite Fathers, Aylesford, Downersgrove, IL with Ecclesiastical approbation.

Whosoever dies clothed in this Scapular shall not suffer eternal fire. - 1251

In 1917 Our Lady requested five things at Fatima:

1. Consecration to her Immaculate Heart
2. Reception of Holy Communion on the first Saturdays of five consecutive months
3. The offering of daily sacrifices for the conversion of sinners
4. Five decades of the Rosary each day
5.* The wearing of the Scapular of Carmel as the sign of our consecration to Mary.

* Our Lady did not use words, but she held Her Scapular out of the skies in her very last appearance at Fatima. Lucia (of whom it was said by Our Lady that she would live in order to spread devotion to her Immaculate Heart) explained that Our Lady did so because "She wants everyone to wear it". The Scapular is our "Sign of Consecration to the Immaculate Heart of Mary".

Whosoever dies clothed in this Scapular shall not suffer eternal fire. - 1251

If you wear Mary's Brown Scapular you should know St. Simon Stock, because you have worn his picture along with Our Lady's picture on your scapular. Actually he is an old friend. It was to him - St. Simon of England - that Our Blessed Mother gave the great Scapular Promise in 1251 saying, "Whosoever dies wearing this Scapular shall not suffer eternal fire."

When a priest enrolled you in the Scapular he said, "Receive this blessed Scapular and ask the most Holy Virgin that, by her merits, it may be worn with no stain of sin and may protect you from all harm and bring you into everlasting life." These stories will give a very brief idea of how Our Blessed Mother keeps her promise.

I saw her keep it one day in a town near Chicago where I was called to the bedside of a man away from the Sacraments for many years. He did not want to see me; he would not talk. Then I asked him to look at the little Scapular I was holding, "Will you wear this if I put it on?" I asked nothing more. He agreed to wear it. Within the hour he wanted to go to confession and make his peace with God. It did not surprise me because for over 700 years Our Lady has been working in this way through her Scapular.

On the very day that Our Lady gave the Scapular to St. Simon Stock, he was hurriedly called by the Lord Peter of Linton: "Come quickly, Father, my brother is dying in despair!"

St. Simon Stock placed his large Scapular over the dying man. He repented immediately and died a friend of God.

That night the dead man appeared to his brother.

"I have been saved through the most powerful Queen and the habit of that man as a shield."

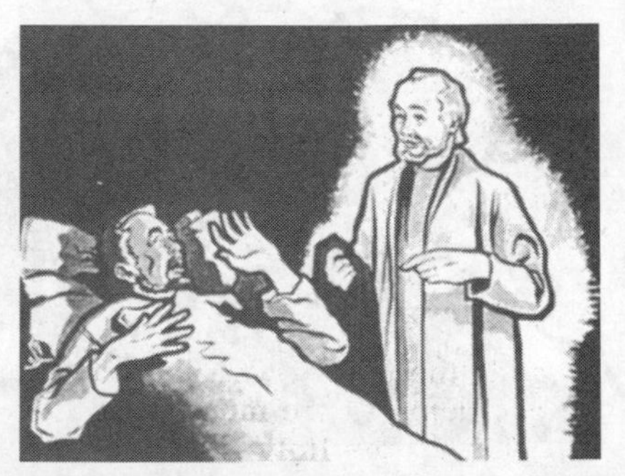

St. Alphonsus tells us: "Modern heretics make a mockery of wearing the Scapular. They decry it as so much trifling nonsense." Yet we know that Pontiffs have approved it.

It is remarkable that just 25 years after St. Simon Stock's vision, Pope Gregory X was buried wearing the Scapular. *When his tomb was opened 600 years after his death, his Scapular was found intact.*

The Scapular was also found LIKE NEW in the graves of SAINT JOHN BOSCO and SAINT ALPHONSUS LIGUORI, although EVERYTHING ELSE in their graves that was corruptible had DECAYED. Saint Alphonsus said that if we did a little more than Our Lady asked of us that we might not even go to Purgatory! All Our Lady asked is in the promise made by those who join her apostolate.

You will understand why the devil works against those who promote the Scapular, when you hear the story of Venerable Francis Ypes. One day his scapular fell off.

As he replaced it, the devil howled, "Take it off! Take off the habit which snatches so many souls from us."

Then Francis made the devil admit that there are three things of which the demons are most afraid: the Holy name of Jesus, the Holy name of Mary and the Holy Scapular of Carmel.

Every month a shipment of 1000 slaves would arrive at Cartagena, Columbia.

Peter Claver organized catechists to give them instruction, and before they were sold, he saw that they were baptized. He used the Scapular to insure the salvation of his converts. Many Ecclesiastics accused the Saint of indiscreet zeal but Peter reminded them that he had baptized and had enrolled all in Our Lady's Scapular. He was confident that Mary would watch over each one.

Imagine! St. Peter Claver was responsible for over 300,000 converts.

In 1845, the English ship, *King of the Ocean*, was lashed by a wild hurricane. The Rev. Fisher, a Protestant minister, together with his wife, children and other passengers, struggled to the deck to pray for mercy and forgiveness as the end seemed at hand.

Among the crew was a young Irishman, John McAuliffe. He opened his shirt, took off his Scapular, made the Sign of the Cross over the angry waves, then threw the Scapular into the ocean.

At that very moment the wind calmed; only one more wave washed the deck, bringing with it the Scapular which landed at the boy's feet.

The Rev. Fisher and his family had observed what he had done.

They questioned the boy. He told them about the Virgin and her Scapular and her Promise of protection in time of danger. So impressed were they that they determined to enter the Church and enjoy a like protection.

This little booklet tells of only very few of the many wonders performed by the Scapular. Our Lady of Fatima appeared with it in her hands just at the end of the Miracle of the Sun at Fatima in 1917, and Lucia, who saw Our Lady and spoke with her said:"She wants EVERYONE to wear it."

A French priest on pilgrimage to Einsiedeln, Switzerland was on his way to Mass when he remembered that he had forgotten his Scapular.

Although late, he retuned to his room for it.

While saying Mass, a young man approached the altar, pulled out a revolver and shot him in the back ... but the priest continued to say Mass.

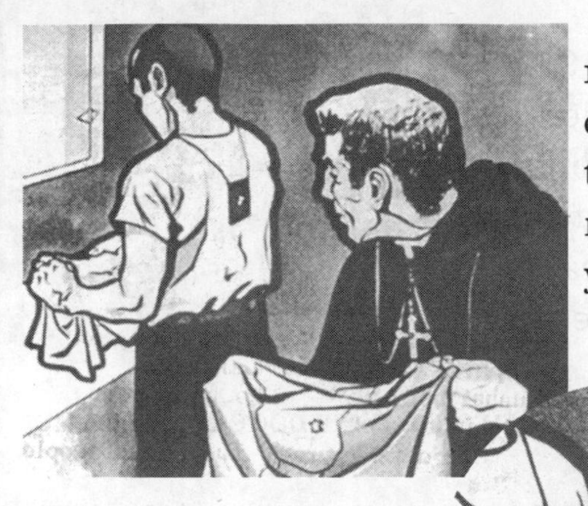

In the sacristy the abbot exclaimed, "I thought the man missed you".

When the vestments were removed, the bullet was found, adhering to his little brown Scapular.

Wear the Brown Scapular as a sign of your CONSECRATION TO THE IMMACULATE HEART OF MARY.

In May of 1957, a Carmelite priest in Germany published the unusual story of how the Scapular saved a home from fire. An entire row of homes had caught fire in Westboden, Germany.

The pious inhabitants of a two-family home, seeing the fire, immediately fastened a Scapular to the main door of the house. Sparks flew over it and around it but it stayed unharmed. Within 5 hours, 22 homes were reduced to ashes and ruins. This one stood unharmed amidst the destruction. Hundreds of people came to see the place Our Lady had saved.

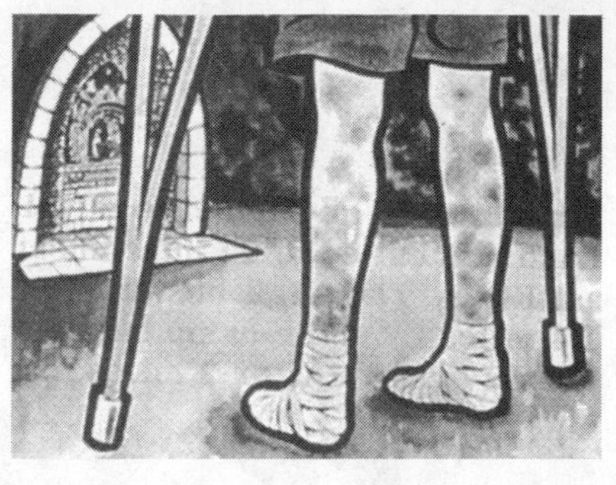

In 1951 the ancient home of St. Simon Stock at Aylesford, England was rededicated and the relics of the Scapular saint returned. Since then thousands of Scapular wearers have come on pilgrimage. In 1957 little Peter came. He was suffering with Leukemia. His arms and legs were covered with ugly sores. He had only a few days to live.

When he returned that very evening, the sores were gone and his strength had returned. His family realized that he was cured. Doctors confirmed his complete cure.

One day in 1944, a Carmelite missionary in the Holy Land was called to an internment camp to give the Last Rites. The Arab bus driver made Father get off 4 miles from the camp because the road was dangerously muddy. After 2 miles had been covered, his feet sank deeper and deeper into the mud. Trying to get solid footing he slipped into a muddy pool. Sinking to death in a desolate place he thought of Mary and her Scapular, for he was wearing the full habit, and looked toward Mt. Carmel.

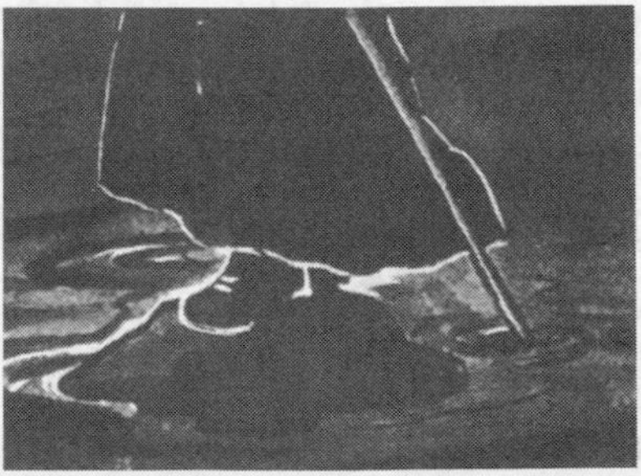

"There, in the distance, was the holy mountain of Carmel, the birthplace of devotion to God's Mother. He cried out, "Holy Mother of Carmel, help me! Save me!" A moment later he found himself on solid ground. He told me, "I know I was saved by the Blessed Virgin through her Brown Scapular. My shoes were lost in the mud and I was covered with it but I walked the 2 miles more through that desolate country praising Mary."

In October of 1952, an Air Force officer in Texas wrote the following: "Six months ago, shortly after I started wearing the Scapular, I experienced a remarkable change in my life. Almost at once I started going to Mass everyday. After a short time I started to receive Holy Communion daily. I kept Lent with a fervor that I had never experienced before. I was introduced to the practice of meditation and found myself making feeble attempts on the way to perfection. I have been trying to live with God. I credit Mary's Scapular".

Mary promises to make easy by grace that which is difficult to nature and to help with more than ordinary graces, as long as we wear the sign of our consecration to Her.

Mary herself has said: **"Take this Scapular whosoever dies wearing it shall not suffer eternal fire. lt shall be a SIGN OF SALVATION - a protection in danger and a pledge of peace."**

The World Apostolate of Fatima USA
PO Box 976 Washington, NJ 07882
908-689-1700 www.wafusa.org

51374

Basic Catechism

of Christian Doctrine

INTRODUCTION

"The time has come and the Kingdom of God is at hand. Repent and believe the good news" (Mk 1:15).

Jesus Christ began his public ministry by challenging everyone to believe in his word and to repent.

In 1917, the Blessed Virgin Mary appeared at Fatima with the same urgent message: Reject sin because it deeply offends God. Believe in Jesus and his Church as the way to eternal life.

Mary lovingly reminded the people of our century of the reality of the fires of hell — and in consequence to believe in Jesus and to repent. The *Basic Catechism of Christian Doctrine* which you hold in your hands, is a simple summary of the Gospel of Jesus. The catechism will help you to understand your Faith and to more perfectly give your life to Jesus Christ. It is a map to the kingdom of heaven.

Our Blessed Mother would surely want you, a member of her Fatima Apostolate, to study and deeply ponder all of the truths of the faith contained in the catechism. Then, as her instrument, you will be ready to share the truths of the Catholic faith with others. By becoming a "missionary" of the Catholic catechism, you will be a herald of the Gospel: "Repent and believe the good news." You will be doing the precise work of Our Lady of Fatima.

Fr. F.L. Miller, S.T.D.

BASIC CATECHISM
OF
CHRISTIAN DOCTRINE

American Version

"The basic prayers and formulas" to be committed to memory are contained in questions 14, 60, 146, 161 and 368, plus the basic prayers pp. 65-67.

(Question 265 revised 1976
Question 248 revised 1978
Questions 81, 194, 221, 236,
258, 305 revised 1984)

This is eternal life: that they may know thee, the only true God, and Jesus Christ, whom thou has sent. — John 17:3

Published by the World Apostolate of Fatima in cooperation with the CMD Apostolate and the permission of the Catholic Truth Society, London. Recommended by Mother Teresa of Calcutta.

2007
WAF, USA
www.wafusa.org
908-689-1700

Catechism of Christian Doctrine

I. FAITH	1. As to Man qq. 1-8	1. His first beginning. 2. His last end.
	2. The Belief qq. 9-134	1. in God the Father; 2. in Jesus Christ; 3. in the Holy Spirit; 4. in the Holy Catholic Church.
II. HOPE	The Our Father qq. 135-157 The Hail Mary qq. 158-168	The seven Blessings. 1. To be hoped for and 2. To be prayed for. Assistance of the Blessed Virgin and of the Angels and Saints.
III. CHARITY	The Commandments qq. 169-248	1. of God; 2. of the Church.
IV. THE SACRAMENTS	The Seven Great Means of Grace corresponding to qq. 249-312	1. the birth 2. the growth 3. the nourishment, 4. the medicine, and 5. the journey of the soul; 6. the Christian Priesthood and 7. the Christian Family.

(a) The Virtues and contrary vices qq. 313-332
(b) The Christian's Rule of Life qq. 333-354
(c) The Christian's Daily Exercise qq. 355-370
(d) Indulgences and Basic Prayers pp. 65-72
(e) 4 week meditation cycle p 73

The Spiritual House of the Soul, says St. Augustine (20 *Sermo in verb. sap.*), is built up in time and solemnly dedicated in eternity. Faith is the foundation, **Hope** the walls, **Charity** the roof, or covering. The **Sacraments** are the great means of grace, or the chief instruments required for the building. The Virtues, the Christian's Rule of Life, and the Daily Exercise, may be likened to the adornment and furniture of the House.

Imprimatur

+ John Cardinal Heenan
Archbishop of Westminster
18 July 1971

ISBN 1-56036-022-4

FAITH

CHAPTER I

1. Who made you?
God made me.

2. Why did God make you?
God made me to know Him, love Him and serve Him in this world, and be happy with Him forever in the next. (See qq. 169, 320, 336, 339, etc.)

3. To whose image and likeness did God make you?
God made me to his own image and likeness.

4. Is this likeness to God in your body, or in your soul?
This likeness to God is chiefly in my soul.

5. How is your soul like to God?
My soul is like to God because it is a spirit, and is immortal.

6. What do you mean when you say that your soul is immortal?
When I say my soul is immortal, I mean that my soul can never die.?

7. Of which must you take most care, of your body or of your soul?
I must take most care of my soul; for Christ has said, "What doth it profit a man if he gain the whole world, and suffer the loss of his own soul?"[1]

[1] Matt. 16:26

8. What must you do to save your soul?

To save my soul I must worship God by faith, hope and charity; that is, I must believe in Him, I must hope in Him, and I must love Him with my whole heart.

CHAPTER II

9. What is faith?

Faith is a supernatural gift of God, which enables us to believe without doubting whatever God has revealed.

10. Why must you believe whatever God has revealed?

I must believe whatever God has revealed because God is the very truth, and can neither deceive nor be deceived.

11. How are you to know what God has revealed?

I am to know what God has revealed by the testimony, teaching, and authority of the Catholic Church.

12. Who gave the Catholic Church divine authority to teach?

Jesus Christ gave the Catholic Church divine authority to teach, when He said, "Go ye and teach all nations."[1]

[1] Matt. 28:19

THE APOSTLES' CREED

13. What are the chief things which God has revealed?

The chief things which God has revealed are contained in the Apostles' Creed.

14. Say the Apostles' Creed.

I believe in God, the Father Almighty, Creator of heaven and earth; — and in Jesus Christ, his only Son, Our Lord; — who was conceived by the Holy Spirit, born of the Virgin Mary; — suffered under Pontius Pilate, was crucified, died, and was buried; — He descended into hell; the third day He rose again from the dead; — He ascended into heaven; is seated at the right hand of God the Father Almighty; — from thence He shall come to judge the living and the dead. — I believe in the Holy Spirit; — the Holy Catholic Church; the communion of Saints; — the forgiveness of sins; — the resurrection of the body; — and life everlasting. Amen.

15. How is the Apostles' Creed divided?

The Apostles' Creed is divided into twelve parts or articles.

FIRST ARTICLE OF THE CREED

16. What is the first article of the Creed?

The first article of the Creed is "I believe in God, the Father Almighty, Creator of heaven and earth."

17. What is God?

God is the supreme Spirit, who alone exists of Himself, and is infinite in all perfections.

18. Why is God called Almighty?

God is called "Almighty" because He can do all things: "With God all things are possible."[1]

19. Why is God called Creator of heaven and earth?

God is called "Creator of heaven and earth" because He made heaven and earth, and all things, out of nothing, by his word.

20. Had God any beginning?

God had no beginning: He always was, He is, and He always will be.

21. Where is God?

God is everywhere.

22. Does God know and see all things?

God knows and sees all things, even our most secret thoughts.

23. Has God any body?

God has no body; He is a spirit.

24. Is there only one God?

There is only one God.

25. Are there three Persons in God?

There are three Persons in God: God the Father, God the Son, and God the Holy Spirit.

[1] Matt. 19:26

26. Are these three Persons three Gods?

These three Persons are not three Gods: the Father, the Son, and the Holy Spirit are all one and the same God.

27. What is the mystery of the three Persons in one God called?

The mystery of the three Persons in one God is called the mystery of the Blessed Trinity.

28. What do you mean by a mystery?

By a mystery I mean a truth which is above reason, but revealed by God.

29. Is there any likeness to the Blessed Trinity in your soul?

There is this likeness to the Blessed Trinity in my soul: that as in one God there are three Persons, so in my one soul there are three powers.

30. Which are the three powers of your soul?

The three powers of my soul are my memory, my understanding, and my will.

THE SECOND ARTICLE

31. What is the second article of the Creed?

The second article of the Creed is, " and in Jesus Christ, his only Son, Our Lord."

32. Who is Jesus Christ?

Jesus Christ is God the Son, made man for us.

33. Is Jesus Christ truly God?
Jesus Christ is truly God.

34. Why is Jesus Christ truly God?
Jesus Christ is truly God because He has one and the same nature with God the Father.

35. Was Jesus Christ always God?
Jesus Christ was always God, born of the Father from all eternity.

36. Which Person of the Blessed Trinity is Jesus Christ?
Jesus Christ is the Second Person of the Blessed Trinity.

37. Is Jesus Christ truly man?
Jesus Christ is truly man.

38. Why is Jesus Christ truly man?
Jesus Christ is truly man because He has the nature of man, having a body and a soul like ours.

39. Was Jesus Christ always man?
Jesus Christ was not always man. He has been man only from the time of his Incarnation.

40. What do you mean by the Incarnation?
I mean by the Incarnation that God the Son took to Himself the nature of man: "the Word was made Flesh."[1]

41. How many natures are there in Jusus Christ?
There are two natures in Jesus Christ, the nature of God and the nature of man.

[1] John 1:14

42. Is there only one Person in Jesus Christ?
There is only one Person in Jesus Christ, which is the Person of God the Son.

43. Why was God the Son made man?
God the Son was made man to redeem us from sin and hell, and to teach us the way to heaven.

44. What does the holy name Jesus mean?
The holy name JESUS means Savior.[1]

45. What does the name Christ mean?
The name CHRIST means Anointed.

46. Where is Jesus Christ?
As God, Jesus Christ is everywhere. As God made man, He is in heaven, and in the Blessed Sacrament of the Altar.

THE THIRD ARTICLE

47. What is the third article of the Creed?
The third article of the Creed is, "who was conceived by the Holy Spirit, born of the Virgin Mary."

48. What does the third article mean?
The third article means that God the Son took a body and soul like ours, in the womb of the Blessed Virgin Mary, by the power of the Holy Spirit.

[1] Matt. 1:21

49. Had Jesus Christ any father on earth?
Jesus Christ had no father on earth: St. Joseph was only his guardian or foster-father.

50. Where was our Savior born?
Our Savior was born in a stable at Bethlehem.

51. On what day was our Savior born?
Our Savior was born on Christmas Day.

THE FOURTH ARTICLE

52. What is the fourth article of the Creed?
The fourth article of the Creed is, "suffered under Pontius Pilate, was crucified, died and buried."

53. What were the chief sufferings of Christ?
The chief sufferings of Christ were: first, his agony, and his sweat of blood in the garden; secondly, his being scourged at the pillar, and crowned with thorns; and thirdly, his carrying his cross, his crucifixion, and his death between two thieves.

54. What are the chief sufferings of Our Lord called?
The chief sufferings of Our Lord are called the Passion of Jesus Christ.

55. Why did Our Savior suffer?
Our Savior suffered to atone for our sins, and to purchase for us eternal life.

56. Why is Jesus Christ called our Redeemer?
Jesus Christ is called our Redeemer because his precious blood is the price by which we were ransomed.

57. On what day did our Savior die?
Our Savior died on Good Friday.

58. Where did our Savior die?
Our Savior died on Mount Calvary.

59. Why do we make the Sign of the Cross?
We make the Sign of the Cross — first, to put us in mind of the Blessed Trinity: and secondly, to remind us that God the Son died for us on the cross.

60. In making the Sign of the Cross how are we reminded of the Blessed Trinity?
In making the Sign of the Cross we are reminded of the Blessed Trinity by the words,"In the name of the Father, and of the Son, and of the Holy Spirit."

61. In making the Sign of the Cross how are we reminded that Christ died for us on the cross?
In making the Sign of the Cross we are reminded that Christ died for us on the cross by the very form of the cross which we make upon ourselves.

THE FIFTH ARTICLE

62. What is the fifth article of the Creed?
The fifth article of the Creed is, "He descended into hell; the third day He rose again from the dead."

63. What do you mean by the words, "He descended into hell"?
By the words, "He descended into hell," I mean that, as soon as Christ was dead, his blessed soul went down into that part of hell called limbo.

64. What do you mean by limbo?

By limbo I mean a place of rest, where the souls of the just who died before Christ were detained.

65. Why were the souls of the just detained in limbo?

The souls of the just were detained in limbo because they could not go up to the kingdom of heaven till Christ had opened it for them.

66. What do you mean by the words, "the third day He rose again from the dead"?

By the words, "the third day He rose again from the dead," I mean that, after Christ had been dead and buried part of three days, He raised his blessed body to life again on the third day.

67. On what day did Christ rise again from the dead?

Christ rose again from the dead on Easter Sunday.

THE SIXTH ARTICLE

68. What is the sixth article of the Creed?

The sixth article of the Creed is, "He ascended into heaven; is seated at the right hand of God the Father Almighty."

69. What do you mean by the words, "He ascended into heaven"?

By the words, "He ascended into heaven," I mean that Our Savior went up body and soul into heaven on Ascension Day, forty days after his resurrection.

70. What do you mean by the words, "is seated at the right hand of God the Father Almighty"?

By the words, "is seated at the right hand of God the Father Almighty," I do not mean that God the Father has hands, for He is a spirit; but I mean that Christ, as God, is equal to the Father and, as man, is in the highest place in heaven.

THE SEVENTH ARTICLE

71. What is the seventh article of the Creed?

The seventh article of the Creed is, "from thence He shall come to judge the living and the dead."

72. When will Christ come again?

Christ will come again from heaven at the last day, to judge all mankind.

73. What are the things Christ will judge?

Christ will judge our thoughts, words, works, and omissions.

74. What will Christ say to the wicked?

Christ will say to the wicked: "Depart from me, ye cursed, into everlasting fire, which was prepared for the devil and his angels."[1]

75. What will Christ say to the just?

Christ will say to the just: "Come, ye blessed of my father, possess ye the kingdom prepared for you."[2]

76. Will every one be judged at death, as well as at the last day?

Everyone will be judged at death, as well as at the last day: "It is appointed unto men once to die; and after this, the judgment."[3]

[1] Matt. 25:41
[2] Matt. 25:34
[3] Heb. 9:27

THE EIGHTH ARTICLE

77. What is the eighth article of the Creed?

The eighth article of the Creed is, "I believe in the Holy Spirit."

78. Who is the Holy Spirit?

The Holy Spirit is the Third Person of the Blessed Trinity.

79. From whom does the Holy Spirit proceed?

The Holy Spirit proceeds from the Father and the Son.

80. Is the Holy Spirit equal to the Father and to the Son?

The Holy Spirit is equal to the Father and to the Son, for He is the same Lord and God as they are.

81. When did the Holy Spirit come down on the Apostles?

The Holy Spirit came down on the Apostles on Pentecost, in the form of "parted tongues, as it were, of fire."[1]

82. Why did the Holy Spirit come down on the Apostles?

The Holy Spirit came down on the Apostles to confirm their faith, to sanctify them, and to enable them to found the Church.

THE NINTH ARTICLE

83. What is the ninth article of the Creed?

The ninth article of the Creed is, "the Holy Catholic Church; the Communion of Saints."

[1] Acts 2:3

84. What is the Catholic Church?
The Catholic Church is the union of all the faithful under one Head.

85. Who is the Head of the Catholic Church?
The Head of the Catholic Church is Jesus Christ Our Lord.

86. Has the Church a visible Head on earth?
The Church has a visible Head on earth — the Bishop of Rome, who is the Vicar of Christ.

87. Why is the Bishop of Rome the Head of the Church?
The Bishop of Rome is the Head of the Church because he is the successor of St. Peter, whom Christ appointed to be the Head of the Church.

88. How do you know that Christ appointed St. Peter to be the Head of the Church?
I know that Christ appointed St. Peter to be the Head of the Church because Christ said to him: "Thou art Peter, and upon this rock I will build my Church, and the gates of hell shall not prevail against it. And to thee I will give the keys of the kingdom of heaven."[1]

89. What is the Bishop of Rome called?
The Bishop of Rome is called the Pope, which word signifies Father.

90. Is the Pope the Spiritual Father of all Christians?
The Pope is the Spiritual Father of all Christians.

[1] Matt. 16:18,19

91. Is the Pope the Shepherd and Teacher of all Christians?

The Pope is the Shepherd and Teacher of all Christians, because Christ made St. Peter the Shepherd of the whole flock when He said: "Feed my lambs, feed my sheep." He also prayed that his "faith" might never fail, and commanded him to "confirm" his brethren.[1]

92. Is the Pope infallible?

The Pope is infallible.

93. What do you mean when you say that the Pope is infallible?

When I say the Pope is infallible, I mean that the Pope cannot err when, as Shepherd and Teacher of all Christians, he defines a doctrine concerning faith or morals, to be held by the whole Church.

94. Has the Church of Christ any marks by which we may know her?

The Church of Christ has four marks by which we may know her: she is One — she is Holy — she is Catholic — she is Apostolic.

95. How is the Church One?

The Church is One because all her members agree in one Faith, have all the same Sacrifice and Sacraments, and are all united under one Head.

96. How is the Church Holy?

The Church is Holy because Jesus Christ, Her Founder is holy, teaches a holy doctrine, and offers to all the means of holiness.

[1] John 21:15-17, Luke 22:32

97. What does the word Catholic mean?
The word Catholic means universal.

98. How is the Church Catholic or universal?
The Church is Catholic or universal because she subsists in all ages, teaches all nations, and is the source of all Truth.

99. How is the Church Apostolic?
The Church is Apostolic because it was founded by Christ on the apostles and, according to his Divine Will, has always been governed by their lawful successors.

100. Can the Church err in what she teaches?
The Church cannot err in what she teaches as to faith or morals, for she is our infallible guide in both.

101. How do you know that the Church cannot err in what she teaches?
I know that the Church cannot err in what she teaches because Christ promised that the gates of hell shall never prevail against his Church; that the Holy Spirit shall teach her all things; and that He Himself will be with her all days, even to the consummation of the world.[1]

102. What do you mean by the Communion of Saints?
By the Communion of Saints I mean that all the members of the Church, in heaven, on earth, and

[1] Matt. 16:18, John 14:16-26, & Matt. 28:20

in purgatory, are in communion with each other, as being one body in Jesus Christ.

103. How are the faithful on earth in communion with each other?

The faithful on earth are in communion with each other by professing the same faith, obeying the same authority, and assisting each other with their prayers and good works.

104. How are we in communion with the saints in heaven?

We are in communion with the saints in heaven by honoring them as the glorified members of the Church, and also by our praying to them, and by their praying for us.

105. How are we in communion with the souls in purgatory?

We are in communion with the souls in purgatory by helping them with our prayers and good works: "It is a holy and wholesome thought to pray for the dead, that they may be loosed from sins."[1]

106. What is purgatory?

Purgatory is a place where souls suffer for a time after death on account of their sins.

107. What souls go to purgatory?

Those souls go to purgatory that depart this life in venial sin; or that have not fully paid the debt of temporal punishment due to those sins of which the guilt has been forgiven.

[1] II Mach. 12:46

108. What is temporal punishment?

Temporal punishment is punishment which will have an end, either in this world, or in the world to come.

109. How do you prove that there is a purgatory?

I prove that there is a purgatory from the constant teaching of the Church; and from the doctrine of Holy Scripture, which declares that God will render to every man according to his works; that nothing defiled shall enter heaven; and that some will be saved, "as one who has gone through fires."[1]

THE TENTH ARTICLE

110. What is the tenth article of the Creed?

The tenth article of the Creed is, "the forgiveness of sins."

111. What do you mean by "the forgiveness of sins"?

By "the forgiveness of sins" I mean that Christ has left the power of forgiving sins to the Pastors of his Church.[2]

112. By what means are sins forgiven?

Sins are forgiven principally by the Sacraments of Baptism and Penance.

113. What is sin?

Sin is an offense against God, by any thought, word, deed or omission against the law of God.

[1] Matt. 16:27, Apoc. 21:27, & I Cor. 3:15
[2] John 20:23

114. How many kinds of sin are there?
There are two kinds of sin, original sin and actual sin.

115. What is original sin?
Original sin is that guilt and stain of sin which we inherit from Adam, who was the origin and head of all mankind.

116. What was the sin committed by Adam?
The sin committed by Adam was the sin of disobedience when he ate the forbidden fruit.

117. Have all mankind contracted the guilt and stain of original sin?
All mankind have contracted the guilt and stain of original sin, except the Blessed Virgin, who, through the merits of her Divine Son, was conceived without the least guilt or stain of original sin.

118. What is this privilege of the Blessed Virgin called?
This privilege of the Blessed Virgin is called the Immaculate Conception.

119. What is actual sin?
Actual sin is every sin which we ourselves commit.

120. How is actual sin divided?
Actual sin is divided into mortal sin and venial sin.

121. What is mortal sin?
Mortal sin is a serious offense against God.

122. Why is it called mortal sin?
It is called mortal sin because it is so serious that it kills the soul and deserves hell.

123. How does mortal sin kill the soul?
Mortal sin kills the soul by depriving it of sanctifying grace, which is the supernatural life of the soul.

124. Is it a great evil to fall into mortal sin?
It is the greatest of all evils to fall into mortal sin.

125. Where will they go who die in mortal sin?
They who die in mortal sin will go to hell for all eternity.

126. What is venial sin?
Venial sin is an offense which does not kill the soul, yet displeases God, and often leads to mortal sin.

127. Why is it called venial sin?
It is called venial sin because it is more easily pardoned than mortal sin.

THE ELEVENTH ARTICLE

128. What is the eleventh article of the Creed?
The eleventh article of the Creed is, "the resurrection of the body."

129. What do you mean by "the resurrection of the body"?
By the resurrection of the body I mean that

we shall all rise again with the same bodies at the day of judgment.

THE TWELFTH ARTICLE

130. What is the twelfth article of the Creed?

The twelfth article of the Creed is, "life everlasting."

131. What does "life everlasting" mean?

"Life everlasting" means that the good shall live forever in the glory and happiness of heaven.

132. What is the glory and happiness of heaven?

The glory and happiness of heaven is to see, love, and enjoy God forever.

133. What does the Scripture say of the happiness of heaven?

The Scripture says of the happiness of heaven: "That eye hath not seen, nor ear heard, neither hath it entered into the heart of man, what things God hath prepared for them that love Him."[1]

134. Shall not the wicked also live forever?

The wicked also shall live and be punished forever in the fire of hell.

HOPE

CHAPTER III

135. Will Faith alone save us?

Faith alone will not save us without good works; we must also have Hope and Charity.

[1] I Cor. 2:9

136. What is Hope?

Hope is a supernatural gift of God, by which we firmly trust that God will give us eternal life and all means necessary to obtain it, if we do what He requires of us.

137. Why must we hope in God?

We must hope in God because He is infinitely good, infinitely powerful, and faithful to his promises.

138. Can we do any good work of ourselves towards our salvation?

We can do no good work of ourselves towards our salvation; we need the help of God's grace

139. What is Grace?

Grace is a supernatural gift of God, freely bestowed upon us for our sanctification and salvation.

140. How must we obtain God's grace?

We must obtain God's grace chiefly by prayer and the Holy Sacraments.

PRAYER

141. What is prayer?

Prayer is the raising up of the mind and heart to God.

142. How do we raise up our mind and heart to God?

We raise up our mind and heart to God by thinking of God; by adoring, praising, and thanking Him; and by begging of Him all blessings for soul and body.

143. Do those pray well who, at their prayers, think neither of God nor of what they say?

Those who, at their prayers, think neither of God nor of what they say, do not pray well; but they offend God, if their distractions are wilful.

144. Which is the best of all prayers?

The best of all prayers is the "Our Father," or the Lord's Prayer.

145. Who made the Lord's Prayer?

Jesus Christ Himself made the Lord's Prayer.

146. Say the Lord's Prayer.

Our Father, who art in heaven, hallowed be thy name; thy kingdom come; thy will be done on earth as it is in heaven; give us this day our daily bread; and forgive us our trespasses, as we forgive those who trespass against us; and lead us not into temptation; but deliver us from evil. Amen.

147. In the Lord's Prayer who is called "Our Father"?

In the Lord's Prayer God is called "Our Father."

148. Why is God called "Our Father"?

God is called "Our Father" because He is the Father of all Christians, whom He has made his children by Holy Baptism.

149. Is God also the Father of all mankind?

God is also the Father of all mankind because He made them all, and loves and preserves them all.

150. Why do we say, "Our" Father, and not "my" Father?

We say "Our" Father, and not "my" Father because, being all brethren, we are to pray not for ourselves only, but also for all others.

151. When we say, "hallowed be thy name," what do we pray for?

When we say "hallowed be thy name" we pray that God may be known, loved, and served by all his creatures.

152. When we say, "thy kingdom come," what do we pray for?

When we say, "thy kingdom come," we pray that God may come and reign in the hearts of all by his grace in this world, and bring us all hereafter to his heavenly kingdom.

153. When we say, "thy will be done on earth as it is in heaven," what do we pray for?

When we say, "thy will be done on earth as it is in heaven," we pray that God may enable us, by his grace, to do his will in all things, as the blessed do in heaven.

154. When we say, "give us this day our daily bread," what do we pray for?

When we say, "give us this day our daily bread," we pray that God may give us daily all that is necessary for soul and body.

155. When we say, "forgive us our trespasses, as we forgive those who trespass against us," what do we pray for?

When we say, "forgive us our trespasses, as

we forgive those who trespass against us," we pray that God may forgive us our sins, as we forgive others the injuries they do to us.

156. When we say, "lead us not into temptation," what do we pray for?

When we say "lead us not into temptation," we pray that God may give us grace not to yield to temptation.

157. When we say, "deliver us from evil," what do we pray for?

When we say, "deliver us from evil," we pray that God may free us from all evil, both of soul and body.

158. Should we ask the angels and saints to pray for us?

We should ask the angels and saints to pray for us, because they are our friends and brethren, and because their prayers have great power with God.

159. How can we show that the angels and saints know what passes on earth?

We can show that the angels and saints know what passes on earth from the words of Christ: "There shall be joy before the angels of God upon one sinner doing penance."[1]

160. What is the chief prayer to the Blessed Virgin which the Church uses?

The chief prayer to the Blessed Virgin which the Church uses is the Hail Mary.

[1] Luke 15:10

161. Say the Hail Mary.

Hail Mary, full of grace; the Lord is with thee; blessed art thou among women, and blessed is the fruit of thy womb, Jesus. Holy Mary, Mother of God, pray for us sinners, now, and at the hour of our death. Amen.

162. Who made the first part of the Hail Mary?

The Angel Gabriel and St. Elizabeth, inspired by the Holy Spirit, made the first part of the Hail Mary.

163. Who made the second part of the Hail Mary?

The Church of God, guided by the Holy Spirit, made the second part of the Hail Mary.

164. Why should we frequently say the Hail Mary?

We should frequently say the Hail Mary to put us in mind of the Incarnation of the Son of God; and to honor Our Blessed Lady, the Mother of God.

165. Have we another reason for often saying the Hail Mary?

We have another reason for often saying the Hail Mary — to ask Our Blessed Lady to pray for us sinners at all times, but especially at the hour of our death.

166. Why does the Catholic Church show great devotion to the Blessed Virgin?

The Catholic Church shows great devotion to the Blessed Virgin because she is the Immaculate Mother of God.

167. How is the Blessed Virgin Mother of God?

The Blessed Virgin is Mother of God because Jesus Christ, her son, who was born of her as man, is not only man, but is also truly God.

168. Is the Blessed Virgin our Mother also?

The Blessed Virgin is our Mother also because, being the brethren of Jesus, we are the children of Mary.

168a. What do we mean by the Assumption of the Blessed Virgin?

By the Assumption of the Blessed Virgin we mean that by the power of God, Mary, at the completion of her life, was taken body and soul into everlasting glory to reign as Queen of heaven and earth.

168b. Is the Assumption of the Blessed Virgin an article of Faith?

The Assumption of the Blessed Virgin is an article of Faith because it has been solemnly defined by the infallible authority of the Church.

CHARITY

CHAPTER IV

THE COMMANDMENTS OF GOD

169. What is Charity?

Charity is a supernatural gift of God by which we love God above all things, and our neighbor as ourselves for God's sake.

170. Why must we love God?

We must love God because He is infinitely good in himself and infinitely good to us.

171. How do we show that we love God?

We show that we love God by keeping his commandments: for Christ says: "If you love me, keep my commandments."[1]

172. How many Commandments are there?

There are ten Commandments.

173. Say the Ten Commandments.

I am the Lord thy God, who brought thee out of the land of Egypt, and out of the house of bondage.

1. Thou shalt not have strange gods before me. Thou shalt not make to thyself any graven thing, nor the likeness of any thing that is in heaven above, nor in the earth beneath, nor of those things that are in the waters under the earth. Thou shalt not adore them nor serve them.
2. Thou shalt not take the name of the Lord thy God in vain.
3. Remember that thou keep holy the Sabbath day.
4. Honor thy father and thy mother.
5. Thou shalt not kill.
6. Thou shalt not commit adultery.
7. Thou shalt not steal.
8. Thou shalt not bear false witness against thy neighbor.
9. Thou shalt not covet thy neighbor's wife.
10. Thou shalt not covet thy neighbor's goods.

[1] John 14:15, Matt. 19:17 & Rom. 13:8-10

174. Who gave the Ten Commandments?

God gave the Ten Commandments to Moses in the Old Law, and Christ confirmed them in the New.

I

175. What is the First Commandment?

The First Commandment is, "I am the Lord thy God, who brought thee out of the land of Egypt, and out of the house of bondage. Thou shalt not have strange gods before me. Thou shalt not make to thyself any graven thing nor the likeness of anything that is in heaven above, nor in the earth beneath, nor of those things that are in the waters under the earth. Thou shalt not adore them nor serve them."

176. What are we commanded to do by the First Commandment?

By the First Commandment we are commanded to worship the one, true, and living God, by Faith, Hope, Charity, and Religion.

177. What are the sins against Faith?

The sins against Faith are all false religions, wilful doubt, disbelief, or denial of any article of Faith, and also culpable ignorance of the doctrines of the Church.

178. How do we expose ourselves to the danger of losing our Faith?

We expose ourselves to the danger of losing

our Faith by neglecting our spiritual duties, reading bad books, going to non-Catholic schools.

179. What are the sins against Hope?
The sins against Hope are despair and presumption.

180. What are the chief sins against Religion?
The chief sins against Religion are the worship of false gods or idols, and the giving to any creature whatsoever the honor which belongs to God alone.

181. Does the First Commandment forbid the making of images?
The First Commandment does not forbid the making of images, but the making of idols; that is, it forbids us to make idols to be adored or honored as gods.

182. Does the First Commandment forbid dealing with the devil and superstitious practices?
The First Commandment forbids all dealing with the devil and superstitious practices, such as consulting spiritualists and fortune-tellers, and trusting to charms, omens, dreams, and such like fooleries.

183. Are all sins of sacrilege and simony also forbidden by the First Commandment?
All sins of sacrilege and simony are also forbidden by the First Commandment.

184. Is it forbidden to give divine honor or worship to the angels and saints?
It is forbidden to give divine honor or worship

to the angels and saints, for this belongs to God alone.

185. What kind of honor or worship should we give to the angels and saints?

We should pay to the angels and saints an inferior honor or worship, for this is due to them as the servants and special friends of God.

186. What honor should we give to relics, crucifixes, and holy pictures?

We should give to relics, crucifixes, and holy pictures a relative honor, as they relate to Christ and his saints, and are memorials of them.

187. Do we pray to relics and images?

We do not pray to relics or images, for they can neither see, nor hear, nor help us.

II

188. What is the Second Commandment?

The Second Commandment is, "Thou shalt not take the name of the Lord thy God in vain."

189. What are we commanded by the Second Commandment?

By the Second Commandment we are commanded to speak with reverence of God and all holy persons and things, and to keep our lawful oaths and vows.

190. What does the Second Commandment forbid?

The Second Commandment forbids all false, rash, unjust, and unnecessary oaths; as also blaspheming, cursing and profane words.

191. Is it ever lawful to swear or to take an oath?

It is lawful to swear, or take an oath, only when God's honor, or our own, or our neighbor's good requires it.

III

192. What is the Third Commandment?

The Third Commandment is "Remember that thou keep holy the Sabbath day."

193. What are we commanded by the Third Commandment?

By the Third Commandment we are commanded to keep the Sunday holy.

194. How are we to keep the Sunday holy?

We are to keep the Sunday holy by praying and participating in Mass and resting from servile works.

195. Why are we commanded to rest from servile works?

We are commanded to rest from servile works that we may have time and opportunity for prayer, going to the Sacraments, hearing instructions and reading good books.

IV

196. What is the Fourth Commandment?

The Fourth Commandment is "Honor thy father and thy mother."

197. What are we commanded by the Fourth Commandment?

By the Fourth Commandment we are commanded to love, reverence, and obey our parents in all that is not sin.

198. Are we commanded to obey our parents only?

We are commanded to obey, not only our parents, but also our bishops and pastors, the civil authorities, and our lawful superiors.

199. Are we bound to assist our parents in their wants?

We are bound to assist our parents in their wants, both spiritual and temporal.

200. Are we bound in justice to contribute to the support of our pastors?

We are bound in justice to contribute to the support of our pastors; for St. Paul says: "The Lord ordained that they who preach the Gospel should live by the Gospel."[1]

201. What is the duty of parents towards their children?

The duty of parents towards their children is to provide for them, to instruct and correct them, and to give them a good Catholic education.

202. What is the duty of masters, mistresses and other superiors?

The duty of masters, mistresses and other superiors is to take proper care of those under their charge, and to enable them to practice their religious duties.

203. What does the Fourth Commandment forbid?

The Fourth Commandment forbids all con-

[1] I Cor. 9:14

tempt, stubbornness, and disobedience to our parents and lawful superiors.

204. Is it sinful to belong to a secret society?

It is sinful to belong to any secret society that plots against the Church or State, or to any society that by reason of its secrecy is condemned by the Church; for St. Paul says: "Let every soul be subject to the higher powers; he that resisteth the power resisteth the ordinance of God; and they that resist purchase to themselves damnation."[1]

V

205. What is the Fifth Commandment?

The Fifth Commandment is, "Thou shalt not kill."

206. What does the Fifth Commandment forbid?

The Fifth Commandment forbids all wilful murder, fighting, quarreling, and injurious words; and also scandal and bad example.

207. Does the Fifth Commandment forbid anger?

The Fifth Commandment forbids anger, and still more, hatred and revenge.

208. Why are scandal and bad example forbidden by the Fifth Commandment?

Scandal and bad example are forbidden by the Fifth Commandment, because they lead to the injury and spiritual death of our neighbor's soul.

[1] Rom. 13:1,2

VI

209. What is the Sixth Commandment?

The Sixth Commandment is, "Thou shalt not commit adultery."

210. What does the Sixth Commandment forbid?

The Sixth Commandment forbids all sins of impurity with another's wife or husband.

211. Does the Sixth Commandment forbid whatever is contrary to holy purity?

The Sixth Commandment forbids whatever is contrary to holy purity in looks, words, or actions.

212. Are immodest plays and dances forbidden by the Sixth Commandment?

Immodest plays and dances are forbidden by the Sixth Commandment, and it is sinful to look at them.

213. Does the Sixth Commandment forbid immodest songs, books, and pictures?

The Sixth Commandment forbids immodest songs, books and pictures, because they are most dangerous to the soul, and lead to mortal sin.

VII

214. What is the Seventh Commandment?

The Seventh Commandment is, "Thou shalt not steal."

215. What does the Seventh Commandment forbid?

The Seventh Commandment forbids all unjust taking away, or keeping what belongs to another.

216. Is all manner of cheating in buying and selling forbidden by the Seventh Commandment?

All manner of cheating in buying and selling is forbidden by the Seventh Commandment, and also every other way of wronging our neighbor

217. Are we bound to restore ill-gotten goods?

We are bound to restore ill-gotten goods if we are able, or else the sin will not be forgiven; we must also pay our debts.

218. Is it dishonest for workers to waste their employer's time or property?

It is dishonest for workers to waste their employer's time or property, because it is wasting what is not their own.

VIII

219. What is the Eighth Commandment?

The Eighth Commandment is, "Thou shalt not bear false witness against thy neighbor."

220. What does the Eighth Commandment forbid?

The Eighth Commandment forbids all false testimony, rash judgment, and lies.

221. Are calumny and detraction forbidden by the Eighth Commandment?

Calumny and detraction are forbidden by the Eighth Commandment, and also tale-bearing and any words which injure our neighbor's character.

222. If you have injured your neighbor by speaking ill of him, what are you bound to do?

If I have injured my neighbor by speaking ill of him, I am bound to make him satisfaction by restoring his good name as far as I can.

IX

223. What is the Ninth Commandment?

The Ninth Commandment is, "Thou shalt not covet thy neighbor's wife."

224. What does the Ninth Commandment forbid?

The Ninth Commandment forbids all wilful consent to impure thoughts and desires, and all wilful pleasure in the irregular motions of the flesh.

225. What sins commonly lead to the breaking of the Sixth and Ninth Commandments?

The sins that commonly lead to the breaking of the Sixth and Ninth Commandments are gluttony, drunkenness and intemperance, and also idleness, bad company and the neglect of prayer.

X

226. What is the Tenth Commandment?

The Tenth Commandment is "Thou shalt not covet thy neighbor's goods."

227. What does the Tenth Commandment forbid?

The Tenth Commandment forbids all envious and covetous thoughts and unjust desires of our neighbor's goods and profits.

CHAPTER V

THE COMMANDMENTS OF THE CHURCH

228. Are we bound to obey the Church?

We are bound to obey the Church, because Christ has said to the pastors of the Church: "He that heareth you, heareth me; and he that despiseth you, despiseth me."[1]

229. What are the chief Commandments of the Church?

The chief Commandments of the Church are:

1. To keep the Sundays and Holydays of Obligation holy, by hearing Mass and resting from servile works.
2. To keep the days of fasting and abstinence appointed by the Church.
3. To go to Confession at least once a year.
4. To receive the Blessed Sacrament at least once a year, and that at Easter or thereabouts.
5. To contribute to the support of our pastors.
6. Not to marry within certain degrees of kindred, nor to solemnize marriage at the forbidden times.
7. To join in the missionary spirit and apostolate of the Church.

230. What is the First Commandment of the Church?

The First Commandment of the Church is, "To keep the Sundays and Holydays of Obligation holy, by hearing Mass and resting from servile works."

231. Which are the Holydays of Obligation observed in the United States?

The Holydays of Obligation observed in the United States are: Solemnity of the Holy Mother of God, January 1; the Ascension; the Assumption of Our Lady, August 15; All Saints' Day, November 1; the Immaculate Conception, December 8; Christmas Day, December 25.

[1] Luke 10:16

232. Are Catholics bound to attend Mass on Sundays and Holydays of Obligation?

Catholics are under a serious obligation to attend Mass on Sundays and Holydays of Obligation unless prevented by other serious duties or by ill-health.

233. Are parents, masters and mistresses bound to provide that those under their charge shall hear Mass on Sundays and Holydays of Obligation?

Parents, masters and mistresses are bound to provide that those under their charge shall hear Mass on Sundays and Holydays of Obligation.

234. What is the Second Commandment of the Church

The Second Commandment of the Church is, "To keep the days of fasting and abstinence appointed by the Church."

235. What are fasting days?

Fasting days are days on which we are allowed to take only one full meal.

236. Which are the fasting days?

The fasting days are Ash Wednesday and Good Friday.[1]

237. What are days of abstinence?

Days of abstinence are days on which we are forbidden to take flesh-meat and anything made from meat.

238. Which are the days of abstinence?

The days of abstinence in the United States are

[1] The obligation of fasting is restricted to those who have completed their eighteenth year until they have begun their sixtieth.

Ash Wednesday and Good Friday and all the Fridays in Lent.[1]

239. Why does the Church command us to fast and abstain?

The Church commands us to fast and abstain so that we may mortify the flesh and satisfy God for our sins.

240. How often should we go to Confession?

If we have been guilty of serious sin we should go to Confession as soon as possible but never less than once a year.

241. How soon are children bound to go to Confession?

Children are bound to go to Confession as soon as they have come to the use of reason, and are capable of serious sin.

242. When are children generally supposed to come to the use of reason?

Children are generally supposed to come to the use of reason about the age of seven years.

243. What is the Fourth Commandment of the Church?

The Fourth Commandment of the Church is, "To receive the Blessed Sacrament at least once a year, and that at Easter or thereabouts."

244. How soon are Christians bound to receive the Blessed Sacrament?

Christians are bound to receive the Blessed Sacrament as soon as they are capable of distinguishing the Body of Christ from ordinary bread, and are judged to be sufficiently instructed.

[1] The age at which abstinence becomes binding is fourteen.

245. What is the Fifth Commandment of the Church?

The Fifth Commandment of the Church is, "To contribute to the support of our pastors."

246. Is it a duty to contribute to the support of religion?

It is a duty to contribute to the support of religion according to our means, so that God may be duly honored and worshipped, and the kingdom of his Church extended.

247. What is the Sixth Commandment of the Church?

The Sixth Commandment of the Church is, "Not to marry within certain degrees of kindred, nor to solemnize marriage at the forbidden times."

248. Which are the times in which it is forbidden to marry with solemnity?

Now, marriage may be contracted at any time of the year. However, the pastor shall advise the spouses to take into account the special character of the liturgical season and abstain from excessive festivity during Advent and Lent.

CHAPTER VI

249. What is a sacrament?

A sacrament is an outward sign of inward grace, ordained by Jesus Christ, by which grace is given to our souls.

250. Do the sacraments always give grace?

The sacraments always give grace to those who receive them worthily.

251. Whence have the sacraments the power of giving grace?

The sacraments have the power of giving grace from the merits of Christ's Precious Blood which they apply to our souls.

252. Ought we to have a great desire to receive the sacraments?

We ought to have a great desire to receive the sacraments, because they are the chief means of our salvation.

253. Is a character given to the soul by any of the sacraments?

A character is given to the soul by the Sacraments of Baptism, Confirmation and Holy Orders.

254. What is a character?

A character is a mark or seal on the soul which cannot be effaced, and therefore the sacrament conferring it may not be repeated.

255. How many sacraments are there?

There are seven sacraments: Baptism, Confirmation, Holy Eucharist, Penance, the Anointing of the Sick, Holy Orders, and Matrimony.

I

256. What is Baptism?

Baptism is a sacrament which cleanses us from original sin, makes us Christians, children of God, and members of the Church.

257. Does Baptism also forgive actual sins?

Baptism also forgives actual sins, with all punishment due to them, when it is received in proper disposition by those who have been guilty of actual sin.

258. Who is the ordinary minister of Baptism?

The ordinary minister of Baptism is a bishop, a priest or a deacon; in case of necessity such as danger of death, any one may baptize.

259. How is Baptism given?

Baptism is given by pouring water on the head of the child, saying at the same time these words: "I baptize you in the name of the Father, and of the Son, and of the Holy Spirit."

260. What do we promise in Baptism?

We promise in Baptism to renounce the devil and all his works and pomps.

261. Is Baptism necessary for salvation?

Baptism is necessary for salvation, beause Christ has said: "Unless a man be born again of water and the Holy Spirit, he cannot enter into the kingdom of God."[1]

II

262. What is Confirmation?

Confirmation is a sacrament by which we receive the Holy Spirit, in order to make us strong and perfect Christians and soldiers of Jesus Christ.

262. Who is the ordinary minister of Confirmation?

The ordinary minister of Confirmation is a bishop.

264. How does the bishop administer the Sacrament of Confirmation?

The bishop administers the Sacrament of Confirmation by praying that the Holy Spirit may come

[1] John 3:5

down upon those who are to be confirmed; and by laying his hand on them, and making the sign of the cross with chrism on their foreheads, at the same time pronouncing certain words.

265. What are the words used in Confirmation?

The words used in Confirmation are these: "N., be sealed with the Gift of the Holy Spirit."

III

266. What is the Sacrament of the Holy Eucharist?

The Sacrament of the Holy Eucharist is the true Body and Blood of Jesus Christ, together with his Soul and Divinity, under the appearances of bread and wine.

267. How are the bread and wine changed into the Body and Blood of Christ?

The bread and wine are changed into the Body and Blood of Christ by the power of God, to whom nothing is impossible or difficult.

268. When are the bread and wine changed into the Body and Blood of Christ?

The bread and wine are changed into the Body and Blood of Christ when the words of consecration, ordained by Jesus Christ, are pronounced by the priest in Holy Mass.

269. Why has Christ given Himself to us in the Holy Eucharist?

Christ has given Himself to us in the Holy Eucharist to be the life and the food of our souls.

"He that eateth me, the same also shall live by me." "He that eateth this bread shall live forever."[1]

270. Is Christ received whole and entire under either kind alone?

Christ is received whole and entire under either kind alone.

271. In order to receive the Blessed Sacrament worthily, what is required?

In order to receive the Blessed Sacrament worthily it is required that we be in a state of grace and keep the prescribed fast; water does not break this fast.

272. What is it to be in a state of grace?

To be in a state of grace is to be free from mortal sin, and pleasing to God.

273. Is it a great sin to receive Holy Communion in mortal sin?

It is a great sin to receive Holy Communion in mortal sin; "for he that eateth and drinketh unworthily, eateth and drinketh judgment to himself."[2]

274. Is the Blessed Eucharist a sacrament only?

The Blessed Eucharist is not a sacrament only; it is also a sacrifice.

275. What is a sacrifice?

A sacrifice is the offering of a victim by a priest to God alone, in testimony of His being the Sovereign Lord of all things.

276. What is the Sacrifice of the New Law?

The Sacrifice of the New Law is the Holy Mass.

[1] John 6:58,59
[2] I Cor. 11:29

277. What is the Holy Mass?

The Holy Mass is the Sacrifice of the Body and Blood of Jesus Christ, really present on the altar under the appearances of bread and wine, and offered to God for the living and the dead.

278. Is the Holy Mass one and the same Sacrifice with that of the Cross?

The Holy Mass is one and the same Sacrifice with that of the Cross, inasmuch as Christ, who offered Himself, a bleeding victim, on the Cross to his heavenly Father, continues to offer Himself in an unbloody manner on the altar, through the ministry of his priests.

279. For what ends is the Sacrifice of the Mass offered?

The Sacrifice of the Mass is offered for four ends: first, to give supreme honor and glory to God; secondly, to thank Him for all his benefits; thirdly, to satisfy God for our sins and to obtain the grace of repentance; and fourthly, to obtain all other graces and blessings through Jesus Christ.

280. Is the Mass also a memorial of the Passion and Death of Our Lord?

The Mass is also a memorial of the Passion and Death of Our Lord, for Christ at his Last Supper said: "Do this for a commemoration of me."[1]

IV

281. What is the Sacrament of Penance?

Penance is a sacrament whereby the sins, whether

[1] Luke 22:19

mortal or venial, which we have committed after Baptism are forgiven.

282. Does the Sacrament of Penance increase the grace of God in the soul?

The Sacrament of Penance increases the grace of God in the soul, besides forgiving sin; we should, therefore, often go to Confession.

283. When did Our Lord institute the Sacrament of Penance?

Our Lord instituted the Sacrament of Penance when He breathed on his Apostles and gave them power to forgive sins, saying: "Whose sins you shall forgive, they are forgiven."[1]

284. How does the priest forgive sins?

The priests forgives sins by the power of God, when he pronounces the words of absolution.

285. What are the words of absolution?

The words of absolution are: "I absolve you from your sins, in the name of the Father, and of the Son, and of the Holy Spirit."

286. Are any conditions of forgiveness required on the part of the penitent?

Three conditions for forgiveness are required on the part of the penitent — contrition, confession and satisfaction.

287. What is contrition?

Contrition is a hearty sorrow for our sins, because by them we have offended so good a God, together with a firm purpose of amendment.

[1] John 20:23

288. What is a firm purpose of amendment?

A firm purpose of amendment is a resolution to avoid, by the grace of God, not only sin, but also the dangerous occasions of sin.

289. How may we obtain a hearty sorrow for our sins?

We may obtain a hearty sorrow for our sins by earnestly praying for it, and by making use of such considerations as may lead us to it.

290. What consideration concerning God will lead us to sorrow for our sins?

This consideration concerning God will lead us to sorrow for our sins: that by our sins we have offended God, who is infinitely good in Himself and infinitely good to us.

291. What other consideration concerning our Savior will lead us to sorrow for our sins?

This consideration concerning our Savior will lead us to sorrow for our sins: that our Savior died for our sins, and that those who sin grievously "crucify again to themselves the Son of God, making him a mockery."[1]

292. Is sorrow for our sins, because by them we have lost heaven and deserved hell, sufficient when we go to Confession?

Sorrow for our sins, because by them we have lost heaven and deserved hell, is sufficient when we go to Confession.

293. What is perfect contrition?

Perfect contrition is sorrow for sin arising purely from the love of God.

[1] Heb.6:6

294. What special value has perfect contrition?

Perfect contrition has this special value: that by it our sins are forgiven immediately, even before we confess them; but nevertheless, if they are serious, we are strictly bound to confess them afterwards.

295. What is Confession?

Confession is to accuse ourselves of our sins to a priest approved by the bishop.

296. What if a person willfully conceals a serious sin in Confession?

If a person willfully conceals a serious sin in Confession, he is guilty of a great sacrilege, by telling a lie to the Holy Spirit in making a bad Confession.

297. How many things have we to do in order to prepare for Confession?

We have four things to do in order to prepare for Confession: first, we must heartily pray for grace to make a good Confession; secondly, we must carefully examine our conscience; thirdly, we must take time and care to make a good act of contrition; and fourthly, we must resolve by the help of God to renounce our sins, and to begin a new life for the future.

298. What is satisfaction?

Satisfaction is doing the penance given to us by the priest.

299. Does the penance given by the priest always make full satisfaction for our sins?

The penance given by the priest does not always make full satisfaction for our sins. We should therefore add to it other good works and penance, and try to gain indulgences.

300. What is an indulgence?

An indulgence is a remission, granted by the Church, of the temporal punishment which often remains due to sin after its guilt has been forgiven.

V

301. What is the Sacrament of the Anointing of the Sick?

This sacrament is the anointing of the sick with holy oil, accompanied with prayer.

302. When is the Sacrament of the Anointing of the Sick given?

The Sacrament of the Anointing of the Sick is given when we are in danger of death by sickness.

303. What are the effects of the Sacrament of the Anointing of the Sick?

The effects of the Sacrament of the Anointing of the Sick are to comfort and strengthen the soul, to remit sin, and even to restore health, when God sees it to be expedient.

304. What authority is there in Scripture for the Sacrament of the Anointing of the Sick?

The authority in Scripture for the Sacrament of the Anointing of the Sick is in the fifth chapter of St. James, where it is said: "Is any one sick among you? Let him bring in the priests of the church; and let them pray over him, anointing him with oil in the name of the Lord. And the prayer of faith shall save the sick man; and the Lord shall raise him up; and if he be in sins they shall be forgiven him."[1]

[1] James 5:14,15

VI

305. What is the Sacrament of Holy Orders?

Holy Orders is the sacrament by which bishops, priests, and deacons of the Church are ordained, and receive power and grace to perform their sacred duties.

VII

306. What is the Sacrament of Matrimony?

Matrimony is the sacrament which sanctifies the contract of a Christian marriage, and gives a special grace to those who receive it worthily.

307. What special grace does the Sacrament of Matrimony give to those who receive it worthily?

The Sacrament of Matrimony gives to those who receive it worthily a special grace, to enable them to bear the difficulties of their state, to love and be faithful to one another, and to bring up their children in the fear of God.

308. Is it a sacrilege to contract marriage in serious sin, or in disobedience to the laws of the Church?

It is a sacrilege to contract marriage in serious sin, or in disobedience to the laws of the Church, and, instead of a blessing, the guilty parties draw upon themselves the anger of God.[1]

309. What is a "mixed marriage"?

A "mixed marriage" is a marriage in which only one partner is a Catholic.

[1] For the marriage of a Catholic to be valid there must be present: 1) either the bishop or the parish priest, or another priest duly delegated, and 2) two witnesses.

310. Does the Church encourage mixed marriages?

The Church does not encourage mixed marriages and considers them dangerous.

311. Does the Church sometimes permit mixed marriages?

The Church sometimes permits mixed marriages by granting a dispensation, and under special conditions.

311a. What does the Catholic partner of a mixed marriage promise?

The Catholic partner of a mixed marriage promises to do everything possible to preserve the faith and have all children of the marriage baptized and brought up in the Catholic religion.

312. Can any human power dissolve the bond of marriage?

No human power can dissolve the bond of marriage, because Christ has said: "What God has joined together, let not man put asunder."[1]

CHAPTER VII

OF VIRTUES AND VICES

313. Which are the theological virtues?

The theological virtues are "Faith, Hope and Charity."[2]

314. Why are they called theological virtues?

They are called theological virtues because they relate immediately to God.

[1] Matt. 19:6
[2] I Cor. 13:13

315. What are the chief mysteries of Faith which every Christian is bound to know?

The chief mysteries of Faith which every Christian is bound to know are the Unity and Trinity of God, who will render to every man according to his works, and the Incarnation, Death, and Resurrection of Our Savior.

316. Which are the cardinal virtues?

The cardinal virtues are "prudence, justice, fortitude and temperance."[1]

317. Why are they called cardinal virtues?

They are called cardinal virtues because they are, as it were, the hinges on which all other moral virtues turn.

318. Which are the seven gifts of the Holy Spirit?

The seven gifts of the Holy Spirit are:

1. Wisdom
2. Understanding
3. Counsel
4. Fortitude
5. Knowledge
6. Piety
7. The fear of the Lord[2]

319. Which are the twelve fruits of the Holy Spirit?

The twelve fruits of the Holy Spirit are:

1. Charity
2. Joy
3. Peace
4. Patience
5. Benignity
6. Goodness
7. Longanimity
8. Mildness
9. Faith
10. Modesty
11. Continence
12. Chastity[3]

320. Which are the two great precepts of charity?

The two great precepts of charity are:

1. "Thou shalt love the Lord thy God with thy

[1] Wisd. 8:7
[2] Isa. 11:2,3
[3] Gal. 5:22,23

whole heart, and with thy whole soul, and with thy whole mind, and with thy whole strength."

2. "Thou shalt love thy neighbor as thyself."[1]

321. Which are the seven corporal works of mercy?

The seven corporal works of mercy are:

1. To feed the hungry
2. To give drink to the thirsty
3. To clothe the naked
4. To house the homeless
5. To visit the sick
6. To visit the imprisoned
7. To bury the dead[2]

322. Which are the seven spiritual works of mercy?

The seven spiritual works of mercy are:

1. To convert the sinner
2. To instruct the ignorant
3. To counsel the doubtful
4. To comfort the sorrowful
5. To bear wrongs patiently
6. To forgive injuries
7. To pray for the living and the dead

323. Which are the eight Beatitudes?

The eight Beatitudes are:

1. Blessed are the poor in spirit; for theirs is the kingdom of heaven.
2. Blessed are the meek; for they shall possess the land.
3. Blessed are they that mourn; for they shall be comforted.
4. Blessed are they that hunger and thirst after justice; for they shall have their fill.
5. Blessed are the merciful; for they shall obtain mercy.
6. Blessed are the clean of heart; for they shall see God.
7. Blessed are the peacemakers; for they shall be called the children of God.
8. Blessed are they that suffer persecution for justice's sake; for theirs is the kingdom of heaven.[3]

[1] Mark 12:30,31
[2] Matt. 25:35-46; Tob. 12:12
[3] Matt. 5:3-10

324. Which are the seven capital sins or vices and their contrary virtues

The seven capital sins or vices and their contrary virtues are:

	Contrary Virtues	
1. Pride		1. Humility
2. Covetousness		2. Liberality
3. Lust		3. Chastity
4. Anger		4. Meekness
5. Gluttony		5. Temperance
6. Envy		6. Brotherly Love
7. Sloth		7. Diligence

325. Why are they called capital sins?

They are called capital sins because they are the sources from which all other sins take their rise.

326. Which are the six sins against the Holy Spirit?

The six sins against the Holy Spirit are:

1. Presumption
2. Despair
3. Resisting the known truth
4. Envy of another's spiritual good
5. Obstinacy in sin
6. Final impenitence

327. Which are the four sins crying to heaven for vengeance?

The four sins crying to heaven for vengeance are:

1. Willful murder[1]
2. The sin of Sodom[2]
3. Oppression of the poor[3]
4. Defrauding laborers of their wages[4]

328. When are we answerable for the sins of others?

We are answerable for the sins of others

[1] Gen. 4:8-16
[2] Gen. 18:20; 19:12,13,24,25
[3] Prov. 14:31
[4] James 5:4

whenever we either cause them, or share in them, through our own fault.

329. In how many ways may we either cause or share the guilt of another's sin?

We may either cause or share the guilt of another's sin in nine ways:

1. By counsel
2. By command
3. By consent
4. By provocation
5. By praise or flattery
6. By concealment
7. By being a partner in sin
8. By silence
9. By defending the ill done

330. Which are the three eminent good works?

The three eminent good works are prayer, fasting and almsgiving.

331. Which are the evangelical counsels?

The evangelical counsels are voluntary poverty, perpetual chastity and entire obedience.

332. What are the four last things to be ever remembered?

The four last things to be ever remembered are death, judgment, hell and heaven.[1]

CHAPTER VIII

THE CHRISTIAN'S RULE OF LIFE

333. What rule of life must we follow if we hope to be saved?

If we hope to be saved, we must follow the rule of life taught by Jesus Christ.

334. What are we bound to do by the rule of life taught by Jesus Christ?

[1] Ecclus. 7:40

By the rule of life taught by Jesus Christ, we are bound always to hate sin and to love God.

335. How must we hate sin?

We must hate sin above all other evils, so as to be resolved never to commit a willful sin, for the love or fear of anything whatsoever.

336. How must we love God?

We must love God above all things, and with our whole heart.

337. How must we learn to love God?

We must learn to love God by begging of God to teach us to love Him: "O my God, teach me to love You."

338. What will the love of God lead us to do?

The love of God will lead us often to think how good God is; often to speak to Him in our hearts; and always to seek to please Him.

339. Does Jesus Christ also command us to love one another?

Jesus Christ also commands us to love one another — that is, all persons without exception — for his sake.

340. How are we to love one another?

We are to love one anotehr by wishing well to one another, and praying for one another; and by never allowing ourselves any thought, word or deed to the injury of anyone.

341. Are we also bound to love our enemies?

We are also bound to love our enemies; not only by forgiving them from our hearts, but also by wishing them well, and praying for them.

342. Has Jesus Christ given us another great rule?

Jesus Christ has given us another great rule in these words: "If any man will come after me, let him deny himself, and take up his cross daily, and follow me."[1]

343. How are we to deny ourselves?

We are to deny ourselves by giving up our own will, and by going against our own humors, inclinations, and passions.

344. Why are we bound to deny ourselves?

We are bound to deny ourselves because our natural inclinations are prone to evil from our very childhood; and, if not corrected by self-denial, they will certainly carry us to hell.

345. How are we to take up our cross daily?

We are to take up our cross daily by submitting daily with patience to the labors and sufferings of this short life, and by bearing them willingly for the love of God.

346. How are we to follow our Blessed Lord?

We are to follow our Blessed Lord by walking in his footsteps and imitating his virtues.

347. What are the principal virtues we are to learn of our Blessed Lord?

The principal virtues we are to learn of our Blessed Lord are meekness, humility and obedience.

348. Which are the enemies we must fight against all the days of our life?

The enemies which we must fight against all the days of our life are the devil, the world and the flesh.

[1] Luke 9:23

349. What do you mean by the devil?

By the devil I mean Satan and all his wicked angels, who are ever seeking to draw us into sin, that we may be damned with them.

350. What do you mean by the world?

By the world I mean the false maxims of the world and the society of those who love the vanities, riches and pleasures of this world better than God.

351. Why do you number the devil and the world amongst the enemies of the soul?

I number the devil and the world amongst the enemies of the soul because they are always seeking, by temptation and by work or example, to carry us along with them in the broad road that leads to damnation.

352. What do you mean by the flesh?

By the flesh I mean our own corrupt inclinations and passions, which are the most dangerous of all our enemies.

353. What must we do to hinder the enemies of our soul from drawing us into sin?

To hinder the enemies of our soul from drawing us into sin, we must watch, pray and fight against all their suggestions and temptations.

354. In the warfare against the devil, the world, and the flesh, on whom must we depend?

In the warfare against the devil, the world, and

the flesh we must depend not on ourselves but on God only: "I can do all things in him who strengtheneth me."[1]

CHAPTER IX

THE CHRISTIAN'S DAILY EXERCISE

355. How should you begin the day?

I should begin the day by making the sign of the cross as soon as I awake in the morning, and by saying some short prayer, such as "O my God, I offer my heart and soul to You."

356. How should you rise in the morning?

I should rise in the morning diligently, dress myself modestly, and then kneel down and say my morning prayers.

357. Should you also hear Mass if you have time and opportunity?

I should also hear Mass if I have time and opportunity, for to hear Mass is by far the best and most profitable of all devotions.

358. Is it useful to make daily meditation?

It is useful to make daily meditation, for such was the practice of all the saints.

359. On what ought we to meditate?

We ought to meditate especially on the four last things, and the life and passion of our Blessed Lord.

[1] Phil. 4:13

360. Ought we frequently to read good books?

We ought frequently to read good books, such as the Holy Gospels, the Lives of the Saints, and other spiritual works, which nourish our faith and piety, and arm us against the false maxims of the world.

361. And what should you do as to your eating, drinking, sleeping, and amusements?

As to my eating, drinking, sleeping, and amusements, I should use all these things with moderation, and with a desire to please God.

362. Say the grace before meals.

"Bless us, O Lord, and these your gifts, which we are about to receive from your bounty, through Christ our Lord. Amen."

363. Say the grace after meals.

"We give you thanks, Almighty God, for all your benefits, who live and reign, world without end. May the souls of the faithful departed through the mercy of God, rest in peace. Amen."

364. How should you sanctify your ordinary actions and employments of the day?

I should sanctify my ordinary actions and employments of the day by often raising up my heart to God whilst I am about them, and saying some short prayer to Him.

365. What should you do when you find yourself tempted to sin?

When I find myself tempted to sin, I should make the sign of the cross on my heart and call on God as earnestly as I can, saying, "Lord, save me, or I perish."

366. If you have fallen into sin, what should you do?

If I have fallen into sin I should cast myself in spirit at the feet of Christ, and humbly beg his pardon by a sincere act of contrition.

367. When God sends you any cross, or sickness, or pain, what should you say?

When God sends me any cross, or sickness, or pain, I should say, "Lord, your will be done; I take this for my sins."

368. What prayers would you do well to say often to yourself during the day?

I should do well to say often to myself during the day such prayers as:

Glory be to the Father, and to the Son, and to the Holy Spirit, as it was in the beginning, is now, and ever shall be, world without end. Amen.

In all things may the most holy, the most just, and the most lovable will of God be done, praised, and exalted above all forever.

O Sacrament most holy, O Sacrament divine, all praise and all thanksgiving be every moment thine.

Praised be Jesus Christ, praised forevermore.

My Jesus, mercy; Mary, help.

369. How should you finish the day?

I should finish the day by kneeling down and saying my night prayers.

370. After your night prayers what should you do?

After my night prayers I should observe due modesty in going to bed; occupy myself with the thoughts of death; and endeavor to compose myself to rest at the foot of the Cross, and give my last thoughts to my crucified Savior.

GRANTS OF INDULGENCES AND BASIC PRAYERS (U.S.A. Ed.)

The 1968 revision attaches indulgences "only to the most important prayers and works of piety, charity and penance." See q. 300 and Paul VI's 1967 Apostolic Constitution in Flannery's *Vatican II* pp. 62-79.

Three General Grants;

1st: "A partial indulgence is granted to the faithful who, in the performance of their duties and in bearing the trials of life, raise their mind with humble confidence to God, adding — even if only mentally — some pious invocation." (See q. 368 and Lk. 18:1, Mt. 7:7-8, etc.)

2nd: "A partial indulgence is granted to the faithful who in a spirit of faith and mercy give of themselves or of their goods to serve their brothers in need." (See qq. 321-322 and Mt. 25:35-36,40; Jn. 13:15, etc.)

3rd: "A partial indulgence is granted to the faithful who in a spirit of penance voluntarily deprive themselves of what is licit and pleasing to them." (See qq. 330, 343-4, 353, 361 and Mt. 8:20, 10:30, 16:24, etc.)

The three conditions for a plenary indulgence: sacramental Confession, sacramental Communion, and prayer for the intention of the Sovereign Pontiff. (One Our Father and one Hail Mary or another prayer.)

Formulas to be committed to memory: the answers to qq. 173, 229, 255, 321, 322, 323 and 324.

Prayers to be committed to memory: the answers to qq. 14, 60, 146, 161, 368 and:

Morning Offering

O Jesus, through the Immaculate Heart of Mary I offer You my prayers, works, joys, sufferings of this day in union with the Holy Sacrifice of the Mass throughout the world. I offer them for all the intentions of Your Sacred Heart: the salvation of souls, reparation for sin, reunion of all Christians. I offer them for the intentions of our bishops, and of all Apostles of Prayer, and in particular for those recommended by our Holy Father this month.

Act of Faith

O my God, I firmly believe that You are One God in three Divine Persons, Father, Son and Holy Spirit; I believe that Your Divine Son became man and died for our sins, and that He will come to judge the living and the dead. I believe these and all the truths which the Holy Catholic Church teaches, because You have revealed them, who can neither deceive nor be deceived.

Act of Hope

O my God, relying on Your infinite goodness and promises, I hope to obtain pardon of my sins, the help of Your grace, and life everlasting, through the merits of Jesus Christ, my Lord and Redeemer.

Act of Charity

O my God, I love You above all things, with my whole heart and soul, because You are all-good and worthy of all love. I love my neighbor as myself for the love of You. I forgive all who have injuried me, and I ask pardon of all whom I have injured.

Act of Contrition

O my God! I am heartily sorry for having offended Thee, and I detest all my sins, because I dread the loss of heaven and the pains of hell, but most of all because they offend Thee, my God, who are all-good and deserving of all my love. I firmly resolve with the help of Thy grace, to confess my sins, to do penance, and to amend my life. Amen.

The Holy Rosary

The Five Joyful Mysteries

1. The Annunciation.
2. The Visitation.
3. The Nativity.
4. The Presentation.
5. The Finding in the Temple.

The Five Sorrowful Mysteries

1. The Agony in the Garden.
2. The Scourging at the Pillar.
3 The Crowning with Thorns.
4. The Carrying of the Cross.
5. The Crucifixion.

The Five Glorious Mysteries

1. The Resurrection.

2. The Ascension.
3. The Descent of the Holy Spirit.
4. The Assumption.
5. The Coronation of Our Lady.

Hail, holy Queen, Mother of Mercy! Our life, our sweetness, and our hope! To thee do we cry, poor banished children of Eve; to thee do we send up our sighs, mourning and weeping in this valley of tears. Turn, then, most gracious Advocate, thine eyes of mercy toward us; and after this our exile show unto us the blessed fruit of thy womb, Jesus; O clement, O loving, O sweet Virgin Mary.

V. Pray for us, O holy Mother of God.

R. That we may be made worthy of the promises of Christ.

A Plenary Indulgence may be gained (under the usual conditions) when the Rosary is prayed in church, in a family group or in a religious community.

V. May the divine assistance remain always with us.

R. May the souls of the faithful departed, through Your mercy, O God, rest in peace.

DEVOTIONAL PRAYERS

The Angelus

During the year (outside Eastertime):

V. The Angel of the Lord declared to Mary,

R. And she conceived of the Holy Spirit.

Hail Mary, etc.

V. Behold the handmaid of the Lord.

R. Be it done to me according to your word.

Hail Mary, etc.

V. And the Word was made flesh.
R. And dwelt among us.
Hail Mary, etc.
V. Pray for us, O Holy Mother of God.
R. That we may be made worthy of the promise of Christ.

Let us pray.

Pour forth, we beseech You, O Lord, Your grace into our hearts; that we, to whom the Incarnation of Christ, your Son, was made known by the message of an angel, may by his passion and cross be brought to the glory of his Resurrection, through the same Christ Our Lord.

R. Amen.

The Regina Coeli

During Eastertime (Easter to Pentecost):

Queen of Heaven, rejoice, alleluia,
For He whom you did merit to bear, alleluia,
Has risen as He said, alleluia.
Pray for us to God, allelulia.

V. Rejoice and be glad, O Virgin Mary, alleluia,
R. For the Lord is truly risen, alleluia.

Let us pray.

O God, who gave joy to the world through the Resurrection of Your Son Our Lord Jesus Christ, grant that we may obtain through his Virgin Mother, Mary, the joys of everlasting life. Through the same Christ Our Lord.

R. Amen.

A Partial Indulgence is granted to the faithful who devoutly recite the above prayer according to the formula indicated for the time of the year (*Enchir. Indul.*,9).

PEACE PLAN FROM HEAVEN

In 1917, at Fatima, Portugal, Our Lady gave us a "Peace Plan from Heaven": Break with sin; do penance and make repartion for sin; pray the Rosary daily; on five first Saturdays: make a good Confession, receive Holy Communion worthily, pray five decades of the Rosary and meditate for fifteen minutes on the mysteries (Do this in a spirit of reparation to Mary's Immaculate Heart); wear the Brown Scapular as a sign of consecration to Mary.

Decade Prayer: "O my Jesus: Forgive us our sins. Save us from the fire of hell. Lead all souls to heaven, especially those in most need of your mercy."

Act of Consecration

O Immaculate Heart of Mary, Queen of heaven and earth, and tender Mother of men, in accordance with your ardent wish revealed at Fatima, I consecrate to you myself, my country, and all my fellow men.

Reign over our hearts, dearest Mother, so that we may be truly followers of Christ and his teachings, in prosperity and adversity, in joy and sorrow, in health and sickness, in life and death.

I want to atone for all my sins and those of all men. I desire God's blessing on my country and the whole world, peace between all nations, with love and justice practiced by all men. Amen.

For Purity

Jesus, Mary and Joseph, I entrust and consecrate myself entirely to you — mind, heart and body. Guard and defend me always from every sin.

May my mind be uplifted to heavenly things, may my heart love God more and more, may I avoid every evil occasion. Hold me close to you, so that I may keep a watch on my internal and external senses. Preserve me from all impurity, and help me to serve you with undefiled mind, pure heart and chaste body, so that in heaven I may join the blessed company of the saints.

Memorare

Remember, O most gracious Virgin Mary, that never was it known that anyone who fled to your protection, implored your help or sought your intercession, was left unaided. Inspired with this confidence, I fly to you, O Virgin of virgins, my Mother. To you I come; before you I stand, sinful and sorrowful. O Mother of the Word Incarnate! Despise not my petitions, but in your mercy hear and answer me. Amen.

Soul of Christ, sanctify me.
  Body of Christ, save me.
Blood of Christ, fill all my veins.
  Water of Christ's side, wash out my stains.
Passion of Christ, my comfort be.
  O good Jesus, listen to me.
Within your wounds, fain would I hide.
  Never more to be parted from your side.
Guard me when the foe assails me.
  Call me, when this life shall fail me.
Bid me come to you above.
  With your saints to sing your love,
World without end. Amen.

Miraculous Medal Prayer

"O Mary, conceived without sin, pray for us who have recourse to thee."

Aspiration

Jesus, Mary, and Joseph, I give you my heart and my soul.

Jesus, Mary, and Joseph, assist me in my last agony.

Jesus, Mary, and Joseph, may I die in peace, and in your blessed company.

A Plenary Indulgence is granted at the hour of death when a priest cannot be present to give the Sacraments and the Apostolic Blessing, provided that during life one habitually said some prayers. The conditions "provided that during life one habitually said some prayers" in this case supplies for the three usual conditions for gaining a plenary indulgence (cf. *Enchir. Indul.*, 28).

Thanksgiving after Communion

Prayer Before a Crucifix: "O good and gentle Jesus, before Thy face I humbly kneel and with the greatest fervor of spirit I beg and beseech of Thee to implant firmly into my heart lively sentiments of faith, hope and charity; contrition for my sins and a firm purpose of amendment. Meanwhile, I meditate on Thy five most precious wounds, having ever before my eyes the words of David, the Prophet, concerning Thee, my Jesus: 'They have pierced my hands and my feet, they have numbered all my bones.' "

St. Michael the Archangel, defend us in the day of battle; be our safeguard against the wickedness and snares of the devil. May God rebuke him, we humbly pray, and do thou, O Prince of the heavenly host, by the power of God, cast into hell, Satan and all the other evil spirits, who prowl through the world, seeking the ruin of souls. Amen.

To prepare for the four week cycle
of the
DIVINE OFFICE
A FOUR WEEK MEDITIATION CYCLE:

Basic Prayers to be memorized & understood:
Sign of the Cross Q 59 ff; Our Father Q 146 ff;
Hail Mary Q 161 ff; Apostles' Creed 14 ff;
Act of Contrition p. 66.

— FAITH SEEKING UNDERSTANDING —

	1st week	2nd week	3rd week	4th week
SUN	Why? 1-8	9th Art. 83-109	1st Command. 175-187	Mass: 266-280
MON	Faith 9-15	10th Art. 110-127	2nd to 4th 188-204	Penance 281-300
TUES	1st Art. 16-30	11th &12th 128-134	5th to 7th 205-218	3 Sacraments 301-312
WED	2nd & 3rd 31-51	Hope 135-140	8th to 10th 219-227	Virtues 313-324
THUR	4th & 5th 52-67	Our Father 141-157	Church Com. 228-248	Vices 324-332
FRI	6th & 7th 68-76	Hail Mary 158-168	Baptism 249-261	Rule of Life 333-354
SAT	8th Art. 77-82	Command. 169-174	Confirm. 262-265	Daily Exer. 355-370

"Say the Rosary every day..."
Our Lady of Fatima
May 13, 1917

The Fatima Apostolate

The World Apostolate of Fatima (The Blue Army) is a spiritual movement dedicated to promoting and living the message given to the world by the Mother of God at Fatima, Portugal, in 1917. In that message, Our Lady of the Rosary, as she identified herself, repeated the timeless Christian message of conversion, prayer and penance for our troubled twentieth century.

Through three small shepherd children, Lucia dos Santos and Venerables Jacinta and Francisco Marto, Our Lady said to mankind, "Do not offend the Lord our God any more, because He is already so much offended" (October 13, 1917). She asked for personal conversion, the daily Rosary for world peace, prayers and sacrifices for sinners who have no one to pray for them and reparation to the Eucharistic Jesus and the Immaculate Heart of Mary.

Mary promised special graces at the hour of death to all who, on the first Saturday of five consecutive months: (1) go to Confession, (2) receive Holy Communion, (3) pray five decades of the Rosary and (4) keep her company for fifteen minutes by meditating on the mysteries of the Rosary, all with the intention of making reparation to her Immaculate Heart.

Members of the apostolate attempt to fulfill these requests in their own lives and to be apostolic witnesses of the Catholic faith in their families, parishes and communities. They are encouraged to read *SOUL* Magazine (Box 976, Washington, N.J., 07882) to keep themselves current on the lastest developments in the Fatima message.

All of our recent popes have given their approbation to Fatima and its message. Pope John XXIII said, "Fatima is the center of all Christian hopes." Pope John Paul II returned to Fatima for the second time on May 13, 1991, to publicly thank Our Lady for sparing his life during the assassination attempt in Rome ten years earlier and for the dramatic changes that have recently occurred in Eastern Europe. Two days later during his general audience at the Vatican, the Holy Father spoke of his visit to Fatima. "Mary's message at Fatima can be synthesized in these clear, initial words of Christ," he said, "'The kingdom of God is at hand. Repent, and believe in the Gospel.'" (Mark 1:15).

World Apostolate of Fatima Pledge

Dear Queen and Mother, who promised at Fatima to convert Russia and bring peace to all mankind, in preparation for my sins and the sins of the whole world, I solemnly promise to your Immaculate Heart:

1. To offer up every day the sacrifices demanded by my daily duty;
2. To pray part of the Rosary* daily while meditating on the mysteries;
3. To wear the Scapular of Mount Carmel as profession of this promise and as an act of consecration to you.
4. To accomplish the devotion of the Five First Saturdays of the month, including fifteen minutes of meditation on the Mysteries of the Rosary.

I shall renew this promise often, especially in moments of temptation.

**Usually understood to mean at least five decades daily.*

Note: The pledge is not a vow and does not bind under sin. Nevertheless it is a promise: your word to your heavenly mother.

www.wafusa.org To Order: 908-689-1700 ext: 18

37502 ISBN 1-56036-022-4

St. Padre Pio & the message of Fatima

Father Andrew Apostoli, C.F.R.

St. Padre Pio & the message of Fatima

In accord with Canon 827 of the New Code of Canon Law, this publication has been submitted to a censor of the Diocese and nothing being found contrary to faith and morals, we hereby grant permission in accord with Canon 824 that it be published.

Rev. Msgr. John B. Szymanski
Vicar General
Diocese of Metuchen
October 9, 2002

N.B. The ecclesiastical permission implies nothing more than the material contained in the publication has been examined by diocesan censors and nothing contrary to faith and morals has been found therein.

First edition, 2002
Reprinted 2005

Photos from The Blue Army Archives

Printed in the United States of America

ISBN 1-56036-117-4

St. Padre Pio & the message of Fatima

World Apostolate of Fatima, USA
Blue Army Shrine
Washington, New Jersey
www.wafusa.org 908-689-1700

— Contents —

FOREWORD

Saint Pio of Pietrelcina, known better to his friends as Saint Padre Pio, is the Spiritual Father of the World Apostolate of Fatima. **Saint Padre Pio said, "I will accept all who sign the World Apostolate of Fatima Pledge as my spiritual children, provided that they live up to the Pledge." The WAF Pledge of Our Lady of Fatima, developed over fifty-five years ago with the help of Sister Lucia of Fatima, is simple in structure, yet profound in its meaning and effect.**

PLEDGE OF THE WORLD APOSTOLATE OF FATIMA

Dear Queen and Mother, who promised at Fatima to convert Russia and bring peace to all mankind, in reparation for my sins and the sins of the whole world, I solemnly promise to your Immaculate Heart:

1. To offer up every day the sacrifices demanded by my daily duty;
2. To pray part of the Rosary † daily while meditating on the Mysteries;
3. To wear the Scapular of Mount Carmel as profession of this promise and as an act of consecration to you.
4. To accomplish the devotion of the Five First Saturdays of the month, including fifteen minutes of meditation on the Mysteries of the Rosary.

I shall renew this promise often, especially in moments of temptation.

†Usually understood to mean at least five decades daily.

NOTE: This pledge is not a vow and does not bind under sin. Nevertheless, it is a promise; your word to your heavenly Mother.

The Spirituality of Saint Padre Pio and the Message of Our Lady of Fatima was written by Father Andrew Apostoli, C.F.R., a great friend of mine and the World Apostolate of Fatima. Originally appearing as a series of articles in *Soul* magazine, Father Apostoli helps the reader to understand that the great holiness and extraordinary mission of Saint Padre Pio is closely related to the Message of Fatima.

The timing of the Blessed Mother's apparitions at Fatima in 1917 and the stigmatization of Saint Padre Pio are seen to be nearly simultaneous. The question asked by Father Apostoli in this booklet: "Did God raise up Saint Padre Pio to be an outstanding witness and example for living the Fatima Message?" is answered in the affirmative. Under the spiritual fathership of Saint Padre Pio, it is the apostolate's mission to promote the Fatima Message of peace and hope for the world.

May this booklet serve to increase devotion to a saint for our time and a model for the holy priesthood. Saint Padre Pio said, "The WAF is the ideal apostolate for our time." When asked by a spiritual child if he should join the WAF, Saint Padre Pio replied, "This (the WAF) is not only an act of prayer—it is also an apostleship. What better thing can you do?" Saint Padre Pio had predicted, "Russia will be converted when there is a World Apostolate of Fatima member for every Communist."

The World Apostolate of Fatima, U.S.A. is pleased and honored to present this booklet on Saint Padre Pio and the Message of Fatima. Father Andrew Apostoli, CFR is to be commended for his insights into Our Lady of Fatima's Message and the spirituality of Saint Pio of Pietrelcina. May this booklet help to bring peace and hope to the reader and to the whole world.

NOTE: For information on becoming a member of THE WORLD APOSTOLATE OF FATIMA, for additional copies of this booklet, or for other information on Saint Padre Pio and the Fatima Message, call toll free at *908-689-1700,* or visit our website at www.wafusa.org.

Saint Padre Pio and the Fatima Apparitions of May and June, 1917

What may appear to many to be a mere coincidence, in God's plan often has great significance. This very clearly appears to be the case with the apparitions of Our Lady of Fatima and the great holiness and extraordinary mission of Saint Padre Pio. The timing of the Blessed Mother's apparitions and the stigmatization of Saint Padre Pio, undoubtedly the most significant mystical event of his life, are nearly simultaneous. The Padre received the "invisible stigmata" of the five wounds of Jesus in his hands, feet, and side (i.e., he felt the pain but there were no visible wounds) on September 20, 1915. Our Lady made six appearances at Fatima on the 13th of each month from May to October 1917. Saint Padre Pio then received the "visible stigmata" (i.e., the five wounds were clearly marked in his flesh) on September 20, 1918, the event that thrust him into an apostolic mission of worldwide influence.

Another consideration is that the spirituality of Saint Padre Pio most strikingly embodies the Message of Our Lady of Fatima! We know that the Fatima Message has played a crucial part in God's plan for the peace and salvation of the world for nearly the past 100 years. We can, then, rightfully ask: Did God raise up Saint Padre Pio to be an outstanding witness and example for living out the Fatima Message? A comparative study reveals remarkable parallels between the two. In this chapter we will focus on some elements of Our Lady's message for May and June, and see them in Saint Padre Pio's life.

ACCEPTED CO-REDEMPTIVE SUFFERING IN REPARATION FOR SINS AND FOR THE CONVERSION OF SINNERS

Our Lady, on God's behalf, asks young Lucia, Jacinta and Francisco: "Do you wish to offer up to God all the sufferings He desires to send you in reparation for the sins by which He is offended, and in supplication for the conversion of sinners?"

The children respond willingly, "Yes, we do!"

Our Lady then assures them they will have much

to suffer, adding, however, "the grace of God will comfort you."

This kind of suffering is called "co-redemptive suffering," since it is joined to Jesus' suffering to make up for sins (reparation) and to obtain the grace of conversion for sinners. Saint Paul describes this suffering clearly: "In my own flesh I fill up what is lacking in the sufferings of Christ for the sake of His Body, the Church" (Col 1:24). We must carefully understand this teaching. There is nothing wrong, or missing, or lacking in what Jesus suffered. Rather, He wants us to share in His great work of redemption. In a similar way, for example, Jesus did not need the five loaves of the young boy to feed the crowd of over 5,000 (cf. Jn 6:1-13), but He chose to use the loaves the boy presented so generously.

Saint Padre Pio, like the Fatima children, was generous in accepting co-redemptive suffering from the Lord. Part of the inscription on his First Mass holy card stressed his desire to offer himself as a "victim of Divine Love" to suffer with Jesus to win souls: "With You may I be for the world the way, the truth, and the life, and through You, a holy priest, a perfect victim!" In an ecstasy, he prayed to Jesus: "I want to help You...It grieves me to see You in this way (suffering from men's sins). Have they committed many offenses against You lately? Make it possible for me to help You with that heavy, heavy cross...You are

are there...what is there to fear?" (*Diary,* pp. 40-41).

As Our Lady promised the children that they would be comforted, Saint Padre Pio knew the same. He wrote to his spiritual director, Padre Benedetto: "It is a happiness that the Lord gives me to rejoice almost only in suffering. In such moments, more than ever, everything in the world pains and annoys me, and I desire nothing except to love and to suffer. Yes, my (spiritual) father, in the midst of all these sufferings I am happy because I feel my heart throb in unison with the Heart of Jesus" (*Letters 1,* p. 194).

DEVOTION TO THE IMMACULATE HEART OF MARY

In the June apparition the children ask if they will go to Heaven. Our Lady answers that Jacinta and Francisco will go soon, but that Lucia must remain for some time longer: "Jesus wishes to make use of you to make me known and loved. He wants to establish in the world devotion to my Immaculate Heart." Lucia then became saddened. Our Lady consoled her: "Do not be disheartened. I will never leave you...My Immaculate Heart will be your refuge and the way that will lead you to God." Then Our Lady opened her hand, and an immense light came forth, enveloping the children and making them see themselves in God. In the front of the palm of Our Lady's right hand, there was a heart encircled with thorns which pierced it. The children understood this was the Immaculate Heart of Mary, wounded by the sins of humanity. Our Lady wanted people to make up for these sins by acts of love.

From early childhood, Saint Padre Pio was devoted to Our Lady. He would call her affectionately, "Mamina," (my little Mother) or "Madonnia" (my little Lady). A little sign over the door of his room summed up how much Our Lady meant to him: "Mary is the inspiration (beginning) of my hope!"

Saint Padre Pio was devoted to Our Lady under various titles. One was Our Lady of Libera, patroness of Pietrelcina, his birthplace. She had freed the city on various occasions from war, plague, and natural disasters. He, no doubt, learned to trust Our Lady in all his trials and concerns.

He also honored Mary as Our Lady of Graces, patroness of the friary at San Giovanni Rotondo. He used to say that all the great graces of his life came to him through the intercession of Our Lady.

Finally, he was greatly devoted to the Immaculate Heart of Our Lady of Fatima. It was she who cured him miraculously in 1959 from an illness that had so weakened him that he was confined to bed for some time. Afterwards, he venerated a special statue of her sent to him by the bishop of Fatima, and he always made his thanksgiving after Mass at the foot of that statue.

Just as little Lucia was assured of Our Lady's constant protection and consolation, Saint Padre Pio enjoyed the same. When a friar once asked him, *"Padre Pio, does Our Lady ever come to your room?"* he answered, *"Why don't you ask me if she ever leaves?"*

ARDENT APPEAL TO PRAY THE ROSARY

In both apparitions, Our Lady asked that the Rosary be prayed. In May, she told of the power of the Rosary: "Pray the Rosary every day, in order to obtain peace for the world and the end of the war." She added that Francisco would have to pray many Rosaries before he could go to Heaven. In June, Our Lady told Lucia: "I want you to pray the Rosary every day. . . ."

Saint Padre Pio is certainly known for his love of the Rosary. When he was old and feeble, he needed the help of some friars to get dressed in the morning. As he was dressing one day, he told Padre Alessio, "Get me my weapon!" Startled, Padre Alessio responded, "Weapon? Padre Pio, you don't have a weapon." Saint Padre Pio answered, "Get me my Rosary!" The Rosary was his weapon to do good and defend against evil.

Saint Padre Pio learned to pray the Rosary many times a day as a young novice, a practice that increased with time. One day a man bragged to Saint

Padre Pio, "I have said the Rosary five times today."

Padre responded, "That's very good! I have said about thirty-five Rosaries!"

The man could not believe that and asked, "Padre Pio, how could you have said thirty-five Rosaries? You have been busy all day long."

The Padre answered, "You do one thing at a time; I do three or four things at a time."

A final quote of Saint Padre Pio sums up his response to Our Lady's request for the Rosary, and why he always urged others to pray it often: "Is there a prayer more beautiful or more pleasing than the one she taught us herself? More beautiful than the Rosary? Always say the Rosary!"

This statue of Saint Padre Pio is located on the grounds of the National Blue Army Shrine of the Immaculate Heart of Mary in Washington, New Jersey. The Shrine is open to the public year round.

Saint Padre Pio and the Fatima Apparitions of July and August, 1917

The apparition of July 13, 1917, occurred at the usual apparition site of the Cova da Iria and was considerably longer than all the other apparitions except that of October.

During this apparition a number of things were revealed that became parts of the "secret" of Fatima. Actually, it might be more accurate to say that there was only one secret, all revealed in this July apparition, but with three parts. But, not to cause confusion, we will simply refer to them as "three secrets." These thrcc messages will be the main focus in our present reflection.

The August apparition, on the other hand, did not occur like all the other apparitions on the 13th of the month, nor did it occur in the Cova. Rather, certain anticlerical government officials, bent on disturbing the apparitions, deceptively kidnapped the visionaries and imprisoned them in a jail in the neighboring city of Ourem.

As a result, the anticipated apparition never happened that day. However, Our Lady suddenly appeared without warning to the visionaries on August 19th (or 15th) at a place called Valinhos, located a short distance from their homes. This unexpected visit was quite brief, but it reinforced the basic Message of Our Lady for prayer and penance for the eternal salvation of souls.

Reminders

As we compare Our Lady's Message for July and August with the spirituality of Saint Padre Pio, we must realize that Our Lady repeated many requests in these apparitions that she had already made in May and June. As Pope John Paul II is quoted as saying, "We do not need a whole lot of new ideas, just a lot of reminders!" So Our Lady often gently reminded her children—Lucia, Francisco and Jacinta, and all of us through them—of the main points of her Message, so that we would remember to carry them out very faithfully.

Let us now consider the main points of Our Lady's July and August Message, and see how Saint Padre Pio also lived these out faithfully.

Hell

One of the most powerful experiences the young visionaries had throughout the course of Our Lady's apparitions was the vision of Hell. This unforgettable vision constitutes the "first secret" of Fatima because the children, directed by Our Lady, would not talk about it initially, except among themselves. It was only publicly revealed later on in the memoirs of Sister Lucia written years afterwards.

God chose to let the visionaries see Hell. It undoubtedly left a lasting impression on them. Here is a part of Lucia's description of what the children saw:

> *"They saw a sea of fire. Plunged in this fire were demons and souls that looked like transparent embers, some black or bronze, in human form, driven about by the flames that issued from within themselves, together with clouds of smoke. They were falling on all sides, just as sparks cascade from great fires, without weight or equilibrium, amid cries of pain and despair which horrified us so that we trembled with fear. . . ."*

Even for these privileged souls, the vision was extremely frightful. What consoled and preserved them through it was that Our Lady had already told them in her May apparition that they were all going to Heaven.

Hell is a reality—it exists! But it is something most people would not care to think about, much less see, because it means admitting even the possibility of going there. Our Lady herself summed up the impact of this vision when she said kindly but sadly to the children: "You have seen Hell where the souls of poor sinners go."

As mentioned above, Our Lady in her earlier apparitions had already requested prayers and sacrifices for the conversion and salvation of souls. But by showing the children Hell, with its grave, unending torments, Our Lady emphasized how urgent and essential was the task of saving souls. The children realized graphically the tragic consequences that awaited any soul that would be lost.

In her brief August apparition, Our Lady again stressed the importance of offering prayers and sacrifices for the conversion of sinners. She said to the children with a sad expression:

> *"Pray, pray very much and make sacrifices for sinners, for many souls go to Hell because they have nobody to pray and make sacrifices for them."*

According to Lucia's memoirs, Jacinta was the one most struck by this urgent Message. The notion of an eternity of suffering affected her greatly. She became extremely zealous in saving souls from Hell by her constant prayer and sacrifices, such as giving her lunch to hungry children or bearing with thirst as a sacrifice.

SAINT PADRE PIO

Saint Padre Pio understood the importance of Hell as a deterrent to sin, especially mortal sin which, if unrepented, would land a person in Hell. A story is told of a man who came to Confession to him who was living a life of mortal sin. Saint Padre Pio told the man, "You had better change your life, or you will end up in Hell."

The man answered, "Padre Pio, I don't believe in Hell."

Saint Padre Pio answered the man, "Well, you will when you get there!" Saint Padre Pio was only too aware of the sufferings of Hell.

In another situation, a widow kept asking him if her husband, who had died recently, was in Heaven. At first, Saint Padre Pio would not answer her. Finally, as she insisted, he told her, "I cannot bear to see your husband in Hell, he is so horrible looking. Although he had made a Confession shortly before he died, he deliberately withheld confessing that he had committed adultery, and so he died unrepentant with these grave sins on his soul."

VICTIM FOR SOULS

In our previous reflection for the May and June apparitions of Our Lady, we touched on Saint Padre Pio's great desire to be a "victim" with Christ for the salvation of souls. Here, let us add a powerful statement of his, clearly showing his ardent longing that

that no soul be lost: "My Jesus, I want to be a victim for others. Punish me and not others, under the condition that I love you and everyone is saved." This is no doubt the reason he spent himself in the work of the confessional, hearing Confessions for over fifteen hours a day when he was younger. It was estimated that he heard over five million Confessions in his lifetime. Why? That sins may be forgiven, and everyone saved!

Yet, the fear of Hell should not be the primary focus of our Christian life; rather, it must be our sincere love for God and for one another. However, fear of Hell, like a safety net, can halt us from mortal sin when love itself may not yet be a strong enough motive. Even St. Dismas, the "good thief," knew its importance when he asked his fellow thief who was resisting repentance even in the very last moments of his life, "Have you no fear of God?" (cf Lk 23:40). Hell is one of the "four last things" along with Death, Judgement and Heaven. St. Augustine once said that if we meditate daily on these "four last things," we would never commit a mortal sin.

Saint Padre Pio and the Fatima Apparitions of September and October, 1917

Of all the apparitions of Our Lady of Fatima in the Cova da Iria, the last two combined what appear to be the most simple (September) and the most spectacular (October) of them all. As we have seen, on August 13th there was no "public" apparition of Our Lady to the shepherd children, Lucia, Francisco and Jacinta, because they had been abducted and imprisoned by disbelieving government officials.

Great crowds of people packed the roads leading to the Cova in September and October. As a result, the visionaries had a difficult time getting to the apparition site. People would throw themselves on their knees before the children, and beg them to offer their petitions to Our Lady: *Heal my crippled son; Cure my daughter who is deaf; Let my husband and son return safely from the war; Let Our Lady convert me, a poor sinner; Ask Our Lady to cure my tuberculosis.*

It seemed as if every kind of human need and suffering was being presented to Our Lady. This is a great example of how instinctively God's children turn to their Heavenly Mother in all their needs and sorrows.

As in the previous chapters, we will now summarize Our Lady's Message for these two months, and then compare it to the spirituality Saint Padre Pio lived out in his own life.

The Rosary and Fatima

In all her apparitions, Our Lady requested the children to "pray the Rosary" or "continue to pray the Rosary." In fact, she specified that they pray the Rosary "every day." How pleasing this prayer is to Our Lady! She wants her children to pray it because it is such a powerful means of doing good and overcoming evil in our daily lives.

Furthermore, it helps us to pray more deeply and more personally by teaching us to combine "formal prayer" and "mental prayer." In formal prayer we use word-formulas composed by others to guide us in how to speak to God, in what to say to Him. In the Rosary, we recite the *Our Father* (the prayer Our

Lord Himself taught us); the *Hail Mary;* the *Glory Be;* the *Apostles' Creed;* and the *Hail, Holy Queen.* We then add "mental prayer" to these inspiring word-formulas. This happens when we reflect or meditate on the various Mysteries of the life (Joyful Mysteries), public life (Luminous Mysteries), death (Sorrowful Mysteries) and resurrection (Glorious Mysteries) of Our Lord— Mysteries in which Our Lady also plays a prominent part. By reflecting on the simple events in these Mysteries, we get to know Jesus and Mary much better, indeed, in a very personal way. This, no doubt, helps to advance us in our spiritual lives.

The Rosary and Saint Padre Pio

We have already seen Saint Padre Pio's great love for the Rosary. He himself prayed it many times a day. What better proof could there be to show how much importance he put on its daily recitation. He used to say that Our Lady herself gave us the Rosary. And why? Because he knew Our Lady was teaching us by it to grow daily in faith, hope and love, and all the other basic virtues of the Christian life.

We can only imagine how much Saint Padre Pio loved Our Lady under her title of "Our Lady of the Rosary." He became one of the most successful salesmen for her Rosary, always encouraging his "spiritual children," all who came to him, and all who sought

sought his assistance to pray the Rosary daily! He knew how effectively the Rosary moved Our Lord, with and through the intercession of His Blessed Mother, to bestow great graces on His people. Our Lady herself told the shepherd children that by praying the Rosary, souls could be saved from going to Hell; wars could be stopped; and peace could be given to the world. After the Holy Sacrifice of the Mass, our Catholic people feel a special attraction and power in the recitation of the Rosary. We can only imagine how many souls Saint Padre Pio saved from Hell, and how much other good he must have done by his daily recitation of many Rosaries. The prayer beads could often be seen passing quietly through his fingers.

The Miracle of the Sun

It was estimated that about 75,000 people had come from near and far for the October apparition. Our Lady had promised Lucia that she would work an undeniable miracle to prove to the people that the apparitions were indeed real. Many devout believers came to pray and honor Our Lady and see a sign of God's love and glory. Others were hardened disbelievers—atheists and agnostics—who came to scoff at any idea of a miracle or, at least, wondering with great hesitancy whether anything at all would happen.

Well, something quite spectacular did happen! The sun began to "dance" in the sky, giving off bright colors that looked like a multi-colored fireworks display. People were mesmerized with wonder and awe! All of a sudden, the mood changed completely to one of overwhelming fear. The crowds saw the sun suddenly begin to hurtle down toward the earth. Many thought it was the end of the world. The earth seemed that it would be consumed in a flaming sun. Many fell to their knees, confessing their sins aloud. Even atheists began to believe and pray.

Suddenly, just before it seemed the sun would impact the earth, it began to recede and return to its normal place in the sky. But what startling effects followed. They were beyond imagination. Many infirm people—the blind, the crippled, and the like—were healed! Many sinners were converted! Hardened atheists became believers! Even the ground and the clothes of the people, which were saturated with rain for days, were perfectly dry! This was the undeniable "miracle" Our Lady had promised Lucia.

And undeniable it was. In fact, it was seen for about fifty miles around Fatima. It brought an appropriate fear of God's justice and punishment to those who needed to turn away from lives of sin, as well as a greater trust in God's goodness, mercy and power, to inspire those who already knew the Lord to grow closer to Him.

Saint Padre Pio, in his great zeal for the salvation of souls, knew how to be God's faithful instrument to provide either a sense of fear or trust in Him, according to the person's need. As he would say, "I do not give candy to those who need strong medicine." One example of "fear" that comes to mind was when an unbelieving couple (both were Masons) came separately to him in Confession. They wanted to mock Saint Padre Pio and the Sacrament of Penance by making a false confession of "sins" they merely made up for the occasion. They went to Confession separately, as he heard men's Confessions at certain times, and women's Confessions at other times. As each of them came to him in the confessional, he was inspired by God to read their hearts. Knowing their deceit, he stopped each one, and he began to tell each of them their real sins—what they were, when they committed them, and how often! Both of these people were so shaken with fear, that a few days later they both went back to Saint Padre Pio, made sincere Confessions and changed their lives. Fear of God's justice is often necessary to touch the hardened hearts of big sinners.

Consolation and Joy

Many of the people at Fatima on October 13, 1917, experienced not only fear, but great consolation as well. These were the devout and simple who already believed and loved God in their hearts. They saw the power and majesty of God in the "dance of the sun." They knew God has the whole world in

His hands, including their lives. Consolation easily comes when we recall the saying: Nothing is going to happen to me today that God and I together can't handle!

Saint Padre Pio knew how to encourage the faithful, even the weak and the fainthearted, and to give "candy" in the form of consolation when good people needed it. He would do this in his work in the confessional, in counseling his "spiritual children," and in responding to the literally thousands of people who wrote to him from all over the world. He often gave as advice something all of us would do well to remember: "Pray, hope, and don't worry!"

He would send the pilgrims to pray to Our Lady, or to visit the nearby shrine of Saint Michael at Monte Sant'Angelo. He knew, like Saint Francis to whom he was so greatly devoted, that the devil rejoices most when he can steal the joy out of the heart of a servant of God. On the other hand, the devil cannot harm the Servant of God he sees filled with holy joy.

Saint Padre Pio was a true channel of God's joy and consolation to others, as Our Lady always is. We can sum up Our Lady's role in the prayerful words of Mother Teresa of Calcutta who, like Saint Padre Pio, was dedicated to Our Lady of Fatima and to her Rosary: "Immaculate Heart of Mary, Cause of Our Joy, pray for us!"

Father Andrew Apostoli, C.F.R.

A special writer for *Soul* magazine, Father Andrew Apostoli, C.F.R., has been a featured celebrant and homilist at Blue Army Shrine events. He has also been the Spiritual Director on numerous World Apostolate of Fatima pilgrimages.

Father Apostoli, a member of the community of the Franciscan Friars of the Renewal, was ordained by Bishop Sheen in 1967. He has been active in teaching, preaching retreats and parish missions, and giving spiritual direction. He is currently an adjunct faculty member of St. Joseph Seminary, Dunwoodie, Yonkers, New York. He is well-known as an author of several books and appears regularly on Mother Angelica's Eternal Word Television Network (EWTN).

World Apostolate of Fatima
The Blue Army, USA
P.O. Box 976
Washington, New Jersey 07882
908-689-1700
www.wafusa.org

World Apostolate of Fatima

Membership Pledge

The World Apostolate of Fatima is a Public Association of the Faithful, approved by the Holy See on the Feast of Our Lady of the Rosary, October 7, 2005.

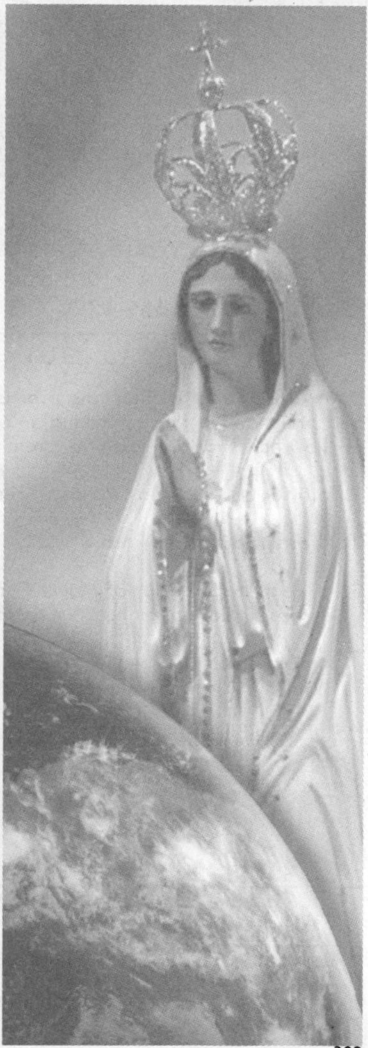

World Apostolate of Fatima, USA
674 Mountain View Rd. Washington, NJ 07882
908-689-1700 x18 www.wafusa.org

PLEDGE TO OUR LADY OF FATIMA

Dear Queen and Mother, who promised at Fatima to convert Russia and bring peace to all mankind, in reparation for my sins and the sins of the whole world, I solemnly promise to your Immaculate Heart:

1. To offer up every day the sacrifices demanded by my daily duty.

2. To pray part of the Rosary* daily while meditating on the Mysteries.

3. To wear the Scapular of Mount Carmel as profession of this promise and as an act of consecration to you.

4. To accomplish the devotion of the Five First Saturdays of the month, including fifteen minutes of meditation on the Mysteries of the Rosary.

I shall renew this promise often, especially in moments of temptation.

____

SIGNATURE

*Usually understood to mean at least five decades.

Note: This pledge is not a vow and does not bind under sin. Nevertheless, it is a promise of love; your word to your heavenly Mother.

The Basilica of Our Lady of the Rosary of Fatima

MORNING OFFERING

O my God, in union with the Immaculate Heart of Mary, *(Here kiss your Brown Scapular as a sign of your consecration. This carries a partial indulgence.)* I offer Thee the Precious Blood of Jesus present on all the altars of the world, joining with It the offering of my every thought, word and action of this day.

O my Jesus, I desire today to gain every indulgence and merit I can, and I offer them, together with myself, to Mary Immaculate—that she may best apply them to the interests of thy most Sacred Heart. Precious Blood of Jesus, save us! Immaculate Heart of Mary, pray for us! Sacred Heart of Jesus, have mercy on us!

"Mary's message at Fatima can be synthe-
'The kingdom of God is at hand. Repent,

The World Apostolate of Fatima is a movement of millions of persons throughout the world responding to the requests made by the Blessed Virgin Mary at Fatima, Portugal in 1917. Through three shepherd children, Our Lady spoke to the world: "Do not offend the Lord Our God any more, because He is already so much offended" (October 13, 1917). She asked for personal conversion, the daily Rosary for world peace, prayers and sacrifices for sinners who have no one to pray for them, and reparation to the Eucharistic Jesus and the Immaculate Heart of Mary.

The Holy Virgin warned, "If my requests are heeded, Russia will be converted, and there will be peace; if not, she [Russia] will spread her errors throughout the world, causing wars and persecutions of the Church. The good will be martyred, the Holy Father will have much to suffer, various nations will be annihilated". However, she prophesied "In the end, my Immaculate Heart will triumph. The Holy Father will consecrate Russia to me, and she will be converted, and a period of peace will be granted to the world." (July 13, 1917).

Mary promised special graces at the hour of death to all who, on the first Saturday of five consecutive months: (1) go to Confession and receive Communion, (2) recite five decades of the Rosary and (3) keep her company for 15 minutes by meditating on the Mysteries of the Rosary, all with the intention of making reparation to her Immaculate Heart.

"The evangelical call to repentance and conversion, uttered in the
relevant than it was sixty-five

sized in these clear, initial words of Christ:
and believe in the Gospel'" (Mk. 1:15).

Pope John Paul II at Vatican City on May 15, 1991

World Apostolate of Fatima members may take advantage of the spiritual privileges associated to authentic devotees of Our Lady of Mount Carmel. Our Lady promised to release from purgatory soon after death all those who (1) wear the Brown Scapular, (2) observe chastity according to their state in life. You must be invested in the Brown Scapular and try to live a Christian Life.

Mother's (Fatima) message, remains ever relevant. It is still more years ago, still more urgent."

Pope John Paul II at Fatima, Portugal, on May 13, 1982

ESSENTIAL CONDITIONS

1. Pray the Rosary daily.
2. Consecrate to God through the Immaculate Heart of Mary and wear the Brown Scapular as a sign of your consecration.
3. Offer reparation (sacrifices demanded by daily duty) through the Morning Offering.
4. Accomplish the devotion of the Five First Saturdays of the month including fifteen minutes of meditation on the Mysteries of the Rosary.

SPIRITUAL PRACTICES

Mass, confession, communion, visits to the Blessed Sacrament, cell holy hours, all-night vigils.

SECONDARY CONDITIONS

1. Send in your pledge.
2. Invite others to join.
3. Wear a sign of membership.

BENEFITS

1. You know you are fulfilling Our Lady's conditions to obtain the conversion and the peace of Christ for the world.
2. You obtain numerous indulgences through the Rosary and the Scapular.
3. You become eligible for the spiritual graces of Our Lady of Mount Carmel. Graces in this life, at the hour of death, and after death.
4. Your name is sent to Fatima and buried near the apparition site.
5. You share in the prayers of millions of members.
6. You become a spiritual child of Saint Padre Pio.
7. You participate in the New Evangelization proposed by the Holy Father.

333296 Printed with ecclesiastical permission

MEMBER INFORMATION

Name: ____

Address: ____

City: ____________________________ State/Province: __________

Postal Code: ________________ Telephone: ____________________

E-mail: ____

Parish: ____

Diocese: ____

Mail to:

World Apostolate of Fatima, USA,
P.O. Box 976, Washington, NJ 07882

☐ I have signed my membership pledge and wish my name sent to Fatima to be buried near the site of the apparitions.

TO THE NATIONAL CENTER:

☐ I would like to make a sacrifice of $ ________________ to Our Lady. For a donation of $9.95 or more we will send you a one year subscription to SOUL magazine.

TO THE INTERNATIONAL CENTER

☐ I would like to make a sacrifice of $ ______________ to Our Lady. For your donation of $18.00 or 12 € or more we will send you an annual subscription to the International Magazine "Messenger of the World Apostolate of Fatima."

____ ______________

SIGNATURE DATE

PLEASE MAKE ONE CHECK PAYABLE TO: WORLD APOSTOLATE OF FATIMA, USA

The Fifteen Promises of Mary to Christians who Pray the Rosary

1. To all those who shall recite my Rosary devoutly, I promise my special protection and very great graces.
2. Those who shall persevere in the recitation of my Rosary will receive some signal grace.
3. The Rosary will be a very powerful armor against hell: it will destroy vice; deliver from sin; and dispel heresy.
4. The Rosary will make virtue and good works flourish, and will obtain for souls the most abundant Divine Mercies; it will substitute in hearts love of God for love of the world, and elevate them to desire heavenly and eternal good. O, that souls would sanctify themselves by this means!
5. Those who trust themselves to me through the Rosary will not perish.
6. Those who shall recite my Rosary piously, considering its Mysteries,

will not be overwhelmed by misfortune, nor die a bad death. The sinner will be converted; the just will grow in grace and become worthy of eternal life.

7. Those truly devoted to my Rosary will not die without the consolations of the Church, or without grace.
8. Those who shall recite my Rosary will find during their life, and at their death, the light of God, the fullness of His grace, and will share in the merits of the blessed.
9. I will deliver very promptly from Purgatory the souls devoted to my Rosary.
10. The true children of my Rosary will enjoy great glory in heaven.
11. What you shall ask through my Rosary you shall obtain.
12. Those who propagate my Rosary will obtain through me aid in all their necessities.
13. I have obtained from my Son that all confreres of the Rosary shall have for their brethren in life and death the saints of heaven.
14. Those who recite my Rosary faithfully are all my beloved children, the brothers and sisters of Jesus Christ.
15. Devotion to my Rosary is a great sign of predestination.

Imprimatur

PATRICK J. HAYES, D.D.

Archbishop of New York

Artwork © World Apostolate of Fatima, U.S.A., Inc.

World Apostolate of Fatima, USA

Washington, New Jersey 07882-0976

www.wafusa.org

419879

OUR LADY'S SPIRITUAL FORMATION PROGRAM: THE FIVE FIRST SATURDAYS DEVOTION

Fr. Andrew Apostoli C.F.R.

PART 3:

Pray the Rosary

"I am the Lady of the Rosary!"

When Catholics think about our Blessed Lady, they almost inevitably think about her beautiful prayer, the Rosary. This is especially true when recalling the message of Our Lady at Fatima. The only request Our Lady made in all six of her apparitions to the young visionaries, Lucia, Francisco, and Jacinta, was "Pray the Rosary every day!" In the final apparition on October 13, 1917, Mary revealed her identity to the children saying "I am the Lady of the Rosary!"

It comes as no surprise, then, that the Rosary would have a very special place in the Five First Saturdays' Devotion. Our Lady knows how much this prayer helps her children to grow in holiness. Like exercise in a physical health program, the Rosary greatly assists our spiritual development. It should daily be an important part of a devout Catholic's training in holiness, in growing in love for God and for one's neighbors. This realization made St. Pio of Pietrelcina a great devotee of the Holy Rosary, exclaim: "Is there any prayer more beautiful than the prayer Our Lady herself taught us than the Rosary? Always pray the Rosary!" And he did! There is a story told that one day a man came to Padre Pio and boasted gently: "Padre Pio, today I prayed five Rosaries!" "Very good!" Padre Pio answered, "I've said about 35 Rosaries!" The man was filled with disbelief and retorted, "Padre Pio, you have been busy all day long! When did you have time to say 35 Rosaries?" The Padre answered, "You do one thing at a time; I do 3 or 4 things at a time!" When it came to praying the Rosary, St. Pio certainly practiced what he preached!

The Rosary: *The Prayer to Go to Jesus Through and With Mary*

There is a traditional Latin saying, "Ad Jesum per Mariam" which is translated, "To Jesus through Mary." It expresses the wisdom and experience of the Church. How many Catholics have found their way to Our Lord through the intercession of His Blessed Mother! The very first Apostles of Jesus "believed in Him" (Jn 2:11) as a result of the miraculous sign Jesus worked at the wedding feast of Cana (cf Jn 2:1-11) through the request of Our Lady: "They have no wine …" (Jn 2:3) And, when it seemed like Jesus would not get involved, He was moved by her unwavering trust, "Do whatever He tells you …" (Jn 2:5). How many other disciples of Jesus, knowing its importance, have sought to approach Jesus more quickly, totally and securely through the assistance of His Mother. The Servant of God, Archbishop Fulton J. Sheen, sought Mary's intercession to her Son, as he expressed it in his episcopal coat-of-arms with the words "Da per Matrem me venire!" which is translated, ***"Grant that I may come to You through Your Mother!"***

Pope John Paul II, in his beautiful Apostolic letter, (The Rosary of the Virgin Mary), teaches clearly that ***in the Rosary Jesus and Mary are inseparably linked together***. For him, the Rosary was both Christ-centered and Mary-centered.

The Rosary, though clearly Marian in character, is at heart a Christocentric Prayer. In the sobriety of its elements, it has all the depth of the Gospel message in its entirety, of which it can be said to be a compendium. It is an echo of the prayer of Mary, her perennial Magnificat for the work of the redemptive Incarnation which began in her virginal womb. With the Rosary, Christians sit at the school of Mary and are led to contemplate the beauty on the face of Christ and to experience the depths of His love. Through the Rosary the faithful receive abundant grace, as though from the very hands of the Mother of the Redeemer. (Par. 1)

No one can help us more than Our Lady to delve deeply into the mysteries of Salvation. As the loving Daughter of God the Father, Mary can enlighten us about the Father's Will for our own lives and how to fulfill it more faithfully each day. As the loving Mother of God the Son, Mary can help us to bring Jesus to others as she did at the Visitation to St. John the Baptist and to his parents. Furthermore, she can teach us to reveal Him to others as she did at Bethlehem to the shepherds and the Magi. Finally, as the loving Spouse of the Holy Spirit, Mary can help us to appreciate the great mystery of Jesus living in us spiritually through Sanctifying Grace (cf Gal 2:19-20) as He lived in her physically through the overshadowing of the Holy Spirit. Without doubt, Mary's preferred instrument to teach us these sacred truths is through the recitation of her Rosary. This is why ***Pope John Paul II referred to the Rosary as a concise summary of the Gospel message***.

The Rosary and Growth in Prayer

Besides teaching us the fundamental truths of our Catholic Faith, the Rosary, especially when prayed daily or at least frequently, helps our prayer-life to develop. Most people are not aware that just as we physically develop through life stages such as childhood, adolescence and adulthood, so we pass through parallel stages in our spiritual life, namely, as a beginner, then as someone advanced, and finally as a mature Christian.

As we pass through these stages, the form of prayer we use changes. The important point here is that the Rosary contains the three forms of prayer most people experience as beginners in the Christian life. By praying the Rosary frequently we become familiar with these three forms of prayer. They soon become "second nature" to us!

The Prayer of the Lips
Formal Prayer

The first prayer beginners experience is called the ***"prayer of the lips"*** because these are the prayers we recite with our lips. They are also called "formal prayers" because we use a set of words or formulas that others have given us. They help a beginner to ***know what to say to God*** in prayer. In the rosary, we use very beautiful "formal prayers." Most important of all are the ***"Our Father,"*** the most perfect prayer taught to us by Our Lord Himself; the ***"Hail Mary"*** composed of words addressed to Our Lady by the Archangel Gabriel at the Annunciation, by her cousin St. Elizabeth at the Visitation, and finally words addressed to Our Lady by the Church; and the ***"Glory be to the Father"*** with which we praise and glorify the most Holy Trinity. Other formal prayers contained in the rosary are the ***"Creed"*** and the ***"Hail Holy Queen."*** We should also recite the powerful little prayer Our Lady taught us at Fatima to recite after each decade of the rosary:

"Oh my Jesus, forgive us our sins, save us from the fires of hell, lead all souls to Heaven, especially those who are most in need of Your mercy."

THESE FORMAL PRAYERS OF THE ROSARY ARE AMONG THE MOST BASIC PRAYERS WE HAVE IN OUR CATHOLIC FAITH. FROM RECITING THEM OVER AND OVER WE LEARN HOW TO SPEAK LOVINGLY AND TRUSTINGLY TO GOD.

The second kind of prayer we learn from reciting the rosary is to meditate. Meditation consists in a reflection of the mind on some incident from sacred Scripture or some teaching of the Church or sayings of a saint. In the rosary, our meditations focus on the mysteries. The Joyful Mysteries deal with the events surrounding the birth of Jesus and His childhood. In the Luminous Mysteries we focus on the events of Jesus' public ministry. In the Sorrowful Mysteries we focus on the agony Our Lord endured in His soul and the sufferings which He endured in His body, during the hours of His passion and death. We also reflect on how Our Lady shared most profoundly in the redemptive sufferings of her Son. In the Glorious Mysteries we focus on Christ's victory over death and the glory He now has in Heaven which Our Lady already shares and we hope to share someday. By meditation we try to penetrate more deeply into the meaning of these mysteries and apply them to our own lives.

As we meditate on the mysteries in our mind, our heart begins to respond with sentiments of love, gratitude, appreciation, and hope. These affections of the heart are precious personal stirrings of our faith and trust in God, our longing to someday share in the glory of Christ and our desire to serve Him in faithful and generous love. It is an important aspect of these affections of the heart that they increase in depth so that we desire to live our Christian life more fully each day and become more conscious of God's presence with us.

From reflecting on these fundamental forms of prayer,

namely, formal prayer, meditation and affective prayer, we can see why the rosary is considered the best instrument for teaching Catholics how to pray. This author remembers an incident on an airplane when a flight attendant came and mentioned to him that she had wanted to learn how to meditate. She was ready to take a course in Transcendental Meditation at a cost of $300.00. She said, "I ended up picking up my rosary and I learned to meditate for nothing!" The rosary is a prayer that costs us nothing, but rewards us with an increase of love and the strengthening of our faith.

One of the things that often discourages people from praying the rosary is they feel that they get so distracted as they pray. It is important to remember a few basic points about distractions. First, everybody gets them. St. Bernard of Clairvaux is quoted as saying that no one can reflect for more than twenty-five seconds without a distraction. Secondly, distractions only disrupt our prayer when they are voluntarily consented to. When our imagination is going wild (St. Teresa of Jesus, an expert teacher on prayer, referred to them as "wild horses running through the attic"), our heart remains focused on the Lord because we have not deliberately desired these distracting thoughts. Distracting thoughts even include temptations that may come when a person is praying the rosary.

We cannot always keep our mind focused on the mysteries in meditation. God made us and knows this. Therefore, our desire to love Him does not end because our imagination goes off in a different direction. ***So don't be discouraged by involuntary distractions. Just try gently to bring your focus back on either the words you are saying, or the mystery you are reflecting on or even just the presence of God with Whom you are speaking.*** The Lord is pleased with your loving desire to pray even though the distractions make the attempt look like a waste of time. It is not. That is only the devil's deceit to discourage you from praying the rosary.

Some people say they find difficulty with the rosary because it is repetitious. They feel that this can turn the recitation of the rosary into a monotonous saying of repeated words. I have not seen a better response to that difficulty than something Archbishop Fulton J. Sheen spoke about. Here is the wisdom of this very saintly Archbishop.

It is objected that there is much repetition in the Rosary, therefore it is monotonous. That reminds me of a woman who came to see me. She said: "I would never become a Catholic. You say the same words in the Rosary over and over again and anyone who repeats the same words is never sincere. I would never believe such a person and neither would God." I asked her who the man was who was with her. She said it was her fiancé. I asked "Does he love you?" "Certainly he does." "But how do you know?" "He told me." "What did he say?" "He said: 'I love you.'" "When did he tell you last?" "About an hour ago." "Did he tell you before?" "Yes, last night." "What did he say?" "I love you." "But never before?" He tells me every night." I said: "Do not believe him. He is repeating. He is not sincere."

THE BEAUTIFUL TRUTH IS THERE IS NO REPETITION IN "I LOVE YOU."

Because there is a new moment of time, the words do not mean the same as before. Love is never monotonous . The mind is infinitely variable in its language, but the heart is not. The heart of man in the face of the woman he loves is too poor to translate the infinity of his affection into different words. So the heart takes but one expression "I love you" and saying it over and over again, it never repeats. It is the only real news in the universe. That is what we do when we say the Rosary. We are saying to the Holy Trinity, to the Incarnate Savior, to the Blessed Mother, "I love you," "I love you," "I love you."

Having reflected on this beautiful prayer Our Lady gave us, we can see why St. Padre Pio often said, "It is Our Lady who gave us the rosary, but the devil is always trying to take it away from us!" Don't ever let him do it!

How to Pray The Rosary

The Joyful Mysteries
(Mondays and Saturdays)

Annunciation
And when the angel had come to her, he said, *"Hail, full of grace, the Lord is with thee. Blessed art thou among women."* (Lk. 1:28)

Visitation
And Elizabeth filled with the Holy Spirit cried out with a loud voice, saying, *"Blessed art thou among women and blessed is the fruit of thy womb!"* (Lk. 1:41-42)

Birth of Jesus
And she brought forth her firstborn Son, and wrapped Him in swaddling clothes, and laid Him in a manger. . . .
(Lk. 2:7)

Presentation
And when the days of her purification were fulfilled. . .
they took Him up to Jerusalem to present Him to the Lord.
(Lk. 2:22)

Finding Jesus in the Temple
And it came to pass after three days, that they found Him in the temple, sitting in the midst of the teachers. . . . (Lk. 2:46)

The Luminous Mysteries
(Thursdays)

Baptism of Jesus
And a voice came from the heavens, saying, *"This is My beloved Son, with whom I am well pleased."* (Mt. 3:16-17)

Wedding Feast at Cana
When the wine ran short, the mother of Jesus said to Him, *"They have no wine"*....[She then said], *"Do whatever He tells you."* (Jn. 2:3-11)

Proclamation of the Kingdom of God
"This is the time of fulfillment. The kingdom of God is at hand. Repent and believe in the Gospel." (Mk. 1:15)

Transfiguration
He was transfigured before their eyes....Out of the cloud a voice: *"This is My Son, My Beloved. Listen to Him."* (Mk. 9:2-8)

Institution of the Holy Eucharist
Then taking bread...[He] gave it to them, saying: *"This is My Body to be given for you. Do this as a remembrance of Me."* (Lk. 22:14-20)

THE SORROWFUL MYSTERIES
(TUESDAYS AND FRIDAYS)

Agony in the Garden
"Father, if Thou wilt, remove this chalice from Me: but yet not My will, but Thine be done"....And His sweat became as drops of blood....

(Lk. 22:42,44)

Scourging at the Pillar
Pilate then took Jesus and had Him scourged. (Jn. 19:1)
From the sole of the foot to the top of the head...wounds and bruises.... (Is. 1:6)

Crowning with Thorns
And they stripped Him and put on Him a scarlet cloak; and plaiting a crown of thorns, they put it on His head....

(Mt. 27:28-29)

Carrying of the Cross
And bearing the Cross for Himself, He went forth to the place called the Skull, in Hebrew, Golgotha. (Jn. 19:17)

Crucifixion
And Jesus cried out with a loud voice and said, *"Father,*
into Thy hands I commend My spirit." And having said this, He expired. (Lk. 23:46)

The Glorious Mysteries
(Wednesdays and Sundays)

Resurrection
"Fear not; for I know that you seek Jesus who was crucified. He is not here, for He is risen, as He said."
(Mt. 28:5)

Ascension
And the Lord Jesus, after He had spoken to them, was taken up into Heaven, and sits at the right hand of God.
(Mk. 16:19)

Descent of the Holy Spirit
And suddenly there came a sound from Heaven, as of a mighty wind coming....And they were all filled with the Holy Spirit.... (Acts 2:2,4)

Assumption
And a great sign appeared in Heaven: a woman clothed with the sun, and the moon was under her feet, and upon her head a crown of twelve stars. (Rev. 12:1)

Coronation
Thou art the glory of Jerusalem...the honor of our people...the hand of the Lord hath strengthened thee, and therefore thou shall be blessed forever.... (Jdt. 15:10-11)

The Rosary Prayers

Sign of the Cross

In the name of the Father, and of the Son, and of the Holy Spirit. Amen.

The Apostles' Creed

I believe in God, the Father Almighty, Creator of Heaven and earth; and in Jesus Christ, His only Son, Our Lord; who was conceived by the Holy Spirit, born of the Virgin Mary, suffered under Pontius Pilate, was crucified, died, and was buried. He descended into hell; the third day He arose again from the dead; He ascended into Heaven, sits at the right hand of God, the Father Almighty; from thence He shall come to judge the living and the dead.

I believe in the Holy Spirit, the Holy Catholic Church, the communion of saints, the forgiveness of sins, the resurrection of the body and life everlasting. Amen.

Our Father

Our Father, who art in heaven, hallowed be Thy name. Thy kingdom come; Thy will be done on earth, as it is in Heaven. Give us this day our daily bread; and forgive us our trespasses, as we forgive those who trespass against us. And lead us not into temptation, but deliver us from evil. Amen.

Hail Mary

Hail Mary, full of grace; the Lord is with thee; blessed art thou among women, and blessed is the fruit of thy womb, Jesus. Holy Mary, Mother of God, pray for us sinners, now and at the hour of our death. Amen.

Glory Be to the Father

Glory be to the Father, and to the Son, and to the Holy Spirit. As it was in the beginning, is now, and ever shall be, world without end. Amen.

Fatima Decade Prayer

O my Jesus, forgive us our sins, save us from the fires of Hell. Lead all souls to Heaven, especially those most in need of Thy mercy.

Hail, Holy Queen

Hail, Holy Queen, Mother of Mercy, our life, our sweetness and our hope. To thee do we cry, poor banished children of Eve. To thee do we send up our sighs, mourning and weeping in this valley of tears.

Turn then, most gracious advocate, thine eyes of mercy toward us; and after this, our exile, show unto us the blessed fruit of thy womb, Jesus. O clement, O loving, O sweet Virgin Mary!

R. Pray for us, O most holy Mother of God.

V. That we may be worthy of the promises of Christ.

Concluding Prayer

Let Us Pray: O God, whose only-begotten Son, by His life, death and resurrection, has purchased for us the rewards of eternal life: grant, we beseech Thee, that meditating on these Mysteries of the most holy Rosary of the Blessed Virgin Mary, we may imitate what they contain and obtain what they promise. Through the same Christ, Our Lord. Amen.

How to Pray the Rosary

- † While holding the Crucifix, make the Sign of the Cross and then recite the Apostles' Creed.
- † Recite the Our Father on the first large bead.
- † Recite a Hail Mary on each of the three small beads for an increase of faith, hope and charity.
- † Recite the Glory Be to the Father.
- † Recall the first Rosary Mystery and recite the Our Father on the next large bead.
- † Recite a Hail Mary on each of the adjacent ten small beads while reflecting on the Mystery.
- † Recite the Glory Be to the Father.
- † Recite the Fatima Decade Prayer.
- † Each succeeding decade is prayed in a similar manner by recalling the appropriate Mystery, reciting the Our Father, ten Hail Marys and the Glory Be to the Father, while reflecting on the Mystery. The Fatima Decade Prayer concludes each Mystery.
- † When the fifth Mystery is completed, the Rosary is customarily concluded with the Hail, Holy Queen.

Rosary Mystery images courtesy of
www.TotallyCatholic.com

printed with ecclesiastical permission

World Apostolate of Fatima, U.S.A.
P.O. Box 976
Washington, NJ 07882

866-513-1917
www.wafusa.org

Fatima Prayer Cell Program

ONE WORLD PRAYING
ORBIS UNUS ORANS
WORLD APOSTOLATE OF FATIMA

Fatima Prayer Cell Program

The World Apostolate of Fatima, USA

Washington, New Jersey

www.wafusa.org

(908) 689-1700, ext. 18

DIOCESAN IMPRIMATUR

In accord with Canon 827 of the New Code of Canon Law, this publication has been submitted to a censor of the Diocese and nothing being found contrary to faith and morals, we hereby grant permission in accord with Canon 824 that it be published.

Rev. Msgr. William Benwell, J.C.L.
Vicar General
Diocese of Metuchen
January 17, 2008

N.B. The imprimatur implies nothing more than the material contained in the publication has been examined by diocesan censors and nothing contrary to faith and morals has been found therein.

2008 Revised Edition

©1996, 2008 World Apostolate of Fatima, USA/
Blue Army, USA

Photos:
©World Apostolate of Fatima, USA/Blue Army, USA

Scripture References from:
The Holy Bible, Douay-Rheims Version
©2000 Tan Books and Publishers, Inc.

Quotations contained in this booklet pertaining to the Apparitions and Miracle of Fatima:
Fatima in Lucia's Own Words, Volume I
©2004 Secretariado dos Pastrorinhos

Icon artwork courtesy of Deacon Charles Rohrbacher

ISBN 1-56036-083-6

Table of Contents

CONTENTS

Introduction

The Fatima Prayer Cell of Holiness is a weekly or monthly spiritual gathering for small group prayer before the Blessed Sacrament or in a home. Members endeavor to grow in holiness by responding to Our Lady's requests for prayer, penance and sacrifice in a spirit of reparation to the Sacred Heart of Jesus and the Immaculate Heart of Mary and for the conversion of poor sinners. Thereby they work to bring about the triumph of the Immaculate Heart and promised era of peace to mankind.

It may be said that the Prayer Cell began in 1916 with the appearance of the Angel of Peace to the three shepherd children, Lucia, Francisco and Jacinta. In 1917, Our Lady appeared and told them to pray and make sacrifices for sinners. The children discussed the meaning of the message given by the Angel and Our Lady. The shepherd children encouraged each other to pray and make sacrifices. Prayer cell members do the same.

Why is it called a "Cell"? Just as cells form the human body by dividing and growing, a Prayer Cell should do the same after there are 8-10 members, or if they have completed a level within the Formation Program. The group then splits and forms a new Prayer Cell. This is how the Prayer Cell grows, multiplies and spreads the holiness of Fatima within the Church, and fills people with the prayerful spirit of Our Lady's Message.

There is nothing difficult in starting the Prayer Cell Program. You can start a Prayer Cell in your parish with only two or more people. Simply get together with your family, several of your friends or fellow parishioners. Contact your pastor for permission to meet in the church on a day and time decided beforehand by the consensus of the group. Follow the prayer program as contained in this booklet. If for some reason you cannot obtain permission to meet in a church, begin a Prayer Cell in your home.

This booklet presents a simple format for use by members of the Prayer Cell Program. Other materials for spiritual reading are also listed towards the end of this booklet for additional study. **It is highly recommended that the *PRAYER CELL FORMATION PROGRAM* (see page 53) be used in conjunction with this booklet for an in-depth study of the Fatima Message** and to help your Cell grow and divide into two, three and four cells as you advance through the formation process.

May God bless you in your love for Our Lady and your desire to grow in holiness for the glory of God and the salvation of souls. By learning, living and spreading Our Lady's Message, you do your part to help bring us another step closer to the promised triumph of the Immaculate Heart of Mary.

Qualification: In this booklet you will notice that Our Lady's pronouns are capitalized. This is to bring to mind the Divine prerogatives which Our Lord has been pleased to grant Her due to His magnanimous generosity.

Suggestions for Keeping the Rosary "Fresh"

Quotes excerpted from *Rosarium Virginis Mariae*
by Pope John Paul II

LEADER'S INSTRUCTIONS:

It is recommended that Prayer Cell members read Pope John Paul II's apostolic letter *Rosarium Virginis Mariae*, which can be downloaded from the Vatican's website, http://www.vatican.va. Listed below are some recommended practices and considerations given by the Holy Father in the recitation of the Rosary. Each Prayer Cell is encouraged to vary the way the Rosary is recited from time to time by using one or more of his many suggestions so as to keep the recitation "fresh" as a method of contemplation.

SCRIPTURE READING [#30]:

"As we listen, we are certain that this is the Word of God, spoken for today and spoken 'for me...' It is not a matter of recalling information but of allowing God to speak."

Read a Bible passage. The leader is free to choose either the one in the booklet, part of which is contained in the passage marked "+", or one of the other passages listed. Passages in this booklet are quoted from the *Douay-Rheims Version* of the Bible except for the Fifth Glorious Mystery, which is taken from the *Office of Readings*. However, any approved version of the Bible may be used.

USE OF ICONS [#29]:

"Announcing each mystery, and perhaps even using a suitable icon to portray it, is as it were to open up a scenario *on which to focus our attention."*

MEDITATIONS [#30]:

"In certain solemn communal celebrations, this word can be appropriately illustrated by a brief commentary."

Two brief commentaries are offered:

- A Scripture meditation and
- A Fatima reflection.

These are optional. One or both may be used.

SILENCE [#31]:

"After the announcement of the mystery and the proclamation of the word, it is fitting to pause and focus one's attention for a suitable period of time on the mystery concerned, before moving into vocal prayer."

THE "OUR FATHER" [#32]:

"...it is natural for the mind to be lifted up towards the Father. *In each of his mysteries, Jesus always leads us to the Father..."*

THE TEN *HAIL MARYS* [#33]:

"These words express...the wonder of heaven and earth; they...give us a glimpse of God's own wonderment as he contemplates his 'masterpiece'...The repetition of the Hail Mary *in the Rosary gives us a share in God's own wonder and pleasure..."*

THE NAME OF JESUS [#33]:

"...it is precisely the emphasis given to the name of Jesus and to His mystery that is the sign of a meaningful and fruitful recitation of the Rosary. Pope Paul VI drew attention ...to the custom in certain regions of highlighting the name of Christ by the addition of a clause referring to the mystery being contemplated."

Particular emphasis should be given to the Holy Name of Jesus - a bowing of the head or an optional clause may be added with each *Hail Mary* after reciting His Name, e.g. "Jesus Incarnate." A clausc is offered in quotes under the name of the Mystery and is taken from *The Secret of the Rosary* by St. Louis de Montfort (except for the Luminous Mysteries).

CONTEMPLATION [#11]:

"Mary constantly sets before the faithful the 'mysteries' of her Son, *with the desire that the contemplation of those mysteries will release all their saving power. In the recitation of the Rosary, the Christian community enters into contact with the memories and the contemplative gaze of Mary."*

GLORY BE [#34]:

"It is important that the Gloria, the high-point of contemplation, *be given due prominence in the Rosary. In public recitation it could be sung..."*

FRUITS OF THE MYSTERY [#35]:

"...it is worthwhile to note that the contemplation of the mysteries could better express their full spiritual fruitfulness if an effort were made to conclude each mystery with a prayer for the fruits specific to that particular mystery.*"*

Program for Prayer Cell of Holiness

Please Stand

***FATIMA AVE*:**

Refrain: *Ave, Ave, Ave Maria.*
Ave, Ave, Ave Maria.

1 *In Fatima's cova*
On the 13th of May
The Virgin Maria
Appeared at midday.

Refrain

2 *To three shepherd children*
The Virgin then spoke
A message so hopeful
With peace for all folk.

Refrain

3 *With sweet Mother's pleading*

She asked us to pray.
Do penance, be modest,
The Rosary each day.

Refrain

SACRIFICE PRAYER:

All of our actions should begin with this prayer. "Make everything you can a sacrifice..." the Angel told us at Fatima.

"O my Jesus, it is for love of You, for the conversion of sinners, and in reparation for the sins committed against the Immaculate Heart of Mary."

MISSION STATEMENT:

In order to establish devotion to Mary's Immaculate Heart in the world, and to place this devotion alongside devotion to the Most Sacred Heart of Jesus, we desire to live and spread Our Lady's Fatima Message, cease offending God, pray and make reparation for sin. By signing the Pledge of Our Lady of Fatima, and trusting in Mary's intercession, we hope to obtain the salvation of souls, the triumph of Mary's Immaculate Heart, and an era of peace for all mankind.

PLEDGE OF OUR LADY OF FATIMA:

Dear Queen and Mother, who promised at Fatima to convert Russia and bring peace to all mankind, in reparation for my sins and the sins of the whole world, I solemnly promise to your Immaculate Heart:

1. To offer up every day the sacrifices demanded by my daily duty.
2. To pray part of the Rosary daily while meditating

on the Mysteries.

3. To wear the Scapular of Mount Carmel as profession of this promise and as an act of consecration to you.
4. To accomplish the devotion of the Five First Saturdays of the month, including fifteen minutes of meditation on the Mysteries of the Rosary.

I shall renew this promise often, especially in moments of temptation.

Please kneel

PRAYERS FROM FATIMA:

These next two prayers were taught by the Angel while prostrate and should be said often in reparation. Prostration is encour aged when possible.

PARDON PRAYER:
"My God, I believe, I adore, I hope, and I love You! I beg pardon for those who do not believe, do not adore, do not hope, and do not love You." *(3x)*

ANGEL'S PRAYER:
"Most Holy Trinity, Father, Son and Holy Spirit, I adore You profoundly, and I offer You the most precious Body, Blood, Soul, and Divinity of Jesus Christ, present in all the tabernacles of the world, in reparation for the outrages, sacrileges and indifference with which He Himself is offended. And, through the infinite merits of His most Sacred Heart, and the Immaculate Heart of Mary, I beg of You the conversion of poor sinners." *(3x)*

EUCHARISTIC PRAYER:

"O most Holy Trinity, I adore You! My God, my God, I love You in the most Blessed Sacrament!"

PETITIONS:

Motivation to pray - Mention personal and apostolic intentions, including all WAF members living and deceased. Conclude with:

"For these and all the intentions of the Sacred Hearts of Jesus and Mary, and in reparation for the sins committed against Them. We ask this through Christ Our Lord. *Amen.*"

The Holy Rosary With Meditations

Alternate Joyful, Luminous, Sorrowful and Glorious Mysteries for each meeting.

Begin the Rosary with the Sign of the Cross.
Recite the Apostles Creed, one Our Father,
three Hail Marys for the virtues of Faith, Hope,
and Charity, and a Glory Be. Announce the Mystery.
Recite five decades of the Rosary, meditating on the
Mystery to be prayed.

Decade Prayer:

After each Mystery, recite the Decade Prayer:

Oh my Jesus, forgive us, save us from the fire of hell. Lead all souls to heaven, especially those who are most in need.

OPTIONAL AVE:

Refrain from the Fatima Ave.
May be sung after the Decade Prayer.

Refrain: *Ave, Ave, Ave Maria.*
Ave, Ave, Ave Maria.

The Annunciation

"Jesus Incarnate"

+Luke 1:26-38

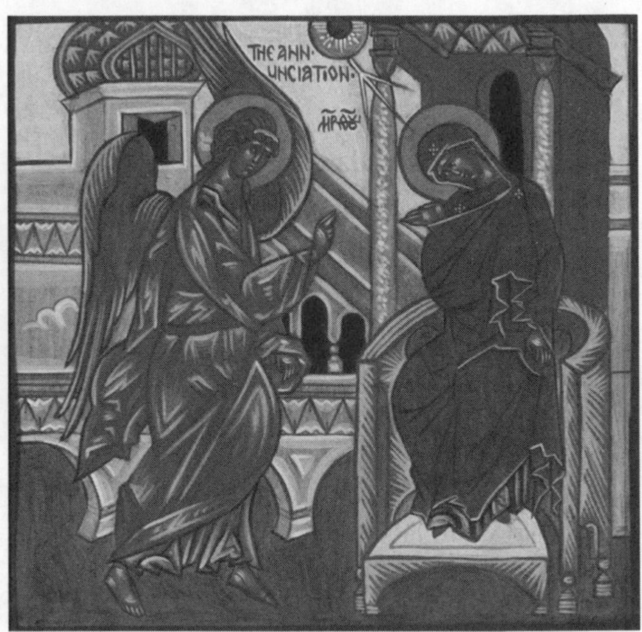

Prayer

We offer Thee, O Lord Jesus, this decade in honor of Thy Incarnation, and we ask of Thee, through this mystery and through the intercession of Thy most Holy Mother, a profound humility.

Scripture

"...the angel Gabriel was sent from God... to a virgin espoused to a man whose name was Joseph, of the house of David; and the virgin's name was Mary. And the angel ...said unto her: 'Hail, full of grace, the Lord is with thee: blessed art thou among women...Behold thou shalt conceive in thy womb, and shalt bring forth a son; and thou shalt call his name Jesus' ... And Mary said: 'Behold the handmaid of the Lord; be it done to me according to thy word.'"

Meditation

The love of God descended upon all of humanity when the power of the Most High came upon Mary. It is in Mary that the Word was made Flesh, and it is in Mary that we receive the graces with which He wishes to visit us. Let us, within the Heart of Mary, open our hearts to receive in faith the love He wishes to pour into our souls.

Fatima Reflection

"What do you want of me?" It is to a heart thus disposed that God sends His tidings of peace, first through the Heart of Mary, and again to us, through the message given to Lucia. We are all called to give our heart to God in asking Him, "What do you want of me?" Let Him enter in.

One Our Father, 10 Hail Marys, One Glory Be, Decade Prayer

Prayer

Grace of the mystery of the Incarnation, come down into my soul and make it truly humble.

The Visitation

"Jesus Sanctifying"

+Luke 1:39-56

Prayer

We offer Thee, O Lord Jesus, this decade in honor of the Visitation of Thy Holy Mother to Her cousin St. Elizabeth, and we ask of Thee, through this mystery and through Mary's intercession, a perfect charity towards our neighbor.

Scripture

"[Mary] entered into the house of Zachary, and saluted Elizabeth...[who] cried out with a loud voice, and said: 'Blessed art thou among women, and blessed is the fruit of thy womb'... And Mary said: 'My soul doth magnify the Lord. And my spirit hath rejoiced in God my Saviour. Because He hath regarded the humility of his handmaid; ...all generations shall call me blessed...holy is his name.'"

Meditation

Mary's faith brought to us our Savior. Her visit to Elizabeth is the sharing of Her Gift of God's Promise, Whom He entrusted to Her. Our Lady's Magnificat is Her Heart's proclamation of God's goodness for those who trust that the Word of the Lord to them will be fulfilled. Let us always proclaim the greatness of the Lord! And our spirit will rejoice in God our Savior!

Fatima Reflection

The angel comes to visit Mary, God's humble handmaid in Nazareth. At Fatima, Our Lady visits poor shepherd children, just as She visited Her cousin Elizabeth. Jesus is with Mary and in Mary. In Her the splendor of God is revealed: *Rays shine forth from beside Him where His power is concealed. (Mulachi 3:4)* Let us approach the Throne of Grace (Mary), as the children did, to ponder the words that proceed from Her lips to bring tidings of hope and peace.

One Our Father, 10 Hail Marys, One Glory Be, Decade Prayer

Prayer

Grace of the mystery of the Visitation, come down into my soul and make it truly charitable.

The Birth of Jesus

"Jesus Born in Poverty"

+Luke 2:1-14

Prayer

We offer Thee, O Child Jesus, this decade in honor of Thy Blessed Nativity, and we ask of Thee, through this mystery and through the intercession of Thy Blessed Mother, detachment from things of this world, love of poverty and love of the poor.

Scripture

"[Joseph] went up...to the city of David, which is called Bethlehem...to be enrolled with Mary...who was with child...And she brought forth her firstborn son, and wrapped him up in swaddling clothes, and laid him in a manger; because there was no room for them in the inn...Glory to God in the highest; and on earth peace to men of good will."

Meditation

In fulfilling the duties of their state in life, Mary and Joseph obey Caesar's decree, bearing patiently with the sufferings and inconveniences this journey entailed. Out of this silent suffering was born our Lord, Who came to be with us, and to accompany us through our own daily trials and sufferings, with a promise of peace.

Fatima Reflection

"Glory to God in the highest and on earth peace among men with whom He is pleased!" What does Our Lady say to those souls who seek peace by embracing the devotion to Her Immaculate Heart, which God willed to be made known at Fatima? *"I promise salvation"*, She says, *"and these souls will be loved by God like flowers placed by me to adorn His throne."* Jesus is born again in the hearts of those who love Him and seek to please Our Lady for His sake.

One Our Father, 10 Hail Marys, One Glory Be, Decade Prayer

Prayer

Grace of the mystery of the Nativity, come down into my soul and make me truly poor in spirit.

The Presentation of Jesus in the Temple

"Jesus Sacrificed"

+Luke 2:22-35

Prayer

We offer Thee, O Lord Jesus, this decade in honor of Thy Presentation in the Temple by the hands of Mary, and we ask of Thee, through this mystery and through the intercession of Thy Blessed Mother, the gift of wisdom and purity of heart and body.

Scripture

"...they carried him to Jerusalem, to present him to the Lord:...And to offer a sacrifice...And behold there was a man in Jerusalem named Simeon...told by God that he should not see death, before he had seen the Christ of the Lord... 'Behold this child *is set for the fall, and for the resurrection of many in Israel, and for a sign which shall be contradicted; And thy own soul a sword shall pierce, that, out of many hearts, thoughts may be revealed.'"*

Meditation

Mary and Joseph presented Jesus in the Temple according to the prescriptions of the law. Marvel with them at Simeon's revelations of what Jesus would accomplish during His life — a glory and tragedy to be fulfilled, both then and *today*: a light to those who are separated from Him, and the glory of His people, the New Israel; yet also a sign of contradiction through divisions found among us — the same sword which pierces the soul of Mary today.

Fatima Reflection

Our Lady reveals Her Heart pierced with thorns on every side, outraged by the sins of humanity, and She seeks reparation. *"...God wishes to establish in the world devotion to my Immaculate Heart." "Do not offend the Lord our God anymore because He is already so much offended."*

One Our Father, 10 Hail Marys, One Glory Be, Decade Prayer

Prayer

Grace of the mystery of the Purification, come down into my soul and make it truly wise and pure.

The Finding of the Child Jesus in the Temple

"Jesus, Wisdom Manifested"

+Luke 2:42-52

Prayer

We offer Thee, O Lord Jesus, this decade in honor of Thy Finding in the Temple among the learned men by Our Lady, after She had lost Thee, and we ask of Thee, through this mystery and through the intercession of Thy Blessed Mother, to convert us and help us amend our lives, and also to convert all sinners, those who have fallen away from the Church, and those who do not believe in God.

Scripture

"And when he was twelve years old, they going up into Jerusalem, according to the custom of the feast, and having fulfilled the days, when they returned, the child Jesus remained in Jerusalem; and his parents knew it not... 'Son, why hast thou done so to us? behold thy father and I sought thee sorrowing'... 'How is it that you sought me? did you not know, that I must be about my father's business?'"

Meditation

Seeking Him, Mary and Joseph find Jesus on the third day. Two days of sorrow, followed by the third day of joy, turns into amazement upon their finding Him. A similar loss and finding was to come later - an event which Mary would forever ponder in Her Heart: Jesus' Death and Ressurection. This loss is one that we should never forget, lest we lose Him forever.

Fatima Reflection

Our Lady comes to a world that has largely lost Christ due to sin. Mary comes seeking Him among us, His members, to teach us how to find Him through prayer and repentance. Let us seek the Holy Face of Christ in the Eucharist - where He is really and truly present, and in each other - where He is veiled under human form, so that in loving God for Himself, and loving each other for His sake, we may experience the joy of finding Him in this life and in the next. Let us show Him to a lost and suffering world.

One Our Father, 10 Hail Marys, One Glory Be, Decade Prayer

Prayer

Grace of the mystery of the Finding of the Child Jesus in the Temple, come down into my soul and truly convert me.

The Baptism of Jesus

"Jesus Baptized"

+Mark 1:2-11,

Matthew 3:1-17 / Luke 3:15-22 / John 1:29-37

Prayer

We offer Thee, O Lord Jesus, this decade in honor of Thy Holy Baptism, and we ask of Thee, through this mystery and through the intercession of Thy Blessed Mother, a firm determination to fulfill our baptismal vows.

Scripture

"It came to pass, in those days, Jesus came from Nazareth of Galilee, and was baptized by John in the Jordan. And forthwith coming up out of the water, he saw the heavens opened, and the Spirit as a dove descending, and remaining on him. And there came a voice from heaven: 'Thou art my beloved Son; in thee I am well pleased.'"

Meditation

As the Lord Jesus submits to John's baptism of repentance and enters the waters of the Jordan River, He not only makes known His willingness to take on our sins as the Lamb of God, but He also sanctifies the waters of our own baptism. We enter into these hallowed waters, are cleansed of all sin and are drawn into the bosom of the Holy Trinity. May we have the faith to see the heaven that was torn open for us and for our salvation.

Fatima Reflection

Jesus comes to communicate His desire to form a binding Covenant of Love with the whole human race. It is already accomplished in the bond He has formed Heart to Heart with Mary – Our Two-in-One Paragon of Love and Love's response. As we have entered the waters of this Covenant at Baptism, let us now enter upon the way Jesus and Mary lived and pointed out to us in the relationship of these Two Hearts revealed in Our Lady's Message at Fatima.

One Our Father, 10 Hail Marys, One Glory Be, Decade Prayer

Prayer

Grace of the mystery of Our Lord's Baptism, come down into my soul and make me truly committed to keep my baptismal vows.

The Wedding Feast at Cana

"Jesus Manifests His Divinity"

+ John 2:1-11

Prayer

We offer Thee, O Lord Jesus, this decade in honor of the Wedding Feast at Cana where Thou didst perform Thy first miracle at the request of Thy Blessed Mother, and we ask of Thee, through this mystery and through Her intercession, the grace of fidelity and generosity in Thy service.

Scripture

"... there was a marriage in Cana of Galilee: and the mother of Jesus was there. And Jesus also was invited, and his disciples...And the wine failing, the mother of Jesus saith to him: 'They have no wine.' ... His mother saith to the waiters: 'Whatsoever he shall say to you, do ye.'"

Meditation

In order to make known to His disciples the New Covenant that will transform the old, Jesus, at the prompting of His Mother, changed water into choice wine. He performs the miracle that anticipates the transformation of wine into Blood in the Passover cup. May we find, in the faith-filled petitions of the Mother of God, a source of new faith; and may we be faithful to the sacramental grace that flows from the open side of the Lamb who was slain.

Fatima Reflection

At the Last Vision, the Eucharistic Cup receives the Blood that flows from Jesus' Face and Side, with Our Lady at His side as though to beckon us to participation: *"Make of everything you can a sacrifice, and offer it to God as an act of reparation for the sins by which He is offended, and in supplication for the conversion of sinners"... "and say many times... 'O Jesus, it is for love of You, for the conversion of sinners, and in reparation for the sins committed against the Immaculate Heart of Mary.'"* Thou has saved the best wine until now!

One Our Father, 10 Hail Marys, One Glory Be, Decade Prayer

Prayer

Grace of the mystery of Our Lord's first miracle, come down into my soul and make me faithful and generous.

The Proclamation of the Kingdom of God & the Call to Repentance

"Jesus Proclaims the Kingdom"

+Mark 1:14-15

Matthew 13:24-34 / Matthew 13:36-43 / Matthew 13:44-52

Prayer

We offer Thee, O Lord Jesus, this decade in honor of the Proclamation of Thy Kingdom and the Call to Repentance, and we ask of Thee, through this mystery and through the intercession of Thy Blessed Mother, an awareness of God's Kingdom within us and to be truly repentant.

Scripture

"And after that John was delivered up, Jesus came into Galilee, preaching the gospel of the kingdom of God, and saying: 'The time is accomplished, and the kingdom of God is at hand: repent, and believe the gospel.' "

Meditation

Jesus spent three years proclaiming the Good News of the Kingdom. All were blessed to witness the tender, yet fierce love of Israel's God. In the Gospels we find not only the immensity of God's saving wisdom in Jesus' public ministry, but also the bewildering array of responses offered by fallen humanity; and in that story we find our own. May we never tire of drinking from the well of Jesus' teachings and reverencing the Gospels as the daily bread that alone can satisfy our soul's hunger for holiness.

Fatima Reflection

"What do you want of me?" Lucia's question at each apparition reveals an eagerness of heart that can be ours in seeking the Will of God. Our Lord instructs, *"Suffer the little children to come unto Me, for of such is the kingdom of Heaven."* Our Lady comes with a Message for childlike souls who wish to learn of the Kingdom of God. *"Are you willing to offer yourselves to God to bear all the sufferings He wills to send you...?"* The faithful fulfillment of duties God seeks and requires.

One Our Father, 10 Hail Marys, One Glory Be, Decade Prayer

Prayer

Grace of the mystery of the Proclamation of God's Kingdom and Call to Repentance, make me hunger and thirst for a deeper union with Christ present in my soul.

The Transfiguration

"Jesus Transfigured"

+Mark 9:1-8

Luke 9:28-36 / Matthew 17:1-9

Prayer

We offer Thee, O Lord Jesus, this decade in honor of Thy Transfiguration, and we ask of Thee, through this mystery and through the intercession of Thy Blessed Mother, spiritual courage.

Scripture

"... Jesus taketh with him Peter and James and John, and leadeth them up into a high mountain apart by themselves, and was transfigured before them... And there was a cloud overshadowing them: and a voice came out of the cloud, saying: 'This is my most beloved son; hear ye him.'"

Meditation

In this mystery of light, the Lord ascends Mount Tabor to manifest His glory to His inner circle of disciples. They witness Moses and Elijah conversing with the glorified Jesus of His upcoming Passion and discover the unity of the Old Testament's witness to Jesus' destiny, as well as the hope that awaits them on the far side of Golgotha. May we also find faith in the mysterious providence of God that penetrates life's darkest corners. *Per Crucem ad Lucem: "Through the Cross to the Light."*

Fatima Reflection

Our Lady, transfigured in Her heavenly state, opened Her hands and bathed the children in light which penetrated their souls, making them see themselves in God. They were caught up in the ecstasy of what participation in the life of God means: *"O most Holy Trinity, I adore You! My God, my God, I love You in the most Blessed Sacrament!"* This memory was to carry them through their trials, just as the Blessed Sacrament will be our strength during ours.

One Our Father, 10 Hail Marys, One Glory Be, Decade Prayer

Prayer

Grace of the mystery of the Transfiguration, come down into my soul and strengthen it in fortitude.

The Institution of the Holy Eucharist

"Jesus Gives Himself as Food"

+Luke 22:14-20

Mark 14:22-26 / Matthew 26:26-30

Prayer

We offer Thee, O Lord Jesus, this decade in honor of the Holy Eucharist, wherein Thou didst sacrificially give Thine own Body and Blood to be our Food, made possible through Mary's gift of self, and we ask of Thee, through this mystery and through the intercession of Thy most Holy Mother, a deep and intimate love for Thee in the Most Blessed Sacrament of the Altar.

Scripture

"And he said to them: ' With desire I have desired to eat this pasch with you before I suffer. For I say to you, that from this time I will not eat it, till it be fulfilled in the kingdom of God.'"

Meditation

In the institution of the Eucharist, the Lord Jesus left us a token of a love beyond all human comprehension. So great was His desire to grant us a total sharing in His Divine Life that He shattered the substance of bread and wine and filled them with Himself. It was the gift of His paschal sacrifice that He left mystically hidden in the Eucharist, that we who receive should become what we eat and drink: living sacrifices of love broken and offered for the life of the world. May the Lord, who offered this precious Gift, preserve us in faith, hope, and love, that we may never be parted from Him now or in the world to come.

Fatima Reflection

The Fatima Message is Christ-centered in the Heart of Mary. Our Lady leads us to be Eucharistic-centered by uniting our heart with Hers. Reparation is an expression of love which consoles the pain of the Beloved. *"Take and drink the Body and Blood of Jesus Christ, horribly outraged by ungrateful men! Make reparation for their crimes and console your God."* Offer it *"in reparation for the outrages, sacrileges, and indifference with which he is offended."* In showing mercy, we are shown mercy.

One Our Father, 10 Hail Marys, One Glory Be, Decade Prayer

Prayer

Grace of the mystery of the Institution of the Holy Eucharist, come down into my soul and inflame me with the fire of love for Christ truly present in the Most Blessed Sacrament.

The Agony in the Garden

"Jesus in His Agony"

+Luke 22:39-46

Matthew 26:36-46 / Mark 14:32-42

Prayer

We offer Thee, O Lord Jesus, this decade in honor of Thy Mortal Agony in the Garden of Olives, and we ask of Thee, through this mystery and through the intercession of Thy Blessed Mother, perfect sorrow for our sins and the virtue of perfect obedience to Thy Holy Will.

Scripture

"... kneeling down, he prayed, saying, 'Father, if thou wilt, remove this chalice from me: but yet not my will, but thine be done.' And there appeared to him an angel from heaven, strengthening him. And being in an agony, he prayed the longer. And his sweat became as drops of blood, trickling down upon the ground."

Meditation

Jesus' participation in the anxieties of His agony lead us to consider how to act when it seems all our strength, supports, and even our friends, have left us in our time of need. It is in that moment we must face the knowledge of our Heavenly Father's Will, and our inner pain of natural resistance, to accept what we have no power to change. *"And being in an agony, He prayed the longer."*

Fatima Reflection

The children were trained in the exercise of prayer, as directed by the angel, to make sacrifices that were necessary to save souls, and as a means to overcome their own natural feelings of recoiling from difficulty. Falling prostrate, they would pray for hours offering to the Lord all that mortified them, repeating the prayer the angel taught them. Jesus said, *"The spirit is willing but the flesh is weak,"* yet, like Jesus, these children exercised their will in prayer to overcome temptation and weakness.

One Our Father, 10 Hail Marys, One Glory Be, Decade Prayer

Prayer

Grace of the mystery of Our Lord's Agony, come down into my soul and make me truly contrite and perfectly obedient to Thy Will.

The Scourging at the Pillar

"Jesus Scourged"

+Luke 23:13-25

Matthew 27:11-26 / Mark 15:1-15 / John 18:37-40; 19:1

Prayer

We offer Thee, O Lord Jesus, this decade in honor of Thy Bloody Scourging, and we ask of Thee, through this mystery and through the intercession of Thy Blessed Mother, the grace to mortify our senses perfectly.

Scripture

"[Pilate] said to them: 'You have presented unto me this man, as one that perverteth the people; and behold I, having examined him before you, find no cause...in those things wherein you accuse him... I will chastise him therefore, and release him' ...but Jesus he delivered up to their will."

Meditation

Vehemently accused by the chief priests, Jesus did not return accusations or justify Himself before Pilate. And in a man-made hour of mercy, a man of death is chosen to be freed of his prison, while Christ our Life is delivered to death - He Who so desires to free us from the prison we create by what we choose to do of our own free will. How forcefully do we impose our will in our dealings with others? How easily do we back down before the insistent force of those who have no respect for the least among us?

Fatima Reflection

The shepherd children, from very early on, had to overcome human respect and the scourging of words: the incessant attention, the false accusations, even threats of death. They held fast to their appointed task, and to the truth, for in Mary they heard His voice. We must all have the determination of martyrs, in the facc of every obstacle, to hold firm to the fullness of our Catholic Faith to the end.

One Our Father, 10 Hail Marys, One Glory Be, Decade Prayer

Prayer

Grace of Our Lord's Scourging, come down into my soul and make me truly mortified.

The Crowning with Thorns

"Jesus Crowned with Thorns"

+ John 19:2-16

Matthew 27:27-31 / Mark 15:16-20

Prayer

We offer Thee, O Lord Jesus, this decade in honor of Thy Cruel Crowning with Thorns, and we ask of Thee, through this mystery and through the intercession of Thy Blessed Mother, a great contempt of the world.

Scripture

"And the soldiers platting a crown of thorns, put it upon his head; and they put on him a purple garment. And they came to him, and said: 'Hail, king of the Jews'; and they gave him blows... [Pilate] saith to them: 'Behold the Man... Shall I crucify your king?' The chief priests answered: 'We have no king but Caesar.' Then therefore he [Pilate] delivered him to them to be crucified."

Meditation

Christ is ridiculed as a mock king. They hailed Him as "the Son of David Who comes in the Name of the Lord" upon His entry into the Holy City; yet shortly thereafter, they said, "We have no king but Caesar!" The only earthly crown Jesus accepts is the crown of thorns. What could possibly be a reason for such a radical rejection of Jesus and of His Kingdom? The terms of accepting Christ's Kingship exclude determining for ourselves the law by which we are to live.

Fatima Reflection

In the humble ways of a child, which Jesus bids us to live, the Fatima children submit to the demands of their parents, Church leaders and government officials. Yet in all of its agonizing circumstances, the children kept their priorities straight. There is no power except that which is given from above. Jesus does not use His Power to assert His personal rights; and the Fatima children surrender themselves to God's Power, Who prevails in the end.

One Our Father, 10 Hail Marys, One Glory Be, Decade Prayer

Prayer

Grace of the mystery of Our Lord's Crowning with Thorns, come down into my soul and make me despise the world.

Jesus Carries the Cross

"Jesus Carrying His Cross"

+Luke 23:26-32

Matthew 27:32-33 / Mark 15:21-22

Prayer

We offer Thee, O Lord Jesus, this decade in honor of Thy Carrying Thy Cross and we ask of Thee, through this mystery and through the intercession of Thy Blessed Mother, to give us great patience in carrying our cross in Thy footsteps every day of our life.

Scripture

"And as they led him away...they laid the cross on [Simon of Cyrene] to carry after Jesus...Women...bewailed and lamented him... 'Weep not over me; but weep for yourselves, and for your children. For behold, the days shall come, wherein they will say: Blessed are the barren...Then shall they begin to say to the mountains: Fall upon us; ...Cover us. For if in the green wood they do these things, what shall be done in the dry?'"

Meditation

Jesus, as if to bear up the lives of each of us as a family upon His shoulders, takes up His Cross. Without Jesus looking to seek relief, they laid hold of Simon; though not for the sake of charity. Women lament Him, but Jesus directs their grief to the source of His affliction – the rejection by those who had experienced His love. (Luke 23:29-31, Is. 2:19, Rev. 6:16-17)

Fatima Reflection

"Penance! Penance! Penance!" was the cry of the avenging angel of the Third Secret whose fiery sword was prevented by Our Lady from striking the earth. *"Pray, pray very much, and make sacrifices for sinners,"* Our Lady pleads, *"for many souls go to hell because there are none to sacrifice themselves and to pray for them."* In imitation of the loving Hearts of Jesus and Mary, let us direct all things to glorify God, and to save souls, to keep the waters of grace flowing.

One Our Father, 10 Hail Marys, One Glory Be, Decade Prayer

Prayer

Grace of the mystery of the Carrying of the Cross, come down into my soul and make me truly patient.

The Crucifixion

"Jesus Crucified"

+John 19:17-30

Matthew 27:33-50 / Mark 15:22-37 / Luke 19:17-30 / Luke 23:33-47

Prayer

We offer Thee, O Lord Jesus, this decade in honor of Thy Crucifixion on Mt. Calvary, and we ask of Thee, through this mystery and through the intercession of Thy Blessed Mother, a great horror of sin, a love of the Cross, and the grace of a holy death for us and for those who are now in their last agony.

Scripture

"...he went forth to that place which is called Calvary...where they crucified him...Now there stood by the cross of Jesus, his mother,...and the disciple standing whom he loved... 'Woman, behold thy son'...to the disciple: 'Behold thy mother.' ...when he had taken the vinegar... bowing his head, he gave up the ghost."

Meditation

Jesus experienced utter desolation, refusing to deliver Himself from death. Who overcomes when even faith is at the brink of being lost? The answer is found where the heart is formed: *"Woman, behold thy son."* After that He said to the disciple: *"Behold thy Mother."*

Fatima Reflection

What could motivate children to want to give up their lunch, or refuse to drink water in the heat of summer, or choose to wear stiff bristled ropes day and night, or to suffer still more when a choice is given to go on suffering or receive now the promise of heaven? Today, children and adults alike, are unwilling to give up anything that pleases themselves. It is only through devotion to Mary that we can take refuge in Her Immaculate Heart and find therein the way that leads us to God.

One Our Father, 10 Hail Marys, One Glory Be, Decade Prayer

Prayer

Grace of the mystery of the Death and Passion of Our Lord and Savior Jesus Christ, come down into my soul and make me truly holy.

The Resurrection

"Jesus Risen from the Dead"

+Luke 24:36-48

Matthew 28:1-15 / Mark 16:1-14 / Luke 24:1-12 / Luke 24:13-35/ John 20:1-10 / John 20:11-18 / John 20:19-29 / John 21:1-14

Prayer

We offer Thee, O Lord Jesus, this decade in honor of Thy Triumphant Resurrection, and we ask of Thee, through this mystery and through the intercession of Thy Blessed Mother, a lively faith.

Scripture

"And he said to them: 'Thus it is written, and thus it behooved Christ to suffer, and to rise again from the dead, the third day: and that penance and remission of sins should be preached in his name, unto all nations...you are witnesses of these things.'"

Meditation

Jesus, having conquered death with life, and sin with love, appears to the women and His followers, at various times and in various ways, to deliver a pro-life message that goes beyond what this finite existence is able to contain. Christ's power is over life and death in this world and in the next! LOVE is more powerful than death; LIFE reaches beyond the grave for those who believe. Suffering has saving power! Penance, and remission of sins in Christ, saves souls.

Fatima Reflection

The day of the miracle had arrived. Not since the resurrection was a miracle of this magnitude ever foretold. Undaunted by the fears of those who said it might not take place, Lucia believed; and her faith was not disappointed. Our Lady keeps Her promises. The sun displayed its power, pilgrims cried out for mercy, some confessed their sins, conversions took place. Let us enter into partnership with Mary and faithfully keep our commitments for true peace. God cannot be outdone in generosity.

One Our Father, 10 Hail Marys, One Glory Be, Decade Prayer

Prayer

Grace of the mystery of the Resurrection, come down into my soul and make me truly faithful.

The Ascension

"Jesus Ascending to Heaven"

+Acts 1:4-12

Matthew 28:18-20 / Mark 16:15-20 / Luke 24:46-53

Prayer

We offer Thee, O Lord Jesus, this decade in honor of Thy Glorious Ascension, and we ask of Thee, through this mystery and through the intercession of Thy Blessed Mother, a firm hope and a great longing for Heaven.

Scripture

"...you shall be witnesses unto me in Jerusalem, and in all Judea, and Samaria, and even to the uttermost part of the earth. And when he had said these things...he was raised up: and a cloud received him out of their sight."

Meditation

All that Jesus said and did, His Life He gave, His Spirit He imparted, was entrusted to His apostles, that they might preach to all nations, giving what they had received. As members of His Body, we, too, have a part in this commission to live out in our own lives what we have received from Christ in body and in spirit. His ascension into heaven is the incense of our presence in Christ before the Father, Who presents all our love and needs to Him, until God's Plan is fulfilled in making Jesus and Mary known and loved.

Fatima Reflection

Our Lady drew all three children to live a way of life that brought them to the heights of holiness in a very short period of time. Jacinta and Francisco were taken to heaven soon. But Lucia was to stay here some time longer. Do we recognize in this invitation the same call for us to spread the Gospel in our own day? *"Jesus wishes to make use of you to make Me known and loved. He wants to establish in the world devotion to My Immaculate Heart."* How will I respond?

One Our Father, 10 Hail Marys, One Glory Be, Decade Prayer

Prayer

Grace of the mystery of the Ascension of Our Lord, come down into my soul and make me ready for Heaven.

The Descent of the Holy Spirit

"Jesus Filling Thee with the Holy Spirit"

+Acts 2:1-18, 34-41

Prayer

We offer Thee, O Holy Spirit, this decade in honor of Pentecost, and we ask of Thee, through this mystery and through the intercession of Mary, Thy most faithful Spouse, Thy Holy Wisdom so that we may know, really love and practice Thy truth, and make all others share in it.

Scripture

"And they were all filled with the Holy Ghost, and they began to speak with diverse tongues...Now when [the multitude] had heard these things, they had compunction in their heart... But Peter said to them: Do penance, and be baptized...in the name of Jesus Christ, for the remission of your sins: and you shall receive the gift of the Holy Ghost."

Meditation

Compunction of the heart, penance, remission of sins: These are the work of the Holy Spirit, Who helps us choose to live without sin, like Mary *"... and they that work by me, shall not sin."* (Eccli. 24:30) As we come to realize our spiritual birth as members of the Church, let us live a new life for God as children of the Hearts of Jesus and Mary.

Fatima Reflection

"Offer prayers and sacrifices constantly to the Most High." Mary, Spouse of the Holy Spirit, can make supple our heart to receive all the inspirations God wishes to send us. When we deny ourselves, we can be moved by inspiration. Jesus can use us to bring light to a world in darkness which is moved only by its lusts and self interests. Let sacrificial love be the moving force of your life as the Fatima children allowed themselves to be moved, no longer acting according to their feelings and personal desires.

One Our Father, 10 Hail Marys, One Glory Be, Decade Prayer

Prayer

Grace of the mystery of Pentecost, come down into my soul and make me truly wise in the eyes of the Almighty God.

Our Lady's Assumption

"Jesus Raising Thee up Body and Soul into Heaven"

+ Ecclesiasticus 24:22-32

Ecclesiasticus 24:1-11 / Ecclesiasticus 24:12-19

Prayer

We offer Thee, O Lord Jesus, this decade in honor of the the Immaculate Conception and the Assumption of Thy Holy and Blessed Mother, Body and Soul into Heaven, and we ask of Thee, through these two mysteries and through Her intercession, the gift of true devotion to Her to help us live and die in holiness.

Scripture

"I am the mother of fair love, and of fear, and of knowledge, and of holy hope. In me is all grace of the way and of the truth, in me is all hope of life and of virtue. Come over to me, all ye that desire me, and be filled with my fruits...He that hearkeneth to me, shall not be confounded...They that explain me shall have life everlasting."

Meditation

"Then the Creator of all things commanded, and said to me: and He that made me, rested in my tabernacle" (Eccli. 24:12). All that can be said of Mary can be expressed in saying that She is all that any of us want to be in loving Jesus with the fullness of that love, which He deserves. She is the perfection of all the love He desires from us. We can offer our hearts to Him, united to Hers, offering a total love, which makes up for our deficiencies. Our Lady's assumption into heaven is `the incense of our presence in Mary's Immaculate Heart before Christ, who presents all of our love and needs to Him, to help us be disposed to fulfill God's Plan.

Fatima Reflection

Our Lady made known Her desire to have the Rosary recited every day. At the last apparition She held out the Brown Scapular because She wants us to wear it. Our Lady was not communicating a mere symbolic presence. She has given us a means to enter into a mystical union with Her, a union which is caught up in the mystery of Mary's bodily assumption. What does this suggest to you in your offering of prayers at Holy Communion?

One Our Father, 10 Hail Marys, One Glory Be, Decade Prayer

Prayer

Grace of the mysteries of the Immaculate Conception and the Assumption of Mary, come down into my soul and make me truly devoted to Her.

The Coronation of Our Lady as Queen of Heaven and Earth

"Jesus Crowning Thee"

+Psalm 44:10-18

Revelation 12:1-8,13-17

Prayer

We offer Thee, O Lord Jesus, this decade in honor of the Glorious Crowning of Thy Blessed Mother in Heaven, and we ask of Thee, through this mystery and through Her intercession, the grace of perseverance and increase of virtue until the very moment of death and after that the eternal crown that is prepared for us. We ask the same grace for all the just and for all our benefactors.

Scripture

"On your right stands the queen in gold of Ophir... So will the king desire your beauty: he is your lord, pay homage to him... The daughter of the king is clothed with splendor, her robes embroidered with pearls set in gold. She is led to the king with her maiden companions... May the peoples praise you from age to age." [Office of Readings]

Meditation

As the world, lost through Adam, was restored through Christ, so also man sinned by the influence of a woman, and by a Woman, the old influence was replaced. Ave reverses Eva, and Live reverses Evil. By means of Mary, Christ crushes the head of Satan; and in the original translation of Gen. 3:15 (*"She shall crush thy head"*), we see Mary's role in playing Her part in God's Plan of salvation. As members of His Body, Jesus gathers us together in Himself, with Mary as Type and Model. In Her let us allow Christ to use us, too, in fulfilling our part in accomplishing His ultimate victory.

Fatima Reflection

"Continue to pray the Rosary everyday in honor of Our Lady of the Rosary, in order to obtain peace for the world and the end of the war, because only She can help you." Our Lady's role as Mother and Queen is intrinsic in our relationship with God, if we are to live according to God's pleasure. Not according to our ways does God see things, but according to His own. Therefore, let us fulfill the desire of Our Lord's Most Sacred Heart: to console Him by relieving the wounds directed against our Mother and Queen by means of the reparation of the Five First Saturdays for the conversion of sinners and for peace.

Prayer

Grace of the mystery of the Coronation of the Blessed Mother in Heaven, convert sinners, help the dying, deliver the Holy Souls from purgatory and give us all Thy grace so that we may live and die well - and please give us the Light of Thy glory later on so that we may see Thee Face to face and love Thee for all eternity. Amen. So be it.

HAIL HOLY QUEEN:

Hail, Holy Queen, Mother of Mercy, our life, our sweetness and our hope. To Thee do we cry, poor banished children of Eve. To Thee do we send up our sighs, mourning and weeping in this valley of tears.

Turn then, most gracious Advocate, Thine eyes of mercy towards us; and after this, our exile, show unto us the Blessed Fruit of Thy womb, Jesus. O clement, O loving, O sweet Virgin Mary!

V. Pray for us, O most holy Mother of God.

R. That we may be made worthy of the promises of Christ.

LET US PRAY:

Oh God, Whose only begotten Son, by his life, death and resurrection, has purchased for us the rewards of eternal life; grant we beseech Thee, that meditating on these Mysteries of the most Holy Rosary of the Blessed Virgin Mary, we may imitate what they contain, and obtain what they promise, through the same Christ, Our Lord. Amen.

ST. MICHAEL PRAYER

St. Michael, the Archangel, defend us in battle. Be our protection against the wickedness and the snares of the devil. May God rebuke him, we humbly pray, and do thou, O Prince of the heavenly hosts, by the power of God, cast into hell Satan and all the evil spirits, who prowl about the world seeking the ruin of souls. *Amen.*

PRAYER FOR THE HOLY FATHER AND HIS INTENTIONS:

May be used in place of one Our Father, Hail Mary, and Glory Be.

O Lord, Source of Eternal Life and Truth, give to Your Shepherd, *[Current Pope's Name]*, a spirit of courage and right judgment, a spirit of knowledge and love. By governing with fidelity those entrusted to his care, may he as successor of the Apostle Peter and Vicar of Christ, build Your Church into a sacrament of unity, love and peace for all the world. We ask this through Our Lord Jesus Christ, Your Son, Who lives and reigns with You and the Holy Spirit, one God forever and ever. *Amen.*

MARY, MOTHER FOR LIFE:

O Mary, Mother of the Life Within, all life we entrust to You: the life of every expectant mother and the child within her womb, the life of every human body, the life of every human soul, the life of every newborn child and the life of all grown old. You held the Lord to Your own Heart and drew Him so close in. So draw us now in all our needs, O Mother of the Life Within.

INVOCATION OF FATIMA PATRONS:

Most Sacred Heart of Jesus, **Have Mercy on us!**

Sorrowful and Immaculate Heart of Mary, **Pray for us!**

Our Lady of the Rosary, **Pray for us!**

Our Lady of Fatima, **Pray for us!**

St. Joseph, **Pray for us!**

St. Pio of Pietrelcina, **Pray for us!**

St. Louis de Montfort, **Pray for us!**

St. Maximilian Kolbe, **Pray for us!**

St. Dominic and St. Simon Stock, **Pray for us!**

St. Therese of the Child Jesus, **Pray for us!**

St. Anthony Mary Claret, **Pray for us!**

Blessed Jacinta and Blessed Francisco, **Pray for us!**

[Saint of the Day], **Pray for us!**

All you holy angels and saints, **Pray for us!**

V. May the Divine Assistance remain with us always.

R. And may the souls of the faithful departed, through the mercy of God, rest in peace. ***Amen.***

Please Stand

***FATIMA AVE*:**

Refrain: *Ave, Ave, Ave Maria.*
Ave, Ave, Ave Maria.

Our thanks to the Godhead
Whose ways are so sure
For giving us Mary
Our Mother most pure.
Refrain

Prayer Cell Formation Program

FORMATION PROGRAM:

Available for purchase separately.

The Formation Program is a step-by-step study guide that includes a 4 level growth process. All 4 levels include:

- Spiritual Reading
- Reflection and Resolution
- Silent Reflection
- Discussion
- Examination by Cell Members
- Apostolic Resolution
- Act of Consecration

Step I forms one in the spirituality of the Message of Fatima through a more in depth look into the words of Lucia Speaks. Once this first level completes its first year, it splits to form a new Prayer Cell moving to Step II using the same process. All levels are on-going to allow for new members to join at any time, attend lessons they missed, or repeat a level before moving on to the next step.

+ Come, Holy Spirit, fill the hearts of Thy faithful and enkindle in them the fire of Thy love.

V. Send forth Thy Spirit and they shall be created.

R. And Thou shalt renew the face of the earth.

LET US PRAY. O God, Who didst instruct the hearts of the faithful by the light of the Holy Spirit, grant us, in the same Spirit, to be truly wise and ever to rejoice in His consolation, through Christ Our Lord. *Amen.*

SPIRITUAL READING:
Read from one of the spiritual books listed below or listen to a talk given by the Spiritual Director or Cell Leader.

- **Prayer Cell Formation Program** -
  Step I: LUCIA SPEAKS
  The Message of Fatima,
  one apparition per month
  Step II: THE TEN COMMANDMENTS
  Section Two of Part Three in the
  Catechism of the Catholic Church
  Step III: "CALLS" FROM THE
  MESSAGE OF FATIMA
  By Sister Lucia dos Santos
  Step IV: ANY APPROVED FATIMA MATERIAL
  Choose from the following,
  or other approved resources:

- *Fatima in Lucia's Own Words*

- *There is Nothing More*

- Articles from *SOUL Magazine*
- The Holy Bible passages
- *True Devotion to Mary, Secret of the Rosary,* or other books by St. Louis de Montfort
- *Aim Higher* by St. Maximilian Kolbe
- *Imitation of Christ* by Thomas a'Kempis
- Encyclicals and writings by the Pope
- Books on Marian Spirituality
- Books by or about Fatima Patrons
- Any World Apostolate of Fatima publication

REFLECTION AND RESOLUTION:

Silently reflect on the readings or talk and after some discussion, determine resolution privately, as a group, or as presented in the lesson.

EXAMINATION BY CELL MEMBERS:

Ask questions like: "How well did we keep our personal and apostolic resolutions?" or "What have we done to further the Message of Fatima?"

ACT OF CONSECRATION:

IMMACULATE HEART OF MARY, Queen of heaven and earth and tender Mother of men, in accordance with Thy ardent wish made known at Fatima, I consecrate to Thee myself, my brethren, my country and the whole human race. Reign over us and teach us how to make the Heart of Jesus reign and triumph in us and around us as It has reigned and triumphed in Thee.

Reign over us, dearest Mother, that we may be Thine in prosperity and in adversity, in joy and in sorrow, in health and in sickness, in life and in death. O most compassionate Heart of Mary, Queen of Virgins, watch over our minds and hearts and preserve them from the deluge of impurity which Thou didst lament so sorrowfully at Fatima. We want to be pure like Thee. We want to atone for the many sins committed against Jesus and Thee. We want to call down upon our country and the whole world the peace of God in justice and charity.

Therefore, we now promise to imitate Thy virtues by the practice of a Christian life without regard to human respect. We resolve to receive Holy Communion on the first Saturday of every month and to offer Thee five decades of the Rosary each day together with our sacrifices in a spirit of reparation and penance. *Amen.*

World Apostolate of Fatima
Prayer Cell Program

World Apostolate of Fatima, USA

674 Mountain View Rd East
PO Box 976
Washington, NJ 07882

908-689-1700 ext:18
www.wafusa.org

48324
406

ISBN 1-56036-083-6

FIRST SATURDAY DEVOTION

Treasure of Fatima

Father Andrew Apostoli, C.F.R.

Treasure of Fatima

Father Andrew Apostoli, C.F. R.

World Apostolate of Fatima, USA
Blue Army, USA
Washington, New Jersey
www.bluearmy.com (866) 513-1917

In accord with Canon 827 of the New Code of Canon Law, this publication has been submitted to a censor of the Diocese and nothing being found contrary to faith and morals, we hereby grant permission in accord with Canon 824 that it be published.

Rev. Msgr. John B. Szymanski
Vicar General
Diocese of Metuchen

N.B. The ecclesiastical permission implies nothing more than that the material contained in the publication has been examined by diocesan censors and nothing contrary to faith and morals has been found therein.

First Printing, 2006

Photos from
©World Apostolate of Fatima, USA/Blue Army,USA

Scripture references from
The New American Bible ©Catholic Book Publishing Co.
unless otherwise noted

Printed in the United States of America
ISBN 0-9776504-0-5

AUTHOR'S PREFACE

Many people today have little or no understanding of the importance of the message given to the world by Our Blessed Lady at Fatima, Portugal, in 1917. She appeared on the 13th of every month from May to October of that year to three little shepherd children: Lucia Dos Santos, Francisco Marto and his sister Jacinta. Our Lady came with a message that was extremely important for the future of the world and its hope for peace. The Catholic Church recognizes that God the Father sent the Blessed Mother to these three shepherd children, and has accepted both the apparitions and the message given.

Today it is essential for the peace of the world that we respond to Our Lady's requests as fully as we can. Our Lady had warned that World War II would happen and Russia would spread the errors of Communism throughout the world if we did not heed her message. Since these evils did occur, we can only conclude that people did not respond as they should to the pleas of our Heavenly Mother. She said that she would come again at a later time to ask for the consecration of Russia to her Immaculate Heart and the Five First Saturdays Devotion.

On March 25, 1984 Pope John Paul II, in spiritual union with the bishops of the world, consecrated the world and Russia to the Immaculate Heart of Mary. Sister Lucia Dos Santos, the only remaining Fatima visionary, declared that Heaven accepted this consecration. What remains for us, now more than ever, is to carry out Our Lady's request for the special First Saturday Devotion.

We live in a time of great crisis in the world and even struggle within the Church. This present booklet is being offered as a means to help all our Catholic people respond with a better understanding and deeper love to what Our Lady has requested. Our Lady, herself, assures us that this devotion plays a significant part in her promise of the ultimate triumph of her Immaculate Heart. Please respond to Our Lady's request.

Fr. Andrew Apostoli, C.F.R.
August 11, 2005
Feast of Saint Clare of Assisi

CHAPTER 1

A Treasure From Fatima: The Five First Saturdays Devotion

One of the most important aspects of Our Lady of Fatima's message was her request for the devotion we call the "Five First Saturdays." I remember as a young boy how many people practiced this devotion in honor of Our Lady on the First Saturdays of five consecutive months. It seemed to be the natural complement to the Nine First Fridays' devotion in honor of the Sacred Heart of Jesus. Our Lord Himself had requested the First Friday devotion at the time of His apparitions to St. Margaret Mary Alacoque in the Visitation Monastery in Paray-le-Monial in France, during which He revealed the overwhelming love of His Sacred Heart for all of us. It was to be a devotion of prayer and reparation for those who offend His infinite love either by hatred, neglect or indifference.

The First Saturday devotion is also meant to be a devotion of prayer and reparation, specifically for those who offend against the Immaculate Heart of Our Lady. When I practiced this devotion as a young boy (and I still practice it today), I did not realize its beauty and depth. It was only years later that I learned that each of the Five First Saturdays was to be offered in reparation for very specific offenses against the Immaculate Heart of Our Lady. I wonder today how many Catholics even know of the devotion of the Five First Saturdays because it does not seem to be widely encouraged. Furthermore, I wonder how many of the people who do practice this devotion actually realize the historical background of this devotion. In subsequent chapters, I will offer reflections on the meaning of the reparation called for on each of the Five First Saturdays.

Our Lady Reveals Her Intention at Fatima

When Our Blessed Mother appeared to Lucia, Francisco and Jacinta on July 13, 1917, she confided the main part of her message to the children. They saw a most frightening vision of Hell, where there were both demons and lost souls in terrifying torment and despair. The young visionaries were completely shaken by the vision. Then Our Lady spoke kindly but sadly to them: "You have seen Hell where the souls of poor sinners go. To save them, God wishes to establish in the world devotion to my Immaculate Heart. If what I say to you is done, many souls will be saved and there will be peace." (Lucia's 4th Memoir)

Our Lady's message was focused on the salvation of souls, and specifically on her Immaculate Heart as God's chosen instrument to bring this about.

As Our Lady continued speaking, she revealed to the children that World War I, then raging, would come to an end. But she warned that a worse war, along with famine and persecution of the Church, especially of the Holy Father, would come about if people did not cease offending God. Then she added in her great maternal love for us: "To prevent this, I shall come to ask for the consecration of Russia to my Immaculate Heart, and the Communion of Reparation on the First Saturdays. If my requests are heeded, Russia will be converted, and there will be peace; if not, she will spread her errors throughout the world, causing wars and persecutions of the Church. The good will be martyred, the Holy Father will have much to suffer, various nations will be annihilated..." We have seen all of these unfortunate evils occur in the world in the 20th century!

Our Lady did add a message of hope when she said, "In the end, my Immaculate Heart will triumph. The Holy Father will consecrate Russia to me, and she will be converted, and a period of peace will be granted to the world." Ever since Pope John Paul II made the collegial consecration requested by Our Lady of Fatima on March 25, 1984, we have begun to see the conversion of Russia back to God, and "a period of peace" beginning to come upon the world. But more must yet be done, and this is where the devotion of the Five First Saturdays plays a vital role.

Our Lady Keeps Her Promise

Our Lady had said to the young visionaries, "I will come (again) to ask for...the Communion of Reparation on the First Saturdays..." Our Lady kept her promise on December 10, 1925. Francisco and Jacinta had already been taken to Heaven. Lucia, the remaining visionary of Fatima, was a postulant for the Dorothean Sisters at a convent in Pontevedra, Spain. Our Lady appeared to Lucia together with the Child Jesus. He spoke first to Lucia: "Have compassion on the Heart of your most holy mother, covered with thorns with which ungrateful men pierce it at every moment and there is no one who does an act of reparation to remove them." We know that all sin ultimately offends God, and so every act of reparation is ultimately directed to Him, to restore His earthly honor and glory that sin has offended and diminished. However, here Our Lord Himself extends the spirit of reparation, to restore the honor of the Immaculate Heart of His Blessed Mother, that sins directly against her have dishonored and diminished. How powerful are the words of His own request: "Have compassion on the Heart of your most holy mother!"

Then Our Lady, showing her Heart to Lucia, spoke, announcing her request: "Look, my daughter, at my Heart, surrounded with thorns with which ungrateful men pierce me at every moment by their blasphemies and ingratitude. You, at least; try to console me and say that I promise to assist at the hour of death, with the graces necessary for salvation, all those who on the first Saturday of five consecutive months shall confess, receive Holy Communion, recite five decades of the Rosary, and keep me company for fifteen minutes while meditating on the 15 mysteries of the Rosary, with the intention of making reparation to me."

What a magnificent promise of Our Lady: that she would assist us with the graces needed for salvation at the most important moment of our lives – the moment of our death! Do we not pray to her for this every time we pray the Hail Mary: "Holy Mary, Mother of God, pray for us sinners, now and at the hour of our death"?

Our Lady states what is required to obtain her promise by practicing the First Saturday devotion. We can summarize these requirements into six points: (1) go to Confession (usually within the week before or after the First Saturday), (2) receive Holy Communion on the First Saturday itself, (3) recite five decades of the Rosary, (4) meditate on one or more of the Mysteries of the Rosary for an additional 15 minutes, (5) do all of these things with the intention of making reparation to the Immaculate Heart of Mary and (6) do these things on the First Saturday of five consecutive months.

In carrying out the 15-minute meditation/ conversation with Our Lady, each person should feel free to follow his or her own individual way of meditating. Furthermore, an individual can focus on one or more of the Rosary mysteries. However, it has been suggested that meditating on one mystery each month is the simplist way to fulfill this part of Our Lady's request.

To complete our understanding of the devotion of reparation on the Five First Saturdays, it is important to know why there are five times of reparation, and what each reparation is for. Sr. Lucia provided this information for us in a letter dated June 12, 1930. In it she tells us that Our Lord appeared to her in the convent chapel on the night of May 29-30, 1930, and revealed to her the meaning of the five Saturdays. Sr. Lucia quotes Our Lord's words to her:

> "Daughter, the motive is simple: there are five ways in which people offend and blaspheme against the Immaculate Heart of Mary: there are blasphemies (1) against her Immaculate Conception, (2) against her Virginity, (3) against her Divine Maternity, refusing at the same time to accept her as the Mother of all mankind, (4) by those who try publicly to implant in the hearts of children indifference, contempt and even hate against this Immaculate Mother, and (5) by those who insult her directly in her sacred images."

It is obvious from all of the above how important this devotion really is. In the following chapters, I will reflect on each of the five reasons why Our Lord wants this reparation paid to the Immaculate Heart of His Blessed Mother and ours, too!

CHAPTER 2

The First Reparation of the Five First Saturdays: For Those Who Blaspheme Against the Immaculate Conception

"I am the Immaculate Conception!" That is the way the Blessed Virgin Mary identified herself at Lourdes to St. Bernadette when the saint had asked who she was. What a marvelous description, one that brings great joy to all who love Our Lady. She is, as a Protestant writer once put it, "our tainted human nature's solitary boast!"

The Immaculate Conception of the Blessed Virgin Mary is especially dear to devout Catholics. It expresses the belief of the Church that Our Lady, through a singular grace and privilege of Almighty God, and through the foreseen merits of Jesus Christ, the Savior of the human race, and in view of her becoming the Mother of God, was preserved free from Original Sin and given a fullness of grace from the first moment of her conception. This was defined as a revealed dogma of the Catholic Faith by Blessed Pope Pius IX in his decree, *Ineffabilis Deus* on December 8, 1854.

This privilege of Our Lady is one of the most cherished of Catholic beliefs. It is also one of the most important. It shows Jesus' complete power and victory over sin. Jesus came to save us from our sins. Did He not say, *"The Son of Man has come to search out and save what was lost"* (Luke 19:10)? He does this in various ways. In Baptism, He takes away the guilt of Original Sin (and of any personal sins that someone over the age of reason may have committed), while at the same time infusing into that soul a share in His own divine life that He merited for us by His redemptive death. In the Sacrament of Penance, Jesus takes away our personal sins committed after Baptism through the power to forgive sins, which He gave to His Apostles on Easter night (cf. *n* 20:22-23), and which has been passed down over the centuries to His bishops and priests.

Now in both these cases, sin has already affected the person, leaving traces of wounds and weaknesses in its wake, even after they have been forgiven! In the case of Our Lady, her privilege was so great that Original Sin (and consequently personal sin as well) never touched her soul. Our Lady would have incurred the guilt of Original Sin because St. Paul says that all men sinned in Adam (cf. Romans 5:12).

But in her case, her privilege was an extraordinary form of Redemption. Our Lady was redeemed by being preserved from Original Sin in view of the foreseen merits of Jesus, her Divine Son rather than being delivered from Original Sin after she had suffered from it. Let us use a comparison by way of example. It would be one thing for a doctor to use his medical skill to heal a patient after an accident. (In a sense, this is what Jesus did for all the baptized!) It would be quite another thing for the doctor to prevent the patient from having an accident in the first place. (This is like what Jesus did for His Mother!) At the same time, she was filled with such an extraordinary fullness of Sanctifying Grace that some saints believed it surpassed the combined holiness of all the angels and saints together!

WHY IS THE "IMMACULATE CONCEPTION" BLASPHEMED?

It Foreshadows Jesus' Complete Victory Over Sin

This blasphemy, no doubt, comes ultimately from Satan himself. The Devil inspires it for many reasons. First, he is angry at Jesus' power and victory which this dogma represents. He knows that at the end of time, any power God allows him to tempt us with will cease completely. He foresees this conquest of Christ over him and his legions, in Our Lady's complete victory of sinlessness all through her life from the first moment of her conception. He deeply resents Our Lady's immaculate holiness. It meant that he did not have, even for one instant, any power or influence over her. Our Lady was like a bright light shining through the darkness of Satan's control and deceit. Satan was helpless to block that light, to stop it, to prevent it from showing the evil he intended to inflict on all mankind. Therefore, he inspires anyone, whether they be among his conscious followers in the occult or simply people who are very weak morally, to express hate, ridicule and contempt against Our Lady's marvelous privilege.

It Reveals Our Lady as the "Woman" who crushes the Head of Satan

Another reason the devil hates the privilege of Our Lady's Immaculate Conception is because he sees the Virgin Mary in a special way under this title as the "Woman" who will crush his head! Immediately after Satan deceived our first parents into committing the Original Sin, God said to him, *"I will put enmity between you and the Woman, and between your offspring and hers; she will crush your head, while you strike at her heel!"* (Genesis 3:15, Vulgate translation) When God spoke of the "Woman," He was obviously not referring to Eve of old to crush Satan's head, since she had just personally sinned by pride (wanting to be as a god) and disobedience (eating the forbidden fruit) at his deception.

Who then is the "Woman?" The Church sees this as a reference to Mary, the Mother of Jesus and our Mother, too! Jesus Himself twice refers to His own Mother as "Woman." (When I was studying Sacred

Scripture in the seminary, they taught us that Jesus' reference to His own Mother as "Woman" was an absolutely unique usage among all ancient Hebrew and Greek literature.) The first usage occurs at the wedding feast of Cana (cf. John 2:1-11), when Jesus says to His Mother, *"Woman, how does this concern of yours involve me? My hour has not yet come."* Moved by the confident trust of His Mother, Jesus then works His first miracle by changing water into wine, thus also inspiring His disciples to believe in Him. The second usage occurs at the cross on Calvary (cf. John 19:25-27) when Jesus gives His Mother the care of all His followers represented by John, the "beloved disciple," saying to her, *"Woman, behold your son!"*

God's words to Satan in Genesis 3:15 are often cited as a "proof text" to support the fact that the dogma of the Immaculate Conception was revealed by God in Sacred Scripture. How is this so? The words we want to focus on are: *"I will put enmity between you* (meaning, the serpent, Satan) *and the Woman"* (meaning, Our Lady, the New Eve). The key word here is "enmity." Enmity means a very bitter hatred. Now, despite how strong our English word enmity is, it cannot convey the full force and intense meaning of the original Hebrew word. The Hebrew root of this word implied such a bitter mutual repulsion between the two, that not for even the briefest moment could they tolerate being in each other's presence. Therefore, Our Lady and Satan would not want to be near each other! So how could Satan have had an influence over the soul of Our Lady, even for

Lady, even for one moment? And without such influence or control, the Immaculate Conception represented the beginning of the destruction of Satan's universal influence over sinful mankind. It was, to use God's words, the beginning of the crushing of his head!

It Prepared Our Lady for Her Divine Maternity

The Immaculate Conception was a marvelous gift from Our Heavenly Father to the Virgin Mary in view of preparing her to become the Mother of His own Divine Son. This privilege separated Our Lady from any direct personal contact with sin. She was as a result sinless and grace-filled! At the moment the Incarnation occurred during the Annunciation, Jesus took His very Flesh and Blood from the absolutely pure body united to the immaculate soul of the Blessed Virgin Mary! This sinlessness is reflected in the Archangel Gabriel's salutation to Our Lady at the Annunciation: *"Hail, full of grace, the Lord is with you. Blessed are you among women!"* (Luke 1:28) In view of this wondrous event, Satan's fury no doubt knew no limits (cf. Revelation 12:12). This is an added reason why he has been relentless in stirring up blasphemy and contempt among his followers against this special privilege of Our Lady!

REPARATION FOR THESE BLASPEMIES IS IMPORTANT

Reparation in this instance is directed at restoring the honor due to Our Lady for God's great privilege to her in view of her becoming the Mother of God. Blasphemy has seriously offended God by dishonoring the extraordinary grace He gave her in her Immaculate Conception. Our reparation atones for this grave dishonor, while praising and venerating the Virgin Mary with appropriate devotion. Did not Our Lady herself, while carrying Jesus physically in her womb, say in her Magnificat: *"God who is mighty has done great things for me, and holy is His name"*? (Luke 1:49)

Besides offering the first of the Five Saturdays' devotion in reparation for the blasphemies against the Immaculate Conception, a person may also choose to wear the Miraculous Medal that was entrusted by Our Lady to St. Catherine Labouré. Since its design was revealed to the saint in a vision, we must truly say it was formed in heaven. It bore the significant prayer to Our Lady, "O Mary conceived without sin, pray for us who have recourse to Thee!" Besides wearing the Miraculous Medal, we should repeat that prayer often, thus making added reparation for blasphemies against the Immaculate Conception. Finally, we should encourage others to practice the Five Saturdays' devotion, and to honor the privilege of Our Lady's Immaculate Conception, thus making further reparation for the blasphemies she has endured. All of this will obtain the special powerful protection of Our Lady against sin and Satan's power in our lives.

CHAPTER 3
The Second Reparation of the Five First Saturdays

For Those Who Blaspheme Against the Perpetual Virginity of Mary

One of the most popular titles of Our Blessed Lady is to call her the "Virgin Mary!" This is very fitting because it is rooted in Sacred Scripture. When St. Luke described the Annunciation event, he twice referred to Our Lady as "virgin." *"In the sixth month, the angel Gabriel was sent from God to a town of Galilee named Nazareth, to a virgin betrothed to a man named Joseph, of the house of David. The virgin's name was Mary"* (Luke 1:26-27).

St. Matthew, in his Gospel account, also stresses Our Lady's virginity, emphasizing that the conception of Jesus occurred without Our Lady having marital relations with St. Joseph. *"Now this is how the birth of Jesus Christ came about. When His mother Mary was engaged to Joseph, but before they lived together, she was found with child through the power of the Holy Spirit. Joseph, her husband, an upright man, unwilling to expose her to the law, decided to divorce her quietly. Such was his intention when suddenly the angel of the Lord appeared in a dream and said to him: 'Joseph, son of David, have no fear about taking Mary as your wife. It is by the Holy Spirit that she has conceived this child. She is to have a son and you are to name Him Jesus because He will save His people from their sins.' All this happened to fulfill what the Lord had said through the prophet: 'The virgin shall be with child and give birth to a son, and they shall call him Emmanuel' (Isaiah 7:14), a name which means 'God is with us.' When Joseph awoke, he did as the angel of the Lord had directed him and received her into his home. He had no relations with her at any time before she bore a son, whom He named Jesus"* (Matthew 1:10-25).

Our Lady's Virginity was Perpetual

These two Gospel passages clearly state that Our Lady was truly a virgin at the moment she conceived Christ within her womb by the power of the Holy Spirit. In fact, Our Lady's virginity was to be perpetual. This is a dogma of the Catholic Church. St. Clement of Alexandria (d. 215 AD) was one of the earliest Fathers of the Church to express this fact: "O great mystery! Mary, an incorrupt virgin conceived, after conception brought forth as a virgin, after childbirth she remained a virgin." The First Lateran Council (647 AD), under Pope St. Martin I, later defined Our Lady's perpetual virginity when it condemned anyone who did not acknowledge with the Fathers of the Church that "the holy and ever virgin and immaculate Mary was really and truly the Mother of God. Inasmuch as she, in the fullness of time, and without seed, conceived by the Holy Spirit, God the Word Himself, Who before all time was born of God the Father, and without loss of integrity brought Him forth, and after His birth preserved her virginity inviolate."

This dogma was traditionally expressed in the formula that Mary was virgin "before, during and after the birth" of Jesus. We have already seen how the meaning of the phrase, "before the birth" of Jesus is clear from the Gospel accounts above. Let us look briefly at the other two phrases. "During the birth" of Jesus grew out of the understanding of the Church, enlightened by the Holy Spirit. It expresses the belief that at the moment of her giving birth to Jesus, through a special divine action, Mary did not lose the physical signs of her virginity. The Fathers of the Church would say that the womb of the Blessed Mother remained closed and intact, and that Jesus passed through the enclosure of her womb much as He passed through the walls of the room where the Apostles were gathered on Easter night with the doors bolted closed (cf. John 20:19). Furthermore, Mary's giving birth to Jesus was painless, as is reflected in the fact that Our Lady herself *"wrapped [Jesus] in swaddling clothes and laid Him in a manger"* (cf. Luke 2:7), something which would have been nearly impossible for a woman who had just suffered the

the excruciating pains of childbirth! If Our Lady did not have a painless virgin birth, St. Joseph would more likely have done these things!

"After the birth" of Jesus requires a somewhat longer explanation because certain objections have been raised against it over the centuries. This phrase refers to the dogmatic belief in Catholic tradition that Our Lady never had marital relations with St. Joseph even after the birth of Jesus, but preserved her virginity intact for the rest of her life. Our Lady, as we shall see, was quite concerned to preserve her virginity before conceiving Jesus, so why should we assume she would surrender her virginity afterwards?

Let us look very briefly at the source of the major objections we find here. The biggest difficulty, raised from early Christian centuries, is that Sacred Scripture speaks of Jesus' "brothers" (cf. Matthew 13:55: Mark 3:31-35; Mark 6:3). How could Our Lady have remained a perpetual virgin if she had other sons after the birth of Jesus? One explanation given by St. Epiphanius (d. 403 AD) was that the "brothers of the Lord" were really sons of St. Joseph by a prior marriage, but there is no evidence at all in the Gospels to support this idea. Another and better explanation is the fact that neither Hebrew nor Aramaic, Our Lord's spoken language, had a specific word for "*cousin*." The word "*brother*" was commonly used to indicate actual cousins. (Even today the word "*brother*" is used broadly in certain ethnic groups to include simple companions, or in my own case as a Franciscan friar to include my fellow religious. Now in neither case is there any blood relationship, but simply a fraternal bond.) Furthermore, these "brothers of the Lord" are never called the children of Mary, and in fact, two of them, James and Joseph (cf. Matthew 13:55; called James and Joses in Mark 6:3), are explicitly said to be the children of another Mary who is certainly not Our Lady (cf. Matthew 27:56). A final observation is that elsewhere in the New Testament, the word *"brother"* is used in a general way to indicate a fellow disciple, not a relative (cf. Acts 1:15; 1 Corinthians 5:11, 15:6).

Our Lady's Intention Was to Remain a Virgin Always

Our Lady's intention to remain a virgin can be seen in her response to the angel Gabriel's message that she was to become a mother: *"How can this be since I do not know man?"* (Luke 1:34). Catholic tradition, going all the way back to the early Fathers of the Church, has always understood Our Lady's question to imply that she had already been inspired by the Holy Spirit to consecrate her virginity to God. If this was not the case, and she was intending to have marital relations with St. Joseph after they lived together as husband and wife, then it logically follows that she would have assumed this was how she would conceive, as the angel had foretold. Thus, her question would make no sense. Therefore, Our Lady's question can only be logically interpreted to mean: *"Not only have I not had marital relations with St. Joseph during this time of our solemn engagement, but even after even after our marriage I will not have marital relations with him!*" We may then conclude that Our Lady is here not only stating the fact that she is a virgin at that moment, but also that she is determined to remain a virgin always!

The Meaning and Importance of Our Lady's Perpetual Virginity

Consecrated virginity, or virginity as a permanent state, was unknown in the Old Testament. It was an aspect of that "*celibacy for the sake of the Kingdom of Heaven*" (cf. Matthew 19:10-12) which Jesus taught for those who were willing to accept it in the New Testament. Our Lady was, no doubt, inspired to her perpetual virginity by the light of the Holy Spirit. Her sinlessness and overwhelming holiness allowed her such openness to the inspirations of the Holy Spirit, that she not only recognized virginity consecrated to God as a spiritual treasure, but she steadfastly consecrated her own virginity to God. St. Therese of Lisieux, our newest Doctor of the Church, was of the opinion that if Our Lady could only become the Mother of Jesus by breaking her vow of virginity to God, she would not have become Jesus' Mother. The Little Flower was convinced that Our Lady would never take back what she had already given to God.

Church historians point out that the doctrine of Mary's perpetual virginity was to become an ideal for many Christian men and women who wanted to give their lives more fully to Christ. Thus, the ideal of consecrated celibacy in both the priesthood and religious life found support in the model of the Virgin Mary! Unfortunately, after Vatican Council II, some liberal Catholic theologians, in an air of theological ferment within the Church at the time, began to reinvestigate long accepted truths with an attitude of complete freedom, as if they were not defined Church teachings. Thus, the perpetual virginity of Our Lady, accepted as dogma for over fifteen centuries since the first Lateran Council (AD 649), began to be questioned and rejected by some within the Church! Could it not be that, in the social climate of the late 1960s and the 1970s, when Western culture was experiencing the devastating effects of the so-called "Sexual Revolution" and some Catholics were promoting a "new sexual morality" that was nothing but a distortion of authentic Catholic moral teaching, that certain people rejected the teaching and example of Our Lady's perpetual virginity, because it was a moral rebuke to the sexual license they were spreading? As Archbishop Fulton J. Sheen put it, "No one becomes a heretic for the way they want to think, but for the way they want to live!"

The late Archbishop, a great devotee of Our Lady, also used to say: "Where devotion to the Blessed Virgin Mary is strong, womanhood, motherhood and purity are all held in great respect!" Devotion to the Virgin Mary is a strong bulwark against the sins of the flesh! If it is rejected, the road to sexual promiscuity would open even wider.

Consecrated or perpetual virginity embraced publicly or privately, is an outstanding sign of the virtue of purity. This is why the sex-crazed society we live in not only rejects it, but attacks it viciously. This author remembers hearing slogans during the turbulent 60s and 70s like "Down with virginity." In the same way, we hear constant demands, both from inside and outside the Church that priestly celibacy should be done away with. Since the perpetual virginity of Our Lady is a model and encouragement for consecrated celibacy, it is no wonder that it has been the object of much blasphemy, which we counter by our First Saturday reparation.

Virginity, seen as the chastity lived by young people before marriage, is another important expression of this virtue. Today, many teenagers are ridiculed by their peers if they admit they are still "virgins." It has become a widespread assumption that every teenager is "sexually active." Thank God and Our Lady, that that is not so. Many young people recognize that their gift of sexuality is meant to be a special gift reserved for married life. They struggle hard to maintain their virginity before marriage. Today, we must encourage young people to look to the Virgin Mary as their example, and to seek her protection with their prayers. There are also a few clever little reminders that help, too! One is a "chastity ring," worn to remind young people to say, "I don't" before they say, "I do!" Another is a chastity button that says, "I'm worth waiting for!"

The Virgin Mary is a great support to all of us in our practice of purity according to our state in life. No wonder the world blasphemes her perpetual virginity!

Let us make reparation for these blasphemies. In this way we will win through the intercession of the Immaculate Heart of Mary, greater graces for purity for the virtuous to remain faithful, and for those whose lives have been caught up in sexual chaos to return to the Divine Mercy of Jesus!

CHAPTER 4
The Third Reparation of the Five First Saturdays (Part One)

For Those Who Blaspheme Against Mary's Divine Motherhood

Belief in Mary as the Mother of God is one of the most cherished beliefs of Catholics. This privilege of Our Lady is the basis and reason for all the other privileges she received from God. It was precisely because she was chosen from all women to be the Mother of Jesus Christ, the Son of God Who took His human nature from her, that she was conceived without Original Sin (the privilege of her Immaculate Conception), that she remained a virgin before, during and after the birth of Jesus (the privilege of her Perpetual Virginity), that she played a very special part with Jesus in His mission of redeeming the world (her privilege as Co-Redemptrix), and that she was assumed body and soul into Heaven when her earthly life was ended (the privilege of her Assumption).

It was only fitting that Our Lady enjoyed all of these privileges in order to fulfill her exalted vocation from God! After all, if we could have chosen our own earthly mother and then be allowed to give her the choicest blessings to make her the best of mothers, would we not have done so?

Then how much more would Jesus do that, since He in fact did choose His own Mother, and then endowed her with all those gifts that would make her the very best of all mothers!

It would be very important to clarify at this point exactly what we mean, as well as what we do not mean, when we call Mary "the Mother of God." Let us start with what we do not mean. When we call Our Lady "the Mother of God," we do not mean she gave birth to Jesus in His Divinity. Many people, especially among our separated brethren, are often under this grave misunderstanding!

As God, the Second Divine Person existed from all eternity. That means He had no beginning, and He will never have an ending! If Mary gave birth to Jesus in His Divinity, then that would mean that Jesus is not God, since God could not have a beginning. It would also make Our Lady appear that she was some sort of "super-goddess" which she is absolutely not!

Mothers are always Mothers of Persons

What then, do we mean when we call Mary "the Mother of God"? To try to explain this simply but clearly, we must use two words taken from Philosophy. They are "nature" and "person." Nature describes the makeup of something, with all its powers and abilities. Nature answers the question, "What is it?" For example, it can be an angel, a man or woman, an animal or even God. All of them have the powers and abilities that are part of their nature.

God, by His Divine Nature, has infinite knowledge and power, and can create things out of nothing. No other nature, because it is created and limited, has the powers of God's Nature! An angel, by his angelic nature, which is totally spiritual, has vast infused knowledge and power, and can do many things human beings cannot.

Men and women, by their human nature, which is partly spiritual (their soul) and partly material (their body), have the ability to reason with their intellect and to freely choose with their wills, as well as the abilities that come from their bodily powers, such as the use of the senses, movement, and reproduction. An animal - whose nature is purely material - has the ability to use senses, move about and reproduce its species, but it lacks the human being's ability to reason intellectually and to choose freely. Animals are governed largely by instinct.

"Person" refers to any being having intelligence and free will, and who is responsible for his or her actions and the consequences of them. We refer to the "person" as the "agent" or the one who acts through the powers of his or her nature. Person answers the question, "Who is it?" It follows, then, that there are only three categories of "persons;" a Divine Person, such as God the Father; an angelic person, such as St. Michael, and a human person, such as St. Therese. Animals, because they lack the ability to reason intellectually and to choose freely, are not "persons" in this philosophical sense.

Let us apply these ideas of "nature" and "person" to Jesus, and therefore to why we call Mary, His Mother, "the Mother of God." What the Catholic Church teaches as her defined dogma is that in Jesus, there are two natures (one Divine and the other human), but only one Person (the Second Divine Person of the Blessed Trinity). From all eternity, without beginning and without end, Jesus was the Second Divine Person, with His Divine Nature, which He possessed with God the Father and God the Holy Spirit. He had the same infinite powers to create, to redeem and to sanctify as They did.

What happened in the moment of the Incarnation was that this Second Person, while keeping His Divine Nature, also took a human nature. He did this by taking His flesh and blood from the womb of the Virgin Mary, when the power of the Holy Spirit came upon her to accomplish this greatest event in human history. As we profess in the Apostles' Creed: "He (Jesus) was conceived by the Holy Spirit, born of the Virgin Mary…" Though Jesus has a human consciousness, a human intelligence and a human free will, He is not a human person. Rather, the Second Divine Person now acts through the human nature

He acquired from Our Lady. In other words, the "agent" responsible for acting through the human nature of Jesus is a Divine Person.

Now, let us apply all this to Our Lady's title of "Mother of God." A human mother is always the mother of a person. Although the mother and father together conceived the child, and God alone infused the soul into the child at the moment of conception (which is why we respect all human life from the moment of conception), the mother is called the mother of the whole person. For example, we say: "This is John's mother" or "This is Anne's mother." We do not say: This is the mother of John's body" or "This is the mother of Anne's body." Motherhood always applies to a person. And the only person in Jesus Christ, Who is fully God and fully man, is the second Divine Person. Therefore, since Mary is the mother of Jesus' human nature, we can say of her: "Mary is the Mother of Jesus;" "Mary is the Mother of One Who is a Divine Person;" "Mary is the Mother of God."

The Important Teaching of the Council of Ephesus

This teaching of the Catholic Church was declared in a special way at the Ecumenical Council of Ephesus in 431 AD. (Ephesus is located in modern Turkey. A strong Catholic tradition says that St. John the Beloved Disciple, who received Our Lady into his care at the foot the cross, later in a time of persecution took her to Ephesus where there was a large Christian community. It was there that Our Lady's life ended, and she was assumed into Heaven. It is still a site of Christian pilgrimage.) At the time, some Christians had asked Nestorius, then Patriarch of Constantinople, if Mary could be called in Greek, *"Theotokos,"* which meant literally the "God-bearer" or "Mother of God." The Patriarch answered that Mary could not be called *"Theotokos,"* but only *"Christotokos,"* "the bearer of Christ" implying that in Jesus there was a human person (Christ) as well as a Divine Person (the Second Divine Person). This teaching became the heresy we call *"Nestorianism"* after its founder. It undermined the whole reality of the Incarnation. What it implied was that God did not really become man, but He simply entered into union with a human person and coexisted there. Thus, according to this heresy, in Jesus of Nazareth, there would have been a Divine Person with a Divine Nature as well as a human person with a human nature. Furthermore, since the "agent" working in the human nature of Jesus would be only a human person, his actions would have had only limited merit. Only a Divine Person can perform an action of infinite merit.

So, if only a human (Christ) died on the cross, the merit of his death would not have been sufficient to redeem the world! That would mean that all of us would still be in our sins, because a purely human person could not atone for our sins.

However, when we maintain the true Catholic teaching that the only Person in Jesus was a Divine Person, then His dying on the cross would be meritorious to redeem the whole world! The Council of Ephesus, led by St. Cyril of Alexandria, condemned the heretical teaching of Nestorious and proclaimed Our Lady as "Theotokos," "the God-bearer" or "the Mother of God." The Christians of Ephesus were so overjoyed that they held a night-long procession throughout the streets of Ephesus chanting, "Theotokos! Theotokos!" It is our same joy to proclaim Mary as the "Mother of God!"

It is the intention for the third of the First Five Saturdays of the month to make reparation for those who, whether from misunderstanding or from deliberate disbelief, deny, or ridicule, or blaspheme this very special Catholic teaching about Our Blessed Mother! As she herself, inspired by the Holy Spirit, proclaimed in her great song of thanksgiving, her "Magnificat:"

> *"From this day all generations will call me blessed; the Almighty has done great things for me, and holy is His Name!"*

CHAPTER 5
The Third Reparation of the Five First Saturdays (Part Two)

For Those Who Blaspheme Mary's Spiritual Motherhood of All God's People

Archbishop Fulton J. Sheen often said that Our Lady has a two-fold motherhood. The first was her physical motherhood. Being the Mother of Jesus, the Eternal Word made flesh, she is truly the Mother of God, and this is her "Divine Maternity." This motherhood was fulfilled when, having conceived by the power of the Holy Spirit at the Annunciation, she gave birth to Jesus at Bethlehem on that first beautiful day we call Christmas. As her conceiving of Jesus was a virginal conception, so her giving birth to Him in the stable at Bethlehem was also a virginal birth. She neither lost her physical integrity, nor did she suffer any pangs of childbirth. The Fathers of the Church offered this explanation of the virgin-birth of Jesus: He miraculously passed through the wall of Our Lady's womb much as He passed through the walls of the Upper Room in Jerusalem when He appeared to the Apostles after His Resurrection (cf. John 20:26). This is because there was no sin involved in either mother or Child. She was the Immaculate Conception; He was innocence itself. Remember that the pangs of childbirth were the result of Original Sin (cf. Genesis 3:16) and Our Lady was spared both the guilt of that sin and its punishment!

Our Lady's second motherhood was spiritual. This is her motherhood of all the brothers and sisters of Jesus, making them also her own true sons and daughters. Since this motherhood is an important part of God's plan of salvation for all mankind, we may appropriately refer to it as Our Lady's "Redemptive Maternity." It actually follows from her "Divine Maternity," and is inseparably connected with it! Why? As St. Louis-Marie de Monfort put it, a mother cannot give birth to a head without also giving birth to its body, composed of its many bodily members. Therefore, by her "Divine Maternity," Our Lady gave physical life to Jesus, the Head of the Mystical Body, the Church. By her "Redemptive Maternity," Our Lady assisted in giving new supernatural life to all the faithful, all the members of Jesus' Mystical Body, the Church. In the first birth, Mary gives life to Jesus in the flesh: *"the Word became flesh and made His dwelling among us"* (John 1:14). In the second birth, Mary cooperates in giving new life in the Spirit to those who are *"begotten of water and the Spirit"* (John 3:5).

Mary's "Redemptive Maternity" Differs From Her "Divine Maternity"

The contrast of Mary's second motherhood with the first is very striking. Her "redemptive Maternity" takes place on Calvary. There was actually a new birth taking place there at the very moment of Jesus' death. When the Roman centurion pierced the heart of Jesus with his lance, we read that *"immediately blood and water flowed out"* (John 19:34). The Fathers of the Church said that the blood here represented the Holy Eucharist, while the water represented Baptism. These are the two main Sacraments of the Church, since Baptism is our birth to new life in Christ while the Holy Eucharist is the Bread of life! Together the blood and water represent the new life in Christ that we have received. It is actually Jesus Himself who is being formed in us or, in a sense, coming to birth in us. Because of this, we can say with St. Paul: *"The life I live now is not my own; Christ is living in me. I still live my human life, but it is a life of faith in the Son of God, Who loved me and gave Himself for me"* (Galatians 2:20). Our new life in the Spirit focuses on Jesus coming to live spiritually within us. So, if Jesus is being born again spiritually within us, Our Lady needs to be there!

Another contrast in Mary's second motherhood was that while her giving birth to Jesus at Bethlehem was painless because there was no sin in either Child or mother, there was great pain on Calvary. Though Our Lady was absolutely sinless and *"filled with grace"* (cf. Luke 1:28), her "new children" were steeped in sin! Because of their sins, they were in danger of being lost forever in Hell. That is why Jesus, with an infinite love, offered Himself in obedience to the Heavenly Father's Will, as a substituted "Victim," *"obediently accepting death, even death on a cross"* (Philippians 2:8) to suffer in reparation for our sins. Her pain then was the sorrow within her pierced motherly heart not only to witness the death of her Jesus hanging in such unspeakable pain upon the cross, but also to unite with Him in His Self-offering to the Father. Our Lady literally had to will, in accordance with the Heavenly Father's plan, the suffering and death of her "first-born Son" so that a multitude of spiritual sons and daughters might come to new life in union with Jesus.

Our Lord confirmed His mother's "Redemptive Maternity" by His own words from the cross: *"Near the cross of Jesus there stood His mother, His mother's sister, Mary the wife of Clopas, and Mary Magdalene. Seeing His mother there with the disciple whom He loved, Jesus said to His mother, 'Woman, there is your son!' In turn He said to the disciple, 'There is your mother!'"* (John 19:25-27). St. Bernard of Clairvaux captures the magnitude of Our Lady's maternal love and suffering at that moment when he writes: "Truly, O Blessed

Mother…were those words: 'Woman, behold your son,' not more than a sword to you, truly piercing your heart, cutting through to the division between soul and spirit? What an exchange! John is given to you in the place of Jesus, the servant in place of the Lord, the disciple in place of the Master; the son of Zebedee replaces the Son of God, a mere man replaces God Himself! How could these words not pierce your most loving heart, when the mere remembrance of them breaks ours, hearts of stone and iron though they are!"

Our Lady's "Redemptive Maternity" Lasts Until the End of the World

Our Lady can never forget her redemptive maternal mission which will continue in the world until the end of time. It is most precious to Our Lady because it was given to her by her Divine Son in the midst of His sufferings and hers! Furthermore, because it involves redemption from our sinfulness, it will never be free of suffering. Well might St. Paul's words regarding his converts apply to Our Lady's relationship to us, her spiritual children: *"You are my children, and you put me back in labor pains until Christ is formed in you!"* (Galatians 4:19) This is why, in connection with Fatima, we speak of Our Lady's "Immaculate and Sorrowful Heart."

This redemptive motherhood is very dear to Our Lady. Her maternal love for us knows no bounds! This is why it offends the honor of Our Lady when people deny her redemptive motherhood or, worse still, ridicule and blaspheme it. Why would anyone do these things? Perhaps our answer can be found in a traditional principle of the spiritual life, "Grace builds on nature." It means, among other things, that many spiritual or religious problems actually have their basis in our human relationships. In other words, many have difficulty accepting Mary's spiritual motherhood because they have significant difficulties relating to their own human mothers. We will look at some of these relationships so as to identify the underlying cause of the problem, and then try to offer some remedies that can free the person to be open to Our Lady's motherhood.

Some Possible Reason for this Blasphemy

Some people experienced a lack of love and affection from their mothers. For example, a situation where a mother never tells her own child that she loves him or her, and yet the child deeply craves being told that! Or a situation where a mother never showed any external signs of affection, such as a kiss or a hug. Such people often experience this lacking as a rejection, as a sense that "I am not good enough!" Because of this hurt and the insecurity it breeds, they may be afraid of reaching out to Our Lady as their mother for fear she may also reject them!

What these people must try to do is to separate their earthly mother from their Heavenly mother. They must recognize the pain of what they did not receive growing up, and try with healing these scars by working at bettering their relationship to their mothers, if this is possible. But they must clearly separate such negative experiences from Our Lady, toward whom they should attempt to reach out trustingly.

Another source of difficulty can be the situation where one's mother played "favorites," thus while obviously loving a brother or a sister, she neglected this one child. This can leave the impression that one must always compete to win the attention and love of a mother, even Our Blessed Mother. To counter this insecurity, the person must be told that Our Lady's love for one of her children does not take away from the love of any of her other children. She loves each of us as if we were her only children on earth! Padre Pio said he experienced Our Lady's motherly love and care in precisely this manner!

A third difficulty would be for people who experienced their mother's love as "manipulative" or "controlling." Mother showed her love clearly when the child was well behaved or did well in school. If not, she withheld her love and affection for very prolonged periods. This can breed in the child the feeling that all love is "conditional," and if I do not meet the conditions, I will not be loved. It also makes love appear as "uncertain," because I will never know when that love will be withheld. To overcome such insecurity, the person must recognize that Our Lady's love is never "hot or cold," or unpredictable. Even when Jesus and Mary withdraw all emotional feelings from their love (this is "spiritual dryness"), they do so only to help us mature in faith, and not to put us on an an emotional roller coaster!

A further difficulty can come when a mother has been abusive, whether verbally, physically or even sexually. This requires a great deal of healing, and may, for a considerable time, prevent one's relationship to Our Blessed Mother from developing as it should. Much prayer is needed to forgive such past hurts and allow reconciliation, if possible, with one's mother. As healing on the natural level grows, there will be greater openness to Our Lady on the supernatural level.

A final area of difficulty stems from various "prejudices." In some cultures, for example, women are looked upon as "second-class" citizens. Their importance and dignity as creatures of God are denied. Such people would most likely have difficulty accepting another woman as "mother." The same applies to many people in our present culture of sexual license and perversion, who lack a healthy orientation toward women. They may well find the childlike trust and confidence involved in accepting Mary as our spiritual mother altogether too much! Those who reject motherhood in general because of a pro-abortion attitude will also likely reject Our Lady's motherhood. Finally, some non-Catholic Christians may reject Our Lady's spiritual maternity because it sounds "too Catholic." Since Marian devotion is strongly linked with Catholic piety, it might require an admission of a truth they might not want to concede. They need to look objectively at Mary's motherhood, and not make it a bone of contention.

When we offer our Five First Saturday devotion to Our Lady, let us pray and sacrifice for all these and many others who experience obstacles to their acceptance of Our Lady's spiritual motherhood in their lives! Our Lady loves them all, and is simply waiting to extend her maternal love and care even to those of her children who out of ignorance, fear, or prejudice reject the motherhood she obtained at so great a price. To quote St. Bernard's sermon once more: "If Jesus could die in body, could Mary not die with Him in spirit? He died in body through a love greater than anyone had ever known! She died in spirit through a love unlike any other since His!"

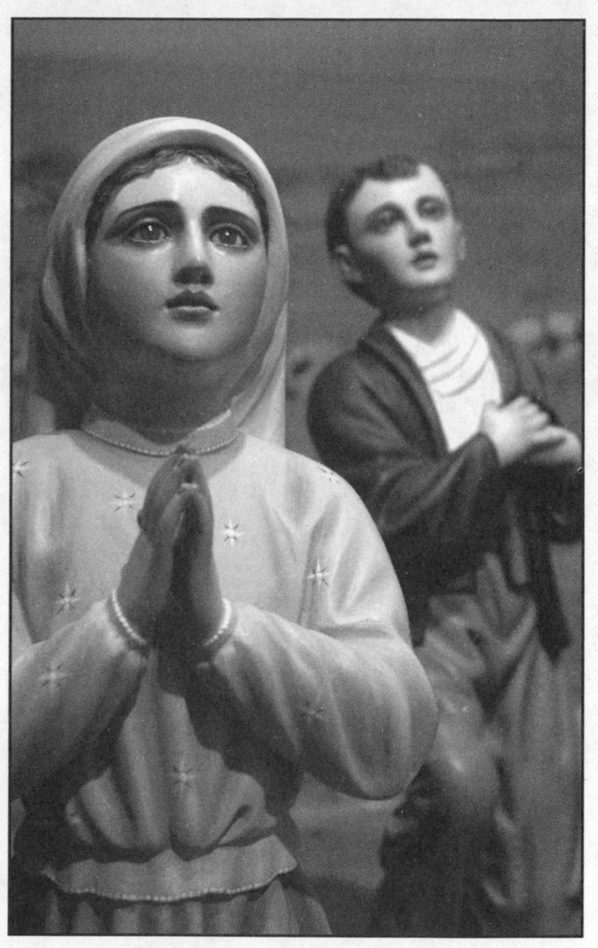

CHAPTER 6
The Fourth Reparation of the Five First Saturdays

For Those Who Alienate Children From Devotion to Our Lady

The Gospel records the story of a group of mothers who were approaching Jesus with their little children in order for Him to place His hands on them and bless them. The Apostles mistakenly thought that the children were at best a distraction to Our Lord, and at worst an annoyance He did not want or need. So the Apostles were stopping the mothers and children from approaching Jesus, turning them away. Our Lord's response was quick and clear:

> *"'Let the children come to Me. Do not hinder them. The kingdom of God belongs to such as these.' And He laid His hand on their heads..."*
> (Matthew 19:14-15)

Begin Speaking about Mary While the Children are Still Young

It is clear from this incident how much Our Lord wants children to come to Him! From their earliest years, the young must be taught about Jesus, about His life, death and resurrection, about His Church, emphasizing her doctrine and Sacraments. This includes in a very special way the Church's rich treasure of teaching and devotion to the Blessed Virgin Mary. She is Jesus' mother, and must therefore be loved, honored and respected along with Him! She is also our mother, given to us by Jesus Himself from the cross of Calvary: *"Woman, behold your son!...Behold your mother!"* (John 19:26-27) And is there anything more instinctive than for a little child to seek his or her mother?

Even from a child's earliest years, he or she can begin to grasp a love for Our Lady in keeping with his or her stage of development. Please allow me to illustrate with two examples drawn from my own family's experience. One involves a niece of mine and the other a nephew. This particular niece would often visit one of her uncles, who had a statue of Our Lady in his backyard. We members of the family would often observe her standing for long periods of time in front of the statue, seemingly engrossed in an animated conversation with the Blessed Mother! One can only imagine what passed between the Immaculate Heart of Our Lady and the innocent heart of a child! The story of my nephew involves a child who was only two years old at the time, or as my brother often put it, in "the terrible twos"! When my brother would bring his little son to Mass on Sundays, he told me that sometimes he was very well behaved, but other times he got quite restless. Well, on one of those occasions when the little guy was restless, my brother walked with him out into the foyer of the church where there was a statue of Our Lady of Grace with her arms reaching outward. As soon as my little nephew saw the statue, he announced to his father, "I'm going to give Mary five!" He promptly went over and gave Our Lady "the high five sign" which he loved to give me (and I suspect others, too!) when I visited! It was my nephew's innocent way, even at the age of two, of showing Our Lady his love for her and that she was special to him! Now, I am not suggesting that we all give Our Lady "the high five sign," but it does represent how easily a child can be taught to honor and revere the Mother of God and our Mother, too!

Silence about Our Lady will have Disastrous Effects for a Child

The foundation of Marian devotion should ordinarily be given in the home. Word and example must go together to assure that it will have a lasting effect. When children hear and see that Our Lady is important to their parents, she becomes important to them also. Many parents today, wanting to adopt what they mistakenly believe is certain "broadmindedness" about religious truths, take the attitude that they will not teach their children anything specific about religion. They say, "I will let my children grow up, and then they can make up their own minds about what they want to believe or not!" (You will notice that they do not allow these same children to make up their own minds about whether they want to go the school or not!)

For a child to wait until he or she grows up to learn basic truths such as those of religion will be too late! The fallacy in this thinking is that to say nothing, is in effect to say something. The human mind at birth is what philosophers would call a "tabula rasa," that is, "a blank sheet." To have any knowledge in the mind, it must come either through experience or by teaching. Therefore, to say nothing about religious truths, - in this case Our Blessed Mother – is to deprive the child of even knowing she exists. After all, you can only come to know the existence of other people when you have been introduced to them, whether by teaching about them, such as when we study about people from history, or by a personal encounter with that individual. Silence on the part of parents, then, conveys to the child either that Our Lady does not exist, or that she is not very important! At the same time, silence on such important religious truths leaves a kind of intellectual vacuum which will very likely sooner or later be filled with erroneous ideas and false moral values. These may come from distorted teachings, the lure of passion which youth experience, or the negative influence of scandal, which Jesus said is unavoidable (cf Matthew 18:7). Left to itself, our fallen human nature tends to follow the law of gravity: it gets pulled down, not up! What lifts us up and strengthens us to resist the downward pull to immorality is God's grace working through the truths of our Catholic Faith!

Now, if these same parents were to speak about the Blessed Mother, especially with a sense of joy, enthusiasm and importance, this is bound to make a deep impact on the child. I have always believed that the initial faith of a child is actually a participation in the faith of the parents, or of other significant people in their lives, such as grandparents, godparents, and teachers. With time, the children will make this participated faith their own personal faith!

What Motivates People to Keep Children from Our Lady?

Through the First Five Saturdays devotion, we make reparation for this failure to teach children about the Blessed Mother due to neglect on the part of parents or others charged with their education. Worse still, however, are those who deliberately sow the seeds of indifference, disrespect, aversion and even contempt for the Blessed Mother. This can result from a number of motives. One would be a deficient religious attitude or prejudice that mistakenly sees Our Lady as one who keeps us from Jesus. A number of our separated brothers and sisters hold the extremely exaggerated notion that Catholics worship Mary or make her into some sort of a "goddess" so that they react to the opposite extreme by minimizing Our Heavenly Father's special predilection for Our

Lady by choosing her to be the Mother of His Son! They argue that we must go to Jesus directly, and not to Jesus through Mary!

But how can the one through whom Jesus came into the world and whose last recorded words in Sacred Scripture are, *"Do whatever He tells you"* (John 2:5) ever possibly keep us from Jesus? In our reparation here, we should pray that such persons, who may be quite sincere despite their mistaken idea, may come to see that Mary is an open gate, not a locked door, on the sure path leading to Jesus!

Radical feminists also oppose love and esteem of Our Lady for themselves and others because, as we have seen in previous reflections, they reject certain essential elements of true feminism, namely, virginity and motherhood. They reject virginity because they want no limits on the promiscuous and often perverted sexual freedom they champion.

Motherhood is rejected because it contradicts their desire for pleasure without responsibility, for which reason they are such determined advocates of abortion. Radical feminists fail to see virginity as a precious gift by which youth, before marriage, preserve the gift of their sexuality for the person with whom they will share a lifelong union of love in marriage. They also reject motherhood, the very glory of womanhood, namely, her privilege through union with her husband to cooperate with God in bringing new life into the world!

In contrast, Our Lady is honored by her faithful children as Virgin and Mother, and as such, she is held up as an example for young people. So as Virgin and Mother, Mary has become for radical feminists an object of distorted teaching, ridicule and even contempt and blasphemy. In their attempts to spread their agenda, they seek to poison the minds and hearts of young people against the Mother of God. Unfortunately, much of the confusion in the Catholic Church today traces back to this source. After all, their mentality is prevalent in our secularized Western society.

The consequence is much like breathing in badly polluted air: it will eventually make one sick. Thus, radical feminist thought has infiltrated the thinking of many Catholic parents and educators, and in turn, like a contagious disease, has been transmitted to a large segment of our Catholic youth, who either do not know Our Lady or are prejudiced against her.

A Bitter Spiritual Battle Rages to Win the Young

There is a veritable battle between good and evil, light and darkness, going on in the world today! It has always existed, but it seems to have reached epidemic proportions in today's society. This can be especially seen in the struggle to win over the minds and hearts of the young. We saw this with the terrible *"isms"* of the 20th century. Communism broke up families by separating little children from their parents at tender ages, so as to prevent proper moral guidance and religious training by parents, especially in a deeply religious country like Russia. Nazism boasted of its "youth camps" where young people were systematically subjected to an indoctrination that rejected God and glorified a "super race" only to have it end in catastrophic destruction in the world. This spirit is still found today in our post-Christian, secularized society. The media bombards the young with false and immoral values. Just imagine the negative moral effects of MTV on youth not only in America, but throughout the world! Even diplomats, such as at the United Nations, have tried to gain control of the young under the guise of legislating "young peoples' rights." These laws are nothing more than attempts to separate children from parental authority and protection. They would leave children helplessly exposed to all kinds of exploitation by unscrupulous adults!

The Church, led by Pope John Paul II and then by Pope Benedict XVI, is well aware of this unrelenting struggle and its importance. Both sides know that whoever controls the minds and hearts of the young, controls the key to the future! Pope John Paul II, as a young priest in his native Communist-dominated Poland, untiringly reached out to the young to save the nation from embracing atheism.

Despite his poor health, John Paul II used a similar approach for the universal Church through his World Youth Days of prayer, and his successor, Pope Benedict XVI, intends to continue on this course. We, too, will assist in this struggle as we carry out the Five First Saturdays devotion, making reparation for the evil done to our young people and winning the graces of conversion for them, as well as for those who attempt to keep them from coming to Jesus through His Mother!

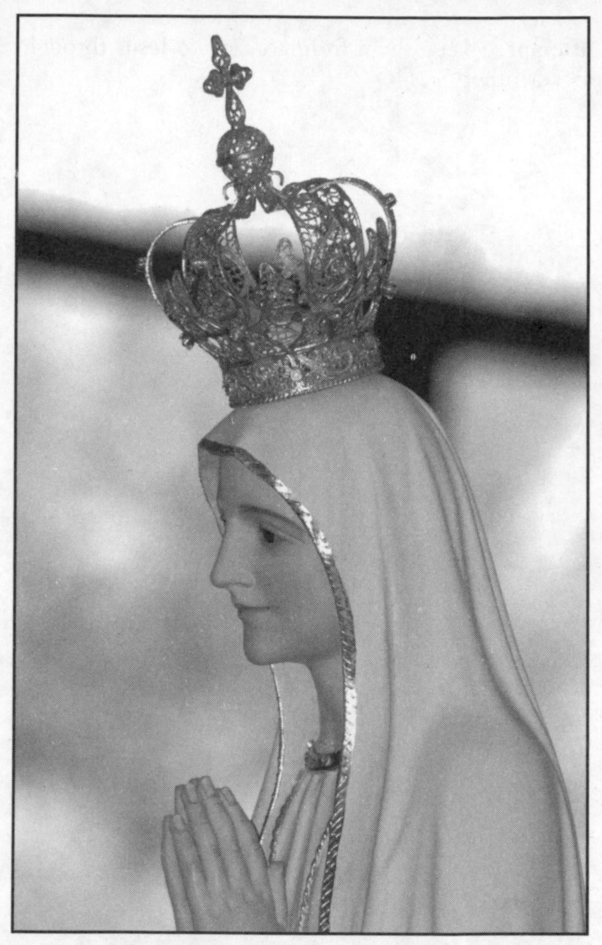

CHAPTER 7
The Fifth Reparation of the Five First Saturdays

For Those Who Dishonor Our Lady in Her Images

Art plays a very important part in the life of any society. In its many forms, the purpose of art is to give expression to the values, the beauty and the aspirations that humans treasure in their hearts. Art can express many a sentiment from joy to sorrow, hope to disappointment, love to loneliness, even reverence to disrespect. It is one of the primary means by which people of a given generation form and express their culture.

The Powerful Influence of Religious Art

Religious art stands out among all these expressions because it touches the most profound and sacred sentiments we have, namely, those stemming from our relationship with God. When sacred art genuinely expresses what transpires between God and the individual in the secret depths of his or her heart, it truly lifts up, inspires and enlightens the human spirit. Such art helps us to feel a sense of the presence of God. This in turn moves us to pray more ardently and trust more confidently in His love and providential care. Devout people instinctively know this by their experience.

The Catholic Church has always used art as part of her mission of evangelization. It has always been an important tool for Christian education. In past centuries, when most of the faithful were illiterate, they would learn much about their Catholic Faith by looking at artistic representations of events in Sacred Scripture and the history of the Church. Scenes from the life of Christ, such as those depicting His birth, public life, death, and resurrection, were extremely popular. They made these events of salvation very real and meaningful for these people of simple faith. The same effect continues today when religious art reinforces what a more educated faithful have already studied about the faith.

As Pope John Paul II wrote in his letter to artists in 1999, "In order to communicate the message entrusted to her by Christ, the Church needs art!"

The Image of Our Lady: A Favorite in Christian Art

Among the most popular images of Catholic art are those of Our Blessed Lady. Without doubt, the theme of the Madonna and Child has inspired some of the most beautiful expressions created by human artists. Even the United States Post Office, despite objections of certain civil libertarians, every Christmas issues its special stamp of the Madonna and Child to meet popular demand.

Special representations of Our Lady have become part of Catholic culture in various countries and even internationally. The image of Our Lady of Guadalupe in Mexico is one of the most outstanding. It was miraculously imprinted on the tilma (a mantle made of cactus fiber) belonging to St. Juan Diego. This tilma, in turn, has been miraculously preserved for nearly five-hundred years.

This image has inspired devotion to Our Lady of Guadalupe as the Queen of the Americas, the Protectress of the Unborn and the Star of Evangelization. Other very popular images of Our Lady include Our Lady of Perpetual Help (Italy), Our Lady of Czestochowa (Poland), Our Lady of Pilar (Spain), Virgin Mary of Kazan (Russia), Our Lady of Walshingham (England) and Our Lady of Loreto (Italy). Over the years, Catholic devotion to Our Lady in these various countries has centered on these images. Many times it was precisely this devotion to Our Lady in these images that preserved a remnant of Catholic culture and identity, especially in times when the Church faced persecution from without and indifference from within.

Devotion to Our Lady through her images has also flourished in connection with places where she has appeared to various members of the faithful over the centuries. Names like Fatima (Portugal), Lourdes and Rue du Bac (France), and Knock (Ireland) are but a few of such places all over the world where the faithful come to honor Our Lady at her shrines. These same faithful and many others keep her image in their homes as reminders of their love for her and of their need to pray to her to seek her motherly protection and intercession.

To Dishonor an Image of Our Lady is a Terrible Offense

Connected to these various images of Our Lady have been certain Marian devotions. These include honoring her joys and sorrows, praying her Rosary, wearing her Miraculous Medal as well as wearing the brown scapular she gave us as Our Lady of Mt. Carmel.

So, when Catholics honor images of Our Lady, there is a considerable sense of piety involved. She is our spiritual Mother who loves and cares for us, our Protectress who defends us from all harm physical and spiritual, our Intercessor with her Son, Jesus Christ.

Therefore, whenever her image is dishonored in any way, it is an offense to devout Catholics because it is a serious dishonor to Our Lady and, consequently, to her Divine Son. It demands reparation for the affront given and intercession for God's mercy for those who caused it!

This Dishonor May Come from Different Causes

Sometimes this dishonor is shown to Our Lady's images by destroying, mutilating, decapitating, spray painting, burning or in any other way disfiguring them. These are outrages that necessitate our reparation. Many times these things are done by members of occult groups who do them to express their contempt for God. Other times it may be the work of people who are violently angry at God for some distorted reason, and who resort to desecration to convey that anger.

Even very famous images of Our Lady have been disfigured over the centuries. For example, the image of Our Lady of Czestochowa suffered desecration. This sacred image was thought to have been painted by St. Luke on a table top made by St. Joseph and used by the Holy Family at Nazareth. In 1430 a group of robbers (said to be Hussites) attempted to rob this priceless image. They put it onto a wagon to carry it away, but the animals pulling the cart would not move. In desperation, the robbers tried to destroy the image with their swords, inflicting a couple of "wounds" on the face of Our Lady. Interestingly, when certain monks charged with repairing the image later tried to cover the scars on Our Lady's face, the wounds only reappeared.

Consequently, the image still today bears those scars, reminding us of how much indignity is heaped upon Our Lady because she is our spiritual mother! Another example closer to our own day involved the very popular Pieta of Michelangelo in St. Peter's Basilica in Rome which was damaged with hammer blows by a distraught man angry at God.

Another equally outrageous dishonor to Our Lady in her images is to produce distorted images or make them from offensive materials. A blasphemous example of this appeared in an art gallery in Brooklyn, New York. The image of Our Lady was made of a most offensive matter and covered with obscene items! Such outrage is certainly a product of the deliberate contempt and mockery fostered by the atheistic, perverted sub-culture that exists in much of our society today. Such desecrations are terribly offensive to the Lord Jesus because they seriously offend His Mother! No doubt the punishment for these sins will also be great. This is why we need first to make reparation for the offense to Our Lord and His Holy Mother by our loving honor to them, and then pray for those who would produce such disgraceful images.

A final form of dishonor to the images of Our Lady is to forbid them to be displayed for prayer and veneration. This can happen in private homes as well as parish churches. Many churches remodeled after Vatican Council II lost much of their religious art. If you walk into some of these churches today, they resemble stark meeting halls rather than places conducive to fervent prayer and worship. They became subject to what might be called a "neo-iconoclasm," a word stemming from the Greek word for "image-breaking." In the 7th and 8th centuries, especially in the Eastern Church, there was an intense controversy over whether religious images could be used or not. Those who opposed their use said religious images were idols, and so they destroyed them (thus the title "iconoclasts"). The Second Council of Nicea (787) finally defined that religious images were worthy of veneration and ordered them to be restored. After all, they had been part of Christian worship since the earliest centuries of the Church, as paintings in the catacombs attest. In fact, one of the earliest known images of Our Lady is found on the wall of the Roman catacomb known as the Cemetery of St. Priscilla. Art experts estimate it dates back to about AD 175. It shows Our Lady seated, holding the Christ Child on her knee!

We Should Honor Our Lady's Images

We can see how important it is that we honor Our Lady for the dishonors shown her. This is our reparation. Then we must pray for those who have so tragically dishonored her, because they will face a severe judgment for such outrages. These are not usually sins of weakness, but very often involve deliberate contempt. As we practice our devotion of the Five First Saturdays, we will be offering this important reparation and intercession. At the same time, we can do even more. We should have images of Our Lady in our own homes, to remind us of her presence, and of her maternal love and care for our families. We should pray before these images of the Mother of God, especially when we gather with family members to pray her Rosary. We should encourage others to do the same. If you have children or grandchildren that, married or single, have their own homes or apartments, you might get them a favorite picture of Our Lady for Christmas, or on some other special occasion, like their wedding.

Another way to foster honor to Our Lady is to put a statue of her in your yard or on the front lawn. I am sure that many people are as impressed as I am when driving by a home with a religious statue out front that expresses the faith of those who live there.

You might also consider working with others to begin a parish or neighborhood "Pilgrim Virgin of Fatima" program, where the image of Our Lady will travel from home to home or in the parish school from classroom to classroom.

If St. Therese of Lisieux, knowing her mission in Heaven would begin soon, could request that she "Be made known everywhere," how much more would Our Lady want us to do that for her? You will only know in Heaven how many you have helped come closer to the Mother of God and our Mother, too!

SUBSCRIBE

to *Soul*

SOUL Magazine keeps you updated on the latest news from the World Apostolate of Fatima and the Catholic Church. SOUL also carries lively features on faith, prayer, Church history, the lives of the saints, Scripture and Marian devotion. It makes a wonderful gift!

SUBSCRIPTION RATES

United States
4 issues - $13.00
12 issues - $35.00

Canada
1 Year (4 issues) - $16.00
3 Years (12 issues) - $42.00

Prices subject to change without notice.

To subscribe, fill out the form below and mail with your payment to: *SOUL* Magazine, Box 976, Washington, NJ 07882.

Name ______________________________

Address ______________________________

____

City ______________________________

State ______________ Zip ______________

Now that you know the Message of Fatima, why not make a difference in the world?

Join the World Apostolate of Fatima

Pope John Paul II has said that the Fatima message is more relevant today than ever (Fatima, May 13, 1982) and that it can be synthesized in Christ's own words: "The kingdom of God is at hand. Repent, and believe in the Gospel"
(Vatican City, May 15, 1991)

WRITE: World Apostolate of Fatrima, USA, Box 976, Washington, NJ 07882
CALL: (908) 689-1700 **WEB:** www.wafusa.org

I wish to further the work of Our Lady of Fatima through the World Aposotlate of Fatima.

Name ______________________________

Address ______________________________

City ______________________________

State ______________ Zip ______________

☐ Please send me the Blue Army Pledge and information about the Apostolate.

☐ Accept my donation of $ ________ to further the work of the Blue Army.

☐ Please send me information on how to honor Our Lady in my Will.

Father Andrew Apostoli, C.F.R.

A special writer for *SOUL* magazine, Father Andrew Apostoli, C.F.R., has been a featured celebrant and homilist at Blue Army Shrine events. He has also been the Spiritual Director on numerous World Apostolate of Fatima Tours pilgrimages.

Father Apostoli, a member of the community of the Franciscan Friars of the Renewal, was ordained by Bishop Sheen in 1967. He has been active in teaching, preaching retreats and parish missions, and giving spiritual direction. He is currently an adjunct faculty member of St. Joseph Seminary, Dunwoodie, Yonkers, New York. He is well-known as an author of several books and appears regularly on Mother Angelica's Eternal Word Television Network (EWTN).

First Saturday Aid

First Saturday Aid

The World Apostolate of Fatima, USA

The Blue Army, USA

Washington, New Jersey

www.wafusa.org

(866) 513-1917

In accord with Canon 827 of the New Code of Canon Law, this publication has been submitted to a censor of the Diocese and nothing being found contrary to faith and morals, we hereby grant permission in accord with Canon 824 that it be published.

Rev. Msgr. John B. Szymanski, Vicar General
Diocese of Metuchen, March 15, 2006

N.B. The ecclesiastical permission implies nothing more than the material contained in the publication has been examined by diocesan censors and nothing contrary to faith and morals has been found therein.

2006 Revised Edition

©1989, 2006 World Apostolate of Fatima, USA/
The Blue Army, USA

Cover photos:
©World Apostolate of Fatima, USA/Blue Army, USA

Inside photos courtesy:
Photos.com and World Apostolate of Fatima Archives

Scripture references from:
The New American Bible
©Catholic Book Publishing Co.

Quotations contained in this booklet pertaining to the Apparitions and Miracle of Fatima:
Fatima in Lucia's Own Words, Volume I
©2004 Secretariado dos Pastrorinhos

ISBN 1-56036-105-0

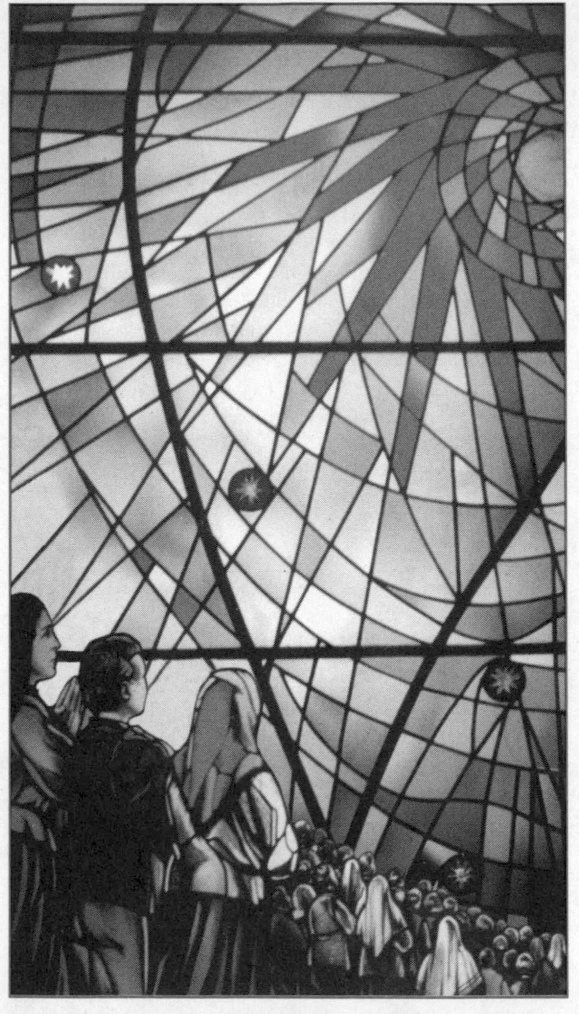

MARY'S GREAT PROMISE AT FATIMA

Mary, the Mother of God, appeared on earth to offer man the instrument of Divine Mercy – the Holy Rosary – that mighty weapon against the evils of this world which call down the wrath of God.

The place Our Lady chose was the small, rustic, obscure village in Portugal called Fatima. Here, at a site known as the *Cova da Iria*, at high noon on Sunday, May 13, 1917, she appeared to three little shepherds – Lucia, ten years old; Francisco, eight; and Jacinta, seven.

As is the custom after lunch in Portugal, they recited five decades of the Rosary. Finishing their prayers, they began to amuse themselves by building a little housc with some loose stones that lay on the ground nearby.

Suddenly, there was a bright flash of lightning in the clear sky. Dreading a thunderstorm, they gathered their flock of sheep to go home.

The children drove their sheep down the hill toward the road. Lightning flashed again as they reached a large holm oak tree. A few steps away, the children were surprised to see a lady all dressed in white, standing just above the branches of a holm oak sapling.

"She was more brilliant than the sun, and radiated a light more clear and intense than a crystal glass filled with sparkling water, when the rays of the burning sun shine through it," Sister Lucia dos Santos wrote of her experience with Our Lady.

"Do not be afraid," the Lady said, "I will do you no harm."

Her indescribably beautiful face was not sad, not happy, but serious. Her hands were clasped before her in prayer with the beads of her rosary hanging down between the fingers of the right hand. Her garments seemed to be made of white light. A mantle covered her head and the simple tunic ran to her feet. The edge of the mantle was of a stronger light which seemed to glitter like gold.

As the children came nearer to her, there followed a dialogue between the Lady and Lucia, during which the Lady invited the children to come to the *Cova* on the thirteenth day of every month until October.

The Ejaculation for Each Decade

There were six apparitions, one on the thirteenth of each month, except in August when the apparition was seen a few days later, at another place, because the children had been imprisoned by the civil authorities.

During these apparitions, Our Lady remained with the children and confided to them a secret which they were not to reveal to anyone. She told them that her home was heaven, asked for the daily recitation of the Rosary and stressed the importance of acts of reparation. She taught them the following ejaculation to be said after each decade:

O my Jesus! Forgive us. Save us from the fire of hell. Lead all souls to heaven, especially those who are in most need.

She advised Lucia to learn how to read and write and insisted on the necessity of prayer and sacrifice. She asked the children to accept all suffering in reparation for the numberless sins which offend the Divine Majesty. She ordered that a chapel be built there in her honor and declared that she was the Lady of the Rosary. In 1925, she appeared again to Lucia, repeated the message and promised to aid at the hour of death anyone who would do the following on five consecutive first Saturdays:

The Five First Saturdays of Reparation to Our Lady

1. Confession *(May be eight days before or after).*
2. Receive Holy Communion.
3. Recite Five Decades of the Rosary.
4. Meditate on the Mysteries of the Rosary for 15 Minutes.
5. The above exercises should be performed on the first Saturday of five consecutive months with the intention of making reparation to the Immaculate Heart of Mary.

No doubt, at Fatima the Lord wished to inaugurate devotion to her Immaculate Heart – the same way our Lord instituted the nine first Fridays devotion to His Sacred Heart at *Paray-le-Monial.*

During the July 13, 1917 apparition, the Holy Virgin said so kindly and so sadly: "You have seen hell where the souls of poor sinners go. To save them, God wishes to establish in the world devotion to my Immaculate Heart..."

The Five Blasphemies Against the Immaculate Heart

Our Lord revealed to Sr. Lucia that there are five ways in which people offend and blaspheme against the Immaculate Heart of Mary:

1. Against the Immaculate Conception.
2. Against Her Virginity.
3. Against the Divine Maternity, while refusing to receive Her as the Mother of mankind.

4. By those who try to publicly implant in the hearts of children indifference, disrespect, and even hate against the Immaculate Mother.
5. By those who insult Her directly in Her Sacred Images.

The Great Promise

Our Blessed Lady promised to Sister Lucia on December 10, 1925:

"Look, my daughter, at my Heart, surrounded with thorns with which ungrateful men pierce me every moment by their blasphemies and ingratitude. You at least try to console me and say that I promise to assist at the hour of death, with the graces necessary for salvation, all those who, on the first Saturday of five consecutive months, shall confess, receive Holy Communion, recite five decades of the Rosary, and keep me company for 15 minutes while meditating on the 15[1] *mysteries of the Rosary, with the intention of making reparation to me."*

The Words of Jesus on the Five First Saturdays Devotion

February 15, 1926 - The Child Jesus to Sr. Lucia concerning the devotion of the consecutive Five First Saturdays:

"It is true, my daughter, that many souls begin the First Saturdays, but few finish them, and those who do complete them do so in order to receive the graces that are promised thereby. It would please me more if they did Five with fervor and with the intention of making reparation to the Heart of your heavenly Mother, than if they did Fifteen, in a tepid and indifferent manner..."

1 Pope John Paul II added the Luminous Mysteries.

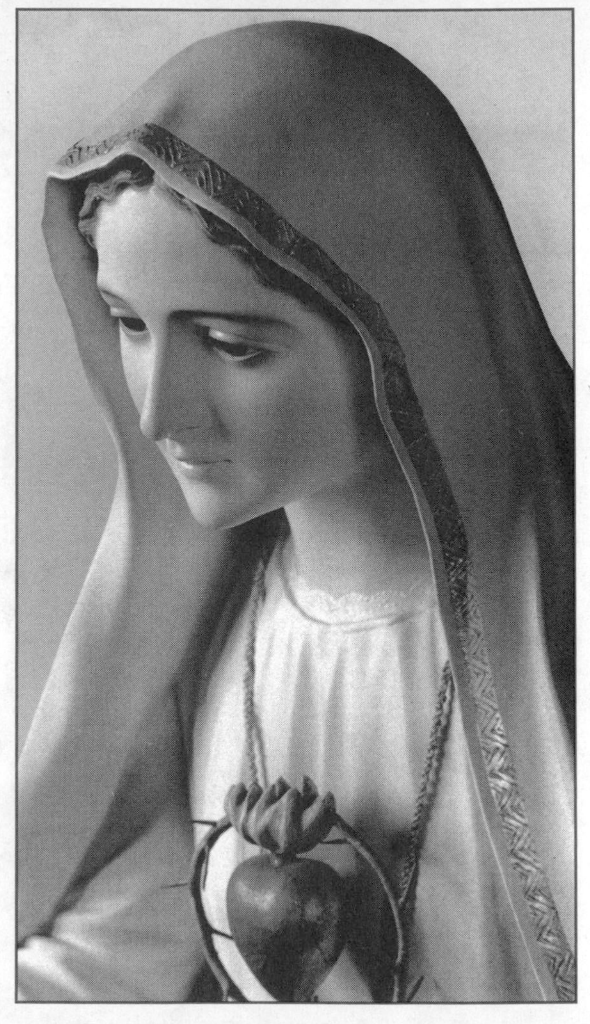

Meditations on the Twenty Mysteries

For The Five First Saturdays of Reparation to The Immaculate Heart of Mary

(Meditation on the mysteries is the most important part of the Rosary. Put yourself in the presence of Jesus or Mary and live the mysteries with them.)

Prayer to Our Lady of Fatima

Most Holy Virgin, you came to Fatima to reveal to three little children the treasure of graces hidden in the recitation of the Rosary. Inspire my heart with a sincere love of this devotion so that, by meditating on the mysteries of our redemption that it recalls, I may gather the fruits and obtain the special grace which I ask of you during these fifteen minutes for the greater glory of God, for your honor, and for the good of souls. Amen.

THE FIVE JOYFUL MYSTERIES

The Annunciation

Luke 1:26-38

Let us consider in this mystery – how the Angel Gabriel was sent from God to a town called Nazareth to a virgin, whose name was Mary, and who was betrothed to a man named Joseph. And when the angel had come to her, he said: "Hail, full of grace, the Lord is with thee. Blessed art thou among women."

When Mary had heard these words she was troubled, and kept pondering what manner of greeting this might be.

But the angel drew near and said to her, "Do not be afraid, Mary, for you have found favor with God. Behold, you will conceive in your womb and bear a son, and you shall name him Jesus. He will be great and will be called Son of the Most High."

And Mary said to the angel: "How can this be, since I have no relations with a man?"

And the angel answered and said to her, "The Holy Spirit will come upon you, and the power of the Most High will overshadow you. Therefore the child to be born will be called holy, the Son of God. And behold, Elizabeth, your relative, has also conceived a son in her old age, and this is the sixth month for her who was called barren; for nothing will be impossible for God."

Mary, bowing her head in humility, answered: "Behold, I am the handmaid of the Lord. May it be done to me according to your word." And the angel departed from her.

Prayer: *Immaculate Heart of Mary, by the message of an Angel, the Holy Spirit overshadowed you. Your most pure and virginal womb became the sacramental tabernacle sheltering the Son of God. At Fatima, the Angel of Portugal came with a message for the three shepherd children to prepare them for your heavenly visit: "Do not be afraid! I am the Angel of Peace. Pray with me: My God, I believe, I adore, I hope, and I love You! I ask pardon of You for those who do not believe, do not adore, do not hope, and do not love You." Help me to pray and live the Angel's prayer at Fatima.*

Recite: *Our Father*, once; *Hail Mary*, ten times
Glory be to the Father, once; and
O my Jesus, once.

The Visitation

Luke 1:39-56

Let us consider in this mystery – how the Blessed Virgin Mary arose and went into the hill country, to a town of Judah, to visit her cousin Elizabeth, who, in her old age, was soon to give birth to Saint John the Baptist.

No sooner did Mary enter into the house than Elizabeth, filled with the Holy Spirit, cried out with a loud voice saying, "Most blessed are you among women, and blessed is the fruit of your womb. And how does this happen to me, that the mother of my Lord should come to me? For at the moment the sound of your greeting reached my ears, the infant in my womb leaped for joy. Blessed are you who believed that what was spoken to you by the Lord would be fulfilled."

Whereupon Mary replied with that canticle of canticles, *The Magnificat.*

The Magnificat

My soul proclaims the greatness of the Lord, my spirit rejoices in God my Savior.

For he has looked upon his handmaid's lowliness; behold from now on will all ages call me blessed.

The Mighty One has done great things for me, and holy is his Name.

His mercy is from age to age to those who fear him.

He has shown might with his arm, dispersed the arrogant of mind and heart.
He has thrown down the rulers from their thrones, but lifted up the lowly.
The hungry he has filled with good things, the rich he has sent away empty.
He has helped Israel his servant, remembering his mercy according to his promise to our fathers, to Abraham and to his descendants forever.

Prayer: *Immaculate Heart of Mary, your visit to your cousin, Elizabeth, filled her heart with song and praise. At Fatima, you visited the three little shepherds. They, too, were captured by your love: "Do not be afraid. I will do you no harm. Pray the Rosary every day, in order to obtain peace for the world, and the end of the war." "When you pray the Rosary, say after each mystery: O my Jesus, forgive us, save us from the fire of hell. Lead all souls to Heaven, especially those who are most in need." Abide in my heart, also, and grant me the grace to remain faithful to your Rosary.*

Recite: *Our Father*, once; *Hail Mary*, ten times; *Glory be to the Father*, once; and *O my Jesus*, once.

The Nativity

Luke 2:1-19

Let us consider in this mystery – how Joseph and his wife, Mary, who was with Child, went to Bethlehem, the city of David, to register according to a decree sent out by the Roman emperor commanding a census of the whole world.

And it came to pass while they were there that the days for Mary to be delivered were fulfilled. But there was no room for them at the inn. Therefore, they took shelter in a stable where she brought forth her first born son and laid Him in a manger. This was the first Christmas.

A multitude of heavenly hosts sang: "Glory to God in the highest and on earth peace to those on whom His favor rests."

Shepherds came to adore the newborn king. And all who heard marveled at the things told by the shepherds. But Mary kept in mind all those things, pondering them in her heart.

Prayer: *Immaculate Heart of Mary, heaven's angels sang in jubilation to witness the birth of Our Lord. The shepherds knelt at the manger. Soon after the great star gleamed in the sky guiding the Magi. At Fatima, you promised a miracle for all to believe. The clouds parted on October 13th, and the great solar star danced through the heav-*

ens, once again showering favors of light upon the earth. Abide with me as I pray the interior prayer the little shepherds received in their hearts as they fell to their knees: "O Most Holy Trinity, I adore You!
My God, my God, I love You in the most Blessed Sacrament!"

Recite: *Our Father*, once; *Hail Mary*, ten times; *Glory be to the Father*, once; and *O my Jesus*, once.

The Presentation

Luke 2:22-39

Let us consider in this mystery – how the Blessed Virgin Mary, on the day of her purification, together with her husband Joseph, took Jesus up to the Temple in Jerusalem to present him to the Lord. They carried with them a pair of young turtledoves, an offering which the poorest were obliged to make.

Now, there was in Jerusalem a devout man named Simeon. It had been revealed to this just and devout man by the Holy Spirit that he should not see death before he had seen the Messiah.

And he came by the inspiration of the Spirit into the Temple at the time when Mary and Joseph brought in the Child Jesus.

Simeon took the Child in his arms and blessed

God saying: "Now, Master, you may let your servant go in peace, according to your word, for my eyes have seen your salvation, which you prepared in the sight of all the peoples, a light for revelation to the Gentiles, and glory for your people Israel."

Joseph and Mary marveled at the things spoken concerning Him. Simeon blessed the Holy Family, and said to Mary, "Behold, this child is destined for the fall and rise of many in Israel, and to be a sign that will be contradicted (and you yourself a sword will pierce) so that the thoughts of many hearts may be revealed."

And when they had fulfilled all things as prescribed in the Law, they returned to Nazareth.

Prayer: *Immaculate Heart of Mary, your Holy Family fulfilled all precepts of the law with profound humility and God's favored blessing, yet your own soul was to be pierced by a sword. Your words to Sr. Lucia grieve me deeply: "Look, my daughter, at my heart surrounded with thorns..." It is my great desire to console you and remove these thorns. I pray that your words to Sr. Lucia may be applied to me: "You, at least, try to console me..."*

Recite: *Our Father*, once; *Hail Mary*, ten times; *Glory be to the Father*, once; and *O my Jesus*, once.

The Finding of the Child in the Temple

Luke 2:41-52

Let us consider in this mystery – how the Blessed Virgin Mary, when Jesus was twelve years old, took Him to Jerusalem according to the custom of the Feast of the Passover. And after they had fulfilled the days, when they were returning, the boy Jesus remained in Jerusalem, and His parents did not know it.

But thinking that He was in the caravan, they had come a day's journey before it occurred to them to look for Him among their relatives and friends.

And they sought Him for a space of three days, and found Him in the Temple, sitting in the midst of the teachers, disputing with them. And all who were listening to Him were amazed at His answers.

And when Joseph and Mary saw Him they were astonished. And His mother said to Him, "Son, why have you done this to us? Your father and I have been looking for you with great anxiety."

And He said to them, "Why were you looking for me? Did you not know that I must be in my Father's house?"

He arose and returned with His parents to Nazareth, and was subject to them. And Jesus advanced in wisdom and age and grace before God and men.

Prayer: *Immaculate Heart of Mary, what joy filled your heart upon finding Him in the Temple. Intercede for me with your Divine Child that I may remain always faithful to the Church and never lose Jesus through mortal sin. If I should offend Him, may I seek the Sacrament of Reconciliation immediately with a contrite heart. I pray for the grace to respond to your request at Fatima: "Are you willing to offer yourselves to God and bear all the sufferings He wills to send you, as an act of reparation for the sins by which He is offended, and of supplication for the conversion of sinners? Then you are going to have much to suffer, but the grace of God will be your comfort."*

Recite: *Our Father*, once; *Hail Mary*, ten times; *Glory be to the Father*, once; and *O my Jesus*, once.

The Five Luminous Mysteries

The Baptism in the Jordan

Matthew 3:1-17

Let us consider in this mystery – how John the Baptist was preaching a baptism of repentance for the forgiveness of sins.

Jesus came from Galilee to the Jordan River to be baptized. Upon seeing Him, John declared that Jesus should be the one baptizing him, not John baptizing Jesus. Yet Jesus assured him that it was proper to be done this way.

After being baptized, Jesus came out of the water and immediately the heavens opened and the Spirit of God descended upon Him in the form of a dove.

Then a loud voice from heaven was heard, saying, "This is my beloved Son, with whom I am well pleased."

Prayer: *Immaculate Heart of Mary, your beloved Son did not have to be baptized for He was God Himself. For this great act of humility, God voiced His profound pleasure. At Fatima, you* *revealed to the three little shepherds that God was pleased with their sacrifices. I offer myself to you, for your promise at Fatima:*

"My Immaculate Heart will be your refuge and the way that will lead you to God." May your Immaculate Heart be my refuge so that my every thought, word, and deed may be pleasing to God.

Recite: *Our Father*, once; *Hail Mary*, ten times; *Glory be to the Father*, once; and *O my Jesus*, once.

The Wedding at Cana

John 2:1-11

Let us consider in this mystery – how a marriage occurred at Cana of Galilee. Jesus and His disciples were in attendance along with Our Blessed Mother.

When the wine began to run out, Mary told this to her Divine Son. He reminded her that the time for His ministry had not yet come. She urged the attendants to do whatever He told them.

There were six stone jars nearby that each held about 20 or 30 gallons. He instructed them to fill the jars with water to the brim. The attendants did as He said. Then Jesus told them to draw some of the water out and bring it to the chief steward. The steward did not know where it came from but tasted the water turned into wine. He then called the bridegroom, telling him that usually the good wine is served first. Then, after the guests had drunk freely, the poor wine is served. Yet he had kept the good wine until now. This was Christ's first public miracle.

Prayer: *Immaculate Heart of Mary, Jesus changed water into wine at your request. Your gracious concern for others is never-ending. As Bridegroom of the Church, Jesus revealed His glory and gave proof that He was the Messiah. At Fatima, the great Miracle of the Sun was proof of your promise. With Lucia I ask: "What do you want of me?"*

As at Cana, I abide to your request: "Do whatever He tells you."

Please pray with me, Mother. Sanctify me so I may bring others to God.

Recite: *Our Father*, once; *Hail Mary*, ten times; *Glory be to the Father*, once; and *O my Jesus*, once.

The Proclamation of The Kingdom of God

Luke 10:1-12

Let us consider in this mystery – how Jesus, after fasting forty days in the desert, traveled through the towns and villages of Galilee, proclaiming His message of belief in the gospel and repentance.

He declared that the time of fulfillment was now, and the Kingdom of Heaven was at hand. He charged the disciples to go forth to preach thus, and if they were rejected to leave that place and move on.

He warned them that He was sending them out like sheep among wolves. But He also encouraged them not to fear the opposition, because the Holy Spirit would give them the words as they proclaimed the Kingdom of Heaven on earth.

Prayer: *Immaculate Heart of Mary, you requested of Sr. Lucia that the Five First Saturdays devotion be promoted for the conversion of sinners and a means of salvation: "I promise to assist at the hour of death, with the graces necessary for salvation, all those who, on the First Saturday of five consecutive months, shall confess, receive Holy Communion, recite five decades of the Rosary, and keep me company for fifteen minutes while meditating on the fifteen mysteries of the Rosary, with the intention of making reparation to me." I realize by your words, "keep me company," that you truly are present when I respond to your request.*

Recite: *Our Father*, once; *Hail Mary*, ten times; *Glory be to the Father*, once; and *O my Jesus*, once.

The Transfiguration

Mark 9:2-8

Let us consider in this mystery – how Jesus took Peter, James and John up a high mountain to pray.

While He was praying, His face changed its appearance and His garments became dazzling white. Then two men appeared, who conversed with Him – they were Moses and Elijah.

They spoke to Him about His forthcoming passion and death in Jerusalem. The three apostles witnessed all that was happening and Peter told Jesus it was good that they were there. He offered to build three booths, one for Jesus and one each for Moses and Elijah, not knowing what he was saying. Then a cloud overshadowed them, and the three apostles were very afraid. A voice from the cloud told them that this was His Beloved Son and to listen to Him. Then Jesus came and told them to rise and not to be afraid. When they raised their heads, Jesus was alone.

Prayer: *Immaculate Heart of Mary, your appearance to the little shepherds at Fatima "was more brilliant than the sun." Opening your hands, you communicated by a reflection emanating from them, a light so intimate, penetrating their hearts to the depths of their souls, enabling them to see themselves in God, "who was that light." Francisco declared: "But what filled me with the greatest joy of all was to see God in this light* *which Our Lady was directing into our hearts." Please direct my ways, Mother, so my heart may be filled with God.*

Recite: *Our Father*, once; *Hail Mary*, ten times; *Glory be to the Father*, once; and *O my Jesus*, once.

The Institution of the Eucharist

Luke 22:14-20

Let us consider in this mystery – how at the Last Supper Christ gave Himself to us.

He took the bread, blessed it and gave it to His apostles saying "This is my body, which is given for you." Next, He took the cup of wine and said it was the new covenant in His blood, which was to be shed on behalf of many for the forgiveness of sins. Here, Christ declares the old covenant with Moses is now replaced with a new covenant. He leaves us His Body and Blood for all generations to share.

Prayer: *Immaculate Heart of Mary, the great gift of the Holy Eucharist, the Real Presence of Jesus, was communicated to the three little shepherds. The Angel appeared for the third time holding a chalice in his left hand, with a Host suspended above it, from which some drops of blood fell into the sacred chalice. Kneeling he prayed "Most Holy Trinity, Father, Son, and Holy Spirit, I* *adore you profoundly and I offer You the most precious Body, Blood, Soul and Divinity of Jesus Christ, present in all the tabernacles of the world, in reparation for the outrages, sacrileges, and indifference by which He is offended..." I beg you, dear Mother, please flood my soul with an increase of faith.*

Recite: *Our Father*, once; *Hail Mary*, ten times; *Glory be to the Father*, once; and *O my Jesus*, once.

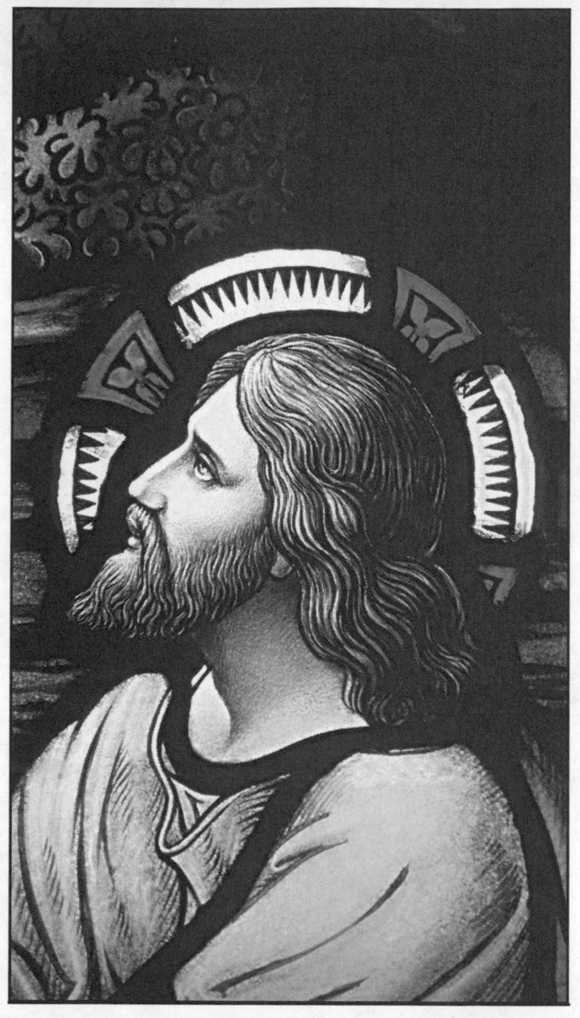

The Five Sorrowful Mysteries

The Agony in the Garden

Matthew 26:36-46

Let us consider in this mystery – how on Holy Thursday after Jesus had instituted the Holy Eucharist, accompanied by His disciples, He went to Mount Olivet, where there was a garden called Gethsemane.

And He said to them, "My soul is sorrowful even to death. Remain here and keep watch with me." Then falling upon His face, He prayed, saying: "My Father, if it is possible, let this cup pass from me; yet, not as I will but as you will."

Thus Jesus prayed three times, and fell into an agony and His sweat became as drops of blood, trickling down to the ground. And there appeared an angel, who strengthened Him. Then Jesus arose, found His disciples asleep and said to them: "Are you still sleeping and taking your rest? Behold, the hour is at hand when the Son of Man is to be handed over to sinners. Get up, let us go. Look, my betrayer is at hand."

Prayer: *Immaculate Heart of Mary, by the overwhelming anguish and grief Our Savior suffered in His Agony, I pray for the grace to respond to your request at Fatima: "Sacrifice yourselves for sinners, and say many times, especially whenever you make some sacrifice: O Jesus, it is for love of You, for the conversion of sinners, and in reparation for the sins committed against the Immaculate Heart of Mary."*

Recite: *Our Father*, once; *Hail Mary*, ten times;
Glory be to the Father, once; and
O my Jesus, once.

The Scourging at the Pillar

Luke 23:1-22 and John 19:1

Let us consider in this mystery – how, in the early morning, Jesus was led before the Roman Governor, Pontius Pilate, to be tried.

But Pilate knew that Jesus had been delivered by the envy of the priests and Pharisees and He said to them: "You brought this man to me and accused him of inciting the people to revolt. I have conducted my investigation in your presence and have not found this man guilty of the charges you have brought against him, nor did Herod, for he sent him back to us. So no capital crime has been committed by him. Therefore, I shall have him flogged and then release him."

Jesus was then led away, stripped of His garments and tied to a pillar, where He was most inhumanly scourged by cruel executioners.

His Precious Blood streamed from His flesh mangled by so many blows.

Prayer: *Immaculate Heart of Mary, Jesus suffered this inhuman punishment to atone for the sins of man. You revealed to Jacinta that many souls go to hell because of sins of the flesh. Grant me the virtue of purity so I may never cause myself or my neighbor the loss of heaven. May the words of Jacinta become my own: "But I offer everything for sinners, and in reparation to the Immaculate Heart of Mary…{Our Lord and our Lady} greatly love those who suffer for the conversion of sinners."*

Recite: *Our Father*, once; *Hail Mary*, ten times; *Glory be to the Father*, once; and *O my Jesus*, once.

The Crowning with Thorns

Matthew 27:26-31

Let us consider in this mystery – how, after Jesus had been scourged, Pilate delivered Him up to be crucified.

The soldiers of the procurator took Jesus into the praetorium and gathered together about Him the whole cohort.

And they stripped Him of His garments and put on Him a scarlet cloak; and plaiting a crown of thorns, they put it upon His head, and a reed into His right hand; and bending the knee before Him they mocked Him, saying "Hail, King of the Jews!" Others spat on Him, and took the reed and struck His head.

At last, they blindfolded Him and renewed all manner of insult and injury.

Prayer: *Immaculate Heart of Mary, at Tuy, Sr. Lucia was blessed to see the Trinity, with Jesus Crucified, above the altar. His Precious drops of Blood were spilling into His chalice. From His side, rivers of water spilled forth over the altar with the words, 'Graces and Mercy.' Your Immaculate Heart was there, also. I pray, be with me as I approach the altar that I may receive worthily His grace and mercy, remembering the words of the Angel at*

Fatima: "Take and drink the body and blood of Jesus Christ, horribly outraged by ungrateful men! Make reparation for their crimes and console your God."

Recite: *Our Father*, once; *Hail Mary*, ten times; *Glory be to the Father*, once; and *O my Jesus*, once.

The Carrying of the Cross

Mark 15:20-26

Let us consider in this mystery – how the soldiers seized Jesus, removed His scarlet cloak and put on His own garments.

A heavy cross is placed upon His bleeding shoulder and He is led away to be crucified. Each step on this agonizing journey causes terrific pain throughout His torn body. The cross cut deeply into His wounded shoulder. He struggled along to Calvary, stumbling and falling beneath the heavy weight of the cross amidst the shouts and jeers of His own people. Finally, they came to a place called *Golgotha*, that is, the Place of the Skull.

Prayer: *Immaculate Heart of Mary, with compassion I recall how painful it must have been for you to see Jesus suffering for the sins of man. Inspire* *me with a keen sorrow for my past sins. In moments of trial, may I remember your promise: "Are you suffering a great deal? Do not lose hope, I will not forsake you." Your words to the three little shepherds bring forth your maternal concern for me: "Do not offend the Lord anymore, because He is already so much offended." I desire never to offend God again.*

Recite: *Our Father*, once; *Hail Mary*, ten times; *Glory be to the Father*, once; and *O my Jesus*, once.

The Crucifixion

Luke 23:33-46 and John 19:16-30

Let us consider in this mystery – how, when Jesus reached the top of Mount Calvary, He was stripped of His garments and then cruelly nailed to the cross.

Then two robbers were crucified with Him, one on His right hand and one on His left. And the people mocked Jesus, saying: "He saved others, let him save himself if he is the chosen one, the Messiah of God."

Jesus spoke: "Father forgive them, for they know not what they do."

One of the thieves who was crucified with Him blasphemed Jesus saying: "Are you not the

Messiah? Save yourself and us."

But the other rebuked him and exclaimed: "Have you no fear of God, for you are subject to the same condemnation? And indeed, we have been condemned justly, for the sentence we received corresponds to our crimes, but this man has done nothing criminal." Then he said: "Jesus, remember me when you come into your kingdom."

Jesus answered: "Amen, I say to you, today you will be with me in Paradise."

Then Jesus looked down from His cross and beheld His Mother, Mary, and John, His beloved disciple. Jesus said to His Mother: "Woman, behold your son." And to John, He said, "Behold your mother." From that hour John took the mother of Jesus to himself, as if she were his own mother.

And when the sixth hour came, there was darkness over the whole land until the ninth hour. And at the ninth hour Jesus cried out in a loud voice, saying: "My God, My God, why have you forsaken me?"

Soon afterward Jesus exclaimed: "I thirst." Then a soldier took a sponge soaked in common wine, put it on a reed and gave it to Him to drink. After He had taken the wine Jesus said: "It is finished." Then He cried out in a loud voice: "Father, into your hands I commend My spirit." He then bowed His head and died.

Prayer: *Immaculate Heart of Mary, for the sake of the bitter anguish you suffered at the foot of the cross, help me to be charitable to all who offend me and to offer and make sacrifices in supplication for the conversion of sinners. At Fatima, you showed the three shepherd children a vision of hell: "You have seen hell where the souls of poor sinners go...." Grant me the grace to overcome evil in moments of temptation, especially at my last hour. Your words to Sr. Lucia sustain me: "I promise to assist at the hour of death, with the graces necessary for salvation, all those who, on the first Saturday of five consecutive months...."*

Recite: *Our Father*, once; *Hail Mary*, ten times; *Glory be to the Father*, once; and *O my Jesus*, once.

The Five Glorious Mysteries

The Resurrection

Matthew 28:1-7

Let us consider in this mystery – how, as the morning of the third day dawned, Our Lord Jesus Christ rose from the dead, and came forth from the grave in all His glory.

At the same time, there was a great earthquake. An angel of the Lord came down from heaven, rolled away the stone from the sepulchre and sat upon it. His countenance was as lightning and His garments white as snow. When the guards saw the angel, they were struck with terror and fell to the ground as if they were dead.

Meanwhile, three pious women brought spices, that they might anoint the body of Jesus. But when they came to the sepulchre they saw that it was empty. And the angel said to them: "Do not be afraid! I know that you are seeking Jesus the crucified. He is not here, for He has been raised just as He said. Come and see the place where He lay. Then go quickly and tell His disciples, 'He has been raised from the dead, and He is going before you to Galilee; there you will see Him.' Behold, I have told you."

Prayer: *Immaculate Heart of Mary, the angel announced to three pious women who came to anoint Our Lord, "Do not be afraid!...." At Fatima, the angel prepared the three shepherd children to see God with the same greeting: "Do not be afraid." It is my desire to keep company with those pleasing to God, so I, too, may hear the words, "Do not be afraid" when I see Him in His Glory. Please grant me the grace to avoid all occasions of sin.*

Recite: *Our Father*, once; *Hail Mary*, ten times; *Glory be to the Father*, once; and *O my Jesus*, once.

The Ascension

Matthew 28:18-20 and Acts 1:9-12

Let us consider in this mystery – how on the fortieth day Jesus appeared to his eleven apostles for the last time in the upper room at Jerusalem.

He ate with them and told them to wait in Jerusalem until they would receive the Holy Spirit. And He said to them: "All power in heaven and on earth has been given to me. Go, therefore, and make disciples of all nations, baptizing them in the name of the Father, and of the Son, and of the Holy Spirit, teaching them to observe all that I have commanded you. And behold, I am with you always, until the end of the age."

Then He went with His apostles to Mount Olivet. Here, He raised His hands and blessed them. And it came to pass that, while He blessed them, He began to ascend, and was raised to heaven. The apostles adored Him and looked after Jesus, until a cloud hid Him from their sight.

But as they were looking after Him, two angels appeared to them, and said: "Men of Galilee, why are you standing there looking at the sky? This Jesus who has been taken up from you into heaven will return in the same way as you have seen Him going into heaven." The apostles rejoiced at these tidings, and they went forth and preached, while the Lord worked with them and confirmed the preaching by the signs that followed.

Prayer: *Immaculate Heart of Mary, you fulfilled your promise in October to perform a miracle. The clouds parted in heaven and the little shepherds were graced to see you with St. Joseph who was holding the Child Jesus in his arms. It is my great desire to go to Heaven, yet I realize by your words for blessed Francisco how deficient I am! "He [Francisco] will go there [Heaven] too, but* *he must say many Rosaries." I pray, dear Mother, for the gift of prayer and self-denial, so I may attend to the Angel at Fatima: "What are you doing? Pray, pray very much! The most Holy Hearts of Jesus and Mary have designs of mercy on you. Offer prayers and sacrifices constantly to the Most High!"*

Recite: *Our Father*, once; *Hail Mary*, ten times; *Glory be to the Father*, once; and *O my Jesus*, once.

The Descent of The Holy Spirit upon the Apostles

Acts 2:1-47

Let us consider in this mystery – when the days of Pentecost were drawing to a close, the apostles, disciples and Mary, the Mother of Jesus, were again assembled together in the upper room.

And suddenly on the tenth day there came a sound from heaven, as of a mighty rushing wind, and it filled the whole house where they were sitting.

There appeared to them parted tongues as of fire, which settled upon each one of them, and they were filled with the Holy Spirit, and began to speak in diverse tongues.

Now there were staying at Jerusalem, Jews and devout men from every nation under the heaven.

And when this sound was heard the multitude gathered and were bewildered in mind, because each heard them speaking in his own language.

They were all amazed and marveled, saying: "Are not all these people who are speaking Galilean? Then how does each of us hear them in his own native language? We are Parthians, Medes, and Elamites, inhabitants of Mesopotamia, Judea and Cappadocia, Pontus and Asia, Phrygia and Pamphylia, Egypt and the districts of Libya near Cyrene, as well as travelers from Rome, both Jews and converts to Judaism, Cretans and Arabs, yet we hear them speaking in our own tongues of the mighty acts of God."

Peter stood forth, and said: "Repent and be baptized, every one of you, in the name of Jesus Christ for the forgiveness of your sins; and you will receive the gift of the Holy Spirit. For the promise is made to you and to your children and to all those far off, whomever the Lord our God will call."

Many believed and were baptized; and the same day about three thousand were received into the Church.

Prayer: *Immaculate Heart of Mary, Sr. Lucia received lights concerning the Holy Trinity which she was not permitted to reveal. It is my heartfelt desire to obtain the virtues necessary to be pleasing to God. Please ask the Holy Spirit Whom Christ* *promised to His apostles and to the world, the gift of fortitude that I may have the courage to be diligent in the pursuit of knowledge and honest in its use. Enlighten my understanding, make me prudent in my undertakings, courageous in adversity and humble in prosperity. I join with the little shepherds in their prayer "O most Holy Trinity, I adore you! My God, my God, I love You in the most Blessed Sacrament!"*

Recite: *Our Father*, once; *Hail Mary*, ten times; *Glory be to the Father*, once; and *O my Jesus*, once.

The Assumption

Revelation 12:1-6

Let us consider in this mystery – how the Blessed Virgin Mary, preserved by a singular privilege from the stain of original sin, was also exempt from that common curse on sinful man, "For you are dirt, and unto dirt you shall return." (Gen. 3:19)

God would not permit her virginal body, from which His own Son took human form, to return to dust. It was the Almighty's wish that her mortal body be assumed into heaven to be reunited with her most pure soul amid the highest demonstrations of jubilee and triumph.

Prayer: *Immaculate Heart of Mary, your appearance above the Cova Tree caused many to question the sincerity of the three little shepherds. However, even nature responded to your grace, for the little branch upon which you stood assumed your heavenly fragrance. I pray for the grace to be emptied of myself so I, too, may be assumed by your holy fragrance. I realize it was through their purity they were blessed to see you "ascend toward the east," into the heavens.*

Recite: *Our Father*, once; *Hail Mary*, ten times; *Glory be to the Father*, once; and *O my Jesus*, once.

The Coronation
Judith 15:9-10

Let us consider in this mystery – how the Glorious Virgin Mary, upon entering the Kingdom of Heaven, was greeted by her Divine Son who placed her by the heavenly throne of the Most Holy Trinity. Exalted above all the choirs of angels, He crowned her before the court of Heaven with the diadem of eternal glory.

At that moment Mary, the Mother of Jesus, is clearly seen as the great Mediatrix of Graces, the lover of mankind, the Refuge of Sinners.

Prayer: *Immaculate Heart of Mary, yours is truly a pilgrim heart. The words of Pope Pius XII ring true today and give perpetual reverence to your name: "Since I crowned Our Lady Queen of the world, she has gone forth like a pilgrim virgin. And the graces and miracles….she has performed along the way are such that we can hardly believe what we are seeing with our own eyes." As Queen of all Hearts, please bless my path and lead me in the ways of God.*

Recite: *Our Father*, once; *Hail Mary*, ten times
Glory be to the Father, once; and
O my Jesus, once.

Prayers at the Conclusion of the Rosary

Hail, Holy Queen

Hail, Holy Queen, Mother of Mercy, our life, our sweetness and our hope. To thee do we cry, poor banished children of Eve. To thee do we send up our sighs, mourning and weeping in this valley of tears.

Turn then, most gracious advocate, thine eyes of mercy towards us; and after this, our exile, show unto us the blessed fruit of thy womb, Jesus. O clement, O loving, O sweet Virgin Mary!

R. *Pray for us, O most holy Mother of God.*

V. That we may be worthy of the promises of Christ.

Let us Pray:

O God, Whose only begotten Son, by His life, death and resurrection, has purchased for us the rewards of eternal life; grant we beseech Thee, that meditating on these mysteries of the most Holy Rosary of the Blessed Virgin Mary, we may imitate what they contain, and obtain what they promise. Through the same Christ, Our Lord. Amen.

Prayer for the Intention of the Holy Father

Our Father, once;
Hail Mary, once;
and *Glory Be,* once. *Amen.*

Prayer of Consecration

Vouchsafe to reign, O most loving Mother, over this family, that it may be your own, and over each one of us who is, and wishes to be, yours in prosperity and in adversity, in joy and in sorrow, in health and in sickness, in life and in death. Reign over our wills, leading them in the path of virtue traced by you for us with your example, in a perfect submission to the will of God.

Reign in our hearts which desire nothing but to be consumed with love for you and Jesus. We want to be pure like you; we want to atone for so many crimes committed against you and against Jesus.

Bring to our country and to the whole world the kingdom of peace in justice and charity.

Therefore, we now promise to imitate your virtues in the practice of a Christian life, and to offer you the wreath of our Rosary and the flowers of our sacrifices, in the spirit of Reparation and Penance.

PRAYERS FROM FATIMA

The prayers taught at Fatima are simple in structure, profound in depth. To a world poor and needy in Faith and Charity these prayers stress ancient Truths of our Holy Catholic Church – especially concerning the Holy Eucharist and Mary, the Immaculate Mother of God.

Pardon Prayer

My God, I believe, I adore, I hope, and I love You! I beg pardon for those who do not believe, do not adore, do not hope, and do not love You.

Sacrifice Prayer

Our Lady requested this prayer be said many times, especially whenever we make some sacrifice:

O Jesus, it is for love of You, for the conversion of sinners, and in reparation for the sins committed against the Immaculate Heart of Mary.

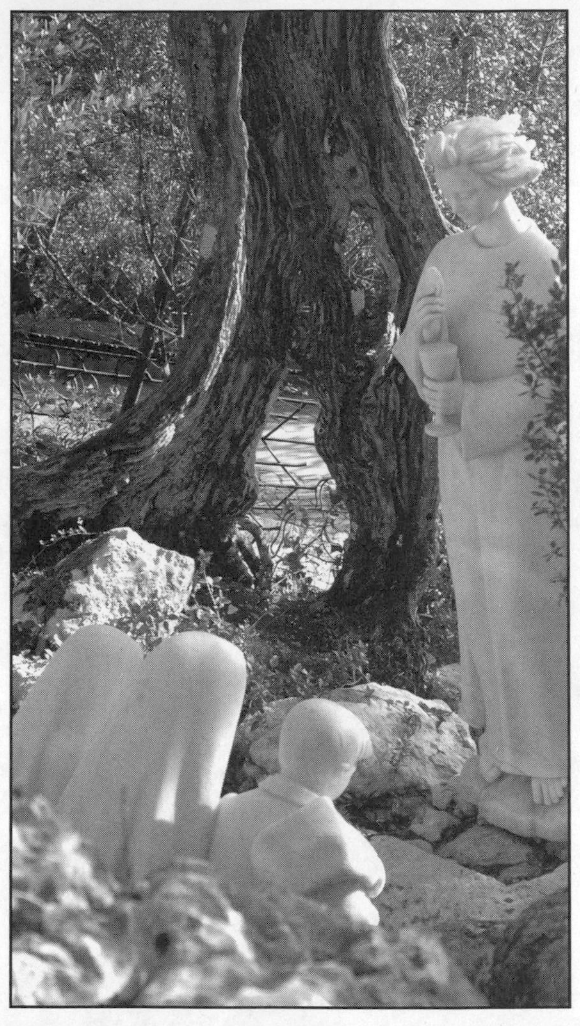

Eucharistic Prayer

This prayer stresses that most beautiful truth – the all-powerful, all-loving God upon our very altars.

Most Holy Trinity, I adore You! My God, My God, I love You in the Most Blessed Sacrament.

The Angel's Prayer

With the Blessed Sacrament suspended in the air, the angel at Fatima prostrated himself, and recited the prayer:

Most Holy Trinity, Father, Son and Holy Spirit, I adore You profoundly, and I offer You the most precious Body, Blood, Soul, and Divinity of Jesus Christ, present in all the tabernacles of the world, in reparation for the outrages, sacrileges and indifference with which He Himself is offended. And, through the infinite merits of His most Sacred Heart, and the Immaculate Heart of Mary, I beg of You the conversion of poor sinners.

The Decade Prayer

O my Jesus! Forgive us, save us from the fire of hell. Lead all souls to heaven, especially those who are most in need.

Prayer for the Canonization of Blessed Francisco and Jacinta

Most Holy Trinity, Father, Son and Holy Spirit, I adore you profoundly and I thank You for the apparitions of the Most Holy Virgin of Fatima.

By the infinite merits of the Sacred Heart of Jesus and through the intercession of the Immaculate Heart of Mary I implore you - if it should be for Your greater glory and the good of our souls - to glorify in the sight of Your Holy Church Blessed Francisco and Jacinta, granting us through their intercession the grace which we implore. Amen.

Recite: *Our Father*, once;
Hail Mary, ten times; and
Glory be to the Father, once.

Sister Lucia on the Importance of the Rosary

Reprinted from
Calls from the Message of Fatima
by Lucia of Jesus and of the Immaculate Heart

And Our Lady ended her Message on that 13th May 1917 with the words: "Pray the Rosary every day, in order to obtain peace for the world, and the end of the war."

Why should Our Lady have told us to say the Rosary every day rather than telling us to go to Mass every day?

This is a question that I have been asked many times, and it is one which I should like to reply to here. I cannot be absolutely certain of the answer, as Our Lady did not explain, and it never occurred to me to ask. Hence, I say only what I think, and what I have come to understand about it all. In fact, I willingly leave all interpretation of the meaning of the Message to Holy Church, because it pertains to the Church to do so; hence, I humbly and willingly submit myself to whatever It may wish to say or to correct, amend or declare.

As regards the question referred to above, I think that God is Father; and as Father He adapts Himself to the needs and possibilities of his children. Now, if God, through Our Lady, had asked us to go to Mass and receive Holy Communion every day, there would undoubtedly have been a great many people who would have said, quite rightly, that this was not possible. Some, on account of the distance separating them from the nearest church where Mass was celebrated; others on account of the circumstances of their lives, their state in life, their job, the state of their health, etc. On the other hand, to pray the Rosary is something everybody can do, rich and poor, wise and ignorant, great and small.

All people of good will can, and must, say the Rosary every day. Why? In order to put ourselves into contact with God, to thank Him for his benefits and ask Him for the graces we need. It is the prayer which places us in familiar contact with God like the son that goes to his father to thank him for the gifts he has received, to talk to him about his special concerns, to receive his guidance, his help, his support and his blessing.

Since we all need to pray, God asks of us, as a kind of daily installment, a prayer which is within our reach: the Rosary, which can be recited either in common or in private, either in Church in the presence of the Blessed Sacrament or at home, either with the rest of the family or alone, either when travelling or while walking quietly in the fields. A mother of a family can say the Rosary while she rocks her baby's cradle or does the housework. Our day has twenty four hours in it. It is not asking a great deal to set aside a quarter of an hour for the spiritual life, for our intimate and familiar converse with God.

On the other hand, I believe that, after the liturgical prayer of the Holy Sacrifice of the Mass, the praying of the Rosary, in view of the origin and sublime nature of the prayers used in it, and of the mysteries of the Redemption which we recall and on which we meditate during each decade, is the most pleasing prayer that we can offer to God, and one which is most advantageous to our own souls. If such were not the case, Our Lady would not have asked for it so insistently.

When I speak of saying the five or fifteen mysteries of the Rosary, I do not want to give the impression that God requires us to count the number of times that we address our supplications, our praise or our thanksgiving to Him. God certainly does not expect this of us: in Him everything is present! But we need to count, in order to have a clear and vivid idea of what we are doing, and to know positively whether or not we have completed what we had planned to offer to God each day, in order to preserve and enhance our relationship of intimacy with God and, by this means, preserve and enhance in ourselves our faith, hope and charity.

I would add that even those people who are able to assist at Mass every day should not, for this reason, neglect to say their daily Rosary. Obviously, the time they devote to saying the Rosary is not the same as that during which they are assisting at Mass. For such people, praying the Rosary can be looked upon as a way of preparing themselves to participate better in the Eucharist, or as an act of thanksgiving after it.

I don't know, but from the little knowledge that I have from my contact with people in general, I see that there are very few truly contemplative souls who preserve and maintain within themselves a relationship of intimate familiarity with God which prepares them for the worthy reception of Christ in the Eucharist. Thus, vocal prayer is necessary for them too, meditated, pondered and reflected upon as much as possible, as the Rosary should be.

There are many fine prayers that can be used as a means of preparing to receive Christ in the Eucharist, and of maintaining our intimate relationship with God. But I do not think that we shall find one more suited to people in general than the praying of the five or fifteen mysteries of the Rosary. For example, the prayer of the Liturgy of the Hours is marvellous, but I do not think it is accessible to all, nor that some of the psalms that one recites will be readily understood by all. It requires a certain degree of instruction and preparation which cannot be expected of all.

Perhaps for all these reasons, and others that we are unaware of, God, who is our Father and understands better than we do the needs of His children, chose to stoop to the simple ordinary level of all of us in asking for the daily recitation of the Rosary, in order to smooth for us the way to Him.

Finally, bearing in mind all that the Magisterium of the Church has said to us over the years about the praying of the Rosary – I shall remind you of some of these things further on – and what God, through the Message, has asked us for so insistently, we can conclude that the Rosary is the form of vocal prayer which is most suited to people in general, which we must appreciate, and which we must make every effort never to abandon. God and Our Lady know better than anyone else what is most appropriate for us and what we most need. Moreover, it will be a powerful means of helping us to preserve our faith, hope and charity.

Even for those people who do not know how, or who are not able to recollect themselves sufficiently to meditate, the simple act of taking the rosary in their hands in order to pray is already to become mindful of God, and the mention in each decade of a mystery of the life of Christ recalls Him to their minds; this in turn will light in their souls the gentle light of faith which supports the still smouldering wick, preventing it from extinguishing itself altogether.

On the other hand, those who give up saying the Rosary and who do not go to daily Mass, have nothing to sustain them, and so end up by losing themselves in the materialism of earthly life.

Thus the Rosary is the prayer which God, through his Church and Our Lady, has recommended most insistently to us all, as a road to and gateway of salvation: "Pray the Rosary every day" (Our Lady, 13th May 1917).

Ave Maria!

How to Pray the Rosary

Make the Sign of the Cross.

1. While holding the crucifix in the hand, recite the Apostles Creed.
2. On the first large bead, recite the Our Father.
3. On the three small beads, recite the Hail Mary for an increase of Faith, Hope, and Charity.
4. Recite the Glory Be to The Father.
5. Call to mind the first mystery and reflect upon it; then recite on the same large bead the Our Father.
6. On the ten small beads, recite the Hail Mary, keeping in mind the mystery.
7. Recite the Glory Be to the Father.
8. After each decade, "O My Jesus. . ."
9. When the fifth decade is completed, the Rosary is concluded with the Hail, Holy Queen.

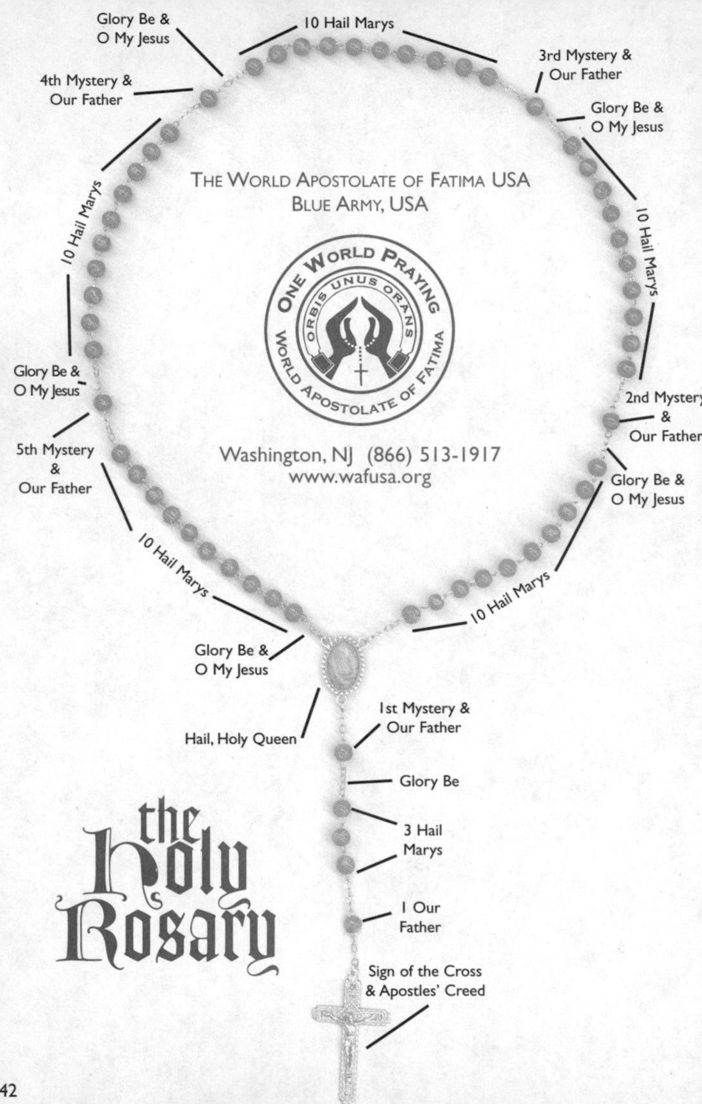

Glory Be &
O My Jesus
10 Hail Marys
3rd Mystery &
Our Father
4th Mystery &
Our Father
Glory Be &
O My Jesus
10 Hail Marys
THE WORLD APOSTOLATE OF FATIMA USA
BLUE ARMY, USA
10 Hail Marys
ONE WORLD PRAYING
ORBIS UNUS ORANS
WORLD APOSTOLATE OF FATIMA
Glory Be &
O My Jesus
2nd Mystery
&
Our Father
5th Mystery
&
Our Father
Washington, NJ (866) 513-1917
www.wafusa.org
Glory Be &
O My Jesus
10 Hail Marys
10 Hail Marys
Glory Be &
O My Jesus
Hail, Holy Queen
1st Mystery &
Our Father
Glory Be
3 Hail
Marys
I Our
Father
Sign of the Cross
& Apostles' Creed
the Holy Rosary

Part 4:

Fr. Andrew Apostoli, C.F.R.

Meditate on the Mysteries

After asking us to confess our sins, receive Jesus in Holy Communion and pray one Rosary, Our Lady then asked that we "keep [her] company for 15 minutes while meditating on the mysteries of the Rosary. "All 4 of these practices make up the Five First Saturdays devotion, and all of them must be carried out "with the intention of making reparation" to Our Lady for all the blasphemies and ingratitude she suffers from evil and ungrateful people. The Child Jesus later appeared to Sister Lucia on February 15, 1926, and explained to her that there are five ways in which people offend and blaspheme against the Immaculate Heart of Mary:

(1) against Her Immaculate Conception

(2) against Her perpetual Virginity

(3) against Her being Mother of God and our Mother, too

(4) by those who publicly implant in the hearts of children indifference, disrespect and even hate against their Immaculate Mother

(5) by those who insult Her directly in Her sacred images.

What is "Meditation"?

Probably of all 4 of the things Our Lady requested, meditating on the sacred mysteries of the Rosary will be the most challenging for Catholics. They would be accustomed to going to Confession, receiving Holy Communion and praying the Rosary. But how do we "meditate"?

In general, to meditate means to reflect on something, to think about some idea or event or situation in life, whether past or present. People meditate, often without realizing it, on things that others have said to them or things that they have experienced. They then try to realize what impact these words or events have already had upon their lives or what they may expect even for the future.

When it comes to prayer, meditation is a step in the normal development of the stages of prayer. When we looked at the third part of Our Lady's spiritual formation program for the Five First Saturdays Devotion, mainly, to pray the rosary, we considered the first three simple steps of growth in prayer. We said that a person begins with reciting "formal prayers" that others have composed. In praying the Rosary, we use very beautiful and important formal prayers such as the Our Father, the Hail Mary, the Glory Be to the Father, the Creed, the Hail Holy Queen, and the "Decade Prayer" which Our Lady taught us to pray after each decade of the Rosary. These formal prayers compose what we called the "Prayer of the Lips" because we recite them.

As prayer develops, we come to the "Prayer of the Mind" and this is meditation. When we meditate in prayer, we can focus on basically one of two things. Sometimes we meditate upon a truth or teaching of our Catholic faith such as Jesus' presence in the Blessed Sacrament, or the role of the Holy Father as the supreme teacher and authority in the Catholic Church. As an example of meditating on a truth of the Catholic faith, let us focus on the Catholic belief of Jesus' Real Presence —Body, Blood, Soul, and Divinity – in the Most Blessed Sacrament. We might begin to meditate or reflect on this profound truth with questions like: Am I sufficiently aware of Jesus' presence in the Blessed Sacrament? Does this make me more reverent and respectful when I am in Church before the Blessed Sacrament? Am I aware of His great love for me that moved Him to give me the Gift of Himself in Holy Communion? Knowing that Jesus Himself is present in every Mass, do I go to Mass faithfully each Sunday and Holy Day? Am I conscious during the week of living a good Christian life so as to be prepared to receive Jesus worthily at Mass on the following Sunday? Do I respect Jesus enough that I would never receive Him if I am in a state of mortal sin?

When we pray the Rosary, we do have some truths of our faith that come through in the mysteries. For example, we Catholics believe in the resurrection of the dead. When we meditate on the first Glorious Mystery, we meditate on Jesus' resurrection. This can allow us to reflect on our own resurrection with questions such as: Do I firmly believe that Jesus has risen from the dead? Do I believe that Jesus will raise up my body on the last day, and that my body and soul will be reunited and I hope to be with Jesus forever in Heaven? Does my faith in the resurrection help me to conquer fear of trials and sufferings for the sake of Jesus since I believe I will be with Him in glory in Heaven? Reflections like these can be helpful as we pray various mysteries of the Rosary.

Meditating on a Gospel Story

However, meditating on the mysteries can also take another form. Our second way of meditating on the mysteries of the Rosary is to reflect on the incident or event and the people involved in such a way as to draw a lesson about Christian virtue or receive an inspiration to love God and do good for our neighbor. All of the stories of the Rosary mysteries can be looked at as events relating to the life of Jesus, Mary, and the Church. Many people like to imagine the scene as a picture in their mind. This is using our imagination to help us to meditate. Another way to achieve this effect is to look at a picture of each mystery of the Rosary as we recite that mystery. A third way that can be helpful is even to read verses of scripture relating to that mystery before each Hail Mary in the decade of the mystery. This is called a "Scriptural Rosary."

After we have the scene of the story either in our imagination or in a picture we are looking at, there are two ways to reflect on the story. One is to think about what happened in the life of Jesus and Mary, including what was said, and then applying it to our own life. Let us take the Second Luminous Mystery as an example, The Wedding Feast at Cana. We can reflect on the scene that Jesus has come with six of His new disciples to a wedding feast at which Our Lady was also present. From the circumstances of the Cana miracle, it seems Our Lady may have had some hand in providing what was needed for the wedding celebration. She makes a comment to her Son: "They have no wine." Then we think of Jesus seemingly telling her He cannot get involved in this situation "because His hour has not yet come," meaning that it was not yet the time for Him to reveal His identity as the Son of God through the miracles He would work. We next reflect on the fact that Mary does not hesitate, despite her Son's answer, to reach out in trust with the last recorded words we have of her in the Bible, "Do whatever He tells you." Jesus goes on then to work His first miracle by changing water into a "choice wine" for the wedding feast. What do we learn from this meditation? Some points would include: imitating Our Lady's concern for those who are in need, especially in spiritual need; persevering in our prayerful requests of the Lord even if He does not at first say "yes"; trusting that the Lord can help us in all of our needs, especially in family life. Such reflections as these can enrich our understanding of the story of each Gospel mystery so that as we are praying the Hail Marys with our lips, our mind is growing in awareness of the rich treasures contained in the Gospel stories.

A second way we can reflect on the Gospel stories of the mysteries is to put ourselves into that story as if we were there when it actually happened. When this author was a young boy, there was a television program entitled, "You Are There." The program showed different events in the history of the United States and the world with characters who reenacted what was said and done at those events. However, there was one difference. The narrator would address questions to various individuals in the story and they would answer these questions so as to give a fuller explanation of what was happening. We can do the same with the Gospel stories of the Rosary mysteries because we can imagine ourselves present at these events, seeing what was happening and hearing what was said. It was as if the people in the story were speaking to us or that we ourselves were taking part in the events that were unfolding. Let us use an example of thinking of the Third Joyful Mystery, the Birth of Jesus. One could imagine oneself as one of the shepherds coming to see the Child Who had been proclaimed by a beautiful choir of angels. What joy might one experience in one's heart! What amazement might we not experience in union with the shepherds when they looked for the first time upon this Child Who was called a "Savior" born for them! What humility, what gratitude, what joy might not well up in our own hearts as we place ourselves in this story.

Or perhaps we could imagine ourselves one of the Magi who brought their gifts to present to the "newborn King." One might imagine oneself honoring Jesus as King of their own life whose Kingship was symbolized by the gift of gold! Or another might imagine adoring Jesus' Divinity, symbolized by the gift of frankincense which was offered in ancient times to the gods. Or finally one might imagine Jesus as the suffering Savior of the world symbolized by the myrrh which was used in ancient times to prepare the body of a dead person for burial. Through meditating we can enter into the very story of the mysteries and in a spiritual sense become part of them. We can relive them in spirit through our love for Jesus and His Holy Mother especially as we pray the Rosary.

With the Intention of Making Reparation

The fruit of meditating, "the prayer of the mind," leads us to the third step in the development of prayer which is "the prayer of the heart." The meditations, in other words, stir up in our hearts affections of faith, love, praise, trust, adoration, joy and every other noble sentiment that we may offer them in praise to the Lord. When we are meditating on the mysteries as part of the Five First Saturdays Devotion, Our Lady asked that these sentiments that arise in our hearts be directed toward her in such a way that they will offer reparation to her for those who have offended her Immaculate

Heart by blasphemies and ingratitude.

What reparation means here is that we offer our love and devotion to the Holy Mother of God to counter or oppose the hatred and outrageous contempt and ingratitude that she suffers from those who deliberately blaspheme all that her Immaculate Heart stands for. (We have already seen above the five blasphemies against Our Lady's Immaculate Heart.) Put more simply, Mary wants us to love her for those who do not love her, to honor her for those who dishonor her, to rejoice in the beautiful gifts and graces God has given her for those who hate what they stand for. We also add to our reparation the prayer of intercession for all those who have offended her by blasphemies and ingratitude. We do this because like Jesus Who on the cross prayed for forgiveness for those who were crucifying Him, Mary wants none of her children to be lost even those who offend her so deeply.

The affections raised while meditating on the mysteries of the Rosary afford us the proper sentiments to offer to Our Lady in this spirit of reparation and intercession. For example, we had mentioned that the first blasphemy we make reparation for is against Our Lady's Immaculate Conception. We can draw from the first Joyful Mystery, beautiful sentiments of reparation. When we have meditated on Mary who was addressed by the Archangel Gabriel as "full of grace," we recognize that God has given her a fullness of grace that implies an absence of all sin, Original as well as personal. At the same time, we reflect on Mary's profound humility in calling herself "the handmaid of the Lord," by which she was saying she was ready to do whatever God was asking of her. We then conclude with Mary's full consent to God to carry out His plan in her life: "Let it be done to me according to your word." Mother Teresa would say, "Our Lady gave God permission." These reflections can stir such a joy, gratitude, and love of Our Lady for all she has done for us that we would naturally respond with praise, gratitude, and our filial love. This is the reparation that brings Our Lady joy from her beloved and faithful children. Surely, she will never forget those of her children who, as she said to Sister Lucia, "kept her company" offering their love for the love others denied her!

Our Lady's Spiritual Formation Program:
The Five First Saturdays Devotion Part 2:

Receive Holy Communion

Our Lady's Spiritual Formation Program: The Five First Saturdays Devotion Part 2: RECEIVE HOLY COMMUNION

One of the best known and most powerful prophecies relating to our time is contained in a dream received by St. John Bosco. He saw the Church as a large wooden ship with the Pope at the helm. Closely surrounding the ship of the Church were many small boats marked by crosses; these were the faithful who followed the Church. Surrounding the ship of the Church at some distance were enemy ships. Some with cannons, others with battering rams, these enemy ships tried to destroy the ship of the Church. Strong winds and waves were also battering the ship of the Church, threatening to destroy it.

Suddenly, from out of the sea two columns arose. At the top of the taller column was the Blessed Sacrament; at the top of the lower column was the Blessed Mother. Wounded first, the Pope was later shot again and killed; his successor guided the ship of the Church safely between the two columns which then protected the Church from enemy fire as well as from the rough seas. If any damage was done to the ship of the Church by the cannon balls or the battering rams, breezes from the two columns "healed" the damage.

Eventually, all the enemy ships, firing their weapons off-balance in the rough sea waters, destroyed one another, and the sea became calm.

When he finished explaining the dream, St. John Bosco said that some of the greatest trials in the Church's history awaited her in the 20th century, but that God was giving two means to protect His Church, namely, devotion to Jesus in the Blessed Sacrament and devotion to Our Lady.

Eucharistic and Marian Devotions Unite at Fatima

In the message of Fatima, these two essential

Catholic devotions are closely united. We get a clear indication of this from the fact that Our Lady's first apparition at Fatima occurred on May 13th, the feast of Our Lady of the Blessed Sacrament.

Even before Mary's apparitions, the Angel of Peace of Portugal in one of his three apparitions to the young visionaries, Jacinta, Francisco, and Lucia, brought the Eucharistic Body and Blood of Jesus to the children. He taught them a prayer of adoration and reparation to Jesus in the most Blessed Sacrament, and led them in adoring Our Eucharistic Lord. Finally, he gave them Jesus in Holy Communion.

Our Lady herself later united devotion to her Divine Son in the Blessed Sacrament with devotion to herself in the Five First Saturdays' devotion by requesting that the people *"receive Holy Communion."*

We can truly say that St. John Bosco's prophecy was uniquely fulfilled in connection with the message of Fatima. Pope John Paul II studied the message of Fatima carefully following the attempt to assassinate him on May 13, 1981, the feast of Our Lady of Fatima. He said that Fatima summed up the whole 20th century, foretelling the Second World War and the rise of Communism and the spreading of its errors throughout the world during the Cold War era. These were among the greatest evils attacking and persecuting the Church that St. John Bosco foretold would happen. But also the saint's prophecy about the powerful effects of devotion to Jesus in the Blessed Sacrament and to Our Lady can be seen in preserving the world from nuclear war. We must continue these devotions if we are to see the complete triumph over the effects of Communism (which must be blamed for the spread of the "Culture of Death" throughout the world), a true world peace and the promised triumph of the Immaculate Heart of Mary. The Five First Saturdays devotion plays a major part in all of these efforts.

Holy Communion: An Extraordinary Spiritual Gift

In one of his most beautiful quotes, Archbishop Fulton J. Sheen said of the Holy Eucharist: "The greatest love story of all time is contained in a tiny white Host!" The Holy Eucharist is truly the "love story" of Jesus for each of us.

St. John in his Gospel, begins the description of the Last Supper at which Jesus gave us the Gift of the

Eucharist with these beautiful words, *"Jesus, knew that his hour had come to pass from this world to the Father, he loved his own in the world and he loved them to the end."* (John 13:1) In the Holy Eucharist, Jesus gave us the Gift of Himself! In one sense, He went away as He said He would by His Death, Resurrection and Ascension into Heaven (cf John 16:5-7). But in another sense, He never went away, for He will be with us in His Eucharistic Presence even until the end of time (cf Matthew 28:20).

Holy Communion:
The Food That Nourishes Us

Jesus called Himself *"the Living Bread that came down from Heaven."* The Israelites had the manna in their forty year journey through the desert to the Promised Land. Jesus in Holy Communion will be our Food for our journey to the Kingdom of Heaven. Jesus insisted on this point: *"Whoever eats My Flesh and drinks My Blood has eternal life, and I will raise him up on the last day. For My Flesh is real Food and My Blood is real Drink."* (John 6:54-55).

We know that if we do not eat the food that nourishes our bodies, we will grow weak. We cannot work, we cannot travel, we cannot carry on our ordinary life activities. We may even become anemic and faint, and if totally deprived we would die. Without the Eucharist, our "daily Bread," we cannot live our spiritual lives fully. We need the strength coming from Holy Communion to pray, to practice our virtues, to resist temptations from the world, the flesh and the devil. Take the example of the great prophet Elijah. He was discouraged because it seemed to him that everyone in Israel at his time had abandoned the true worship of Yahweh and had gone over to the worship of false pagan idols. Exhausted and depressed, Elijah lay down under a tree. But an angel woke him twice and both times he ate and drank the food the angel had brought him. We read that Elijah, *"strengthened by that food, he walked forty days and forty nights to the mountain of the God, Horeb."* (cf 1 Kings 19:8) We will persevere in our journey through the reception of Holy Communion.

Holy Communion: The Food That Changes Us

When we eat ordinary food, we change that food into ourselves. Our last meal is now becoming part of us in terms of its nourishment to our body, our blood cells and the like. Why is this? Because we are greater than the food we eat. The greater changes the lesser into its likeness. But with regard to Jesus in the Eucharist, He is greater than we are. Therefore, when we receive Him in Holy Communion, He changes us into His own likeness. In this sense, we can apply the expression, "You are what you eat!" What does this change consist in? It is a spiritual transformation into the likeness of Christ. First, He changes our values, our thoughts, our attitudes. He gradually makes these more like His own. He begins to fill our minds with concern for the things that are above and not those of earth, and so our value-system begins to change dramatically. In the words of St. Paul, *"Your attitude must be that of Christ."* (Philippians 2:5) Our thoughts become stronger in terms of our faith to believe, our mercy to forgive, our kindness that keeps us from being critical. Our attitude changes because we look at life more and more with the eyes of Christ. We begin to see "God in all things and all things in God" as some of the Fathers of the Church put it.

"Whoever eats My Flesh and drinks My Blood has eternal life in him, and I will raise him up on the last day. For My Flesh is real Food and My Blood is real Drink." (John 6:54-55)

Secondly, Jesus changes our hearts into a greater likeness to His own when we receive Him in Holy Communion. He fills us with the fire of love from His own Eucharistic Heart, that Flame of Love who is the Holy Spirit Jesus gives us. He enables us to love God more ardently, being more grateful for all He has given us and done for us. His providence in governing our lives, His mercy in forgiving us our sins, His patience with our shortcomings, His generosity in meeting our needs, all become more real to us. As a result, we begin to experience a more ardent desire to love God in return. As St. Francis of Assisi would often say: "Greatly to be loved is the love of Him Who loved us so much!" This increasing love of God will overflow into an increasing love of our neighbor, as we shall see.

But this change into the likeness of Christ through reception of Holy Communion does not happen by itself. We must cooperate and do our part. First, we must prepare to receive the Lord worthily in Holy Communion. This means first and foremost to be in the state of grace, that is, not conscious of any mortal sin on our soul. Mortal sin separates us from the love of God and renders us unworthy to receive Jesus in Holy Communion. We should go to Confession to have mortal sin(s) removed before we receive the Lord. To receive Jesus into a soul that lacks His life and love is a great dishonor to Him. If we knowingly receive Holy Communion in mortal sin, that act itself would be a mortal sin called a "sacrilege."

On the other hand, the thought of wanting to receive Jesus worthily in Holy Communion can be one of the best motivations to avoid mortal sin. This is what St. Maria Goretti used as her resistance to the young man (who on a second occasion killed her for resisting) when he first approached her and asked her to commit a sin of impurity with him. The saint's response was: "If I do that, I cannot receive Jesus in Holy Communion!" St. Maria Goretti knew her soul had to be in the state of grace to receive Jesus worthily!

Holy Communion:
The Food That Challenges Us

The increase of love that Jesus gives us for Himself when we receive Him in Holy Communion must overflow to others. At the same Last Supper at which Jesus gave us the Holy Eucharist, He also gave us "His commandment": *"Love one another as I love you!"* (John 15:12) His sacramental presence in us and His gift of the Holy Spirit Whom He leaves with us are the sources of a surge of charity in our hearts. We must become concerned with the needs of our neighbors. Their need for salvation and sanctification are their greatest needs. The Lord makes us share His thirst for souls expressed on the cross when He cried out, *"I thirst."*

Through the whole message of Our Lady of Fatima, we learn to offer intercessory prayer for the salvation of others and to offer reparation for their sins, as well as, our own by little daily sacrifices and by fulfilling faithfully the duties of our state in life. Then there are the bodily needs of our neighbor. These are covered by the works of mercy. Assisting the hungry, the thirsty, the homeless, the naked, the sick and the imprisoned in whatever way we can should be the fruits of our Eucharistic love. Then there are the spiritual needs of our neighbors. These may not be as urgent as meeting their physical needs, but they will be more important in the long run! Instructing those who do not know their Faith, counseling those in doubt, consoling those in sorrow, admonishing those living sinful lives and praying for the living and the dead are among the important spiritual needs our neighbors may have.

Our Communion with Jesus calls us to these works of mercy. His love shared in Holy Communion also enables us to do these works. A little story involving Mother Teresa of Calcutta illustrates this point. A reporter once asked her how she found the strength to do all the good works she did – with dying destitutes in the streets of Calcutta, AIDS patients, lepers, abandoned children, the homeless and the hungry? Mother Teresa's answer was simple and clear. She said, "I begin each day with Holy Mass, receiving Jesus hidden under the appearance of a simple piece of bread. Then I go out into the streets and I find the same Jesus hidden in the dying destitutes; the AIDS patients, the lepers, the abandoned children, the hungry and the homeless. It's the same Jesus!" This is the kind of love Our Lady in her message from Fatima wants us to have for her Divine Son and for all her other sons and daughters because they are at the same time Jesus' brothers and sisters!

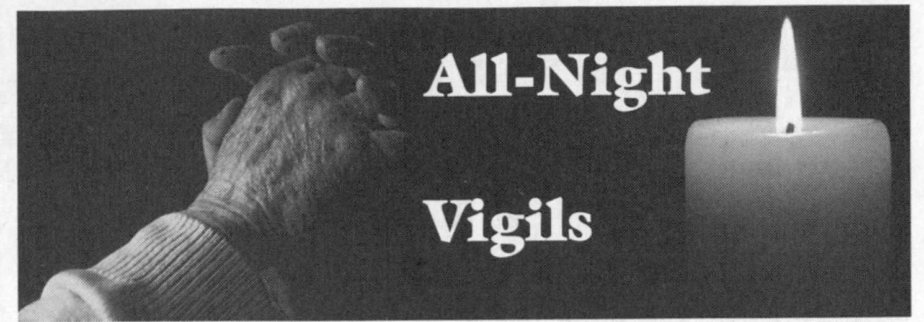

The idea for the All-Night Vigil of prayer and penance is not new, but the vigils are the product of the response of many Marian apostles to the appeals of Fatima for increased prayer, penance and reparation for the offenses committed against Our Lord and Our Lady.

The first All-Night Vigils were made by Our Lord Himself, for the Gospels say that He frequently went off "to a private place" and prayed all night. Our Lord made a "vigil" in the Garden of Gethsemane the very night He was betrayed to his enemies.

Over three hundred years ago, in a little chapel in a Visitation convent in Paray-le-Monial, France, Sr. Margaret Mary Alacoque was praying before the altar when Our Lord appeared before the monstrance revealing his Sacred Heart. He asked for devotion to His Sacred Heart, Eucharistic reparation and specifically for a night hour in His Presence in preparation for the First Friday of the month.

Impetus Given at Fatima

But it was not until our own day – following the great visitations of Our Lady at Rue du Bac, Paris; LaSalette; Lourdes and Fatima – that night adoration began to emerge from the cloisters and to become an organized lay movement. Indeed, it would be more proper to say that only in recent years, following the appeals of Our Lady of Fatima for reparation, that All-Night Vigils suddenly became an international phenomenon of faith – following the example of the pilgrims at Fatima and the pioneering efforts of the late Henrietta Bower of England.

When the pilgrims visiting Fatima began to number in the hundreds of thousands, it became the custom to have the Blessed Sacrament exposed all night on the vigil of the anniversary of Our Lady's appearances. Prayers and exhortations before our Eucharistic Lord sounded from the loudspeakers in the great natural amphitheater of the Cova da Iria until Communion was distributed in the early morning hours by dozens of priests to tens of thousands of joyfully tired pilgrims. These All-Night Vigils grew out of necessity, for there were no accommodations for the majority of the pilgrims. It seemed that Our Lady, who had appeared there for reparation, was literally drawing people to Our Lord in the Blessed Sacrament and to a night of sacrifice and prayer.

In 1960, a recognition of the importance of the vigil came from Pope John XXIII. He had termed Fatima "the hope of the world." The Bishop of Fatima wrote to all the bishops of the world to announce a special All-Night Vigil of reparation at Fatima on October 13 of that year. He suggested that the bishops might do something similar in their own dioceses. Over three hundred bishops agreed. Following the vigil, Pope John XXIII sent a cablegram to the Bishop of Fatima expressing gratitude and a special blessing on all who took part in this vigil, not only at Fatima but everywhere in the world.

In the All-Night Vigils (which are in themselves special acts of penance and sacrifice), we find the devotions of the Sacred Heart of Jesus and the Immaculate Heart of Mary are closely united. The Mass which is celebrated at the opening of the vigil is that of the Sacred Heart of Jesus and the Mass which closes the vigil is that of the Immaculate Heart of Mary.

During the hours in between, meditative Rosaries, Exposition of the Blessed Sacrament, Confessions, talks, processions of the Blessed Sacrament and the Pilgrim Virgin statue, and a coffee break, enable the time to pass quickly.

The entire night is given by each individual who participates, from the opening evening Rosary and Mass the night before to the closing Mass the next morning.

When the First Saturday precedes the First Friday of the month, the vigil is held the following week where First Friday comes before Saturday.

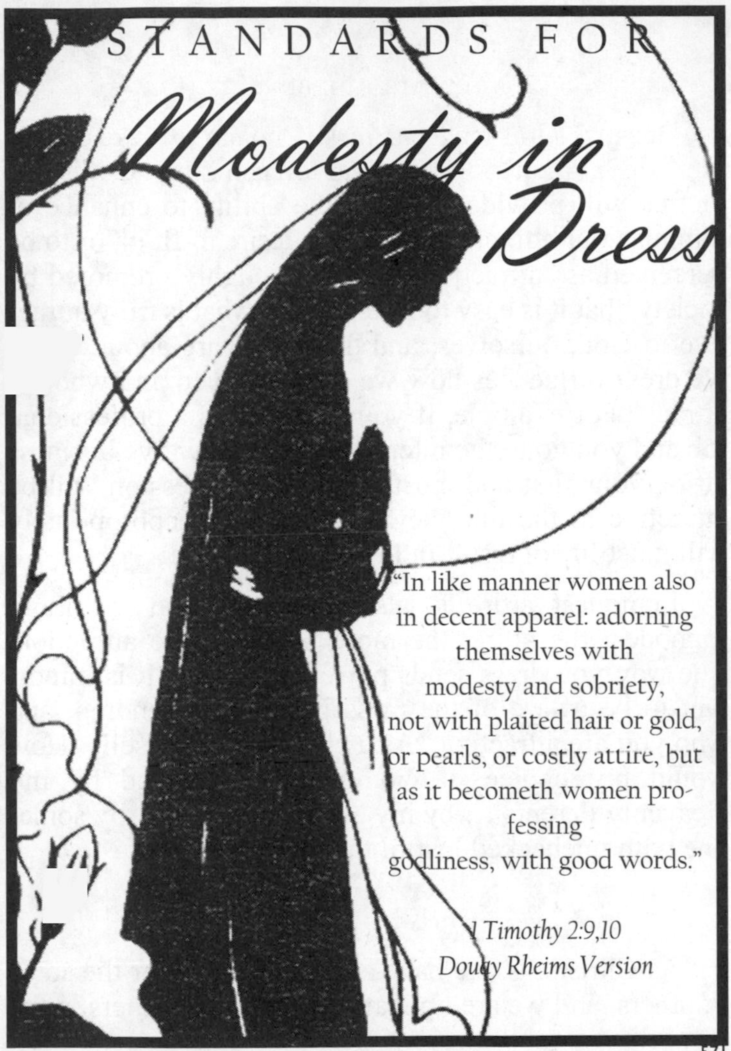
STANDARDS FOR
Modesty in Dress
"In like manner women also
in decent apparel: adorning
themselves with
modesty and sobriety,
not with plaited hair or gold,
or pearls, or costly attire, but
as it becometh women pro-
fessing
godliness, with good words."
1 Timothy 2:9,10
Douay Rheims Version

You Are Attractive!

Because God made us in His image, we are fundamentally attractive to Him and to each other. God's gift of free will provides us with the ability to enhance or diminish our attractiveness. The desire to fit in, or to be perceived as "attractive," is so thoroughly promoted by society, that it is easy to lose track of what is truly attractive to God, ourselves, and those we care about. How we dress influences how we are perceived and who we attract. For example, if you are seeking a professional job and you go to the interview in conservative business attire, your first and most important impression will be attractive to the interviewer. Dressing inappropriately will most likely result in lost opportunity.

Immodest attire is also attractive, and the more immodest the attire, the more powerful the attraction. The way you dress sends powerful signals. It is important to be aware of the message you are sending, and who you are attracting. As a check, ask yourself, "How would my choice of clothing be perceived by my Heavenly Parents … by my earthly parents … by someone with unchecked lustful thoughts?"

Christian Charity

As Christians, we have a responsibility for the souls of others, and we are obligated not to place others in the near occasion of sin. Charity requires that we pay particular attention to this grave responsibility in a matter as serious as sexual attraction. Sexual sin often begins with an unchecked lustful thought. Lustful thoughts often lead to more serious sin.

Let's consider differences in perception between the sexes to better understand the need for modesty.

What About the Other Sex?

Differences between the two sexes are obvious. What may not be so obvious is how these differences affect feelings and perception. Most women tend to be self-conscious about how they look. Recognizing this tendency in themselves, women should take extra care to preserve both dignity and integrity, as well as beauty.

While a scantily clad man is not likely to elicit lustful desires in most women, the same cannot be said about the exact situation in reverse. Why is this so? In His infinite wisdom, God created woman to be instinctively appreciative of feelings, and man to be instinctively attracted by the sight of a woman. He did not intend that these instincts be misused. Just as care should be exercised by men to avoid unduly attracting a woman emotionally, so women should exercise the same care to avoid unduly arousing sexual desire among men.

Let's explore how exercising this care would affect how we dress.

Standards of Dress

Since we can agree that prevailing standards have been forced well below what Christian charity would dictate, let's re-evaluate what is modest. The purpose for setting moral standards is to answer the rising question from those who honestly want to know: "What is the dividing line? How far is too far? What can be worn safely within limits?" While one may not intend to be a temptation to sin, dress and deportment can speak louder, sending a different message.

There are general standards of modesty that both men and women should abide by:

- ✦ The body should be clothed in such a way so as to <u>protect and foster the dignity of the human person</u> and awaken consciousness of that proper respect due to each one as an image of God.
- ✦ Clothing should *conceal* rather than *reveal* the figure of the body.
- ✦ Clothing should cover and protect the skin against the weather and sun, while protecting the eyes from images that incite the imagination.
- ✦ The covering should include the front and back of the body, the shoulders and mid-section.
- ✦ A generous expression of this intention would be to cover the body at least to the elbows and knees.

- ✦ Clingy, flesh-colored and transparent material should be avoided. Special care should be taken with swimming apparel.
- ✦ Jeans and slacks should be loose-fitting and held up around one's waist.
- ✦ In church, special care should be taken to dress modestly as we are in the presence of Jesus in the Blessed Sacrament; one should not be a distraction.

Children's Standards

Babies and young children should be properly prepared by prudently getting them accustomed to wearing modest clothing, so they do not lose their sense of modesty.

Special care should be taken in choosing dresses for children's religious ceremonies, such as for First Holy Communion, Marian processions and May crownings.

The sports industry and other forms of entertainment, dances and dating challenge Christian youth to change what has been widely accepted as the norm in public and private appearance.

Besides these general standards, women have a special call to modesty because of their unique dignity as sacred vessels of life-giving potential and because of man's weakness. Clothing should never cheapen one who is destined for glory, or used for selfish pleasure or personal comfort if a soul's risk could be involved. For this reason, here are some helpful standards:

- ✦ Dress Mary-like, without compromise.
- ✦ Dresses should cover the knees when seated.
- ✦ Neckline cuts should not exceed 2-3 inches.
- ✦ If wearing a dress, sit in front of a full length mirror and observe what can be seen from someone sitting across and facing you. Try various positions: crossing your legs; turn to the side and lift your arms to observe what is seen from the side with short sleeves, or in front with shorts when legs are in an open casual relaxed position, etc.
- ✦ Avoid :
    - Sleeveless shirts and dresses, including tank tops
    - Tight fitting clothing such as slacks, jeans, sweaters, shorts, and bathing suits
    - Wedding and bridesmaids dresses, fashion gowns, and other formal attire that violate decency

- ✦ As a practical consideration, during warmer seasons, 100% cotton breathes and lighter colors, especially white, reflect the sunlight, diverting rays from the body, while darker colors absorb heat.

Conclusion

In this world which is increasingly filled with immodesty leading to serious sin and the loss of salvation for many poor souls, we are all called upon to exercise prudence and charity, beginning with ourselves, whether we refrain from being a means of temptation or whether we take steps to control our eyes and imagination. As we have shown, what the world considers proper clothing is many times far short of what a modest Christian should want to wear. It is up to each of us to consider prayerfully our standard of dress. Where souls are concerned, it is always better to err on the side of charity and modesty.

RECOMMENDATION: *Modesty would be a good topic of a moderated discussion for Christian youth groups, CCD classes, parents and teens, and among friends, to discover how fashion affects others, thereby reinvigorating the desire to improve the standard prevalent in the world today. Young people have a powerful ability to influence society for good when they partner together to begin new trends in dress. With a mind to be leaders of the new generation, and approaching store managers to make requests for changes in clothing, a united, determined effort can begin "to restore all things in Christ."*

Are Standards Really Necessary?

When Our Lady visited Jacinta of Fatima, She told her, "The sins which cause most souls to go to hell are the sins of the flesh," and "Fashions will much offend Our Lord. People who serve God should not follow the fashions." [1] Yet, raising the issue of a need for standards in modesty in dress will often raise objections: "Standards are unnecessary," it is said, "since common sense will dictate reason in all cases. Women should be respected to be allowed the freedom to make their own judgments on a personal matter such as this."

Unfortunately, after two generations of the sexual revolution, many good Catholics are desensitized by the media glut of impurity. Years of increasingly suggestive fashions, seductive advertisements, and now rampant pornography on billboards, in movies, magazines, and on the internet have combined to bring about a loss in the sense of the sacredness of the human body.

Isn't it time for us to re-evaluate what is modest and what effect our fashions have on others?

Treasure:

Life

Your Dignity

A New Respect

Treasure Modesty!

Dress to be Attractive to Your Divine Bridegroom –

Jesus Christ

To Those You Care about

To Those Who Care about You!

Other Quotes

"When I think of the United States, I think of this: One of the things Our Lady especially asked was for modesty in dress. There seems to me to be not much modesty in the life of the women of your country. But modesty would be a good sacrifice to offer to Our Lady, and it would please her.

If the Catholics in your country could make a league for modesty in dress…it will greatly please Our Lady."
Sr. Lucia to an American couple

"The good of our soul is more important than that of our

body; and we have to prefer the spiritual welfare of our neighbor to our bodily comforts…If a certain kind of dress constitutes a grave and proximate occasion of sin, and endangers the salvation of your soul and others, it is your duty to give it up… O Christian mothers, if you knew what a future of anxieties and perils, of ill-guarded shame you prepare for your sons and daughters, imprudently getting them accustomed to live scantily dressed and making them lose their sense of modesty, you would be ashamed of yourselves and you would dread the harm you are making for yourselves, the harm which you are causing to these children, whom Heaven has entrusted to you to be brought up as Christians."

Pope Pius XII to Catholic Young Women's Groups of Italy

© World Apostolate of Fatima,USA

PO Box 976
Washington, NJ 07882
866-513-1917
www.wafusa.org

This publication has been examined by diocesan censors and nothing contrary to faith and morals has been found therein.

100150

581

Examination of Conscience

1. I am the Lord your God. You shall not have strange gods before me.

Do I give God time every day in prayer?
Do I seek to love Him with my whole heart?
Have I been involved with superstitious practices or have I been involved with the occult?
Do I seek to surrender myself to God's Word as taught by the Church?
Have I ever received Communion in the state of mortal sin?
Have I ever deliberately told a lie in Confession or have I withheld a mortal sin from the priest in Confession?

2. You shall not take the name of the Lord your God in vain.

Have I used God's name in vain: lightly or carelessly?
Have I been angry with God?
Have I wished evil upon any other person?
Have I insulted a sacred person or abused a sacred object?

3. Remember to keep holy the Lord's Day.

Have I deliberately missed Mass on
Sundays or Holy Days of Obligation?
Have I tried to observe Sunday as a family
day and a day of rest?
Do I do needless work on Sunday?

4. Honor your father and your mother.

Do I honor and obey my parents?
Have I neglected my duties to my spouse and children?
Have I given my family good religious example?
Do I try to bring peace into my home life?
Do I care for my aged and infirm relatives?

5. You shall not kill.

Have I had an abortion or encouraged
anyone to have an abortion?
Have I physically harmed anyone?
Have I abused alcohol or drugs?
Did I give scandal to anyone, thereby
leading them into sin?
Have I been angry or resentful?
Have I harbored hatred in my heart?
Have I mutilated myself through any
form of sterilization?
Have I encouraged or condoned sterilization?

6. You shall not commit adultery.

Have I been faithful to my marriage vows
in thought and action?
Have I engaged in any sexual activity
outside of marriage?
Have I used any method of contraception
or artificial birth control?
Has each sexual act in my marriage been
open to the transmission of new life?
Have I been guilty of masturbation?
Have I respected all members of the
opposite sex, or have I thought of other
people as objects?
Have I been guilty of any homosexual activity?
Do I seek to be chaste in my thoughts,
words and actions?
Am I careful to dress modestly?

7. You shall not steal.

Have I stolen what is not mine?
Have I returned or made restitution
for what I have stolen?
Do I waste time at work, school or at home?
Do I gamble excessively, thereby denying
my family of its needs?
Do I pay my debts promptly?

Do I seek to share what I have with the poor?

8. You shall not bear false witness against your neighbor.

Have I lied?
Have I gossiped?
Have I spoken behind someone else's back?
Am I sincere in my dealings with others?
Am I critical, negative, or uncharitable in my thoughts of others?
Do I keep secret what should be kept confidential?

9. You shall not desire your neighbor's wife.

Have I sought to control my thoughts?
Have I consented to impure thoughts?
Have I caused them by impure reading, movies, conversation, or curiosity?
Do I seek to control my imagination?
Do I pray at once to banish impure thoughts and temptations?

10. You shall not desire your neighbor's goods.

Am I jealous of what other people have?
Do I envy other people's families or possessions?
Am I greedy or selfish?

Are material possessions the
purpose of my life?
Do I trust that God will care for all of my
material and spiritual needs?

Helps to Grow in Holiness

Do I consciously seek to imitate Christ in all of my dealings with others?
Do I have a confessor who gives me spiritual direction?
Do I try to go to Confession at least once a month as part of the First Saturday Devotion?
Do I ask Our Lady to help me examine my conscience and make a sincere and honest Confession?
Do I seek to lead others to make frequent use of the sacraments?

Imprimatur
Rev. Msgr. John B. Szymanski
Vicar General, Diocese of Metuchen

World Apostolate of Farima, USA
PO Box 976
Washington, NJ 07882
(866) 513-1917 www.wafusa.org

97690 11/0

Our Lady's Spiritual Formation Program: The First Saturday Devotion

Father Andrew Apostoli, C.F.R.

Editor's Note: In this issue of SOUL, Fr. Apostoli begins a new series, entitled Our Lady's Spiritual Formation Program. The first installment will discuss the importance of Confession and its impact on our lives and the world in general.

> IN HIS INSPIRING APOSTOLIC LETTER ON THE MOST HOLY ROSARY, ENTITLED ROSARIUM VIRGINIS MARIAE, POPE JOHN PAUL II STATES, "WITH THE ROSARY, THE CHRISTIAN PEOPLE SIT AT THE SCHOOL OF MARY AND ARE LED TO CONTEMPLATE THE BEAUTY ON THE FACE OF CHRIST AND TO EXPERIENCE THE DEPTHS OF HIS LOVE."

We do not often think of Our Lady as having a "school," but the words of the late Vicar of Christ assure us that she does. And it is a school which all of us as her spiritual children must attend for instruction and spiritual formation for her children to grow in holiness. One aspect of this school is education – we must continue to learn more and more about the mysteries of the Kingdom of Heaven which we do as we meditate on the beautiful mysteries of her Rosary.

"... I promise to assist at the hour of death with all the graces necessary for salvation all those who, on the first Saturday of five consecutive months, confess their sins, receive Holy Communion, recite five decades of the Rosary and keep me company for a quarter of an hour while meditating on the mysteries of the Rosary, with the intention of making reparation to me."

Our Lady to Sister Lucia, December 10, 1925

But in addition to education, we also need spiritual formation. Our Lady guides us on how to live in a way that we put the mysteries of her Rosary into practice, by living lives of virtue and carrying out faithfully the Will of Our Heavenly Father. This was the goal of Jesus' life: "The world must know that I love the Father and do as the Father has commanded me." (John 14:31) Our Lady herself grew in virtue through the perfect accomplishment of the Father's Will in her life.

Jesus and Mary Revealed the Devotion of the Five First Saturdays

One of the most important programs Our Lady offers is the devotion we call the Five First Saturdays. In her apparition at Fatima on July 13, 1917 the Blessed Mother forewarned that if people did not heed her message calling for prayer, sacrifice, and penance, an evil would begin in Russia that would spread throughout the world, provoking wars, famine, annihilation of nations and persecution of the Holy Father and the Church. Of course Our Lady was speaking of Atheistic Communism which began in Russia.

To counter this evil, Our Lady said she would come again to request two things. First, she wanted Russia to be consecrated to her Immaculate Heart. Our Lady appeared to Sister Lucia on June 13, 1929 and asked her to petition the Holy Father along with all the bishops of the world to consecrate Russia to her Immaculate Heart. After a number of attempts that did not completely fulfill the request, Pope John Paul II carried out this important consecration on March 25, 1984. When asked if this consecration was made correctly, Sister Lucia declared that Heaven accepted this consecration.

The second thing Our Lady would come again to request was the devotion of the "Communion of Reparation" or, as we call it today, the "Five First Saturdays" devotion in reparation for the offenses against her Immaculate Heart. Our Lady fulfilled this promise when she appeared with the Christ Child to Lucia on December 10, 1925.

The Child Jesus and Our Lady appeared in her convent room which is now a chapel. Lucia saw the heart of Our Lady surrounded by a crown of piercing thorns.

The Child Jesus spoke first: "Have pity on the heart of your most holy Mother. It is covered with the thorns with which ungrateful men pierce at every moment, and there is no one to remove them with an act of reparation."

Then Our Lady spoke, "My daughter, look at my Heart surrounded with the thorns with which ungrateful men pierce it at every moment by their blasphemies and ingratitude. You, at least, try to console me, and say [to all the people] that I promise to assist at the hour of death with all the graces necessary for salvation all those who, on the first Saturday of five consecutive months, confess their sins, receive Holy Communion, recite five decades of the Rosary and keep me company for a quarter of an hour while meditating on the mysteries of the Rosary, with the intention of making reparation to me."

In this simple apparition the Child Jesus and Our Lady summed up a devotion that is important for both the peace and the salvation of the world. So important is it that the Child Jesus appeared to Sister Lucia about two months later on February 16, 1926, and asked "What was being done to establish in the world this devotion to the Immaculate Heart of His Mother?" In her later writings, Sister Lucia frequently referred to this devotion. She said that this devotion should be practiced "because Jesus asked for this, the preferred act of reparation. Do it simply out of love for your Blessed Mother to remove the thorns that continuously pierce her Immaculate Heart through man's blasphemies and ingratitude."

"Confess their Sins"

The first essential part of Our Lady of Fatima's spiritual formation program was that her children "confess their sins." Prior to Vatican II, many Catholics went to confession frequently. It was an accepted and expected part of Catholic living, especially in the United States. But after Vatican II, things changed drastically. In fact, many Catholics are in danger of losing the practice of this sacrament which is absolutely essential for our salvation as well as our spiritual growth. Our Lady foresaw in 1917 what would happen. The devotion she gave us was meant to assure that her faithful children would seek her Son's forgiveness in the Sacrament of Penance at least once a month.

Some Practical Reasons for the Decline in Confessions

We must ask here the question: Why has the practice of confession fallen off so drastically? Let us see some practical reasons. First, there are fewer priests to hear the confessions of a growing number of Catholics in the United States.

More significant, however, is the fact that a number of priests – probably influenced by liberal moral theologians who have downplayed the malice of sin – do not seem to value confession in their own personal lives as they did years ago and so fail to see its importance for their flock.

A final practical reason can be seen in the practice of "general absolution." There has been much abuse concerning the original purpose for which general absolution was permitted namely, where penitents would be deprived of absolution for long periods of time. This practice has also "de-personalized" the sacrament as a personal encounter with our merciful Savior through His priest-representative.

The greatest reason why Catholics are not going to confession now as they did years ago is that we have lost a sense of sin! Why? Let us look at some of the reasons.

First, there has been a great decline in faith. When faith is strong, we have a real sense of God's presence in our lives. But when faith declines God is no longer seen as important, no longer thought of as the center of daily life. Therefore, sin is no longer seen as offending the living God Who is worthy of all our love. Rather, sin becomes merely the breaking of rules proposed by organized religion.

Secondly, widespread immorality is accepted in society today. Things that were clearly seen as "wrongs" and as morally evil years ago (e.g., abortion, euthanasia, homosexuality), are now socially accepted and even protected as "rights." We can only wonder if Our Lord's words about the End Times apply to our present situation: "Because of the increase of evil, the love of most will grow cold." (Matthew 24:12) It is easy to drift morally downstream; it takes courage and effort to resist the current of sin!

Thirdly, self-deceit easily leads to the denial of sin. Quoting Archbishop Fulton J. Sheen again: "The worst of all evils is not sin, but the denial of sin." St. Paul tells us that we are led astray morally "through illusion and desire." (cf Ephesians 4:22) "Desire" refers to our passions which, if undisciplined, keep pulling us down, tempting us to go against the law of God. Yet Jesus tells us clearly: "He who obeys the commandments he has from Me is the man who loves Me." (John 14:21) "Illusion" allows us to indulge our passions in sinful desires by enabling us to deceive ourselves. This usually happens through the "Everybody does this today!" rationalization.

Others "shop around" until they find some priest or theologian who will tell them what they want to hear. These are "illusions" which justify sin. To quote Archbishop Fulton J. Sheen once again: "People do not become heretics for the way they want to think, but for the way they want to live!"

How Confession Helps Us

To go to the Sacrament of Reconciliation on a monthly basis as Our Lady asks for in the Five First Saturdays devotion will help to counter the loss of a sense of sin while providing many positive helps to our spiritual growth. Let us look at some of these.

Frequent confession reminds us of the reality of sin in our lives. In order to confess to a priest, a person must acknowledge and accept the fact that he or she has sins to confess. Let us take an example from Alcoholics Anonymous. A penitent must acknowledge his or her sins and admit: "I am a sinner!" Then they must acknowledge that they cannot take their own sins and guilt away but that they need God's mercy and forgiveness.

We also come to know ourselves in the sense of how we are doing in our relationship with God and with our neighbor. This "self knowledge" is necessary for all spiritual growth. If people are neglecting prayer or praying with deliberate distraction, they can work on correcting these situations. Again, if they see that they easily get annoyed at the faults of others, they can resolve to practice greater patience. But how will people know their sinful behavior unless they take time to examine their consciences? This is precisely what going to confession regularly requires them to do. Furthermore, after confession they should make one or more resolutions to amend their lives. But for many people today, none of this is done.

Most important of all, confession brings us God's forgiveness for our sins. The word used in the Sacrament of Penance by which a priest confers God's forgiveness on us is the word "absolve." The root of this word comes from two Latin words meaning to untie or loosen someone as from a burden. Sacramental absolution sets us free from the burden of our sins and gives us a chance to renew the living of our Christian life. There is a sense of a new beginning, a fresh clean start. At the same time we experience a peace through the sacrament. This peace assists us to practice the virtues more completely by preserving us from strong feelings of sinful inclinations and passions.

Finally, with our sins forgiven we have greater purity of heart. This means that when we strive to love God and to do good to our neighbor, our motivation to love more generously will increase. At the same time, confession has a way of preparing us to receive greater graces when we receive Jesus in Holy Communion. This is why Our Lady added that after confessing our sins on each First Saturday, we are to receive Jesus in Holy Communion. As we shall see in our next meditation, our soul will be better prepared for Jesus to come in the "Communion of Reparation" as Our Lady called it.

It is no wonder, then, that Our Lady links the peace of the world, the overcoming of the evils spread by

Communism, and the triumph of her Immaculate Heart to the First Saturday Devotion which, with monthly confession, deepens peace in the soul of each person. When a sufficient number of people have this peace of God in their hearts, then like a bud in Spring, nurtured by gentle rain and warm sun, this peace will blossom throughout the whole world.

A GUIDE TO CONFESSION

Rev. Fredrick L. Miller

A GUIDE TO CONFESSION

Rev. Frederick L. Miller, S.T.D.

The World Apostolate of Fatima
The Blue Army, USA
Washington, New Jersey
www.wafusa.org
(866) 513-1917

In accord with Canon 827 of the New Code of Canon Law, this publication has been submitted to a censor of the Diocese and nothing being found contrary to faith and morals, we hereby grant permission in accord with Canon 824 that it be published.

Rev. Charles T. O'Connor, Delegate,
Diocese of Metuchen, August 6, 1997

N.B. The ecclesiastical permission implies nothing more than the material contained in the publication has been examined by diocesan censors and nothing contrary to faith and morals has been found therein.

Seventh Printing - July 2005,
1997 Revised Edition

Cover photos: Front cover: photos.com Back cover: The statue of Our Lady in the Cova da Iria at Fatima, Portugal by Foto Iris.

Portions of this booklet are copyrighted by
The Blue Army, USA - 1989

ISBN 1-56036-105-0

By the Blood of His Cross

You are able to be at peace with God, to call Him "Father" and live with Him forever in heaven because of Jesus Christ Who "loved you and gave Himself for you" (Gal. 2:20). Jesus, offering Himself as a sacrifice on the cross, "paid the price" for your sins and reconciled you to His Father "in his blood." St. Paul says: "For in him all the fullness of God was pleased to dwell, and through him to reconcile to himself all things, whether on earth or in heaven, making peace by the blood of his cross" (Col. 1:19-20).

Although Christ's entire ministry was a ministry of reconciliation, He principally instituted the Sacrament of Penance on Easter night. Appearing to His Apostles, He gave them the power to forgive all sins in His name. In that first meeting of the risen Christ with the Apostles, the Lord said to them, and, in fact, to all priests of every time and place: "Receive the Holy Spirit. If you forgive anyone's sins, they are forgiven. If you retain anyone's sins, they are retained" (Jn. 20:22-23).

In giving His Church the Sacrament of Reconciliation in this way, Christ taught us that He wants all sins committed after Baptism to be confessed to one of His priests. The Council of Trent teaches that this Confession is necessary by Divine Law. The *Catechism of the Catholic Church* explains why Christ established this sacrament:

"Christ instituted the sacrament of penance for all sinful members of His church; above all for those who, since baptism, have fallen into grave sin, and have thus lost their baptismal grace and wounded ecclesial communion. It is to them that the sacrament of Penance offers a new possibility to convert and to recover the grace of justification. The Fathers of the Church present this sacrament as 'the second plank (of salvation) after the shipwreck which is the loss of grace'" (no. 1446).

Christ, risen from the dead and ascended into heaven, continues to exercise His ministry of reconciliation through His priests. In Confession, you open your heart to Christ in the person of the priest and through the absolution, you are reconciled to God and the Church. In fact, Catholics believe that the priest not only receives the power to forgive all human sins in the Sacrament of Holy Orders, but also acts as a doctor, teacher, father and judge when he administers the Sacrament of Penance.

As doctor, the priest comforts and heals. He "prescribes medicine" (penances) to cure the wounds inflicted by sin and to strike at the deep roots of sin. He teaches his penitent how to avoid sin and the occasions of sin in the future, how to grow in all of the Christian virtues. Never showing anything but love, mercy and gentleness to the person who has sinned, the confessor helps the penitent experience the tender love of God the Father. When the priest is confident that the penitent is sincerely sorry for the sins confessed and firm in the resolution to turn away from them, his judgement is forgiveness and mercy. Consider the consoling fact: the sins that you bring to the tribunal of penance will not be held against you when you stand before the judgement seat of Christ at the moment of your death. This explains how thoroughly your sins are "destroyed" in this sacrament of Christ's mercy. All are forgiven and "forgotten" by God.

On your part, what must you do to experience the forgiveness of your Savior? First of all, it is important to examine your conscience before you approach the priest. Spend some time thinking about your life since your last worthy Confession to see how you may have offended God. Ask the Holy Spirit to help you know your sins and humbly confess them.

In the examination of conscience you seek to know the truth about yourself. You try to see yourself as God sees you. The simplest way to do this is to meditate on your observance of each of the Ten Commandments. This booklet contains a more or less detailed examination of conscience to help you prepare for Confession.

After you admit your sins to yourself, ask the Holy Spirit for deep sorrow for your sins. Catholics call sorrow for sins "contrition." It is helpful in preparing for Confession to meditate on the sufferings of the crucified Christ and to recall that He bore the penalty of your personal sins as He hung on the cross. This prayer will convince you that sins wound Christ and the Church.

"Perfect contrition" is sorrow for sins motivated by love of God. "Imperfect contrition" is sorrow for sin motivated by the fear of punishment in hell. Whenever you fall into sin, you should approach God with perfect contrition. Because we are such complicated people, we never know with certitude that our contrition is perfect. However, the Church assures us that God will forgive all of our sins in the Sacrament of Penance even if our contrition is "imperfect." This is another indication of the goodness and mercy of God.

If your contrition (perfect or imperfect) is real, it will include a desire to confess your mortal sins to a priest, abandon sin and all the circumstances that lead to sin (purpose of amendment) and make satisfaction for the sins committed.

Mortal sin is a direct, conscious and free violation of one or another of the Ten Commandments in a serious matter. (See the *Catechism of the Catholic Church*, no. 1854-1864). Mortal sin, also known as grave or deadly sin, destroys the life of grace in our souls.

All mortal sins must be confessed to a priest. You must "name" the sin. For example, "I committed adultery." "I had an abortion." "I gambled away a week's salary." You must also tell the number of times you committed the mortal sin. For example, "I used a contraceptive device three times since my last Confession." Our confessions must always be integral, that is complete. If you deliberately refuse to confess a mortal sin, none of your sins are forgiven and you commit a new mortal sin. By resisting the grace of the Holy Spirit and lying to Christ in the person of His priest, you commit the sin of sacrilege. The necessity of the confession of mortal sins by name and number is not the invention of the Church or any member or members of the Church. Rather, it is a law established by the Lord Himself (cf. Jn. 20:22-23). It is for our benefit!

If you are guilty of mortal sin, you must go to Confession before you receive the Body and Blood of Christ in Holy Communion. St. Paul says, "anyone who eats the bread or drinks the cup of the Lord unworthily will be guilty of desecrating the body and blood of the Lord" (1 Cor. 11:27). We should make the following consideration: If I die with an unrepented mortal sin on my conscience, I will forfeit the eternal enjoyment of God in heaven and find myself in the fires of hell.

The Church suggests that you go to Confession frequently even if you are not guilty of mortal sin. (Not all sin is mortal, that is, deadly. See 1 John 5:16.) The *Catechism of the Catholic Church* defines venial sin in this way: "One commits venial sin when, in a less serious matter, he does not observe the standard prescribed by the moral law, or when he disobeys the moral law in a grave matter, but without full knowledge or without complete consent" (no. 1862). Many priests are convinced that monthly Confession of venial sin is helpful for every Christian. These "devotional Confessions" will help you grow in humility and charity. They help you, above all, to root out all sins and attachment to sin in your life. The grace of Confession always increases and strengthens the love of God and neighbor. If there is mortal sin, especially habitual mortal sin, more frequent Confession is necessary.

If you are having difficulty understanding the difference between mortal and venial sin or struggling with whether a particular sin is mortal or venial, do not hesitate to ask the priest to help you resolve these problems when you go to Confession. Remember, he is your doctor, your teacher, your father.

In order to be forgiven you must sincerely desire to make reparation to God for your sins through acts of prayer, penance and charity. The priest in giving you a penance has as his goal the healing of the wounds caused by the sins you committed. In performing the penance, you begin to make reparation for the harm your sins have caused you, others and the Church. The penance imposed by the confessor reminds you that you need to be one with Christ in His sufferings so as to share in the glory of His risen life.

Once you have expressed sorrow for your sins by humbly confessing them to the priest, and resolved to make amends for them by accepting the penance the priest gives you, you pray the Act of Contrition and receive sacramental absolution.

As the priest prays the words of absolution over you, be certain that Christ exalted at the right hand of the Father in heaven is forgiving all of your sins. It is worthwhile to meditate on the words of absolution through which we receive the Lord's forgiveness:

"God the Father of mercies through the death and resurrection of His son has reconciled the world to Himself and sent the Holy Spirit among us for the forgiveness of sins. Through the ministry of the church, may God give you pardon and peace, and I absolve you from your sins in the name of the Father, and of the Son, and of the Holy Spirit. Amen."

The Introduction to the *New Rite of Penance* (no. 6) beautifully explains the effect of the absolution of the priest:

"In the sacrament of penance the Father receives the repentant son who comes back to Him, Christ places the lost sheep on His shoulders and brings it back to the sheepfold, and the Holy Spirit sanctifies this temple of God again or lives more fully within it. This is finally expressed in a renewed and more fervent sharing of the Lord's table, and there is great joy at the banquet of God's Church over the son who has returned from afar."

You may have been away from the sacraments for a long time, even for years. Reading through the following examination of conscience, you may realize that you have offended God in many different ways. You may feel embarrassed to open your heart in such a personal way to a priest. (Remember you may always go to any priest for Confession. It does not have to be your "parish priest." Also, you always have the right to go anonymously, that is, behind a screen.) You may be deeply troubled by some sin from the past that you never adequately confessed or even deliberately refused to confess. Or, it may be that your life is basically in order with God but you have abandoned the practice of regular Confession. Did someone possibly tell you that the confession of venial sins is without value? Or was a priest rough with you on some occasion in the past? Perhaps you've just become lax regarding this sacrament. Reading this booklet may be an important moment of grace for you! **Make the resolution now to go to Confession as soon as possible.**

Satan loves sin and hates the grace of Confession that comes to us through the power of the cross of Christ. The devil will try to stop you from going to Confession. He will make you feel frightened, embarrassed, proud, filled with despair or anger. The holy Bishop, Saint Antoninus said, "The devil takes our shame away so that we sin with ease and then gives it back when we think about going to confession." In other words the suppression of shame that makes sin possible, flares up again to make Confession seem impossible.

If the idea of Confession makes you feel uneasy, turn for help to the Mother of God. Ask her to fill your heart with confidence in Christ's love for you, His desire to forgive your sins. She will help you think of Him hanging on the cross in agony, praying for you and your conversion. He is thirsty for your love. Quench that thirst by confessing your sins. Ask the Virgin Mary to take you by the hand and bring you to Jesus in the Sacrament of Reconciliation. Through her motherly help you will feel the freedom to open your heart to the mercy that flows from the wounded Heart of Jesus Christ.

What inner peace you will feel when you hear the priest say to you at the end of your meeting with him: "The Lord Jesus has freed you from your sins. Go in peace."

Examination of Conscience

1. I am the Lord your God. You shall not have strange gods before me.

—Do I give God time every day in prayer?

—Do I seek to love Him with my whole heart?

—Have I been involved with superstitious practices or have I been involved with the occult?

—Do I seek to surrender myself to God's Word as taught by the Church?

—Have I ever received Communion in the state of mortal sin?

—Have I ever deliberately told a lie in Confession or have I withheld a mortal sin from the priest in Confession?

2. You shall not take the name of the Lord your God in vain.

—Have I used God's name in vain: lightly or carelessly?

—Have I been angry with God?

—Have I wished evil upon any other person?

—Have I insulted a sacred person or abused a sacred object?

3. Remember to keep holy the Lord's Day.

—Have I deliberately missed Mass on Sundaysor Holy Days of Obligation?

—Have I tried to observe Sunday as a family day and a day of rest?

—Do I do needless work on Sunday?

4. Honor your father and your mother.

—Do I honor and obey my parents?

—Have I neglected my duties to my spouse and children?

—Have I given my family good religious example?

—Do I try to bring peace into my home life?

—Do I care for my aged and infirm relatives?

5. You shall not kill.

—Have I had an abortion or encouraged anyone to have an abortion?

—Have I physically harmed anyone?

—Have I abused alcohol or drugs?

—Did I give scandal to anyone, thereby leading them into sin?

—Have I been angry or resentful?

—Have I harbored hatred in my heart?

—Have I mutilated myself through any form of sterilization?

—Have I encouraged or condoned sterilization?

6. **You shall not commit adultery.**

—Have I been faithful to my marriage vows in thought and action?

—Have I engaged in any sexual activity outside of marriage?

—Have I used any method of contraception or artificial birth control in my marriage?

—Has each sexual act in my marriage been open to the transmission of new life?

—Have I been guilty of masturbation?

—Have I respected all members of the opposite sex, or have I thought of other people as objects?

—Have I been guilty of homosexual activity?

—Do I seek to be chaste in my thoughts, words and actions?

—Am I careful to dress modestly?

7. **You shall not steal.**

—Have I stolen what is not mine?

—Have I returned or made restitution for what I have stolen?

—Do I waste time at work, school or at home?

—Do I gamble excessively, thereby denying my family of their needs?

—Do I pay my debts promptly?

—Do I seek to share what I have with the poor?

8. You shall not bear false witness against your neighbor.
 —Have I lied?
 —Have I gossiped?
 —Have I spoken behind someone else's back?
 —Am I sincere in my dealings with others?
 —Am I critical, negative, or uncharitable in my thoughts of others?
 —Do I keep secret what should be kept confidential?

9. You shall not desire your neighbor's wife.
 —Have I sought to control my thoughts?
 —Have I consented to impure thoughts?
 —Have I caused them by impure reading, movies, conversation, or curiosity?
 —Do I seek to control my imagination?
 —Do I pray at once to banish impure thoughts and temptations?

10. You shall not desire your neighbor's goods.
 —Am I jealous of what other people have?
 —Do I envy the families or possessions of others?
 —Am I greedy or selfish?
 —Are material possessions the purpose of my life?
 —Do I trust that God will care for all of my material and spiritual needs?

Helps to Grow in Holiness

—Do I consciously seek to imitate Christ in all of my dealings with others?
—Do I have a confessor who gives me spiritual direction?
—Do I try to go to confession at least once a month as part of the First Saturday Devotion?
—Do I ask Our Lady to help me to examine my conscience and to make a sincere and honest confession?
—Do I seek to lead others to make frequent use of the Sacraments?

How to go to Confession

1. You always have the option to go to confession anonymously, that is, behind the screen or face to face, if you so desire.
2. After the priest greets you in the name of Christ, make the sign of the cross. He may choose to include a reading from Scripture for reflection. Then say: "Bless me Father for I have sinned. It has been (state how long) since my last confession. These are my sins."
3. Tell your sins simply and honestly to the priest.

(You might even want to discuss the circumstances and the root causes of your sins and ask the priest for advice or direction.)

4. Listen to the advice the priest gives you and accept the penance from him. Then make an Act of Contrition for your sins.
5. The priest will dismiss you with the words of praise: "Give thanks to the Lord for He is good" or "the Lord has freed you from your sins. Go in peace. " And you respond by saying either: "His mercy endures forever" or "Thanks be to God."
6. Spend some time with Our Lord thanking and praising Him for the gift of His mercy. Try to perform your penance as soon as possible.

An Act of Contrition

O my God, I am heartily sorry for having offended Thee and I detest all my sins because I dread the loss of heaven and the pains of hell, but most of all because they have offended Thee, my God, Who art all good and deserving of all my love.

I firmly resolve, with the help of Thy grace to confess my sins, to do penance and to amend my life. Amen.

An Act of Contrition*

My God,
I am sorry for my sins with all my heart.
In choosing to do wrong
and failing to do good,
I have sinned against you
whom I should love above all things.
I firmly intend, with your help,
to do penance,
to sin no more,
and to avoid whatever leads me to sin.
Our Savior Jesus Christ
suffered and died for us.
In his name, my God, have mercy.

*From the Rites of the Catholic Church as revised by decree of the Second Vatican Ecumenical Council and Published by Authority of Pope Paul VI.

English translation prepared by The International Commission on English in the Liturgy.

Litany of the Most Precious Blood of Jesus

Lord, have mercy.
Christ, have mercy.
Lord, have mercy.
Christ, hear us.
Christ, graciously hear us.
God, the Father of Heaven, *have mercy on us.*
God, the Son, Redeemer of the world, *have mercy on us.*
God, the Holy Spirit, *have mercy on us.*
Holy Trinity, One God, *have mercy on us.*
Blood of Christ, only-begotten Son of the Eternal Father, *save us.*
Blood of Christ, Incarnate Word of God,*
Blood of Christ, of the New and Eternal Testament,
Blood of Christ, falling upon the earth in the Agony,
Blood of Christ, shed profusely in the Scourging,
Blood of Christ, flowing forth in the Crowning with Thorns,
Blood of Christ, poured out on the Cross,
Blood of Christ, price of our salvation,
Blood of Christ, without which there is no forgiveness,

**Save us.*

Blood of Christ, Eucharistic drink and refreshment of souls,*
Blood of Christ, stream of mercy,
Blood of Christ, victor over demons,
Blood of Christ, courage of martyrs,
Blood of Christ, strength of confessors,
Blood of Christ, bringing forth virgins,
Blood of Christ, help of those in peril,
Blood of Christ, relief of the burdened,
Blood of Christ, solace in sorrow,
Blood of Christ, hope of the penitent,
Blood of Christ, consolation of the dying,
Blood of Christ, peace and tenderness of hearts,
Blood of Christ, pledge of eternal life,
Blood of Christ, freeing souls from purgatory,
Blood of Christ, most worthy of all glory and honor,*
Lamb of God, You Who take away the sins of the world, *spare us, O Lord.*
Lamb of God, You Who take away the sins of the world, *graciously hear us, O Lord.*
Lamb of God, You Who take away the sins of the world, *have mercy on us.*

V. You have redeemed us, O Lord, in your blood.

R. And made us, for our God, a kingdom.

**Save us.*

Let us pray

Almighty and eternal God, You have appointed your only-begotten Son the Redeemer of the world and willed our redemption through his blood. Grant we beg of You, that we may worthily adore this price of our salvation, and through its power be safeguarded from the evils of the present life, so that we may rejoice in its fruits forever in heaven. Through the same Christ our Lord.

Amen.

For almost fifty years SOUL Magazine has been an integral part of the World Apostolate of Fatima. SOUL is a valuable source of information on the latest developments in the apostolate and the Church relating to Fatima. At the same time, SOUL publishes inspiring articles on Fatima, the Catholic Faith, prayer, Marian devotion, the lives of the saints, scripture and the spiritual life. Reading SOUL is a wonderful way for you to remain current on the latest news about Fatima and the World Apostolate of Fatima. Reading SOUL can also help to recharge your "spiritual batteries." For some, reading SOUL has even offered a point of conversion, reminding them of the ultimate realities in life.

WAF division leaders and members alike should read SOUL to stay abreast of apostolate news and remain current on the Fatima message. By doing so they will help themselves be more informed, credible and effective Blue Army representatives both to potential members and the Church at large.

While SOUL supports the work of the WAF on all levels, we depend on you to support SOUL. We have no sales force and no advertising department. By helping us to increase our family of readers, both within the apostolate and on the outside, you are helping to insure the future of this important publication.

We encourage all WAF divisions to establish and maintain an active SOUL promotion committee in their diocese. The World Apostolate of Fatima National Center will be happy to provide promotional copies of SOUL for the price of shipping and handling, as well as SOUL subscription cards. Opportune times to promote SOUL include visits to the diocese of the National Pilgrim Virgin Statue, All-Night Vigils, Rosary rallies and processions and other apostolate events. Some divisions have promoted SOUL at county and state fairs. The possibilities for this type of work are unlimited.

If you have questions about promoting SOUL, please contact us at SOUL Magazine, PO Box 976, Washington, NJ 07882 or call (908) 689-1700 x18. We are also very interested in hearing your comments about SOUL.

WAF Prayer Cells

The first level of organized Blue Army activity is the Prayer Cell. A Blue Army Prayer Cell is a weekly spiritual gathering for small group prayer before the Blessed Sacrament or in a home. Members endeavor to grow in holiness by responding to Our Lady of Fatima's requests for prayer, penance and sacrifice in a spirit of reparation.

God has always required perseverance in prayer from the faithful in the Old and New Testaments (Sir. 17:24; 18:22; Luke 21:26; Rom. 12:12; Eph. 6:18; Col. 4:2; I Thess. 17 and I Peter 4:7). At Fatima, the angel and the Blessed Virgin reinforced to the children and all Christians the scriptural imperative to remain constant in prayer. Participating in a Blue Army Prayer Cell is an excellent means of putting these healthy spiritual admonitions into practice.

It may be said that the first prayer cell started with Our Lady and the three children at Fatima. During her six apparitions at Fatima in 1917, Our Lady and the children prayed together.

The Prayer Cell Program

We follow a ten-point program of prayer, based on the spiritual exercises of Saint Ignatius of Loyola, which includes the Rosary and prayers taught by Our Lady and the Angel of Peace at Fatima:

Opening Prayer

1. Eucharistic, Sacrifice and Angel's prayers
2. WAF Pledge
3. Meditative Rosary
4. St. Michael Prayer, Petition for Life and Pardon Prayer
5. Invocation of WAF Patrons
6. Motivation Report (prayer petitions)
7. Suggested Spiritual Reading:

a. Lucia Speaks- (The Message of Fatima: on apparition at each meeting for beginners)
b. Fatima in Lucia's Own Words-(Sister Lucia's memoirs)
c. Articles from the special Fatima issue of SOUL magazine
d. Articles from regular issues of SOUL magazine
e. The Catechism of the Catholic Church or other approved catechism
f. The Gospels and other New Testament readings
g. True Devotion to Mary or the Secret of the Rosary by St. Louis de Montfort
h. My Imitation of Christ by Thomas A Kempis
i. My Daily Bread: A Summary of the Spiritual Life by Fr. Anthony J Pavone, S.J.

8. Examination by cell members (report on previous week's resolutions)

9. Resolutions for the week
10. Eucharistic Prayer and Angel's Prayer

Just as the cells in a body divide and grow, a prayer group should do the same. After there are between eight and ten members, part of the group splits and forms a new prayer cell to grow and form new cells again. In this manner, more and more people will be filled with the prayerful spirit of the Fatima message.

The prayer cell offers members the joy of holy friendships, of praying together and helping each other to respond to Our Lady's Fatima message.

If there is an established WAF Prayer Cell in your parish or in a nearby home, you can join it. If not, contact your local WAF diocesan division and inquire about prayer cells in your diocese. If a diocesan division does not exist, contact the WAF National Center. Interest others in participating in a prayer cell. By all means approach your pastor. Show him the ten-point program and explain your reason for wanting to pray in a group. If you cannot obtain permission to meet in a church, begin a prayer cell in your home. Two or three persons are sufficient to form a prayer cell.

Details of Prayer Cell operations are available in the WAF Prayer Cell kit which includes the Leader's manual and a sample copy of all literature each prayer cell member should have for a meeting. The kit is available from your WAF diocesan division or the National WAF Center.

In her apparitions, Our Lady of Fatima asked for prayer, penance and sacrifices. She especially asked for the daily recitation of the Rosary and that we pray very much and make sacrifices for sinners because many souls go to hell since there is no one to pray and make sacrifices for them.

Our Lady was instrumental in the collapse of communism in Russia which has opened the way for its conversion. The World Apostolate of Fatima has much to do to help fulfill Our Lady's promise that Russia would be converted. We must also work for the conversion of America that is being overshadowed by the corruption of materialism and immorality. Prayer and sacrifices are the tools needed to accomplish this. You can make a difference! Won't you join a prayer cell group today?

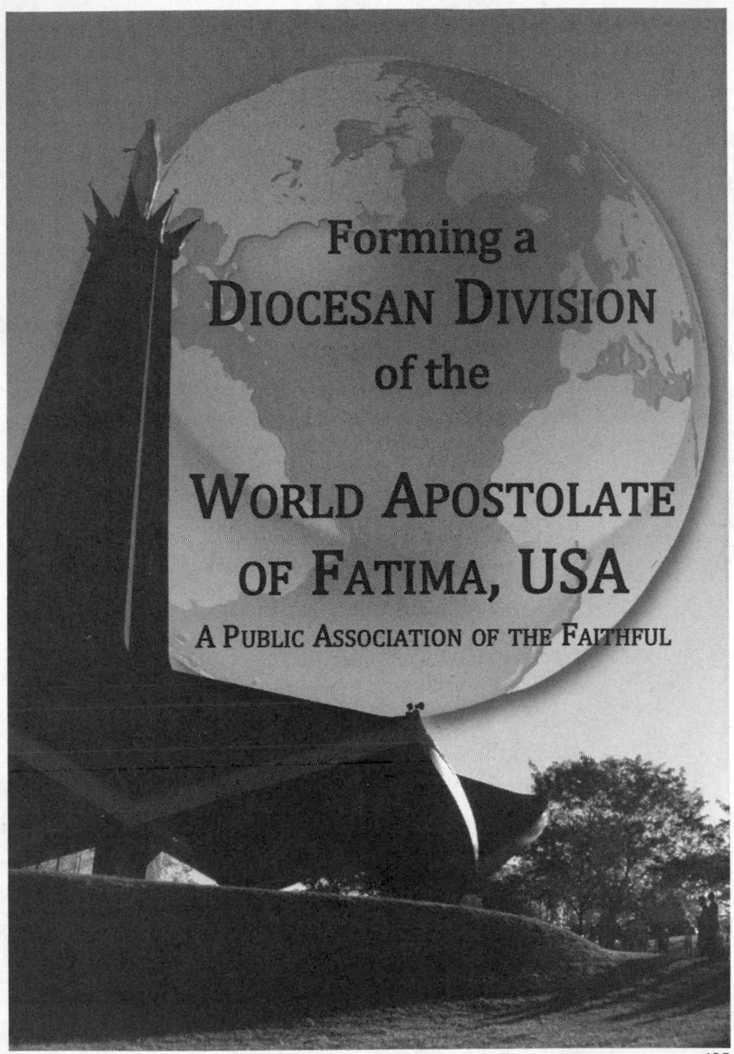
Forming a
DIOCESAN DIVISION
of the
WORLD APOSTOLATE
OF FATIMA, USA
A PUBLIC ASSOCIATION OF THE FAITHFUL

Forming a Diocesan Division of the
World Apostolate of Fatima, USA
A Public Association of the Faithful

Contents

Introduction

This booklet is intended as a guide for your efforts to establish a new World Apostolate of Fatima Diocesan Division in your diocese. It does not answer all your questions; it does not address every situation. It does point you in the right direction; it does give you a framework within which you can work, while at the same time allowing you the flexibility to address circumstances unique to your diocese.

Some very important guidelines must be presented at the very beginning of this process, so that the diocesan division which will result from your efforts will be formed according to the mission, programs and structure of the worldwide International World Apostolate of Fatima. And the national World Apostolate of Fatima, USA, Inc., previously known as the Blue Army of Our Lady of Fatima.

Organization Structure

The World Apostolate of Fatima is a Public Association of the Faithful under the Pontifical Council of the Laity. Under Canon law (Church law) we are privileged to be one of very few lay apostolate's that are officially part of the Catholic Church, and we are the only Fatima organization. With this privileged comes great responsibility to the Holy Father and to the Vatican to fulfill our mission in communion with the Bishops of the world. Pope John Paul II worked closely with us to establish the World Apostolate of Fatima in its present form, partly because he felt the "Message of Fatima is More Important now Than Ever."

International headquarters is not based in any country but is comprised of 9 board members who represent different continents and are elected by representatives from member nations every four years. The International office is maintained in Fatima, Portugal at a hotel owned and operated by the World Apostolate of Fatima, USA, Domus Pacis, the International President oversees international operations. Each member nation establishes "Divisions" within the dioceses of its country to carry out the work of the Apostolate. A Division is authorized by the National Center and is established only with the approval of the National Center and the local Bishop. Each Division has a Spiritual Director who is assigned by the local Bishop.

Representatives from Divisions meet annually to elect National Board of Trustee Members and to do the business of the apostolate. A National center is maintained in Washington NJ at the National Blue Army Shrine of the Immaculate Heart of Mary. Many tens of thousands of pilgrims visit the shrine each year and the National Center supports the work of the Apostolate and its Divisions. The National Board of Trustees determines and oversees the work of the Apostolate in concert with its mission, constitution and by-laws.

Our Mission is to promote and spread the message that

Mary brought to the three little shepherd children at Fatima in 1917. The message of Fatima contains everything we as Catholics need to do in order to please God and help convert the world. Because this is true, the Fatima message is commonly referred to as the "Peace Plan from Heaven." Mary promised an era of peace and the triumph of her Immaculate Heart if we do what she asks. Focusing on this mission does not, of course, exclude us from referring to other Church-approved apparitions in so far as they show similarity with or support for the Fatima message. As members of a Church-approved organization we must, however, be very careful not to reference alleged apparitions which have not received Church approval.

All World Apostolate of Fatima programs and all aspects of our apostolate spring from what Mary said to Lucia, Francisco and Jacinta, and from what she asked of them. As you get more deeply involved in formal apostolate programs you will see this connection.

The structure of your division should be a smaller version of the World Apostolate of Fatima, USA as it now exists, having been reorganized in 2006 as a result of the adoption of a new International Constitution read by and approved by Pope John Paul II. Initial planning for a new division should work towards developing a diocesan division council comprised of 3 delegates from each parish, and an elected board of trustees and officers. The Division adopts a constitution and bylaws in concert with the National Constitution and by-laws, incorporates under state law and receives federal IRS not-for-profit-corporation tax-exempt status, and obtains insurance coverage.

No doubt this sounds like a rather overwhelming undertaking, fear not! The above is an explanation of the ultimate structure of a diocesan division. Fully organizing a division will take time; however the division can begin to respond to Our Lady's request with the establishment of a "skeletal" structure that is described within these chapters. As time progresses and the Division builds you will find that the accomplishment of what was said above will not be an overwhelming process at all, because you will be carrying it out one step at a time. Assistance throughout the entire process will always be available from the National Center, primarily through contact with the National Coordinator. May God bless your efforts!

Forming a Diocesan Division of the
World Apostolate of Fatima, USA

The following information will help you through the process that leads to the establishment of a new division of the World Apostolate of Fatima in your diocese. ("Diocese" also refers to "Archdiocese.") The process is not one step-by-step list of actions to be undertaken in a fixed sequence. The flow of the process is determined by the particular set of circumstances in each diocese. Some of the factors determining the flow of the process are:

1. The source of the idea to start a World Apostolate of Fatima, USA Division (a priest, a lay person, a group of lay people, an existing organization or group already doing something that is part of the total Apostolate).

2. The availability of a priest to serve as spiritual director from the outset of the start-up effort. This priest may or may not become the permanent spiritual director. He should be a priest who is Marian-oriented in general and, if possible, Fatima-oriented.

3. The disposition of the bishop toward Marian devotion is a real factor, as are his feelings relative to the World Apostolate of Fatima, USA. Your knowledge of this is very important as you begin this process.

4. The availability of and access to other individuals, lay and cleric, for assistance and involvement as the process move forward.

The World Apostolate of Fatima is a spiritual apostolate. This cannot be emphasized enough.

We must first learn the message of Fatima, then live the Fatima message in our own lives. By doing this we respond to the Vatican Council II call to holiness. Then we must spread this very important message to others so that they too will learn, live and ultimately evangelize the Fatima message. By our efforts in this area we respond to the Vatican Council II call to the apostolate of the Laity.

Our organization exists to teach people to learn, live and spread the Fatima message. This is not simply an academic exercise. Our goal is to change peoples lives – to get them to live the Fatima message, not just know about it. We must carry to others the "good news" of Fatima and inspire them to respond to it in their lives. As a result, members provide spiritual nourishment to our world.

In the framework of what has been said, let us move on

to the process of starting a World Apostolate of Fatima, USA Division in your diocese.

Two things must be done initially to establish a solid spiritual base for your new division. It is not necessary to do these two things in the order in which they are presented here. One thing that must be done in this overall process is to have a priest who will act as the spiritual director for those involved in leading the effort to establish a Division in the diocese. The entire process and every facet of activity must be spiritually based and under the guidance of a spiritual director. Without spiritual nourishment, your efforts will suffer. Following the initial idea to form a division, acquiring the assistance of a temporary or permanent spiritual director has to be high on the list of things to accomplish.

Another thing that must be done is to establish a foundation in prayer for the success of your efforts and for guidance in maintaining proper focus and perspective in your efforts. To do this, you must set up at least one Apostolate prayer cell. The prayer cell is a fundamental element of the worldwide Apostolate. Just as the cells of a body grow and multiply and develop that body, so too the Prayer Cells grow and multiply and develop the apostolate. Prayer cells are small gatherings of people – two to eight members – who meet once a week in their parish church preferably, or in someone's home. There is a prayer cell kit available that explains in detail how to establish a cell and how to conduct it. When the prayer cell grows to eight or ten members it should divide in two – just like body cells – thus continuing to grow and develop the prayer support for the apostolate and to fulfill Our Lady's request for prayer for the salvation of souls and to bring about an era of peace. If you check with the National Center, you may be able to find out if there are any Prayer Cells already in your diocese; you can build on them and get the members involved in the new diocesan division.

It is necessary to obtain the blessing and authorization of your bishop to formally establish a World Apostolate of Fatima, USA Division in your diocese. The National Center of the apostolate will not recognize, as part of the organization, any group which does not have the approval of its bishop. The official status of the diocesan division is derived from its affiliation with the National and International organization. The bishop's permission to establish the division confers no official status from the diocese; it only gives approval for the division of the World Apostolate of Fatima to operate in his diocese. Even though the bishop's approval is necessary, the particular point in the process where this approval is sought is dependent upon the preference of the bishop. The decision when to approach the bishop could perhaps best be made by the spiritual director who presumably, especially if he is a diocesan priest, will know the bishop's preference, and, therefore be the best equipped person to decide when to approach him for his approval.

This acceptance of the organization and the appointment or confirmation of the spiritual director must be in written form, a copy of which must be forwarded to the National Center.

An Organization Begins to Take Shape

With these items clear in your mind, let's look at the actual setting up of the division. The initiator(s) of the idea of establishing a Division, along with the spiritual director – and with the prayer support of prayer cells which have already been established – are now ready to sit down together to begin the development of an "organization." This first meeting will have a minimum of two attendees – the spiritual director, and the lay person who initiated the idea. Depending on what "recruitment" has been done before this meeting, it could be attended by a significant number of people. As with every Apostolate gathering, the meeting should start with a prayer.

The purpose of this first meeting is to discuss among those in attendance the proposal to start a World Apostolate of Fatima, USA, Inc. Division. If there are very few people at this meeting – perhaps five or fewer – the thrust of your discussion may be directed to the level of interest and dedication to this project on the part of those few people. If it is the consensus of those present that there is not enough support within this group to justify continuing the effort to form a division, then you will have to attempt to reach out to other people. Those at this first meeting may all participate in this new recruitment effort, or perhaps some will simply decide not to be involved further and the remainder will continue recruiting until they feel there is enough support to convene another "initial" meeting.

When, in one of these "initial" meetings, you achieve a consensus that it is time to proceed, you are ready to select temporary officers. This may be done, depending on circumstances, by election, appointment, or volunteering. You will have to decide in your meeting the most appropriate method of doing this. These will be only temporary officers to serve in the start-up phase of the organization efforts. When you broaden your efforts at recruitment, it will be to your benefit to be able to approach prospective members in the framework of an existing structured group.

If you have not yet approached the bishop for official approval, it is at this point that you may wish to have your spiritual director seek the bishop's approval for the establishment of the division and for the bishop to confirm or appoint him as your spiritual director – presuming, of course, that he wants to continue. If the people who have been selected to fill the temporary officer positions are people already known to the bishop because of other service to the diocese, so much the better.

Your approach to the bishop could include (according to your particular circumstances) the explanation of the role of the World Apostolate of Fatima, USA Division in the diocese. The division will be a benefit to the bishop, because all the division's efforts are directed to help all who participate in World Apostolate of Fatima programs to more fully respond to the Second Vatican Council's Universal Call to Holiness, and to the Vatican's call for the World Apostolate of Fatima to serve the Church as a Public Association of the Faithful under the Pontifical Council of the Laity. Similarly, your division members and leaders have responded to the council's call to the Apostolate of the Laity.

Before leaving the topic of obtaining your bishop's approval for the formation of an approved World

Apostolate of Fatima, USA Division, you should know that the National Center will help you with this in any way we can. All you need to do is call the National Coordinator at the National Center.

Another service of the National Center is also available to you at this point in your organization process. We will assist you by doing a mailing to "World Apostolate of Fatima, USA people" in your diocese so that you may inform them of an upcoming major organizational or kickoff meeting. You provide to us the first three digits of all the zip codes in your diocese, and we will do a mailing in your diocese. The National Coordinator will work with your representative to develop the letter and arrange for the mailing. If you do not have any funds available or donors to contribute to this mailing, the National Center will advance the money for the mailing. The agreement is that when you receive sufficient financial support from your members you will reimburse the National Center in whole or in part depending on your means. Once you are formally established and functioning, we will give you a list of all people in your diocese to whom the mailing went. The letter cannot be sent out until you have a date, time and place for the meeting, and the agenda as well.

The First General Organizational Meeting

This brings us to the next step in this process – planning the organizational meeting. You should plan to start the meeting on a strong spiritual foundation; working with your spiritual advisor you can determine the agenda for the first meeting. Consider starting with a Holy Hour, which will include Exposition of the Blessed Sacrament, five decades of the Rosary, a short homily, and Benediction. Holy Hour should be conducted by the spiritual director and the homily can be very effectively used to develop interest in the Fatima message in general and the formation of the division in particular. Immediately after Benediction the acting president (or another leader) should announce that there will be refreshments in the church hall (or other location) and the organization meeting will take place there after refreshments or during refreshments, whichever is appropriate.

Whenever the organizers of the division decide it will be beneficial to the establishment or ongoing work of the division, they can invite someone from the National Center to attend their meeting to give a presentation or advice. The person to invite would be the National Coordinator, since it is he who is primarily responsible for assisting in the establishment of new divisions, or the Executive Director. If schedule conflicts prevent his attending, he may be able to send someone else. Circumstances may make it impossible for anyone from the National Center to attend. In this event, we will arrange to have a volunteer from a neighboring division attend your meeting and represent the National Center. Whoever comes, there will be no expense to the new division.

For this organizational meeting there should be a prepared agenda with certain responsibilities:

1. The spiritual director should explain (if he has not already done so in his homily at the Holy Hour) the spiritual thrust of the Apostolate. This should be a general explanation of the responsibilities of the pledge, the need for reparation, the emphasis on personal sanctification and evangelization of others. Even though Mary appeared at Fatima in 1917, her message is "pure Vatican II" in so far as it relates to the Universal Call to Holiness and the Apostolate of the Laity. The emphasis must be on the fact that Fatima is a message for today.

2. The interim president should then explain what organizational activities have taken place up to this point in the process and who has been involved. Interim officers should be introduced. Also report on the approval of the bishop, and mention that there will be an election

of permanent officers later in the meeting.

3. There should be a brief explanation of each of the major programs of the World Apostolate of Fatima, USA. Special emphasis should be given to national programs. For all the other programs, a brief few words can be said just to give people a general idea of the scope of activity in which the Apostolate is involved.

4. At any point in this meeting you may schedule the presentation by the representative of the National Center. This presentation will include an explanation of the relationship between the National Center and the individual divisions as well as current National and International news and events.

5. A question and answer period would be appropriate at some time during the meeting, perhaps as a separate agenda item. It could be made known at the outset of the meeting that questions may be asked at any time.

6. Election of officers should be held at this meeting. The interim officers or others may be elected to be the "permanent" officers. Nominations must be made from the floor to nominate candidates for all the offices: president, vice-president, secretary, treasurer, or combination secretary-treasurer or a corresponding secretary

and a recording secretary. Interim officers can be nominated individually if they wish to continue, or a motion can be made to elect all the interim officers for a three-year term if they are all willing to continue. The usual term for officers is three years.

7. If it is possible committees and chairpeople should be appointed at this meeting who will take individual responsibility for promoting specific programs such as membership growth and retention and growth and development of prayer cells. The newly elected president can ask for volunteers or, if he or she is familiar with the interests of some of the attendees, he or she can appoint those persons.

8. If committee chairpersons are appointed at this meeting, it should be announced that an "executive committee" meeting will be held before the next general meeting in order to discuss plans for various aspects of apostolate work so that reports can be presented at the next general meeting and members can be asked to volunteer to work with specific chairpersons in various aspects of apostolate activities.

9. Finally, a time, place and date should be suggested for the next meeting. Suggestions should be solicited for the type of spiritual activity to begin the meeting.

A few words need to be said about officers' three year terms mentioned above. From the very beginning of a division, members must be thinking about its continued viability, its growth, its openness to change and to new ideas. A primary way to assure the success of the new division is to have officers elected for specific terms, and also to have a limit on the number of consecutive terms which an officer can serve. A three-year term of office is the most common in our divisions, and a limit of two consecutive terms is quite common. Provision can be made for election of a former officer after a one term hiatus. Experience has shown that when someone gets elected to office and continues year after year, there is a general although not universal, tendency for the division to stagnate. People lose interest and the division begins to lose previously active people and ultimately, a division exists "on the books," but there is no or minimal activity taking place. These are considerations to be addressed formally in your constitution and/or bylaws. More on this follows.

You've Organized – Now What?

If you have proceeded according to the plan explained above, you should now be able to look at what you have done and find yourself in an established World Apostolate of Fatima Diocesan Division, approved not only by your diocesan bishop, but also by the National Center of the World Apostolate of Fatima, USA. You should have at this time a slate of elected officers beginning their three-year term. You should have most, if not all, of your committee chairpersons selected and, with the aid of volunteers, be carrying out specific aspects of the Apostolate. What comes next?

You should immediately start establishing a "formal" World Apostolate of Fatima presence throughout your diocese. You are THE ONLY World Apostolate of Fatima Division in your diocese. You need to develop your diocesan organization so that it involves all parishes in the diocese. In small dioceses, this is relatively simple. In larger dioceses this can be a formidable challenge, but you must do it. If you do not make distant areas of your diocese feel as much a part of the division as do the people in the principal diocesan city or in the parish from which most of the officers may come, you will be headed for stagnation. The most vibrant divisions in the USA are those organized similar to the structure described in the next paragraphs.

At this point, your new diocesan division has a spiritual director, a slate of officers, and a group of committee chairmen and volunteers. You are ready to begin work on setting up what will become the formal structure when you adopt your constitution. The foundation of this structure is laid by meeting with pastors on a parish by parish basis. Tell them about the new diocesan division of the World Apostolate of Fatima, USA. There are different approaches to doing this. One is for the president of the new division to contact pastors by phone or letter asking for a meeting with him to explain the new Division and its programs. Another way is to utilize people who have been involved already in the organization of the new division and have them contact their own pastors to explain the new division and its programs.

Whatever approach is used, two things must be asked of the pastor during this meeting: (1) Appoint two parishioners as the official representatives to the diocesan division of the World Apostolate of Fatima, USA. (The pastor would be the third parish representative to the diocesan division.) (2) Indicate a willingness to allow Apostolate programs and devotions to function in the parish with approval on a case by case basis.

It is to be expected that you will not be able to set up an appointment with every pastor you contact. When you do meet with a pastor, he may not agree to either of the two items mentioned above. Do not be discouraged; just move on. You may certainly use your spiritual director as a contact person with pastors in order to help "open doors" for the meeting. Remember, don't focus on the fact that your diocese has 100, 200, or 300 parishes. Simply focus on the one you are going to contact. Each time you are successful with one parish, you have added three "official" parish representatives to your division.

These parish representatives become the governing body of the diocesan division – usually called the diocesan division council – and at their annual meetings pass resolutions, act on major issues of division activity, and also elect trustees to represent them during the time between the annual meetings. In formed Divisions, the number of trustees is usually nine. The National Apostolate has nine, as do many of the divisions. Details of election of trustees and officers will be addressed when you develop your constitution. For now, proceed with your present set-up.

This is a good time to prepare a news release to distribute to your diocesan newspaper and to all the secular newspapers in your diocese. Don't forget! You are a Diocesan Division of World Apostolate of Fatima, USA a Public Association of the Faithful. That means that you function on a diocesan-wide level. Your news release should reflect this "universal" presence within the diocese. A properly prepared news release will most likely bring you more volunteers. In fact, you should ask for volunteers. The people of your diocese need to know that you are there. Keep this in mind as you schedule events and plan activities. Announce events in your diocesan newspaper, parish bulletins and elsewhere. If you are planning something very public like a procession or a Rosary rally, inform the secular press as well. People may see it there but not in the diocesan paper. You should have as one of your volunteers a "public information" person who is good at writing news releases.

Looking to the Future

After you've been functioning for a while and feel confident enough, after prayer and discernment under the guidance of your spiritual director, you should start thinking about a constitution and bylaws for your new organization. You will also want to think about incorporating and getting tax exempt status. These are all things with which the National Center will help you. When you actually are going to get involved in these items of business, you should contact the National Center to get assistance and direction in your efforts. Much of this assistance will come to you in the form of the World Apostolate of Fatima, USA Manual which will be provided to you. We will make available to you copies of our National constitution and bylaws, upon which your diocesan documents should be modeled. We will also provide a sample copy of a division's actual documents to facilitate your efforts. Another source of help available to you is our corporate attorney. He will be happy to talk to you or your attorney to assist you and answer questions (at no charge to you).

It is appropriate to mention here at the conclusion of this document what was stated so strongly at the beginning. Unless ALL your efforts are rooted in the basic concept that the World Apostolate of Fatima is a spiritual apostolate, you will be doomed to failure. Your division will not grow and thrive. It will suffer the fate of the seed that falls on ground with soil too shallow to properly nurture its growth. It will spring up, but it will soon die for lack of nourishment. The food of Apostolate and its division is prayer and spirituality; it is the grace of God which we must constantly seek and for which we must constantly pray; it is the love of Our Lady of Fatima as shown in our dedication to her message without thought of personal benefit.

We live in the world; we function in the world; our divisions need resources of the world. That is our human conditions. As long as we seek and use the resources of the world only for the glory of God and for our spiritual mission, God and his Blessed Mother will bless our efforts, the Apostolate and we will produce fruit one hundred fold.

Know that you are not alone or without resources. Do

not hesitate to contact the National Coordinator or the Executive Director at the National Center at any time for direction, advice, assistance or for answers to questions.

May God bless all your efforts, and may Our Blessed Lady of Fatima be your constant companion and guide.

The Blue Army Shrine of the
Immaculate Heart of Mary

PO Box 976
Washington, NJ 07882
908-689-1700
www.wafusa.org

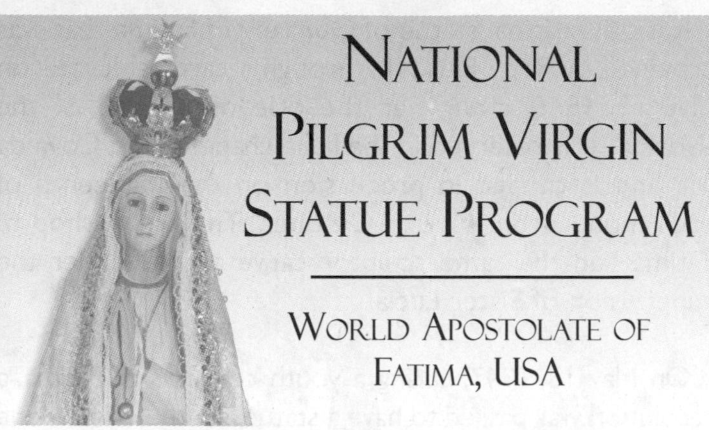

National Pilgrim Virgin Statue Program

World Apostolate of Fatima, USA

Filled with bitterness for reasons known only to himself, a wealthy Portuguese man named Gilberto went to Fatima on May 13, 1920, just three years following the first apparition. His pilgrimage plans did not include prayers like the intentions of most of the pilgrims. He went there with the intention of throwing bombs at the pilgrims he would find praying there. Heaven, however, intervened, and Gilberto returned to his home converted.

In thanksgiving for the peace he now felt within himself through this conversion, he hired the most widely acclaimed sculptor in Portugal, Jose Thedim, to carve a statue in the likeness of the vision of Our Lady seen by the three children.

It is this original statue of Our lady of Fatima that was crowned by Pope Pius XII, through a cardinal legate, on May 13, 1946, giving her the title of "Queen of the World." It is reserved in the little chapel at the Cova da Iria and is carried in procession on the thirteenth of each month from May to October. The first Bishop of Fatima had the same sculptor carve a copy under the supervision of Sister Lucia.

On May 13, 1947, during a youth congress at Fatima, a resolution was passed to have a statue like the original one at the Cova carried throughout Europe and into Russia. Sister Lucia suggested the bishop give his statue for this purpose and that it be known as the "Pilgrim Virgin."

Since then, the Fatima sanctuary has commissioned a number of International Pilgrim Virgin Statues that have been carried far and wide throughout the world as a means of making the Fatima message known. For several years one of these statues was in the custody of the World Apostolate of Fatima, USA and which used it extensively in evangelizing through the Fatima message.

U.S. NATIONAL PILGRIM VIRGIN

On the fiftieth anniversary of the Fatima apparitions on May 13, 1967, Pope Paul VI blessed twenty-five national Pilgrim Virgin Statues of Our Lady of Fatima to be presented to individual countries around the world. The Pilgrim Virgin statue for the United States was received in Columbus, Ohio, and is presently traveling throughout the country under the auspices of the World Apostolate of Fatima, USA. In 1997 it celebrated its thirtieth year of diocesan visitations.

The message of Our Lady of Fatima carried by her Pilgrim Virgin statue is the same: Christ, and Christ alone is our Redeemer; He is Love and mercy and the Giver of every grace. Because Mary is the Mother of Jesus, and His most perfect imitator, she can intercede for us, her children. Mankind offends God by sin; therefore we must offer reparation for our sins, and the sins of others.

SCHEDULING THE PILGRIM VIRGIN IN YOUR DIOCESE

The ultimate goal of the National Pilgrim Virgin Statue Program is to have the statue spend at least twenty-two days in each diocese of the United States. Wherever there is an established World Apostolate of Fatima Diocesan Division, one of the main goals of the division should be to have the national Pilgrim Virgin Statue visit the diocese. Requests should be sent to the World Apostolate of Fatima, USA to reserve the statue for your diocese. Be aware that the statue is often booked more than a year in advance. After the statue is scheduled for your diocese, planning for the visit should begin anywhere from six months to a year in advance. A general chairman and a spiritual director should be in charge. Following verification of the date, the World Apostolate of Fatima, USA will assist you in contacting your bishop for diocesan approval. When a letter of approval is received at the World Apostolate of Fatima from your bishop, you will receive your Pilgrim Virgin kit, containing all the tools you will need in planning this very special event.

Hosting a visit of the National Pilgrim Virgin Statue offers a wonderful opportunity for Diocesan Divisions to recruit new WAF members through the pledge and SOUL Magazine. Advantage should be taken of such opportunities by having a good supply of WAF materials, especially pledges, and a good supply of SOUL subscription forms (available from the National Center) along with sample copies for viewing.

Sponsoring groups such as Holy Name or Altar Rosary Societies, Knights of Columbus and Legion of Mary can also schedule the statue if there is no active World Apostolate of Fatima diocesan division.

The World Apostolate of Fatima – A Marian Apostolate for Our Times

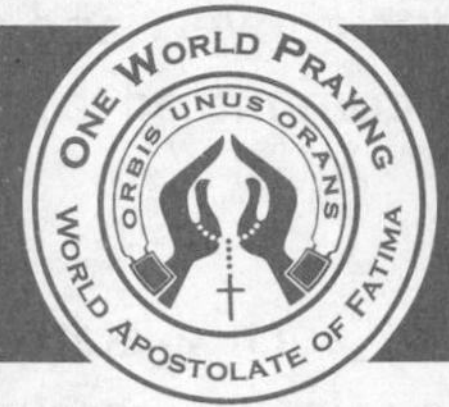

Prof. Américo Lopéz-Ortiz
International President of the
World Apostolate of Fatima

Our times are characterized by a spirit of confusion, dissatisfaction, insecurity and indifference. The multiplying effect of humanity's sins, the contempt for the issues concerning God and the order established by the Creator, and the violence present in human relations, have a devastating effect over the collective spirit of our societies which become sick, weakened, old and agonizing. Many people are conscious of this conditions but feel there is nothing they can do to remedy it.

The Most Holy Virgin of Fatima, echoing the Gospel of her Beloved Son, Jesus Christ, prophesied this state of affairs if humanity was not going to change its way of life and if it did not convert and do penance for the horrendous sins committed by so many unfortunate people.

What to do when confronted by such a state of affairs? We must put into practice the spiritual measures prescribed by Our Lady of Fatima. These measures can and must change the course of history as we human beings put them into practice in our personal lives and in our relations with others. The World Apostolate of Fatima is a public association of the faithful who have undertaken the mission to spread and make live the message of Our Lady of Fatima as a very powerful tool in the New Evangelization proposed by the Holy Father, John Paul II, the Great and his successor, Benedict XVI, as a task to be performed by the Universal Church.

At the commencement of this third millennium of Christendom we must face the crisis of our times with the spiritual weapons prescribed by the Most Holy Virgin of Fatima: PRAYER, PENANCE, CONVERSION, CONSECRATION TO HER IMMACULATE HEART, ADORATION AND EUCHARIST REPARATION. These spiritual means represent the best of our FAITH and it is these, and only these, that can change the course of history.

THE MIRACLE OF THE CENTURY

What has happened in Russia from the time the Holy Father John Paul II made a collegiate consecration of Russia and the world on 25 March, 1984, as per the requests of the Virgin of Fatima, is an indication of greater graces being bestowed upon humanity waiting to be asked. This is because many of the graces that are available are not granted because no one requests them. Instead of becoming confused by our inability to understand the roads of God, and being dominated by the uneasiness felt by witnessing the laborious and difficult task of the conversion of the peoples of Russia and of the whole world, we should concentrate all our energy and resources to evangelize our own society and our cultural environment.

THE EFFORT OF THE CENTURY

God, Our Lord, has done His part, with the assistance of Our Lady of Fatima. This has changed the direction of history and has opened a wonderful range of possibilities. It is now our turn, as Disciples of Christ, to carry out our work, our commitment. The historical responsibility rests on our shoulders. It is our turn to carry out the effort of the century through the spiritual means offered by Our Lady of Fatima to transform the societies of the present world by means that facilitate the salvation of souls, so that they stop being what they are, true instruments for ruining souls. The task is formidable, but possible with God's help, that can do all. Let us put into practice the PLAN FROM HEAVEN:

1, The meditative prayer of the daily Holy Rosary, preferably carried out with the family, at the most convenient time.

2, The revitalizing penance will crush the evil in our soul; it will forgive our faults, thus improving the spiritual health of the Mystical Body of Christ, the Church, "which today suffers and bleeds for so many afflicted parts".

3, The true conversion or return to God by the repentant heart does wonders, because "in heavens there is more joy for a sinner who repents than for ninety-nine righteous men who remain righteous".

4. The consecration to the Immaculate Heart of Mary will be the antidote against the threats of evil. By giving ourselves to Mary as her possession ("TOTUS TUUS"), she will defend us against all attacks and dangers that threatens our spiritual life, and despite not being exempt from falls and hard tests, we will always return to God in the knowledge that by her intercession, we will reflect and grow in the life of sanctity and presence of the Lord.

5. Eucharistic adoration and reparation will be the principal means through which our faith will attain the greatest victories, because "this is the sign that has been given to us". In the context of the message of Fatima, the Eucharistic devotion of the Communion of Reparation of the Five First Saturdays is linked to obtaining the grace of unity among all Christians and the internal strength of the Universal Church. In order for this to take place, first it is necessary to spread the true message of Our Lady in a much greater manner than it is now, and to achieve through our apostolic effort the conversion of many sinners and that many souls put into practice the PLAN FROM HEAVEN announced in Fatima. Once numerous Christians return to the adora-

tion and reparation of the Eucharist ("Hidden Jesus" as quoted from Francisco Marto), then will the great obstacles of this world crumble with the formidable strength of the power of God.

THE PRIMACY OF GOD IN THE MESSAGE OF FATIMA

Pope John XXIII said: "Fatima is the centre for all Christian hopes". When we consider our human frailties, and when all hope seems to vanish, THE MESSAGE FROM FATIMA SHINES THROUGH LIKE THE LIGHT OF A LIGHTHOUSE IN THE DENSEST FOG. This is so because, as Pope Paul VI said, the message from Fatima brings up to date the Gospel of our Lord Jesus Christ for all to know.

Through the words of Our Lady of Fatima the "Good News" of her beloved Son comes to life. The Virgin Mary came to Fatima to warn us of the dangers that threaten humanity. The atheism of the totalitarian Marxist governments, as well as the materialism of the masses are denounced as serious impediments to the establishment of the Kingdom of God. In simple words which could easily be understood by the children.

1. Even if what has to be done strikes us as formidable, it is important to point out the practical character of Our Mother's prophesy in Fatima. The message from Fatima is an EXISTENCIAL CALL TO HUMANITY for a change in lifestyles, a rejection of sin, and reparation for the crimes committed. Our Lady offers a SAFE AND REALISTIC METHOD that can change the course of Human History. The requests from Our Lady are the following:

2. Meditative Prayer – through daily recitation of the Holy Rosary (at least five of the mysteries, a tertiary) as an effective method for the development of souls in harmony with Our Lord capable of applying to their lives "the spiritual direction" which meditation on the events of the lives of Christ and Mary has to offer.

a. Reparation – which becomes life-giving penance, whose principal manifestation is the joyous acceptance of God's will, offering Our Lord through the Immaculate Heart of Mary, our prayers, good deeds, sufferings, joys and happiness, in other words, all our being and existence, in order for us to become like Christ.

b, In Fatima, Reparation is offered to us through three paths, which are:

Penance – in its dual acceptance of our submission to the will of God, which implies that we carry our daily cross, accepting the suffering that God sends us, as well as the mortification we inflict on ourselves by voluntary privation and sacrifice.

C, Reparatory Prayer – with a profound adoration for the Majesty of God which we offend with our lack of love, and which is superbly contained in the prayer by The Angel from Fatima and addressed to the Holy Trinity with the purpose of "consoling Our Good Lord, who is greatly offended".

2, Reparatory Holy Communion – through the Holy Sacrament of the altar transformed into a Banquet through the Eucharist, the Virgin offers THE GREAT PROMISE OF HER IMMACULATE HEART

Consecration to the Immaculate Heart of Mary, SOUL OF THE MESSAGE OF FATIMA, which consists of entrusting our past, present and future existence to the Lord through Mary. This is the true realization of our baptismal promises, in which we renounced Satan and all his works, the corrupt world, and our own egocentric weaknesses, in order to become the "new man", the "new being", raised up to the dignity of an adopted son of God, a true "ALTER CHRISTUS", with all that that implies. Through our consecration to the Immaculate Heart of Mary we become true spiritual children of Mary, conceived in her own heart, beating in union with all the Sacred Hearts, in an ineffable harmony of loving.

For now, we can point to several levels of consecration suggested by the Story of Fatima, which are as follows:

---

a. A rejection of sin, timidity, and indifference in favour of an imitation of Christ, his virtues and teachings, through a Marian spirit of joyous acceptance of the will of God, with all its repercussions for the human soul.

---

b. A deepening in the inner life of prayer, through the

discovery of a personal God who beats within our hearts, and a desire to please "the Good Lord" even in the smallest details so that "the fire of Our Lord burns our heart."

C, The highest mystical peaks can be reached as the priceless gift of the Heart of such a Holy Mother who gives sublime gifts to her favourite children revealing her most unimaginable treasures. BLESSED ARE THOSE WHO REACH SUCH A STATE OF SPIRITUAL PERFECTION, THAT PERSERVE AND TRIUMPH, FOR THEY TRULY BECOME OTHER MARYS, ADORNING THE CREATION OF THE FATHER WITH THEIR LOVING PRESENCE AND SAINTLY FRAGRANCE. They are the ones, more than anyone else that will make triumph that is imminent in our times, the twenty-first century.

PORTUGAL

Nuno Prazeres

WAF International Secretariat - Portugal

One World Praying for Life and Peace is an International Spiritual Fatima Event sponsored by the World Apostolate of Fatima.

The World Apostolate of Fatima coordinated Worldwide Fatima Sanctity of Life Day, in more than forty-two countries. Rooted in the Message of Fatima, this day was dedicated to prayer for the sanctity of human life.

This initiative came from the National Blue Army Shrine of the Immaculate Heart of Mary, USA, the American nucleus of the World Apostolate of Fatima, launched the challenge to all other member nations affiliated with this international movement. The aim was to gather and offer God more than one hundred million prayers for life.

After spreading this appeal worldwide, the

International Secretariat, located in Fatima, received more than 30 million prayer pledges, coming from all corners of the globe.

In Fatima, the program of the activities started with the International Mass at the Shrine of Our Lady of Fatima, presided by His Excellency Serafim Ferreira da Silva, Bishop of Leiria-Fatima and concelebrated by ninety priests. It is estimated that more than 150,000 people participated in this celebration. The Eucharist was followed by the blessing and dedication of the wonderful statue of Our Lady, Mary, Mother of the Life Within, at *Domus Pacis*, the international headquarters of the organization.

In the afternoon, a Rosary for the Sanctity of Life was prayed in the Chapel of the Apparitions and two conferences about the same subject were given at the auditorium of *Domus Pacis*.

International results were very positive; the Message of Fatima was associated, in an unprecedented way, with movements that strive to defend human life from conception to natural death.

At the national level, there were echoes from various associations and mass media agencies which, through their outlets, spoke about this event.

ECHOES FROM THE INTERNATIONAL CATHOLIC PRESS

Margaret M. Russell

Catholic News Service/

U.S. Conference of Catholic Bishops

Multitudes of people filled the square outside the Shrine of Our Lady of Fatima for Mass to mark the day of prayer for life. Bishop Serafim de Sousa Ferreira e Silva of Leiria-Fatima celebrated this Mass, which also served as the annual pilgrimage for lay Franciscans from throughout Portugal and for the people of the diocese. The World Apostolate of Fatima sponsored the day of prayer with the goal of getting 100 million prayers said for the intention of upholding the sacredness of life.

Before the Mass, thousands of families gathered at the shrine to offer prayers in thanksgiving for the intercession of Mary. Hundreds at a time prayed the rosary in the Chapel of the Apparition, while others crawled on their knees through the square and around the chapel in devotion to Mary.

After the Mass, His Excellency Serafim Ferreira da Silva went to the guesthouse Domus Pacis to bless a statue, "Mary Mother of the Life Within." Another statue was being blessed and placed at the U.S. headquarters in Washington, N.J., the same day. Bishop Serafim, said Mary was trying "to think, to do new things" for a better world. "Each of us has something to do. And the boss wants us to produce."

"If 60 years ago mankind could build an atomic bomb to destroy Hiroshima, why are we not able to neutralize a destructive hurricane?" the bishop asked. Nuno Prazeres said the initiative for the international day of prayer came from the Blue Army USA. "We hope that in the coming years it can become the largest day in the world for prayers for life," he added.

He said the international headquarters in Fatima has received prayer pledges from about 500,000 people. He said the Apostolate divisions in 42 countries were involved in the prayer day, and no figure for the total number of prayers had been tallied."

ARGENTINA

Mr. Ruben Tarcaya, WAF Salta-Argentina

The WAF in Argentina organized a detailed program for One World Praying Day, which included the prayer and meditation of the rosary, the Holy Mass and candlelight procession with Our Lady of Fatima through the streets of Salta. It was a wonderful day of prayer that ended with a procession, the ringing of bells and fireworks.

Many people pledged their prayers for this intention. We estimated 2,000 formal registers. In other WAF centers in Argentina, this initiative was also promoted through the mass media and e-mail.

INDIA

Francis S. Barreto, WAF Vice Chairman, India

The WAF Goa Unit and the Indian National Center had begun a Rosary chain praying for this intention a month before One World Praying Day, which culminated in a well attended Full Day Prayer Service at the *Institute Piedade* in Panjim.

The day started with the WAF Vice Chairman Francis S. Barreto highlighting Our Lady's Message. The Executive Trustee, Dr. Alvaro da Costa, began the Rosary with a special prayer between each decade: "Mary Queen of Christian Families, Pray for us and send us holy priests." Mr. Francis Barreto led the Holy Hour with "Calls From the Message of Fatima" by the late Sr. Lucia.

Back in the chapel, Filipe Goes led the Sorrowful Mysteries for holiness of Lay Faithful. Mass followed with Rev. Fr. Carmo Martins, Parish Priest of St. Alex Church, Dean of Calangute Deanery and Spiritual Advisor of the WAF.

After Mass, the Glorious Mysteries were recited in thanksgiving for the gift of the grace filled day and for the intention of holiness for members of the WAF all over the world. All left with grateful hearts and praising God for all He had done.

MEXICO

Jorge Gutierrez,
National President of WAF Mexico

Mexico responded enthusiastically to the invitation made by the World Apostolate of Fatima in USA to pray. National President of WAF Mexico, Jorge Gutierrez, said "It is important to give a response as human beings about preserving life from birth till death. But as followers of the Message of Fatima we believe that prayer, and the simple but demanding act of laying our hopes and fears before God, is a vital part of that response. . . I want you to continue saying the Rosary every day. . . Let's remember, the Rosary is a means to achieve a goal. Our goal is to do Our Lord's will to sanctify our lives."

SWITZERLAND

Mr. George Inglin,

WAF International Vice-President - Switzerland

"We had a great prayer feast in Einsiedeln. The World Apostolate of Fatima, in collaboration with other religious organizations, invited people to pray together. Over 200 people followed this call on a cold and rainy day. Our wonderful church was completely full during the Mass at 11 o'clock and also during the rosary in the afternoon. Not only in Einsiedeln, but also in many congregations, private houses and parishes, people prayed, and we think that we got one million prayers on that day in Switzerland. We do not know the exact number, but this does not matter, heaven surely knows the exact number of prayers. We thank all praying people who followed our request and offered Mary, Mother of the Life Within their prayers for the sanctity of life."

CZECH REPUBLIC

Hana Frankakova, WAF National Secretary,
Czech Republic

The WAF Fatima centre in the Czech Republic was united to the many people engaged in the One World Praying event.

In our country, members prayed with our novena to the Infant Jesus of Prague (it is a great treasure of our Country) and we also travelled to the Sanctuary of Our Lady - Protection of Life, located in one of our regional centres. We also prayed the joyful mysteries of the Rosary, with all attendees of the conference of the Czech WAF. Everything on that day was so blessed.

SPAIN

Fr. Carlos Lumbreras, WAF
National President, Spain

"The WAF in Spain celebrated last September at the Shrine of the Immaculate Heart of Mary – Pontevedra, with its national assembly, attended by numerous delegates from Spain. On this occasion, Fr. Carlos Lumbreras took the opportunity to inform all delegations of the World Apostolate of Fatima about the worldwide celebrations on October, 2nd to pray for the sanctity of life.

On October 2nd, at the national centre of Madrid, the rosary and Holy Mass were offered for that intention. Many people all over the country contributed with their prayers for life."

PHILIPPINES

Nida Ruiz, WAF National President, Philippines

"In the Philippines many wonderful events took place with regards to the One World Praying day for life and peace. Every (Arch-)diocese was informed and each held their own prayer program of activity. A chain rosary in all Parishes started at 1 am of One World Praying Day until midnight."

TANZANIA

Joseph Mwita, WAF National Secretary, Tanzania

"In Tanzania, in order to pray for protecting the sanctity of life through the intercession of Our Lady of Fatima, two major events took place on One World Praying Day.

First, it was requested to all bishops in Tanzania to allow all priests during Holy Mass on this day to give a special message on the fight to preserve the sanctity of life from conception to natural death, and they accepted.

Second, there were prayer groups all over the country that prayed the rosary, first in the group and later each one with their families."

BLUE ARMY SHRINE WASHINGTON, NJ - USA

Michael La Corte,
Executive Director WAF, USA

Citizens of all faiths gathered to pray for the sanctity of life on Worldwide Fatima Sanctity of Life Day in locations around the world and 100 million prayers were sent to Heaven.

The World Apostolate of Fatima/Blue Army has, for the past year, been organizing Worldwide Fatima Sanctity of Life Day. People of all faiths rallied from around the world to confront the evils of war, abortion, terrorism, genocide, child slavery, assisted suicide, and other Sanctity of Life issues with prayer. The culmination of all the United States planning took place at the Blue Army Shrine in Washington, NJ as well as many other World Apostolate of Fatima/Blue Army sponsored events at locations around the U.S.A.

Millions of people from around the world joined together in prayer. It was indeed a glorious day. Hard work coupled with the power of prayer, penance and sacrifice will lead to the ultimate triumph – peace on earth! It is encouraging to know that our heavenly Father listens and responds to our needs. So, for twenty minutes we asked people from around the world to raise their hearts to heaven in humility, and ask for help from above.

Four thousand people were on hand to listen to renowned speakers including Bishop Bootkoski of the Diocese of Metuchen, NJ, Fr. Andrew Apostoli, well known from EWTN and pro-life champion and former presidential candidate Dr. Alan Keyes. After the uplifting speeches, Christian Artist Tony Melendez had everyone on their feet and singing. Bishop Bootkoski also blessed the Sanctity of Life statue "Mary, Mother of the Life Within."

Thousands more were on hand in California to listen to the encouraging words of Mike Galloway, president and founder of CatholicOnline.com. Dozens of other events were held from Arizona to Vermont.

With your spiritual and financial support and the guidance of Our Lady, we reached our goal and created the largest day of organized prayer for life the world has ever seen.

THE MESSAGE OF FATIMA:
Our Lady's Peace Plan

The message of Fatima is increasingly relevant to the world we live in today. In 1917 Our Lady told us:

"War is a result of sin"

"Do not offend the Lord our God any more, because He is already so much offended"

"I have come to ask the faithful to amend their lives and ask pardon for their sins, they must cease offending God"

"Pray the Rosary every day in order to obtain peace for the world, and the end of the war"

"Continue to pray the Rosary in order to obtain the end of the war"

"Continue to pray the Rosary every day in honor of Our Lady of the Rosary, in order to obtain peace for the world and the end of the war, because only she can help you"

"Pray, pray often especially the Rosary"

"If my requests are not heeded... various nations will be annihilated"

"My Immaculate Heart will triumph ... an era of peace will be granted to mankind"

Through these words Our Lady made clear the cause of war and the path we must follow to bring about peace on earth.

Our Lady also made it clear that if we do not spiritually nourish the world, greater wars will follow that will-result in the annihilation of nations. These few words answer many questions we are faced with today.

God created us and by nature we are good; perhaps this is most evident when we are in need. Whether it is a tsunami, earthquake, flood, act of war, a family crisis, a stranger on the street or a friend in need people want to help. We respond immediately with an outpouring of love, spiritual support or financial support.

There was a touching story in the news today of a young Jewish man who was heartbroken when his brother was killed by a missile. Although his loss and pain was tremendous he saw that some good could come by donating his brother's organs to those in need. Political and religious boundaries that separated this man from his "enemy" were ignored and one of his brother's eyes was used to give sight to a Muslim who lived in the country that delivered the missile that killed his brother.

When told of this the man whose loss was great asked to meet with the man whose sight was restored. When they met, the Jewish man excitedly approached the Muslim man and thanked him for allowing the tragedy of his brother's death to provide him with sight. Both men embraced as children of God.

Political, cultural, racial, and religious boundaries are artificial artifacts created by man. We are all God's children and by nature we all want peace for ourselves and for each other. So we ask ourselves, why do we war with each other, especially after the development of weapons that could annihilate nations? What overpowers the good nature that God gifted us with when He created us?

The answer lies in Our Lady's message. "War is a result of sin." Our problems have both a human and a spiritual nature. Perhaps a simple way to look at it would be that our offenses against God nourish the diabolical, and when we do good we thwart diabolical power. Perhaps Our Lady was telling us that sin empowers Satan, who can then co-opt and empower political leaders to rally otherwise rational people to war against their neighbor. Thus, as spirituality in the world decreases, evil is empowered and our strife increases and as spirituality increases evil is weakened and our strife decreases.

In order to bring peace to earth we must please God. To bring war we must act in ways that please Satan. Our Lady promised that through her intercession, Divine intervention would bring an era of peace on earth. The only question is "when will this happen": before our strife increases and nations are annihilated or after? The answer depends on our actions, on our ability to spiritually nourish the world.

How do we spiritually nourish the world? Our Lady answered this with clarity:

1. FOLLOW THE COMMANDMENTS
2. PRAY, PRAY OFTEN ESPECIALLY THE ROSARY
3. PERFORM ACTS OF PENANCE AND REPARATION FOR YOUR SINS
4. MAKE SPIRITUAL AND FINANCIAL SACRIFICES
5. MAKE FIRST SATURDAY DEVOTION

1. Following the Commandments is fairly self-explanatory except for the tendency to redefine the commandments using the "follow your conscience" clause. It is correct that we should follow our conscience; however, if it "waters down" the commandments we must be sure that we have: worked to properly form a conscience that can be relied upon, deeply searched our souls, and asked for God's guidance. We must be sure that we are not simply choosing the most convenient path.

2. The need for prayer was pointed out by Our Lady more often then anything else she mentioned. World Apostolate of Fatima members make a commitment to pray the Rosary daily. If you are a spiritual athlete your commitment is vital; if you or someone you know is not ready to commit to at least twenty minutes of daily prayer, or you are not Catholic, or you do not know how to pray the rosary, it is still important that you pray and pray often. Everyone prays; for those that don't think they pray it may take a bus coming at them at 60 mph, but they will pray. Prayer takes many forms and all of them are valuable.

To some degree, you can draw an analogy between prayer and health. It is obvious to all that physical exercise and good nutrition strengthens the body and mind and allows you to feel better, accomplish more and live longer. I was amazed when a doctor who practiced at the Mayo Clinic told me that 80% of the patients he sees would not need him if they walked just ten minutes a day.

The best approach to good physical health is to start small, don't get discouraged when you slip, and work your way into a habit. For many, the same is true for sound spiritual health. If everyone said hello to God and our Blessed Mother when they awoke and before sleep and worked to increase the time they spent praying, this would be a much different world. If you can't start with 20 minutes start with 20 seconds a few times a day. You will be amazed at the difference it makes. Prayer is spiritual nourishment for your soul, other souls and the world. Prayer also helps you achieve personal peace, and strengthens your communion with Heaven.

Our Lady's Message was a message meant for all of God's children, not just Catholics. It is important that all people pray more and you should encourage your non-Catholic friends to pray according to their faith.

3. Penance and reparation renew us.

We can take great solace in knowing that although we will sin there is no sin so big that God can't forgive us. It is important that we recognize our offenses to God rather then deny them, that we are truly sorry, and that we repent. As Catholics we are also blessed to have the sacrament of confession. A major benefit of confession, penance and reparation, is to know that God has forgiven us so that we may be spiritually healed, leave our past behind, and live more productive and spiritual lives. The renewal that results from losing the weight of our past sins and the strength we are then able to receive from the Holy Eucharist frees us to spiritually nourish ourselves, our loved ones, the faithfully departed and the world.

4. Our Lady asked us to make spiritual and financial sacrifices. Sacrifice may take the form of denying oneself something of value, perhaps fasting or "giving up..." Sacrifice can also take the form of a good deed or can be performed as a matter of attitude. During our daily lives we are going to encounter many things that are "trying," we can willingly accept these challenges and offer the pain up to God as a sacrifice rather then curse our condition, blame someone, or want to "kick the wall."

Jacinta battled pleurisy, a very painful disease, until her early death. She rejoiced, knowing that offering her pain to God as a sacrifice saved many souls. Francisco tied a rope tightly around his waist to create pain that he could offer as his sacrifice. Our Lady pointed out to Francisco that sacrifice should not result in self induced damage to one's body.

In August of 1917 Our Lady asked the children to take up a collection so that a chapel may be built, a place where people could learn, live, and spread her message. Many more spiritual and financial sacrifices have been made and consequently a large shrine exists in Fatima, Portugal where the original chapel was built. Millions of pilgrims come to learn, live, and spread her message. The World Apostolate of Fatima, USA offers pilgrims a shrine with a similar purpose in New Jersey and operates a guest house in Fatima that receives many thousands of pilgrims each year. We also have many Divisions hard at work throughout the world, publish much literature on the message of Fatima, and sponsor many programs to reach young and old alike.

We will employ the power of radio and TV to help people of all ages, from all faiths, and from all countries put Our Lady's plan for peace into action. We set a goal of One Billion Prayers for Life and Peace in One Day; many people will begin to understand the power of prayer to bring peace to their daily lives and to the world. Of course this is only possible to the extent that people are willing to follow the example of those people in Fatima who almost 90 years ago made the first financial sacrifice at Our Lady's request.

Part of the reason we are here is to learn, even if the lessons may be painful. When we sacrifice we feel better, live better lives, help others, and recognize and appreciate God more fully and more often.

5. First Saturday Devotion contributes to the salvation of your soul, and spiritually enriches the world through prayer and sacrifice.

Our Lady said to Sister Lucia: "I promise to assist at the hour of death, with all the graces necessary for salvation, to all who on the First Saturday of five consecutive months:

1. CONFESS
2. RECEIVE HOLY COMMUNION
3. PRAY FIVE DECADES OF THE ROSARY
4. KEEP ME COMPANY FOR FIFTEEN MINUTES WHILE MEDITATING ON THE MYSTERIES OF THE ROSARY, ALL WITH THE INTENTION OF MAKING REPARATION TO MY IMMACULATE HEART"

Father Andrew Apostoli has authored a booklet on First Saturday Devotion that we have published in this book.

Acting on Our Lady's plan for peace will spiritually nourish a world in desperate need and perhaps on the brink. Spiritual athletes must put all their talents to use and everyone else needs to take a step forward. The political problems we are facing today will either result in peace or the annihilation of nations. We are not victims, we need to become active participants in this spiritual battle. If peace was not possible Our Lady would not have given us specific instructions on how to create a world where we accept our differences, put God first, and live in harmony.

Great Blessings Bring Great Responsibility

ABRIDGED ADDRESS TO THE PONTIFICAL COUNCIL FOR THE LAITY ON THE CEREMONY OF PROCLAMATION OF THE DECREE OF APPROVAL OF THE WORLD APOSTOLATE OF FATIMA AS A PUBLIC ASSOCIATION OF THE FAITHFUL, AULA MAGNA, 3RD OF FEBRUARY, 2006

Professor Americo Pablo Lopez-Ortiz

International President
World Apostolate of Fatima

Blessed be Jesus Christ!

Today with joy the World Apostolate of Fatima celebrates its approval by the Holy See as a public association of the faithful for the Universal Church. A great blessing and at the same time a great responsibility to carry out with hope and excellence!

Under the umbrella of the World Apostolate of Fatima (WAF), all associations and apostolic movements propagating the authentic Message of Fatima may encounter an example of faithfulness and loyalty to the Holy Father and the Diocesan Bishops in communion with the Successor of St. Peter. The WAF will serve the Church as a worldwide intent of the New Evangelization proposed by Pope John Paul II, the Great, and by his Successor, Pope Benedict.

The WAF, (World Apostolate of Fatima) will live its charisma of formation of lay people by transmitting:

- The authentic Message of Fatima and its profound spirituality, centered in the Primacy of God in our society and our civilization;

- The reverent meditation of the mystery of God, the Holy Trinity as the center of our lives;

- The Most profound love for Jesus present in the Blessed Sacrament;

- The practice of the prayer of meditation – the Holy Rosary – as the instrument to achieve world peace and rebuild families as the main institution of our Societies;

- The daily offering of our duties to follow Christ as His beloved disciples, bearing our daily cross and learning from it to become saints (friends of God), living His Grace and Mercy;

- Practicing the reparatory devotion of the Five Consecutive First Saturdays of the Month, to obtain from God the special grace of unity and strength of the Universal Church against its enemies and inner dissention, as well as a promise of perseverance and all the necessary means of salvation at the moment of death, crowned by the "entrustment" of our lives to God, through Jesus Christ, by the intercession of the Immaculate Heart of Mary, a true school of sanctity for men and women of our era, consecrating our lives as a renewal of our baptismal pledge, a pledge that is resembled in our WAF Pledge to convert ourselves and be instruments to live and make alive the Gospel in our days.

The Brown Scapular of Our Lady is the sign of such a consecration, a sign of personal conversion and group solidarity. A sign of love, of true charity, of solidarity with the poor and oppressed, so that **OUR CHARITY, THE *AGAPE* OF THE GOSPEL, WILL TURN INTO DEEDS, NOT MERELY WORDS,** so that people can turn to the WAF members and exclaim: "Look how much they love each other, how much they resemble true Disciples of Christ!"

This is our faith, this is our commitment, and this is our responsibility to God, to the Church, to history!

DO NOT REST UNTIL THE PLEAS OF OUR LADY OF FATIMA ARE HEARD BY HUMANITY...DO NOT REST UNTIL HER REQUESTS ARE RESPONDED TO BY MANY!

An era of peace, a century of hope, a new Marian Pentecost, a new spring for the Church and for the world, was promised by Our Lady, if we are faithful to her message. The message of Fatima is more urgent now than ever before, more actual, and more essential to the present state of moral and spiritual crisis of our civilization.

Our Apostolate must contribute as much as possible to offer a new criteria, a new option to solve the present crisis by turning to the ever new, ever actual, ever efficient tall of the Gospel: "Repent and do penance! Convert yourselves while there is still time!"

May the Holy Spirit renew our hearts with the peace and joy of Jesus Christ ever present in the Immaculate Heart of Mary so that we all may remain in his Grace and Mercy! *"Semper fidelis!'*

> AN ERA OF PEACE, A CENTURY OF HOPE, A NEW MARIAN PENTECOST, A NEW SPRING FOR THE CHURCH AND FOR THE WORLD, WAS PROMISED BY OUR LADY, IF WE ARE FAITHFUL TO HER MESSAGE. THE MESSAGE OF FATIMA IS MORE URGENT NOW THAN EVER BEFORE...

Archbishop Stanislaw Rylko, president of the Pontifical Council for the Laity, presented Professor Americo Lopez Ortiz, the International President of the World Apostolate of Fatima, with the great news that the World Apostolate of Fatima has been approved by the Holy See as a Public Association of the Faithful for the Universal Church. The decree is dated on the 7th of October, 2005 the Feast of Our Lady of the Rosary. On this same day, our Apostolate offered worldwide Holy Hours with children and young people to renew the channels of grace and mercy. The Apostolate held Worldwide Fatima Sanctity of Life Day, "One Day 100,000,000" Prayers on Sunday the first day of this same week.

A public ceremony to officially announce this wonderful news was held at the Vatican on the 3rd of February, 2006. Only eleven similar organizations exist within our Church, and the World Apostolate of Fatima is the only Fatima organization to receive official recognition by the Holy See. Almost sixty years of hard work, prayer, penance, and sacrifice offered by the Apostolate coupled with this recognition is a calling to a higher responsibility to live and spread the message of Fatima. We invite you to celebrate with us as we thank you for all of your support. We are now called to do even more as we ask for your continued spiritual and financial sacrifice.

We were honored to have Father Roland, WAF Board member from Africa light candles and celebrate Holy Mass at the Capelinha in Fatima Portugal as we placed rosary prayer pledges at Our Lady's statue for those who participated in Worldwide Fatima Sanctity of Life.

Angel of Peace

Pardon Prayer

Prayer taught by the Angel of Peace to the three children during his first apparition in 1916.

My God, I believe, I adore, I hope and I love Thee! I beg pardon for those who do not believe, do not adore, do not hope, and do not love Thee.

Angel's Prayer

With the Blessed Sacrament suspended in the air, the Angel of Peace prostrated himself and recited the prayer during his third apparition to the children in 1916.

O Most Holy Trinity, Father, Son and Holy Spirit, I adore Thee profoundly. I offer Thee the most precious Body, Blood, Soul and Divinity of Jesus Christ, present in all the tabernacles of the world, in reparation for the outrages, sacrileges and indifference by which He is offended. By the infinite merits of the Sacred Heart of Jesus and the Immaculate Heart of Mary, I beg the conversion of poor sinners.

Eucharistic Prayer

Prayer communicated to the seers by an interior impulse during apparition of May 13, 1917.

Most Holy Trinity, I adore Thee! My God, my God, I love Thee in the Most Blessed Sacrament!

Sacrifice Prayer

During the July 13, 1917 apparition, Our Lady taught this prayer to say this prayer when they would have some sacrifice to offer God.

O Jesus, it is for love of You, for the conversion of sinners, and in reparation for the sins committed against the Immaculate Heart of Mary.

Decade Prayer

During Her July 1917 apparition, Our Lady asked that the following prayer be inserted after each decade of the Rosary.

O my Jesus, forgive us our sins, save us from the fires of hell. Lead all souls to Heaven, especially those most in need of Thy mercy.

Imprimatur: Most Rev George W. Ahr,
Bishop of Trenton

© The World Apostolate of Fatima,
The Blue Army , USA
Washington, NJ 07882
www.bluearmy.com (866) 513-1917

328475
704

Mary for Life

O Mary, Mother of the Life Within,
all life we entrust to you;
The life of every expectant mother
and the child within her womb;
The life of every human body,
the life of every human soul;
The life of every newborn child
and the life of all grown old.
You held the Lord to your own heart
and drew Him so close in.
So draw us now in all our needs,
O Mother of the Life Within.

Artist: Joe DeVito
Copyright © 2002 DeVito/Birchfield Design Group

printed with ecclesiastical permission

World Apostolate of Fatima, U.S.A.
Washington, NJ 07882

328762

706

The Twelve Promises of the Sacred Heart to St. Margaret Mary

1. I will give them all the graces necessary for their state of life.

2. I will give peace in their families.

3. I will console them in all their troubles.

4. They shall find in my Heart an assured refuge during life and especially at the hour of death.

5. I will pour abundant blessings on all their undertakings.

6. Sinners shall find in my Heart the source and infinite ocean of mercy.

7. Tepid souls shall become fervent.

8. Fervent souls shall speedily rise to great perfection.

9. I will bless the homes in which the image of my Sacred Heart shall be exposed and honored.

10. I will give to priests the power to touch the most hardened hearts.

11. Those who propagate this devotion shall have their name written in my Heart, and it shall never be effaced.

12. The all-powerful love of my Heart will grant to all those who shall receive Communion on the first Friday of nine consecutive months the grace of final repentance; they shall not die under my displeasure, nor without receiving the Sacraments; my Heart shall be their assured refuge at that last hour.

"And He showed me that it was his great desire of being loved by men and of withdrawing them fromthe path of ruin into which Satan hurls such crowds of them, that made Him form the design of manifesting His Heart to men, with all the treasures of love, of mercy, of grace, of sanctification and salvation which it contains, in order that those who desire to render Him and procure for Him all the honor and love possible, might themselves be abundantly enriched with those divine treasures of which His Heart is the source. He should be honored under the figure of this Heart of flesh, and its image should be exposed. . . . He promised me that wherever this image should be exposed with a view to showing it special honor, He would pour forth his blessings and graces. This devotion was the last effort of His love that He would grant to men in these latter ages, in order to withdraw them from the empire of Satan which He desired to destroy, and thus to introduce them into the sweet liberty of the rule of His love, which He wished to restore in the hearts of all those who should embrace this devotion."

- St. Margaret Mary

Imprimatur
E. Morrogh Bernard
Vic. Gen. Westmonasterii, 1954
World Apostolate of Fatima, USA
Washington, New Jersey 07882-0976

419877

Jacinta Marto was born at Fatima, Portugal on March 11, 1910. She died in the hospital at Lisbon, February 20, 1920.

She was the youngest and most favored of the three shepherds. With her companions, she saw an angel three times and Our Lady six times. She also had the special privilege of seeing other appearances of the Blessed Virgin, and of the Holy Father. The theme of her life was to pray and make every possible sacrifice, for the conversion of sinners and in reparation to the Immaculate Heart of Mary.

Before she died, she said: "In heaven I'm going to love Jesus very much, and the Immaculate Heart of Mary too."

God has granted countless extraordinary graces through her intercession. On May 13, 2000, Pope John Paul II proclaimed the heroic virtues of the Servant of God, Jacinta Marto, granting her the title of Blessed.

Prayer for the Blessed Jacinta's Canonization

FOR PRIVATE RECITATION

Most Holy Trinity, Father, Son and Holy Spirit, I adore You profoundly. I thank You for the Apparitions of the Most Holy Virgin at Fatima. They have made manifest to the world the treasures of the Immaculate Heart of Mary.

By the infinite merits of the Sacred Heart of Jesus and through the intercession of the Immaculate Heart of Mary I implore You - if it should be for Your greater glory and the good of our souls - to glorify in the sight of Your Holy Church Jacinta the shepherdess of Fatima, granting us through her intercession the grace which we implore. Amen.

Our Father, Hail Mary, Glory Be to the Father.

Please send details of favors received through the intercession of Jacinta Marto to:
Vice-Postulator da Causa de Jacinta Marto, Apartado 6, P-2496 Fatima, Portugal

with ecclesiastical permission
Rev. Msgr. John B. Szymanski
Vicar General, Diocese of Metuchen
April 28, 2000

World Apostolate of Fatima
Washington, NJ 07882
5/2000 329395

Francisco Marto was born at Fatima, Portugal on June 11, 1908 and died there April 4, 1919. With his companions, he saw an angel three times and Our Lady six times.

At his third appearance, the angel said to the three young shepherd children: "Console you God." These words impressed Francisco very deeply. He made every sacrifice he could to give consolation to Jesus. He would pray alone for long hours in church, or hide himself in prayer in some lonely place. Shortly before he died, he said, "In heaven I'm going to console Our Lord and Lady very much."

God has granted countless extraordinary graces through his intercession. On May 13, 2000, Pope John Paul II proclaimed the heroic virtues of the Servant of God, Francisco Marto, granting him the title of Blessed.

Prayer for the Blessed Francisco's Canonization

FOR PRIVATE RECITATION

Most Holy Trinity, Father, Son and Holy Spirit, I adore You profoundly. I thank You for the Apparitions of the Most Holy Virgin at Fatima. They have made manifest to the world the treasures of the Immaculate Heart of Mary.

By the infinite merits of the Sacred Heart of Jesus and through the intercession of the Immaculate Heart of Mary I implore You - if it should be for Your greater glory and the good of our souls - to glorify in the sight of Your Holy Church Francisco the shepherd of Fatima, granting us through his intercession the grace which we implore. Amen.

Our Father, Hail Mary, Glory Be to the Father.

Please send details of favors received through the intercession of Francisco Marto to:
Vice-Postulator da Causa de Francisco Marto, Apartado 6, P-2496 Fatima, Portugal

with ecclesiastical permission
Rev. Msgr. John B. Szymanski
Vicar General, Diocese of Metuchen
April 28, 2000

World Apostolate of Fatima
Washington, NJ 07882
5/2000 333298

God Bless America

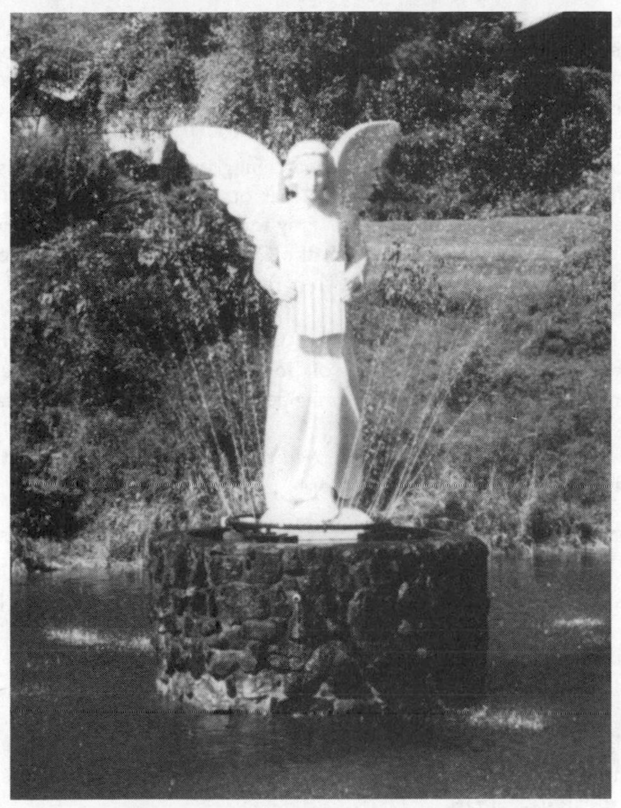

Guardian Angel of the United States

National Blue Army Shrine
of the Immaculate Heart of Mary
Washington, New Jersey

Prayer to the U.S. Guardian Angel

O Glorius Guardian Angel of the United States, to whom God has entrusted the care of our beloved country, we honor you and thank you for the care and protection you have given to this great nation from the first moments of its inception.

O Powerful Angel Guardian, whose watchful glance encompasses this vast land from shore to shore, we know that our sins have grieved you and marred the beauty of our heritage. Pray for us, O Holy Angel, before the throne of God. Obtain for us, from the Queen of Heaven, the graces we need to overcome the forces of evil so rampant in our beloved land.

Help us, our God-given protector and friend, to respond wholeheartedly to the urgent pleas of the Mother of God at Fatima. Assist us to offer the prayer and sacrifice necessary to bring peace and goodness to our nation.

We want to make you known and loved throughout our land, so that with your help we may become once more "a Nation under God!"

July 4, 1982 - Dedication of the statue of the Guardian Angel of the United States at the National Blue Army Shrine of the Immaculate Heart of Mary.

This unique statue of the Guardian Angel of the United States has been raised by the Blue Army of Our Lady of Fatima in order to initiate and foster devotion to the Great Angelic Protector under whose dominion God has placed our beloved nation. The impetus for this endeavor stems from the three apparitions of the Guardian Angel of Portugal to the three children at Fatima in 1916.

Printed with Ecclesiastical Permission

The Blue Army
Washington, NJ 07882